The American Exploration and Travel Series

NAVAHO EXPEDITION

NAVAHO
EXPEDITION

JOURNAL OF A
MILITARY RECONNAISSANCE
FROM SANTA FE, NEW MEXICO
TO THE NAVAHO COUNTRY
MADE IN 1849 BY
Lieutenant James H. Simpson

Edited and Annotated
by Frank McNitt

UNIVERSITY OF OKLAHOMA PRESS
Norman

BY FRANK MCNITT

Richard Wetherill: Anasazi (Albuquerque, 1957)

The Indian Traders (Norman, 1962)

(editor) *Navaho Expedition,*
by Lieutenant James H. Simpson (Norman, 1964)

Copyright 1964 by the University of Oklahoma Press, Publishing Division of the University. Composed and printed at Norman, Oklahoma, U.S.A., by the University of Oklahoma Press. First Edition.

THIS BOOK

IN FRIENDSHIP, RESPECT,

AND GOOD MEMORIES,

IS FOR JUAN—

John Arrington

Preface

MY FIRST ENCOUNTER with Lieutenant Simpson's Navaho journal occurred thirteen years ago, in one of the quiet rooms of the library of the University of California at Los Angeles. The journal was one of perhaps a score of books brought down from the stacks, to be used in the early phases of work on the biography of Richard Wetherill. What the other books were I do not remember. A few weeks later the library provided me with a photostatic copy of the complete journal. After the first hurried reading, I knew that I must have it. Its discovery—and so I thought it to be—was, and still remains, a most happy accident. Only later did I realize how many others had made the same discovery before me. Our interest in the history or archaeology of the Southwest had led us to the same source.

Those who are familiar with the journal and the contributions to it of the Kern brothers' map and drawings know that for more than a century the journal has been entombed between the dry boards and extraneous dull pages of a Senate executive document—available in a few of our best libraries, but, of all forms of printed works, in format the most repellent. In turning the pages on the tome's arthritic spine, I felt that Simpson's unusual narrative cried out for liberation. I felt then, and do still, that the journal is one of the enduring landmarks of Western Americana, that it has been denied the very wide appreciation it deserves only because of its official shroud and relative inaccessibility.

During the next ten years, as other work interposed, Simpson's journal traveled about with me in its large manila envelope. Nothing very much was done about it in this time because I knew that it was quite a bit more than I was ready to handle. If Simpson abominated the Navaho country, at least he knew it from close observation; I did not. Not in the least sharing his dislike, even for the mud holes or sand drifts where over the years our several different cars bogged down, I tried to learn something about it. A photographic enlargement of Edward Kern's map of the 1849 expedition was helpful. During the years when I was working in Farmington, New Mexico, and later in Albuquerque, it was possible to take Kern's map for a few days or a week at a time and explore small sections of the route traveled by Colonel Washington's command. On one such trip, backtracking the troops from Naschiti to Chaco Canyon, one conventional car surrendered unconditionally; we were buried to the hubs in sand on a hogan road, a mile or two west of the White Rock Trading Post.

In late summer and early fall of 1961 the entire route followed by the military expedition was traced in a four-wheel-drive Land-Rover. The model used for this we named "The Beast." Slightly larger than an American Jeep, this canvas-top vehicle in coursing rough terrain had the kick of an army mule—but, like an army mule, once really prodded, would grind through sand, crunch over rocks and Simpson's ubiquitous artemisia, and halt panting only before vertical canyon walls. Like Wetherill's mule Nephi, the Land-Rover we could love and bitterly hate at exactly the same moment. As with Nephi, though, what really counted was that The Beast took us there and brought us back.

Unlike Lieutenant Simpson and the troops in 1849, we did not cover the ground in one direct march, but took it in easy stages of a week at a time, retreating on week ends for fresh supplies of food, water, and gasoline to Albuquerque, Farmington, or Gallup. More than one thousand miles were traversed in this way, my son Ben being with me for the first half of the military route, from Santo Domingo Pueblo to Canyon de Chelly, and John Arrington riding with me and helping to shorten the miles from de Chelly to Albuquerque. The first and last miles of the route, beginning and ending at Santa Fe, I traveled alone.

The limited cargo area of the Land-Rover really determined our progress, as we could carry only enough food and fuel for a week. On the front seat between us we carried the UCLA copy of Simpson's journal, maps, and two cameras and a camera tripod. In the truck bed behind were one spare wheel, four five-gallon cans divided equally between water and gasoline, bedrolls, a tent, a two-bitted ax and two shovels, a gasoline stove and gasoline lantern, a cardboard box of groceries and aluminum pots and dishes and a .30–.30 rifle, lashed with rope to the top hoops and never taken down. An ice chest was left behind—no room—which meant warm beer at night and eating from cans. I mention these details, not knowing whether anyone cares, because Simpson omitted such housekeeping notes from his journal and I wish that he had included them. We used everything I have mentioned (except the rifle and the tent) every day for nearly two months. I have not mentioned, but will now, a compass attached to the Land-Rover's instrument panel, which, next only to a long-handled shovel and the gasoline, was more useful than anything else aboard.

Colonel Washington's expedition was favored by little rain, which allowed his troops to move with celerity and comparative ease. In the same months—August and September, 1961—the rainfall was heavy and the nights correspondingly colder and windier. At the military campsite near Pintado a gale wind and frigid rain drove us at midnight to raise the tent. Quicksand in the wet Chaco Wash made it impossible for two weeks to trace Simpson's small diversionary party from Penasco Blanco to the vicinity of Juan's Lake. Instead, and reluctantly, we followed the route of the troops out of the Chaco, and even then, with all four wheels churning, were forced to shovel out of mud. On the day John Arrington started out with me from Farmington, a true gully-washer unwound between Mexican Water and Dinnehotso, and from Dinnehotso south there was no road but only a darkening and deepening plain of water and gluey adobe. The last twenty miles we traveled in two hours. Not far above Many Farms—the headlights on, the windshield muddied and visibility about ten feet—the road dropped away beneath us, and we fell into a branch of the Chinle Wash. For two hundred yards, perhaps, The Beast, now lost and beaten, followed the wash, and then, with a sucking sound, sank. We sank to the floorboards in red, oozy clay which could have been quicksand, but happily was more like liquid cement.

The gear necessary for the night was waded to higher, but not dry, ground, and after two cups of coffee, in the middle of a raining nowhere, we shook out the bedrolls. In early morning light, when the tent came down, John found a tarantula evacuating a warm spot directly under the place where he had slept. With dawn also came Navahos, one of whom, Hostine Harrison, agreed to help extricate the Land-Rover from the middle of the wash, where it rested as immobilized as an expensive tombstone. The ruin of an abandoned hogan stood some distance away. We looted it of timbers, cut them up, and with these and with rocks and a tripod jack managed, after four hours, to hoist each wheel of The Beast to surface-water level. I do not believe that Colonel Washington's artillerymen, at any point of crossing Washington Pass, opened their palms with larger blisters. Anyway, once more mobile, we trundled south for six miles and then across a mud lake to Harrison's hogan. Here we left him, surrounded by small children and several dogs, he speeding us on our way with the gift of two melons and a newspaper bundle of meat-filled corn-cakes, each wrapped in corn husks.

Against John's mild remonstrance, I determined several days later that our maps and compass were faulty. John, who cares nothing for maps and not much more for a compass, suggested that perhaps—down where the canyon opened—we might bear gradually to the southwest. Rather crossly, I assured him that he was mistaken, too. We turned east and traveled east for many miles, until we sank again, in the mud of a middle-aged Navaho widow's front yard. This was country that Lieutenant Simpson never saw. If the story were not so interminably long, it would stand telling; briefly, we would probably be there still if John had not charmed that lonely and suspicious widow into telling him where we had gone astray. Of course, it was where I had turned east instead of southwest.

Soon afterward we reached the Río Puerco, below the tankard-rock that somehow reminded Richard Kern of William Penn. Like the Chaco, the Puerco was in flood. We waited ten days before we could cross it, and then almost lost The Beast again in a wilderness of sand and scrub piñon on the way to Zuñi. Eastward from Zuñi our journey was free of mishaps or detours. Excepting three segments of the military's route—from the vicinity of Borrego Dome to Jemez Pueblo, a small section of the Chaco Wash, and through the Zuni Mountains to Canyon del Gallo—some twenty-five miles in all, we had stayed well within the vanished prints of Colonel Washington's trail.

Quite early in the preparation of this work I felt that if a new edition of Simpson's journal were submitted to a publisher, it should offer the reader something more, a sketch at least that would satisfy a natural curiosity about Simpson himself and about his military career, in which the Navaho expedition was merely one part. As always happens, this archival search led to complications. Simpson's life, during his western period, was linked so closely to the lives of friends and companions that the search imperatively was extended to include the Kern brothers, Henry Linn Dodge, James Calhoun, and several others of lesser importance here. Finally, because all of these men were so concerned, if for only a short time, with the Navaho and Pueblo people, it seemed necessary to explore tentatively into tribal history.

Of Simpson's friends or companions, I will admit to stronger feelings of kinship for Calhoun, Henry Dodge, and Richard Kern than I have for Simpson, who—for all of the lasting values found in his Navaho journal—somehow excuses himself from their company by coupling with his dislike of the country an air of aloof, cool detachment.

Of the Kern brothers, Edward seems the least interesting to

me; Richard the most warm-hearted, convivial, and talented; and Benjamin—least strong of the three—the strongest claimant upon our sympathies. While in Washington, more than a year ago, I first stumbled on the old army records that cast new light on the murder of Benjamin Kern and Old Bill Williams. Interesting as this was, I thought the material too remote from the affairs of Lieutenant Simpson, and so took only a few hurried notes. Later, when I realized that the fate of the doctor and the old mountain man were closely woven into an early part of this story, I returned to the archives to examine the documents more critically. I regret that what I have found does not remove the uncertainty of what happened in the mountains when the two men were killed—and perhaps only widens the area of mystery and speculation. On the evidence, however, I cannot help but believe that the muleteers accompanying Kern and Williams were accessories to their death.

In editing Simpson's journal, an effort has been made to preserve the original manuscript faithfully. Changes have been made in punctuation, and the names of several individuals, misspelled in the original, have been corrected.

In writing of the Indian tribes we are confronted always with the question of how tribal names should be spelled. Historically, from 1538 and the days of the Spanish chronicler Father Gerónimo Zarate-Salmeron to the present, the name of the *Diné* has evolved from Nabahu or Nabajoo, to Navajoe or Navajo, and since 1948—among scholars and due mainly to the late Clyde Kluckhohn—to Navaho. Lieutenant Simpson spelled the name Navajo, as does the Department of Indian Affairs, the Navajo Tribal Council itself, and the *Navajo Times,* the tribal newspaper which in 1963 was published at Window Rock "for" and "by . . . the Navajo People." My own feelings in the matter, due in part to an aversion to tinkering with historical spellings of things, places, and people's names, include me strongly to *Navajo.* The University of Oklahoma Press, like most of today's anthropologists and the Bureau of American Ethnology, finds good reason to prefer *Navaho.* Therefore, to avoid confusing shifts in spelling, and because of my wholehearted agreement with my publishers that Navajos are Navahos regardles of spelling, the latter form will appear throughout except in direct quotations.

I have deleted Simpson's references in his narrative to the numerical sequence of Richard Kern's accompanying drawings. Also, I have deleted several passages—in all not more than two or three paragraphs—relating to the geology of the region traveled. Several of Simpson's footnotes have been omitted, and, again from the narrative, a philosophical discussion of quotations from Psalms, Chapter 107, verses 35 and 37. The changes, in truth, are so few and inconsequential that I do not believe that Simpson himself would detect them.

For his assistance to me thirteen years ago, when he was UCLA's librarian, and for his encouragement and many kindnesses since, I would like to express my deep appreciation to Lawrence Clark Powell. I am indebted to two members of his staff, Everett Moore and Robert Vosper, who also helped me in the discovery of Simpson's journal.

Bill Bromberg of the National Park Service, who in 1961 was stationed at Chaco Canyon, offered the friendliest co-operation and permitted me to borrow four maps, which were invaluable in retracing Simpson's route in 1849. Superintendant Merritt S. Johnston, who had then just arrived in the Chaco, trusted me with a key to the east gate of the monument. Without that key we could not have traveled into the canyon on the approach from Pueblo Pintado.

Mrs. Louise Southwick of the War Records Division of the National Archives spent hours of her good time, in that vast catacomb, finding old army documents, manuals, and other materials which no one but she could have known existed.

I am especially grateful to Mrs. Carmelita Ryan of the Indian Records Division of the National Archives, who for nearly ten years and with fine patience and wisdom, has helped me over many shoals.

For certain episodes in the lives of the Kern brothers I am indebted to Miss Haydée Noya of the Department of Manuscripts at the Henry E. Huntington Library for her assistance in making available copies of documents from the Fort Sutter Papers collection, and to Robert O. Dougan for granting permission to use these documents and other materials in the library's collection. These same materials previously were consulted by Robert V. Hine. I wish to acknowledge the pioneering use Mr. Hine has made of these documents and the guidance I have derived from his biography, *Edward Kern and American Expansion*.

Annie Heloise Abel's *The Official Correspondence of James S. Calhoun* has been a major source of information—as invaluable to me in this work as it has been in the past. In nearly the same measure I am indebted to the late Richard Van Valkenburgh, and to John Adair, whose writing in closely parallel fields I have drawn upon freely.

Captions accompanying the drawings by Richard Kern are those which he used.

Frank McNitt

NORTH WOODSTOCK, CONNECTICUT
FEBRUARY 24, 1964

Contents

Illustrations

Introduction

BY FRANK MCNITT

THESE WERE RAW RECRUITS, for the most part, lifting the dust in August heat and tired with their long march. They were used to hunting or farming but not to marching, nor were they accustomed to the discipline of orders. From Fort Leavenworth, in June, they had marched to Bent's Fort on the Arkansas. After a rest and regrouping they picked up and moved again, down Timpas Creek and over the Raton Mountains. They were raggedy and unruly, sixteen hundred cocky, overconfident, and untrained men of Stephen Watts Kearny's Army of the West. Back home they had signed up for President Polk's war with Mexico, signed up for Senator Benton's Manifest Destiny. Santa Fe received their invading arms quietly, without resistance.

A few Americans—our first expatriates and today reunited to their country by conquest—were on hand in the small adobe capital to welcome them. More would come down in a day or so from Don Fernando de Taos, ten- and twenty-year men of experience in overland commerce and the mountain fur trade, men who were familiar with this strange land and the ways of its people, Indian and Mexican.

If not in the mountains, Bill Williams might have been there. Kit Carson was not there, but soon would meet Kearny on the Río Grande and return with the army to California, as guide. James Magoffin, the trader, and Charles Bent of Bent, St. Vrain and Company were there. Their advices to officials in Washington, particularly the information given by Magoffin, had proved accurate: Governor Manuel Armijo had neither troops nor stomach for repelling this invasion. He had quit the undefended capital and left to the acting governor, Juan Bautista Vigil, the honor of greeting the American horde and surrendering Santa Fe to General Kearny.

The General felt a sense of urgency and communicated this to his officers. On August 19, 1846, the morning after his arrival, he ordered construction of a fort "for the defence and protection of this city," assigning Lieutenants William H. Emory and Jeremy F. Gilmer "to make a reconnoissance . . . and select a site." Three days later the location was approved. On the fourth day, August 22, the officers' "complete plan of the work . . . for a garrison of 280 men" also was approved, and construction was started the day following. A labor detail of one hundred men was ordered out from the ranks, and to this force shortly were added twenty Mexicans, who were put to work molding adobe bricks.

With this much accomplished, the capital in quiescence except for rowdyism among his own troops, Kearny departed for a probing scout of some ninety miles south along the Río Grande, as far as Tome. The ranchos of the valley he found hushed, their owners inclined to peace. On his return he was pleased to discover that Colonel Alexander W. Doniphan, whom he had left in command, had prevented his Missourians from tearing down the Palace of the Governors—the General's temporary abode— and that work on the fort was progressing well.

The fort occupied an eminence north and slightly to the east of the capital's plaza, the foundation walls eventually enclosing an area of a trifle more than seventeen acres and, because of the uneven formation of this hill, laid out in a tri-decagon longer than it was wide and resembling three five-pointed stars fused together and then very badly pounded out of shape.

"The fort will be an important and a permanent one," Kearny wrote on September 16.[1] "I have this day named it 'Fort Marcy'"

[1] Kearny to Adjutant General Roger Jones, September 16, 1846. National Archives, War Records. Record Goup 94, Mexican War, K173, 1846. Important, yes—but not permanent. The fort's garrison was finally withdrawn in October, 1894, and in the following June the deserted post came under the jurisdiction of

—a memorial for William L. Marcy, then secretary of war and later secretary of state.

One week later the General escorted young Susan Magoffin on a tour of the fortification, and she noted in her diary how he had arrived punctually at her door "on a spirited bay charger" and taken her through the town's clogged streets. They first inspected rows of artillery drawn up on one side of a street, then "ascended a long and rather steep hill, on the summit of which stands fort Marcey, sole master of the plain below."

This was, thought Susan, "the most perfect view I ever saw. Not only every house in the city can be torn by the artillery to attoms, but the wide plain beyond is exposed to the fullest view— and far beyond this still are the majestic mountains. . . . The Fort occupies some two acres of ground, has double walls built of adobes, the space between being filled with stones and morter. Dwellings, store houses &c. are to be built within the wall, in the center under ground is the magazine for ammunition."[2]

Fort Marcy was completed and garrisoned before the month was out, an ugly, many-angled but heroic accomplishment. To the keen eyes of Lieutenant J. W. Abert, freshly arrived and filled with enthusiasm, the fort looked then very nearly the same as it would to Lieutenant James Hervey Simpson less than three years later: "October 2. In a little while we reached Agua Fria [south of Santa Fe]. Soon Fort Marcy came into view and our glorious flag with its graceful stripes playing in the wind. . . . In the evening we visited Fort Marcy. It is situated on a prominent point of the bluff commanding the city. The distance of the center of this work, from the flagstaff to the plaza, is but 644 yards. The whole of the interior is defiladed from all the surrounding heights with-

the Department of the Interior. Record Group 94, Post Returns, Fort Marcy, Box 387.

2 Susan Shelby Magoffin, *Down the Santa Fe Trail and into Mexico: The Diary of Susan Shelby Magoffin, 1846–47* (ed. by Stella M. Drumm), 140–41. Susan was eighteen years old and a bride of less than eight months when, in June, 1846, she started west from Independence with her husband, the Santa Fe trader Samuel Magoffin. They reached Santa Fe in a train with other traders on August 30. Susan was James Magoffin's sister-in-law.

in range; ten guns may be brought to bear upon the city"—which reveals the insecure position of the small American garrison then, and for some years to come.

Abert continues: "The slopes are revetted with adobes. The block house and magazines are constructed of pine logs one foot square. The only approachable point is guarded by the block house, which also assists to protect the entrance to the fort."[3]

Adobes, two feet long and one foot wide, six inches thick. And pine logs, which actually would mean piñon, hauled from the higher slopes of the Sangre de Cristos. Adobes and piñon, the only readily available building materials, both easily fractured under persistent pounding and, in the case of the latter, source of profane disgust to the conquering army's quartermasters. Their problem it was to keep gun carriages and army wagons ready for the field. Spokes and axles of eastern oak or hickory would crack on New Mexico's atrocious roads. Replacements of soft cedar, softer piñon, or the impossible cottonwood threatened the army's mobility. Captain L. C. Easton, assistant quartermaster at Fort Marcy, urgently advised Washington that New Mexico timber would never do. He begged for immediate shipment of metal axles and spare wagon parts—and prepared to wait three or four months for delivery.

General Kearny, meanwhile, would get to California the best way he could and damn the broken axle that meant abandoning another wagon. But first was the safeguarding of what had been won. Affairs of this new territory, civil and military, must be entrusted to capable men. Among other appointments, Kearny, on August 28, named Henry Linn Dodge, a young Missourian whom he had found in the capital on his arrival, treasurer of Santa Fe, replacing the ailing Francisco Ortiz.[4] Charles Bent, possibly in reward for services, he named civil governor of the

[3] Ralph Emerson Twitchell, "The Story of the Conquest of Santa Fe," *Historical Society of New Mexico*, No. 24 (n.d.), 36.

[4] National Archives, War Records. Record Group 94, Mexican War, K173, 1846.

territory on September 22. Three days later, at the head of the major part of his army, he started for California—so passing from the scene of present concern, but soon to meet the bitter rivalry pressed upon him by another figure in this work, the ambitious John Charles Frémont.

Colonel Doniphan remained behind, left in military command of Fort Marcy and the several companies detached for territorial duty. His orders were to await the arrival of fresh troops under Colonel Sterling Price, who was to replace him, and then proceed to join General Wool in the conquest of Chihuahua.

If he enjoyed such things as the fandangos or *bailes* which the capital afforded, it was not for long. Even before Kearny's departure, Doniphan and the General had discussed the recurrent raids on Mexican settlements by encircling Indian tribes—Navahos and Southern Utes, three or four tribal divisions of the Apaches, and the closely allied Kiowas and Comanches. The Pueblos, Charles Bent assured them in fatal error, could be counted as friendly.

The Navahos at the moment were the principal aggressors. Mounting depredations by this tribe in recent weeks—murders, livestock stolen, children taken in captivity—presented an increasing challenge. If the Navahos knew, they certainly did not care; but in claiming New Mexico for the United States, General Kearny had pledged his government to maintain order in the territory and provide protection to its citizens against any hostile enemy. Kearny's promise would be fulfilled, not with immediate effectiveness but only in time and within the capacities and limited means of this new military and civil establishment.

Colonel Doniphan received orders during the first week of October to take the field against the Navahos and, if possible, bring them to terms. His superiors contemplated a punitive expedition. Doniphan evidently interpreted his orders in terms as lenient as he might while staying just short of disobedience. Eight years earlier, as a brigadier general of Missouri militia and in this role plunged into the center of anti-Mormon hysteria, he had stonily refused orders to execute Joseph Smith and other Mormon leaders. A onetime lawyer and Missouri legislator, he was a man of strong personal convictions.

With considerable courage, it would appear, but with no knowledge whatever of the country he was entering or of the adversary he would meet, Colonel Doniphan left Fort Marcy with a pack train of mules and supplies for one month. He divided his command, sending Major William Gilpin northwest to the San Juan with a detachment of dragoons and about sixty-five conscript Mexicans and Pueblos serving as "spies" and scouts. With his own columns, Doniphan moved down the Río Grande to the ranchos of Albuquerque and then continued due west until he reached the Mexican pueblo of Cubero. The plan was in a sense an enveloping or a pincers movement, but not precisely warlike. Major Gilpin was instructed, after reaching the San Juan, to proceed down the Tunicha, or Chuska, Valley, summoning all Navahos he should meet on the way to a council at a place somewhere to the south known to the Mexicans as Ojo del Oso and to the Navahos as *Shash Bitoo,* or Bear Spring.

Doniphan's intentions were clearly understood back at Fort Marcy, and from there on November 11, by which time his troops had reached Cubero and were resting, this message was sent to army headquarters in Washington: "Col. Doniphan's Regt. is in the Navijo country attempting to make a treaty with those Indians; there is no doubt the Indians will Treat, but it is very doubtful if they will comply with the treaty when the troops are removed from their Country."[5]

The skepticism may have been shared by Doniphan himself, and almost certainly was by Captain John Henry K. Burgwin, commanding Companies G and I, First Dragoons, and escorting a train of American traders to Chihuahua in Mexico. Burgwin's orders were to get the train safely to the vicinity of "El Passo," where the traders were to await favorable military developments

[5] Captain W. M. D. McKissack to Major General Thomas S. Jessup. National Archives, War Records. Record Group 92, Office of the Quartermaster General, Consolidated Correspondence, 1794–1915, Box 987.

before proceeding. In any event, Burgwin took the merchant wagons down the Río Grande and in so doing, in the Mexican settlements he passed through, picked up useful information about the warring traits of Apaches and Navahos. To most soldiers, as to Burgwin, the present atmosphere in the territory would make treaty-making seem of dubious value.

As Colonel Doniphan poised about Cubero, giving Major Gilpin time to scout the San Juan and turn south through the Chuska Valley, Captain Burgwin arrived back at the hacienda of walled adobes and spreading ranchos called Albuquerque. At this place, on the seventeenth of November, Burgwin's dragoons went into camp, from that date establishing a military post that would remain here on the river's east bank until it was abandoned in 1867. Burgwin's first garrison included 5 officers, 13 non-coms, 3 buglers, a blacksmith, and 115 privates.[6]

Time came, meanwhile, for Doniphan to move toward the Ojo del Oso meeting place. To his biographer, John T. Hughes, we are indebted for descriptive side lights that, for sheer imagination, challenge the best of Swift's Brobdingnag. Gilpin, in the Hughes version, braved "perils, hardships and sufferings . . . almost incredible." The major's eventless ride over rolling prairies is compared to "the passage of the Carthaginian general over the Apenines . . . the march of Bonaparte and McDonough over the snow-capt peaks of the Alps." Stirring indeed, nor did Doniphan, proceeding quietly up the Wingate Valley from Cubero, escape hardship. The green slopes of the Zuni Mountains to Doniphan's left, the red rock bluffs forming a low bastion to his right startlingly become "colossal granite peaks [that] shoot almost perpendicularly out of the plain, more than six thousand feet high."[7]

The divided forces of Colonel Doniphan's First Regiment, Missouri Volunteers, were rejoined at Ojo del Oso, the future site of new Fort Wingate, there meeting a camp of some five hundred Navahos, including the tribe's principal chiefs and head-

[6] National Archives, War Records. Record Group 94, Post Returns, Albuquerque, Box 6.

[7] John T. Hughes, *Doniphan's Expedition.*

men. Only the most meager account of what took place is possible, as we have yet to discover letters or journals of any of the troops present (Hughes, then a private in Company C, was in camp near Socorro), and the Navaho version has been lost to the oldest generation of the tribe now living. Thanks, nevertheless, to Hughes, we do know that it was on a Sunday that a treaty was signed. And because of the date—November 22—and the usual climate of the region, we might assume an early-morning frost chilling the shadows of tents and thin smoke rising from many small cook fires. Later, the oratory on both sides, with the interruptions for translation, would have seemed nearly endless to the lower-ranking soldiers and Navahos, lounging about or astride their horses, motionless or moving restlessly on the outer edges of the council circle.

Congress failed to ratify the treaty, an omission of small moment, since, with the best of intentions, neither party to the agreement at that time was in any position to enforce its terms.

A memorandum by Hughes gives the substance of the treaty's five articles.[8] First, between Navahos and Americans, "firm and lasting peace shall henceforth exist." Second, "the people of New Mexico and the Pueblo tribe of Indians" were embraced in the term "American." Third, a free and mutual trade should be carried on between the several mutual parties "without molestation, and full protection shall be *mutually* given." Fourth, women and children taken as captive slaves—both Indian and Mexican—must be restored to their people. Fifth, all property taken by either side, since the day General Kearny entered Santa Fe and claimed New Mexico for the United States must be returned.

With Doniphan's name on the agreement appeared the signatures of Lieutenant Colonel Congreve Jackson and Major Gilpin. Navahos who signed with their marks—and not one of them would sign Colonel Washington's treaty in 1849—represented a majority of the tribe's actual leaders. First among them was Zarcillas Largo (in Spanish, Long Earrings, but called "Nataal-

[8] *Ibid.*, 307.

lith" by the Navahos), generally accepted as head chief of the Navahos. Below his mark were the marks of thirteen others: Caballada Mucho, Alexandro, the renegade Sandoval of the *Diné Ana 'aii*, Cayatanita, José Largo, Narbona of the Chuska Valley, Narbona Segundo, Pedro José, Narbona's son-in-law Manuelito, Tapio, Archuleta of the San Juan, Juanico, and Savoietta García.

Doniphan deserves credit for drafting a treaty that dealt directly—from the Americans' point of view—with the basic areas of disagreement or antagonism between the Navahos and their white and Indian neighbors. The Navahos, however, were not ready for this treaty, or for any other that was not implemented by force. The fault in this treaty, as in Colonel Washington's treaty, was the assumption of something not so—a willingness of the Navahos to make important concessions in exchange for vague promises, or for what to them were meaningless virtues of unwanted peace.

His treaty with the Navahos concluded, Colonel Doniphan led his Missourians southward through valleys and across pine-wooded hills to the pueblo of Zuñi. He was greeted with expressions of friendship, but after one night in the village he turned eastward again to the Río Grande. His role in the affairs of this unsettled territory was ending. In early December, 1846, we leave him at the river, preparing to march south to engage and defeat Mexican forces near El Paso; from there his regiment would go on to fresh victories at Sacramento and Chihuahua.

Far across the empty plains to the Missouri and from there eastward, the attention of the country centered, as well it might from that distance, on the progress of the war in Mexico and California. Scarcely a ripple of concern was felt back in the States, then, when news came late of the murder in New Mexico of Governor Bent and four others, all on the morning of January 19 in an insurrection at Don Fernando de Taos. More than the people in the States then knew or cared, the incident at Taos marked the end of General Kearny's bloodless conquest and the beginning of more than twenty years of intermittent warfare.

Governor Bent and the others were killed, perversely enough, by usually peaceful Indians of Taos Pueblo. A clique of Mexicans, plotting revolt, used the puebloans to strike this blow against the new American regime. The uprising was put down, and quickly, but not before the traditional Indian foes of the towns and ranchos—Comanches and Utes, Apaches and Navahos —appraised the situation rather well. American troops left here in garrison were far too few to be troublesome.

The first demonstration of Indian reaction came at once after the Bent murders. From their new post at Albuquerque, Captain Burgwin's two companies of dragoons took a bad clawing in what was referred to afterward as "the battle of Pueblo de Taos." Wounded in the chest on February 4, Burgwin died three days later. Before the fighting ended, the losses mounted to one sergeant and six privates killed, and twenty others wounded.[9] The Pueblo casualties were not given, but what mattered to observant Navahos was that mounted dragoons were not protected by strong medicine and could be shot out of their saddles.

From an Indian point of view, the Taos insurrectionists (save a few who were hanged) came out of the affair rather well. This may possibly have been a factor causing the Navahos, early in February to forget their recent council with Doniphan and turn again to raiding the Río Grande settlements. From Fort Marcy, where the small garrison could make only a token resistance, Captain W. M. D. McKissack reported that "the Nabajoe Inds. have broken their treaty and recommenced depredations, and if a new expedition is sent to their country to bring them to subjection and managed similar to the other [Doniphan's] it will cost $20,000 more."[10]

Burgwin's blooded dragoon Companies I and G, meanwhile, remained on duty at Taos under a new commander, Captain William N. Grier, and then in late March returned to their post in rented adobe quarters at Albuquerque. As other tribes joined the

[9] National Archives, War Records. Record Group 92, Office of the Quartermaster General, Consolidated Correspondence, Box 9.

[10] *Ibid.*, Box 987. McKissack to Jessup, February 16, 1847.

Navahos in sporadic raids, there was talk among the officers here, as at Santa Fe, of "a new expedition." But so long as the war with Mexico continued, replacements at the two posts were reduced to stringy and callow boys—the men of any real fighting ability were needed in Mexico or California. There was, indeed, a small territorial force of New Mexico volunteers to augment these regular army troops, an effective force because the volunteers knew the country and knew better than the fresh Missouri and Illinois recruits the ways of the Indians. Even so, all that this came to was a modest containing effort until some months after the war with Mexico ended and a treaty of peace was ratified on March 10, 1848.

A hiatus of more than a year followed. Army troops of occupation during this time remained in Mexico and California, and—spread too thin to count for anything—in the new territory taken from Mexico between the Río Grande and the Sierras.

The first omen of change in this situation was the arrival in Santa Fe, on October 10, 1848, of a stern, beak-nosed veteran campaigner, Lieutenant Colonel John Macrae Washington. He entered the capital at the head of one company of mounted troops and a battery of artillery, all parched dry, all tattered and very tired after a march of seventy-seven days across the deserts and plains from Monterey, California. A scant two years before, Colonel Washington's troops were farm boys who gee-ed a fat farm horse down a furrow or, in time off, drew a bead with nothing deadlier than a squirrel gun. They talked still in Missouri farm accents, but they talked with the experience of cavalry maneuvers in battle or of the logistics and killing capacities of a field or mountain howitzer. They went into quarters at Fort Marcy; and on the day following their arrival, Colonel Washington assumed his duties as civil and military governor of New Mexico.

Among the officers and civilians soon to figure in Lieutenant Simpson's journal of the Navaho campaign of 1849, Colonel Washington is first to appear on the scene, excepting only Henry Linn Dodge, who seems to have reached Santa Fe before the summer of 1846. Two other young men who would be important to the expedition were, with their elder brother, at about the same time embarking on an ill-starred adventure that brings them into the sphere of this and Lieutenant Simpson's story. Richard and Edward Kern in this same October of 1848 were in Westport, Missouri, there joining forces with Frémont and, as artists and topographers, awaiting the momentary start of Frémont's fourth expedition. With them was their brother, Dr. Benjamin Kern, listed officially on the party's roster as physician but, as were all of the others, expected to do his share of the mulewhacking and guard-duty chores that were a part of driving a pack train across the plains.

Edward, the youngest of these brothers, had accompanied Frémont's third expedition to California in 1845. As impressionable at that time as his twenty-one years would suggest, knowing nothing of the world beyond the realm of books and his studio and the streets and social life of Philadelphia, Edward, overwhelmed, surrendered to two overpowering emotional forces. One of these would last; the other would not. To a point, the vastness of the western country excited his interest and aroused a deep, growing urge for exploration. That emotion he would not lose. The other, amounting to hero worship, centered on the mercurial, seemingly infallible Frémont, who embodied for him what he believed were the virtues of a great man.

With these strong motivations, Edward Kern had persuaded his brothers, with the grace of Frémont's assent, to join him in one of the most harebrained exploring expeditions ever undertaken in this country. Censured publicly by his government for his insubordination during the recent war in California, Frémont hoped to regain favor with a dazzling success of this new expedition. His object was to discover a central route for a transcontinental railroad connecting St. Louis with the Pacific Coast—a dream that was entirely reasonable, providing that a route could be found over the high barrier of the south-central Rocky Mountains. The balance between reasonableness and disaster lay in Frémont's timetable. A winter passage of the Rockies, if not impossible, most certainly would be hazardous. This, with his pre-

JAMES HERVEY SIMPSON
*From a steel engraving made after Simpson
was brevetted brigadier general in 1865.*

SOLDIERS' QUARTERS, FORT MARCY, SANTA FE.

vious experience in these mountains, Frémont knew. The effort would be a spectacular gamble, but if he succeeded in taking his pack train through, presumably he would have demonstrated the all-weather feasibility of his chosen route. Frémont was aiming toward one of the most formidable sections of the Rockies—the peaks and high passes along the thirty-eighth parallel.

Frémont's party was about two weeks out of Westport when, in early November, Colonel Washington reorganized his forces in New Mexico. "With a view more effectively to secure the principal settlements against Indian incursions," he reported, "and to obtain the necessary supplies of forage for the public horses," he divided his troops between six military posts, all in the Río Grande Valley.[11] One company of dragoons was assigned to each of the towns of Taos, Albuquerque, and Socorro. Detachments of twenty and twenty-five men were removed from the two latter places to posts at Tome and Doña Ana. Fort Marcy, in Santa Fe, retained the largest garrison—one company of the Third Artillery, and a company of the Second Dragoons.

At Bent's Fort, meanwhile, Frémont's party paused late in November, observed chunks of ice floating in the Arkansas, and pressed upstream to the adobe settlement of Pueblo de Carlos (now Pueblo, Colorado). Here, where the plains merged with the lower slopes of the Rockies, Frémont engaged Old Bill Williams as guide. His personal magnetism again may have had a part in this arrangement, for early snowstorms already gave unmistakable warning that an unusually severe winter had set in. Some mitigation of our judgment of Frémont's foolhardiness is found in Williams' willingness to go along, for probably no other mountain man shared his knowledge, in all seasons, of the terrain ahead. His mere presence in the party indicates that, even in this hard winter, by one pass or another, the Rockies could be crossed.

Snow lay deep in Wet Mountain Valley and was drifted saddle-high over Robidoux Pass. Beyond, and still climbing, the party

---

[11] Washington to Secretary of War Marcy, November 8, 1848. 31 Cong., 1 sess., *House Exec. Doc. 5*, Part 1.

encountered Williams Pass, named earlier for their guide, on the lower approaches to the San Juan Mountains. By mid-December the Frémont expedition was in serious trouble and on December 25, split by a division of loyalties, faced with disaster.[12] The Kern brothers, especially Benjamin Kern whose slender strength ebbed first, were among those of the party who agreed with Bill Williams that Frémont, in his determinedly headlong assault upon the San Juans, was leading them to their death. When their foundering, starving mules could no longer make more than staggering progress through the deep snow, Williams urged turning from the thirty-eighth parallel to an easier pass to the north or to a course south that would skirt the San Juan range entirely. Frémont held adamantly to his plotted route until Christmas Day, when, too late, he admitted defeat and told his desperate followers they would turn back for the Río Grande.

The retreat was a disorganized nightmare. One by one, eleven of the party's thirty-three men were left behind in the snow to die of starvation, exhaustion, or sub-zero temperatures. Edward Kern's high esteem for Frémont, never shared by his brothers, turned to something like hatred when the great pathfinder, sending Bill Williams and a few of the strongest men on ahead for help, soon after abandoned those who were slower and more weakened than himself. The Kern brothers and six others, the weakest of all who survived, straggled on at the rear. At Taos a French mountain man named Lablond, learning of their plight, went out to meet them and bring them through the snow to the pueblo town, which they reached in early February.[13]

At Taos, where Frémont rested, there was no reunion. The Kerns, Old Bill Williams, and two others, already thoroughly disillusioned, were angered more when Frémont placed all the blame for his costly failure on Williams. Without them, but with all the remaining supplies and at the head of a fraction of his original command, Frémont departed for California now following a well-traveled southern route.

[12] Robert V. Hine, *Edward Kern and American Expansion*, 58.
[13] John Greiner to Richard Kern, January 27, 1851. Fort Sutter Papers, 129.

An epilogue to the fiasco remained to be acted out. Somewhere in the San Juan Mountains on the back trail, to spare what strength they had left, the Kerns had cached several hundred pounds or more of equipment belonging to themselves and others of the expedition. Richard and Edward stayed on in Taos while Benjamin Kern, with Bill Williams and a party of eight Mexicans, started back to recover the property. From their departure in late February the progress of their pack train may be traced, conjecturally, northward on the Río Grande to the vicinity of Zebulon Pike's old stockade on the north bank of the Conejos, perhaps then to Willow Creek, and then certainly into the mountains. Here they disappear.

Before they left Taos, we may safely presume, Dr. Kern and Bill Williams knew something of the Indian depredations that were then engaging Major Benjamin Lloyd Beall's dragoons, quartered in the town. Beall himself rode out on February 10 with part of his command, and was now near Bent's Fort campaigning against a war party of Kiowas who had taken a number of Mexican captives. Another detachment of dragoons under Lieutenant J. H. Whittlesey at the same time was tracking a band of Southern Utes—either Moaches or Capotes—who had been raiding the river settlements. Trails dragged in the snow by the lodgepole travois led into the San Juans.

Lieutenant Whittlesey's dragoons came upon and attacked a Ute camp on March 13. Later in the day there was a second encounter with another band of the same tribe. By their own account, the Utes suffered greater losses than Whittlesey later reported, their dead numbering seventeen and not ten, and including two chiefs or headmen.[14] Even so, most of the Utes escaped, leaving their lodges and most of their possessions to be burned.

[14] Beall to Lieutenant J. H. Dickerson, assistant adjutant general, Ninth Military Department., Santa Fe, March 26, 1849. This and other army post documents found in the same file shed an entirely new light on the murder of Kern and Williams. National Archives, War Records. Record Group 98, Records of U.S. Army Commands, Department of New Mexico, Letters Received, Box 1. Whittlesey reported the engagement to Beall on March 15, 1849, and his account of the fight was printed in the Santa Fe *Weekly Gazette*, March 12, 1853.

Eight days later (not the same day or the next, as other accounts have had it), members of one of these bands, still smoldering from their defeat, presumably crossed the trail of Benjamin Kern's pack train. What happened then is not nearly so certain as it first appeared to Major Beall a few days afterward. One of Kern's eight muleteers brought word that the Doctor and Old Bill Williams had been murdered by Utes.

"I would state," Major Beall reported on his return to Taos, "that an express arrived here from Red River late last evening [March 25] by which I draw information that two American Citizens were killed by the Eutaw Indians on the 21st inst. They were of Col. Fremont's party, who had left here, during my absence on my late expedition, for the purpose of recovering some property which had been left by the Colonel's party in the Mountains, and they were on the return to this post accompanied by eight Mexicans, with the property when they were killed by the Indians. The Mexicans were released, and one of them brought me the news of their death."[15]

Another account of the affair was related afterward by Assistant Army Surgeon Horace R. Wirtz, who was then stationed with Beall's dragoons at Taos. Until now, the Wirtz version of the murder of Dr. Kern and Williams has been accepted without question. Perhaps this is due as much to an oversight of army records (previously undiscovered) as to our knowledge that Dr. Wirtz, at the time of the murder, was close to the scene and a participant in at least the first part of the episode he described. Wirtz, in fact, was a member of Lieutenant Whittlesey's command. He tells how Whittlesey's patrol set out from Taos to punish the Indian raiders, and continues: "We met a band of Utes the second day out, and after a sharp hand to hand action, in which neither party gained much advantage, we succeeded in maintaining possession of the battle ground. After burying our dead, we met in the afternoon another band of Utes, and as they were encumbered with their families, we gained an easy victory and killed a large number.

[15] *Ibid.*, Beall to Dickerson, March 26, 1849.

"But this victory was attended with sad results. A portion of the band we defeated fled in the direction of the upper Del Norte, and at night came upon the little party that were encamped at Fremont's cache."

Dr. Wirtz was not present at this encounter. "Uncle Dick" Wootton, who was not present either, said the Utes met Kern's pack train early in the morning.[16] Only those who were present and survived could be certain. Dr. Wirtz continues: "From the account given by the Mexicans who escaped, it appears that about a dozen Utes came upon them as Bill Williams and Dr. Kern were sitting quietly by their camp fire, after having opened the cache and packed everything preparatory to starting. Williams and the Doctor were unsuspicious of any evil design, and treated the Indians well. But the savages had prepared a dire revenge for the death of their friends, and while the two white men were conversing, seated on the ground, two of the Utes suddenly raised their rifles and fired. One bullet struck Bill Williams in the forehead, and another passed into the heart of the Doctor. The Mexicans prepared to fly, but the Indians called to them and said they were at war only with the whites, and did not intend to harm them. The murderers however took possession of the mules and packs, and ordered the Mexicans to remain where they were till morning."[17]

[16] H. L. Conard, *Uncle Dick Wootton*, 200.

[17] The Wirtz account, taken from his notebook years later when he was medical director of Arizona, was published in the *Arizona Miner* of August 20, 1870, under the heading "How Bill Williams was Killed." Wirtz prefaces the remarks quoted here by relating circumstances of the disaster that befell Frémont's party a few months before in the San Juan Mountains. Favour, in *Old Bill Williams* (205–207), relied solely upon Wirtz, allowing himself to be misled, and in turn so misleading others who since have written on the same episode. Several documents among the Fort Sutter Papers in the Huntington Library collection, quoted or referred to below, bear on the matter without doing much to illuminate it. Other Kern documents of this period are held, at this writing, in the private collection of Fred Cron of Dingmans Ferry, Pennsylvania, and are not available for inspection. Mr. Cron, however, informed me that there are two letters in his collection which relate to the murder of Dr. Kern and Williams—"one letter from a man inquiring about their deaths, and a letter of reply written by Edward Kern." Mr. Cron indicated that the letters add nothing conclusive to what is

Major Beall and Dr. Wirtz both derived their information, contradictory on several minor points, from the muleteers who accompanied the murdered Kern and Williams. Beall soon had reason to question the Mexicans' story. Dr. Wirtz, whom—we meet again presently on the Navaho expedition, accepted the Mexicans' explanation at face value and evidently never learned that at least in one detail (the disposal of the property) it was untrue.

Richard and Edward Kern stayed on in Taos. For a time they considered going into the mountains to bury or bring back the bodies of their brother and Williams, and then gave up the idea. Strange rumors, meanwhile, filtered back to Taos, presenting the murder of the two men in a strange new light.

Early in April the brothers learned that some of the property recovered from the mountain cache was reported to have been found in a Mexican settlement in the vicinity of Abiquiu. So positive was the information that Richard wrote on April 6 to Captain John Chapman, commanding a militia company of New Mexico mounted volunteers stationed at Abiquiu, requesting his aid in securing the property. Major Beall was temporarily absent, leaving the post at Taos under the command of Captain Henry B. Judd, to whom the Kerns also turned for help. Judd at once sent instructions for an investigation, bringing this reply from Captain Chapman: "Sir: A young man arrived here this morning with some dispatches from you to the Prefect liveing in this vicinity, and also a note from Mr. [Richard] Kern to me, respecting the property of Col. Fremont and the late Doct. Kern, which was supposed to be concealed in this neighbourhood.

"I perhaps varied from your instructions, to some extent believeing from information that I have been able to obtain since my arrival here that the Prefect here is more of a friend to the Eutaws than he is to the Americans, and I have also heared a

---

known about the death of the two men, but said that Edward Kern's letter of reply is accompanied by a map, this indicating a rock and presumably the place of the cache.

rumor that he himself has purchased some property belonging to Americans who have been murdered. I have had spies out to try and ascertain the fact.

"I therefore took the responsibility of detaining the package, and took a sergeant and one man and went with the young man in search of the Goods; we proceeded to a village about six miles above this place and found three Mexicans who were recognized by the young man as being with Doct. Kern at the time he was murdered. I searched their Houses and found the goods the young man takes with him to Taos. I found the villians with some of the cloathing of the Decd on them, which they gave up. I also found a pick belonging to the Doctor. I arrested them and will keep them confined until I hear from you believeing that they should be sent to Taos for trial. . . .

". . . The prisoners inform me that the Ballance of the property belonging to the late Doct Kern that was in their possession is in the Moro [a Mexican settlement in the Mora River valley of the Sangre de Cristos, southeast of Taos].

"Two of my men returned last night from the Eutaw camp some fifty miles from this place. They brought in with them a Dragoon saddle and a pistol belonging to the soldiers who were killed in the battle that Lieut. Whitelsy [Whittlesey] had with them. They passed through their camp, under the character of Mexican traders with some tobacco and beads and were very well treated they saw the cloathing, arms & bugle belonging to those who were killed in the fight."[18]

Chapman, whom we shall meet again on the Navaho expedition, wrote on the same day to Richard Kern. He repeated substantially the information he communicated to Captain Judd—that he was returning to Richard and Edward some of the property recovered and that he was holding three of the muleteers "in Confinement, untill I hear from Taos. I believe that they

[18] Chapman to Judd, April 10, 1849. National Archives, War Records. Record Group 98, Records of U.S. Army Commands, Department of New Mexico, Letters Received, Box 1.

should be sent there for trial, as I do not feel warranted in turning them over to the Civil Authorities at this place."[19]

Nine days later Chapman cryptically informed Colonel Washington that he had in custody at Abiquiu a Ute chief who, if released, "purposes to bring in all of the property of Col. Freemonts ... but the murderers he says will never be given up as long as his men can fight."[20] The letter obviously appears to be an admission by Chapman's captive that Utes had murdered Williams and Kern. The proposal of the Ute prisoner to return "all" of the property is relayed without comment by Chapman, who already had found much of the property in Mexican hands. In its contradictions and vagueness the letter provides baffling evidence. Chapman fails to identify his prisoner by name, but describes him as "the head chief of the Eutaw tribe"—which is improbable; at most he would have been a chief or headman of one of the three tribal divisions of the Southern Utes.

Only three letters more and a special order of the day posted by Major Beall shed light on the case. In the first of these letters Captain Judd reports that he had arrested the prefect of Abiquiu in connection with the murder of Kern and Williams and was "sending him under escort to Santa Fe for investigation."[21] Judd gives no hint of the prefect's supposed part in the affair, and what happened to him after he reached the capital is not disclosed.

"From a source to be relied on," Major Beall noted two days later in Special Orders No. 6, he had learned "that a considerable amount of property belonging to Colonel Fremont's party is now concealed in some of the houses of the Rio Collarado [the Red River, north of the Mora]." Sergeant Batty and six dragoons were instructed to "proceed to that point and make strict search. . . . Should he [the sergeant] find any portion of the property he will

[19] Chapman to R. H. Kern, April 10, 1849. Fort Sutter Papers, 127.

[20] Chapman to Washington, April 19, 1849. National Archives, War Records. Record Group 98, Records of U.S. Army Commands, Department of New Mexico, Box 1.

[21] *Ibid.*, Judd to Dickerson, April 25, 1849.

bring the same to this post, together with the person or persons in whose possession the same may be found."

Sergeant Batty evidently recovered more of the Kern property because he returned shortly with two companions of the three Mexican muleteers previously arrested by Captain Chapman near Abiquiu. The two birds in hand, however, quickly turned to five in the bush. There is no doubting Major Beall's annoyance over this development in his note to headquarters in Santa Fe, May 1: "The Mexican prisoners who were suspected of having been concerned in the murder of Dr. Kern and Mr. Williams have been turned over to the *civil* authority, and have since been *bailed out*. I had lately caused two others to be taken up near this post on whom property belonging to Col. Fremont's party was found.

"I would respectfully state, that if such persons are turned over to the civil authority of this place, justice will never be executed upon the guilty. Must I turn over Montoya—the Eutaw prisoner, to the civil authority?"[22]

As far as the records indicate, the Mexican prisoners, once free on bail, disappeared and were never brought to trial. Their part in the murder of Dr. Kern and Old Bill Williams therefore remains unproved and conjectural. Even greater uncertainty surrounds the Ute, Montoya, who presumably was the same person as Captain Chapman's captive at Abiquiu, who was "known to be the head chief of the Eutaw tribe." If Montoya was indeed a headman of his tribe, his position was considerably less important than he led Captain Chapman to believe: no Ute chief of that name appears in other documents of the time or as a signatory to Ute treaties made in 1849 and later. We do not know whether Montoya was put on trial or released; the records do not say.

Richard and Edward Kern were never more certain than we are today of the identity of the murderers. Regardless of the evidence implicating the Mexican muleteers, suspicion continued to center upon the Utes. Months after the brothers first started their inquiries, Major John Greiner wrote to Richard

[22] *Ibid.*, Beall to Dickerson.

Kern that he believed Chico Velásquez, a Ute chief, was principally to blame. "I am more than half inclined to believe that [he] is the Captain of the Band who murdered your brother & Williams," Greiner wrote, "and I have had my eye on him closely for some time, and shall embrace the first opportunity of paying him his deserts—He is the fellow no doubt most deeply implicated in the murders of the White & Mail party—and I think his scalp sits very loosely upon his head."[23]

That Chico Velásquez was a murderous character there is little doubt. The French trader Auguste Lacome advised Indian Agent James S. Calhoun to place no trust in the Ute, as in his treaty negotiations with the Americans he "did not act, nor did he intend to act in good faith . . . he has sworn eternal hatred & enmity both to Americans & Mexicans, & that his mark of distinction among his tribe, are the ornaments of his 'legings,' being the finger nails of Americans on one side & of Mexicans on the other." Lacome, too, noted that Chico Velásquez "was engaged with the Apaches in their massacre of the party of Mr. J. M. White, & that he boasts of the part he took in that disaster."[24]

[23] Greiner to R. H. Kern, January 27, 1851. Fort Sutter Papers, 129. Major Greiner was appointed by Calhoun as one of four agents to the Indians of New Mexico in April, 1851.

[24] Lacome to Calhoun, March 16, 1850, reporting on a mission to which he and the trader Encarnacion Garcia were appointed by Calhoun in February, 1850, "to visit the Utes and Apaches . . . of northeast New Mexico, determine their numbers and state of mind." James S. Calhoun, *Official Correspondence*, enclosure E.) Their scouting mission resulted directly from the massacre of the James White and F. X. Aubrey party of St. Louis in October, 1849, near Point of Rocks on the Cimarron Cutoff of the Santa Fe Trail. In the raid by Jicarilla Apaches and a group of Utes (possibly Moache), all members of the train were killed except Mrs. White, her daughter, and a Negro servant. Through the offices of Lacome and Garcia, going to the Utes and Apaches as traders and supplied with trade goods, Calhoun had hoped to effect the ransom of the three, whom he believed to be alive and held captive. Elsewhere in this communication Lacome informs Calhoun that Mrs. White and her daughter had been murdered by their Indian captors as they fled from a troop of dragoons led by Major William N. Grier. The fate of the Negro servant has never been determined. I have found nothing that establishes definitely the band to which Chico Velasquez belonged, but his frequent association with the Jicarilla Apaches, in the region north and east of Taos, suggests that he was a Moache.

Lacome, who probably knew the Utes as well as any other trader did, unfortunately offered no opinion, so far as the present writer has determined, concerning those who killed Dr. Kern and Old Bill Williams.

Until such time as additional evidence may be found, the questions raised by their deaths have no final answer. Major Beall appears to have been convinced that the eight Mexican muleteers did not stand by innocent and helpless when Kern and Williams were murdered. His reasons for thinking so are not explicitly stated, although obviously he attached much importance to the muleteers having in their possession the clothing, the doctor's metal pick, and other Kern property taken from Dr. Kern's pack mules. Captain Chapman's Ute prisoner, whether Montoya or another, implicated other Utes in the murder; Chico Velásquez, who ornamented his buckskin leggings with finger joints of Americans and Mexicans, is implicated only circumstantially—by his bad record and by John Greiner's unspecified but deeply grounded suspicions.

Proof that was lacking in 1849 is lacking still, but we may believe that a band of Moache or Capote Utes perhaps was responsible for the murder of Benjamin Kern and Old Bill Williams. It is conceivable, though difficult to believe, that after killing the two Americans, the Utes would have spared the lives of the Mexican muleteers. It is not at all conceivable that the Utes would have spared the Mexicans and rewarded them with the loot from the Kern packs. Utes simply did not act that way. If slim evidence points to the Utes as the murderers, there is tangible evidence suggesting one other tenable conjecture: Kern and Williams were alone at the time they were killed. Sometime before the Utes discovered their campfire, the Mexican muleteers, with no motive worse than larceny, had deserted them in the mountains, running off with most, if not all, of the mules and packs forming the train.

On another point, finally, there is no uncertainty. Richard and Edward Kern, painfully concerned over their brother's death, lingered in Taos as May and then June turned to summer. Only by this turn of circumstance were they present in the territory and able to participate in Colonel Washington's expedition against the Navahos.

From his quarters at the Governor's Palace in Santa Fe and from his office at Fort Marcy, Lieutenant Colonel John Macrae Washington performed as best he could in his demanding dual role as civil governor and military commander of an unruly and generally unknown territory stretching from somewhere east of the Río Grande to somewhere this side of the California Sierras. Obviously, his tasks were beyond the capabilities of any one or even a dozen men. He could, and no doubt did, reduce his geographical problem to a known equation: into the territory he governed could easily be dropped, and swallowed up, all of the Atlantic seaboard he was intimately familiar with, from Virginia to Florida. And because nine-tenths of the territory was populated—if at all—only by Indians, he gave his attention to preserving the security of the Spanish-American settlements. The burden rested most heavily on the military arm of government.

Colonel Washington had had previous experience in Indian campaigns that probably recommended him to his present post. A Virginian, he was assigned with artillery units to duty in the South after his graduation in 1817 from the Military Academy at West Point. He was first at Charleston Harbor, South Carolina, then on the Florida frontier, and then back to Savannah Harbor, Georgia, and Fort Moultrie, South Carolina. As a first lieutenant, he transferred for advanced artillery practice to Fort Monroe in Virginia, and then was shipped back to Fort Marion in Florida—this in 1826-27, when he was about thirty years old and still a lieutenant. He won a captaincy and his first taste of Indian fighting against the Creek Nation in 1833-34. There were interludes at Fort Macon, North Carolina, and again in his native Virginia, and then he fought against the Seminoles in Florida in 1836. As an artillery expert, Washington had a passive part in helping to move the Cherokee Nation to the Oklahoma plains; after that he returned to fighting the durably stubborn Seminoles.

Nine years before we find him in Santa Fe, he was marking time at Dearbornville, Michigan, and then at Buffalo, New York —frontier country in the early 1840's, though offering nothing so exciting as the Seminole War and his combat at Locha-Hatchee. At the outbreak of the war with Mexico, when he was no longer young and seemed immobilized in the backwash of Carlisle Barracks, Pennsylvania, he was promoted to major and sent off to join General John Ellis Wool's column on the march from San Antonio to Saltillo, Mexico. For his gallant action in the battle of Buena Vista he was brevetted lieutenant colonel, became Wool's chief of artillery, and in 1847 was acting governor of Saltillo. Thereafter, he remained in the "army of occupation" until orders came to him in California to report to Santa Fe.

From this record we must derive our principal impressions of the man, since in his official orders and letters as military governor he reveals nothing of himself beyond the vague, faceless image of authority—stern, though not overbearing, and among his own officers inclined less to gregariousness than to aloof reserve. We might assume a relaxing or some thawing-out of the colonel's reserve when he and Lieutenant Simpson, a man of good intellect and education, were brought together by the hazards and hardships of the Navaho campaign. Between them certainly existed a basis for mutual respect and sharing of interests. If there was a relationship more than coolly formal, however, there is no indication of it in Simpson's journal. Nothing in the journal, in fact, gives any sort of clue to Colonel Washington's personality. Here, even as in Richard Kern's diary of the Navaho expedition, Colonel Washington remains, with an absence of speculation or comment, the distant, capable commander. Kern provides, though, a few engaging hints. On the final pages of his diary, otherwise empty, appear several perfunctory sketches of landscape intermingled with doodles and caricatures. One of these last brings together a long-stemmed clay pipe, a tin of tobacco, and a glass or tankard from which seems to be emerging a bearded goat labeled "Dick Kern" in block print. Wistful memories of Philadelphia, no doubt. On two other pages are three sketches, in profile, of obviously the same man—an officer. In each, the dark brows are lowered in a frown over a big blade of a nose that in one sketch is emphasized to a pronounced beak. The lips are set grimly, partly obscured under a heavy, dark mustache. Above the eyebrows the forehead rises to a balding dome, with wavy hair pushing back almost wiglike. In one sketch a toy-sized officer's hat is perched ludicrously on the officer's head. The sketches are not identified, but the fierceness and dignity which they convey somehow suggest that Kern's subject was Colonel Washington.

In early spring of 1849, before the Navaho campaign was conceived, Colonel Washington took additional measures to protect the Spanish settlements of the river valleys. Since the previous fall and his establishment of six military posts along the Río Grande, the raiding tribes of Indians had been causing more trouble. "Some change has taken place in the aspect of our Indian relations in this territory," he reported.[25] "The depredations, which were but few, have . . . become of frequent occurrence. . . . In order, therefore, to suppress them . . . I have felt it my duty to call in an auxiliary force of volunteers."

Four companies were mustered in at Santa Fe on March 23— a total of 393 privates enlisting for six months. The cost, estimated by Colonel Washington at $43,433, included transportation of 65,640 rations from Fort Leavenworth; the transportation of ordnance, ammunition, arms and medical supplies; and such miscellaneous items as fuel and forage; rent of quarters, stables, and storehouses; the cost of shoeing horses, the payment of guides and interpreters, and the purchase of camp and garrison equipage. All of this had been figured out carefully: each soldier's ration was weighed at three pounds and cost twenty-seven cents to bring across the plains from Leavenworth; the militia would need 164 fresh horses and 20 pack mules.[26]

[25] Washington to Adjutant General Jones, March 29, 1849. 31 Cong., 1 sess., *House Exec. Doc. 5*, Part I.

[26] National Archives, War Records. Record Group 92, Quartermaster's Consolidated File, Colonel J. M. Washington.

"The prompt manner in which these troops were raised," Colonel Washington reported two months later, "has produced a most salutary effect upon the interests of this territory. . . . The volunteer companies have done good service in the way of protecting the frontier settlements, which, but for their presence, must have been partially, if not wholly destroyed. . . . It will take some considerable time for the various Indian tribes inhabiting and adjacent to New Mexico, numbering at least twenty thousand warriors, to become acquainted with our national strength."

Two of the volunteer companies deserve passing attention here, as they will soon be joined with Colonel Washington's regular troops in the Navaho campaign. One was commanded by Captain John Chapman, whom we have encountered already at Abiquiu. He was then thirty-one years old and, on the evidence of letters written in his own hand, encumbered with only the most rudimentary education. Very little about him can be gleaned from the same archival sources that reveal considerably more of Captain Henry Linn Dodge. The records offer nothing that tells us where John Chapman came from or what happened to him. In fairness, he cannot be held entirely responsible, if responsible at all, for the performance of some of his militia during the two months of the Navaho expedition. Relieved of duty under Colonel Washington before the command completed its march, Chapman served later as a captain of Santa Fe Guards of Mounted Volunteers, again at Abiquiu, and under the command of Major Steen and Lieutenant Colonel Beall in campaigns against the Apaches and Utes. After that we lose him.

Of Captain Dodge there will be more later, but now—observing the chronology of these events—only this brief reference. He was born at Ste Genevieve, Missouri, in 1817, and was described, at the time of the Navaho expedition, as being five feet, nine inches tall, with a florid complexion, gray eyes, and dark hair.[27]

---

[27] National Archives, War Records. Record Group 15, 1817–SC–1773. Van Valkenburgh (1941) says that Dodge "was the fourth child of the thirteen children of the pioneer Henry Dodge and his stalwart Scotch wife, Christina McDonald. . . . By the time he was a stripling of twenty, he had volunteered for

Just when he came to Santa Fe and under what circumstances is not certain. But we find him there, twenty-nine years of age and a practicing lawyer, when General Kearny arrived in the capital with his army and, as we have seen, named him to serve as Santa Fe's treasurer.

In July of the year following, Dodge enlisted for service in the Mexican War as a private in Company A, Light Artillery, Santa Fe Battalion of New Mexico Mounted Volunteers. For thirteen months his battery was attached to Beall's First Dragoons and then, the war over, Dodge was mustered out at Las Vegas. Instead of claiming bounty land, his due as a veteran, Dodge requested instead that he be given one hundred dollars—an alternative, which he received presently in script. In 1848 and for at least fifty years more, federal currency in New Mexico was in low supply.

Colonel Washington's call for volunteer militia found Dodge again in Santa Fe, enlisting as the captain of a company of foot soldiers. His unit was stationed at Jemez Pueblo and in addition to himself included two Mexican lieutenants, four American-born sergeants, seventy-three Mexican privates, and one musician—a bugler, probably. The muster rolls show that during their six months of service none of these men received pay, but performed with loyalty and bravery.

From their quarters at Jemez, Dodge's militia was in almost daily contact with small parties of Navahos moving on mountain and valley trails to the pueblo of Jemez and on to the Río Grande. If it was their intention to raid, the presence of the militia discouraged them; through spring and until early July the Navahos were quiet. Sixty miles air-line over the Jemez Mountains, in the Chama Valley, Captain Chapman's mounted volunteers found life less agreeable.

---

service in the Black Hawk war of Illinois. Serving under his father, Henry fought in the final battle of Bad Axe River and saw the defeat of Black Hawk and Keokuk, the Sac and Fox chieftains. . . . The seventeen years after the close of the Black Hawk war are obscure." Van Valkenburgh has Dodge arriving in Santa Fe in 1849, which is late by at least three years.

BENJAMIN J. KERN

RICHARD H. KERN

EDWARD M. KERN

"Pueblo of Jemez from the East."
By R. H. Kern, August 20, 1849.

On May 30, Colonel Washington reported, "a large party of [Jicarilla] Apache Indians entered the valley . . . and murdered a number of the inhabitants, amounting, it is reported, to not less than ten." The raid occurred at a time when Chapman's cavalry were still off on a scout of Ute camps to the north and near the San Juan. Those murdered at Abiquiu were not long dead, however, on Chapman's return. He followed the Jicarillas' trail with about forty of his troops and "succeeded in routing the Apaches, killing about twenty of them, and having three of his own men wounded—one mortally—and a servant boy killed."[28]

Drifting clouds of early summer swept over the plains and river valley when Richard and Edward Kern, all but the last few dollars of their money spent, left Taos. Unable to afford horses or other conveyance, they walked. In Santa Fe, if they were fortunate, they would find work that would pay passage home. At the moment they owned nothing more than the clothes on their backs. And so, with their youth, they walked briskly; four days, about, would bring them to the adobe capital.

Like their late brother, Benjamin, the bothers were unmarried and so would remain for the rest of their short lives. Richard was twenty-eight, Edward almost three years younger. They both were serious in their craft but of a merry disposition—the rather round and stocky Richard leaning to cakes and ale as he could afford them, to music and poetry, and to putting a flute to his bearded lips and from this pipe enticing a flow of silvery notes. Both were gregarious, Edward's good humor coming, perhaps, from deeper within a frame that was tall and angular and, at certain periods, shaken by seizures of epilepsy. On their walk from Taos to Santa Fe, however, we can imagine the Kerns' mood as not merry at all. In letters home to their family and friends, first from Taos and soon from Santa Fe, they revealed strong depths of feeling—for the loss of their brother, for their present improverishment, and increasingly of bitterness over

[28] Washington to Jones, June 4, 1849, 31 Cong., 1 sess., *House Exec. Doc. 5,* Part I.

Frémont's libel of Williams and self-exoneration for the disaster in the mountains.

Our continuing interest in the Kerns, which grows rather than diminishes, is not rooted entirely in their talent as artists, which is the talent they cared most about and which induced Frémont to make them part of his company. In their drawings and water colors a similarity of technique is apparent, and it is a technique in the manner of Alfred Jacob Miller, whose proficiency far excelled theirs. In the period that concerns us, the productivity is almost entirely from the hand of Richard; Edward's western sketches survive, but they are few, and his efforts for Frémont and soon for Simpson center on cartography. Richard's best work, like Miller's, appeals to us now for its blithe simplicity and directness, his total unconcern for studio artfulness, the fresh and sometimes naïve concern for the little, absurd details that somehow—together—can become more significant than the blank fictions of well-ordered, ponderous selection. Richard was awkward in his treatment of the human figure and of animals. This failing his eastern lithographers set about correcting. While they were at it, when they found it necessary, they improved upon his work with lyrical interpretations of their own. In consequence of this, a small number of Richard's plates for Simpson's Navaho journal—the sketches of a Navaho warrior and of Fahada Butte are two startling examples—bear little resemblance to the original in nature.

Edward's map of the country explored by Colonel Washington's command was important in its time and retains documentary interest now because it was the first map with any semblance to accuracy that was made of this vital section of New Mexico and present Arizona. Mountain ranges, river courses, canyons, and valleys may be a bit askew, but for practical use—first by the military—Edward's map basically was reliable and charted a vast terra incognita, known only "in the heads" of a few Mexican, French, and American traders and mountain men. Two years later, Edward's pioneer charting of 1849 would be encompassed and supplanted by a considerably more ambitious map—of virtually the entire Southwest—produced mainly by Richard Kern, under the supervision of Lieutenant John G. Parke of the Topographical Engineers. From these valuable originals came later maps that charted military expeditions, directed emigrant trains on their southern routes to Los Angeles, and eventually aided in the selection of Indian reservations, a transcontinental railroad, and the first non-Spanish occupation of land westward from the Río Grande for one thousand miles.

Their western sketches, water colors, and maps were enough to place Richard and Edward Kern lastingly, if in the minor ranks, among the most memorable twoscore of men who variously and colorfully unlocked the floodgates of our western expansion to the Pacific slope. To the dream and substance of Senator Thomas Hart Benton's Manifest Destiny, Richard and Edward contributed rather fascinating fragments simply by virtue of being present, as observant or active participants, when our western history was being made. Their diaries and letters happily survive, offering pungent and illuminating, if not very literary, footnotes to the unfolding events of their time.

Edward was the youngest, and Richard next, of eight children; their father, John Kern, managed to support the family in modest comfort from his income as custom-house collector for the port of Philadelphia. An older brother, John, Jr., was the first to choose a career of painting and possibly influenced Richard and Edward to follow him. Edward's biographer, Robert Hine, says that there is no record of enrollment for any of the Kerns at the Pennsylvania Academy of the Fine Arts, which would have been their obvious choice had they attended an art school. Possibly the brothers were briefly apprenticed to or took lessons from one of the established artists of their city. In any event, all three in time took in students themselves and by this means derived the steadiest if not largest, source of their incomes.

The friendly intervention of Joseph Drayton, another Philadelphia artist then working in Washington, in the spring of 1845 helped to secure Edward's appointment as topographer and artist to Frémont's third California expedition. Frémont's object, after following the Arkansas to Bent's Fort and then crossing the Rockies, was to survey the region in the vicinity of the Great Salt Lake and then to discover suitable passes through the Sierras to the Pacific Coast. In pursuit of the company's main objectives, Edward's duties included taking celestial observations and helping to chart the territory surveyed, and making sketches of the plant, animal, and bird life encountered on the way.

In spite of Edward's youth and greenness, his eagerness to learn earned Frémont's confidence even before the party divided, on the approach to the Sierras in early winter.[29] After various misadventures, and some time after his command was reunited at San José in the middle of February, Frémont named the Kern River for the expedition's young cartographer. (Years afterward a town and county in California also would take Kern's name.) The outbreak of war with Mexico projected Edward suddenly into a new role that left little time for his sketch pad and brushes. The property of the neutralist John Sutter was rudely expropriated, and command of Sutter's Fort was turned over by Frémont, before his departure for the shifting battlefronts, to Kern. Perhaps to his amusement, the unwarlike artist was commissioned a first lieutenant of the California Battalion, on detached duty. From July, 1846, through the following January, Edward devoted himself to maintaining his small garrison, fighting off recurrent attacks of illness, and raising volunteer forces for his absent commander.

The collapse of Mexican resistance in early spring of 1847 brought the disbandment of the California Battalion, but Ed-

[29] Edward Kern, who was born October 26, 1823, was twenty-one at the start of this expedition. On the strength of Frémont's own version later, Allan Nevins (*Frémont, the West's Greatest Adventurer*, 246–47) says that in late November, fearing the heavy snows in the Sierras, Frémont divided his command into two parties. The smaller group he led directly over the mountains, "sending the main body under Kern south along the Sierras" to cross on the lower passes. The larger of the parties actually was led by Theodore Talbot, with the veteran Joe Walker as guide. As Hine points out (22–23), Frémont erred in recalling Kern's role, and Edward merely was "placed in full charge of the topography."

ward stayed on at Sutter's Fort without commission or official rank. He had remained loyal to Frémont through the latter's insubordinate refusal to recognize General Kearny as his superior officer. He was still partisan to his hero when Frémont was ordered east to appear before a court martial—disillusionment, as we have seen, came later.

Edward remained in California through the summer and fall, finally in November sailing for home on the schooner *Commodore Shubrick*, out of San Francisco. Exactly a year later Frémont's grand new endeavor would have Edward and his two brothers along with the others, preparing to make an assault on the Rockies. Our references to that episode end now, with Benjamin Kern dead in the San Juans and Richard and Edward making their way on foot from Taos to Santa Fe.

As unaware as the Kerns were of the fate bringing them together, Lieutenant Simpson, accompanying the command of Captain Randolph Barnes Marcy and a train of emigrants out of Fort Smith, Arkansas, was approaching Santa Fe about the same time. A first lieutenant in the Corps of Topographical Engineers, Simpson had never before been west of the Missouri or, as he would put it, "outside of the United States." He was thirty-six years old. On receiving his present orders in March, he was occupied with the relatively mundane construction of a lighthouse near Monroe, Michigan. But he liked this work and the Michigan country, too, and so may not have been pleased by the change. His orders required him to report for duty to General Mathew Arbuckle at Fort Smith; on arrival there he would join Captain Marcy's escort of John Dillard's California-bound emigrants; most important, he was to explore, survey, and direct the construction of a wagon road from Fort Smith to Santa Fe by way of the south bank of the Canadian River. Upon reaching Santa Fe, he was to detach himself from Marcy's escort, which would return to Fort Smith, and continue with Dillard's wagons to California.

Captain Marcy's instructions also emphasized the government's interest in discovering "the best possible" southern route to California—an alternative to the Santa Fe Trail and the Gila River route. Marcy's safe conduct of the Dillard party was, of course, another immediate concern; beyond this, he was directed to carry presents to the Comanche Indians and remind them, pointedly, of their 1835 treaty promise to allow Americans to travel through their country unmolested.[30]

Simpson arrived at Fort Smith in the company of his brother-in-law, Thomas A. P. Champlin, a citizen of Buffalo, New York. Champlin's shadowy presence among the forming company, as later in the Navaho campaign, is explained only by Simpson's brief comment that Champlin was with him as his assistant. At Fort Smith they found their Santa Fe–California expedition grouping and moving off in separate contingents, Marcy's troops having preceded them by a day or two, and a week before Marcy's departure, a small force under Captain Frederick T. Dent going ahead to prepare a wagon road as far as Chouteau's trading post on the border of the High Plains. The emigrant train was to leave Fort Smith still later, rendezvousing with the escort at Chouteau's on May 17.

Marcy left camp near Fort Smith on the morning of April 5 at the head of twenty-five dragoons and fifty infantry, his train including eighteen wagons, a six-pound field gun and traveling forge, and a *remuda* of mules. The mules were booty taken in the war with Mexico and now so travel-weary that they slowed Marcy's progress to a crawl. Simpson and his brother-in-law caught up with the column twenty-six miles west of the fort; and at Edwards' trading post on the Canadian, on the riverbank

---

[30] The treaty was made on the eastern border of the Grand Prairie, in the vicinity of Augustine A. Chouteau's trading post and old Camp Holmes, and near the Canadian River, August 24, 1835. For free hunting privileges, the Comanches and Wichitas and neighboring bands of Cherokees, Choctaws, Muskogees, Osages, Quapaws, and Senecas agreed to allow free passage to "citizens of the United States . . . through their settlements or hunting ground . . . to any of the provinces of the Republic of Mexico." As always, both parties to the treaty violated its terms, and the Comanches, especially, in 1849 were harassing every small group of whites that came their way.

opposite a settlement of Shawnees, they were joined by a Delaware guide named Black Beaver.

Simpson's wide-ranging interests, as reflected in his journals, extended to Indians only impersonally. Those he encountered in his travels excited his curiosity—almost never his interest. The prehistory of the Aztecs could absorb him, but not the traits or background of a Delaware guide. It is Marcy, then, not Simpson, who tells us that Black Beaver was an unusually colorful member of this unusual tribe—the Delawares appearing again and again, after their removal to the lower plains, in fabled roles of aggressiveness against their High Plains and mountain cousins. Marcy's guide probably told only the truth when he said he knew all of the western country from the Canadian to the Columbia. He had spent five years in Oregon and California, two more in the country of the Crows and Blackfeet. On the Gila and the Columbia and on the upper Pecos and the Río Grande he had trapped beaver. He had crossed the Rockies so many times he had lost count, knew their passes as well as he knew Shawneetown, opposite Edwards' post, where at the moment he lived. With Kiowas and Arapahos, or any other Plains tribe, he could converse in sign language. The Comanche tongue he spoke as easily as his own. "He proved most useful," Captain Marcy observed.[31]

Evening of June 1—and by chain measurement, 418 miles out on the plains from Fort Smith. The separate camps of Dillard's emigrants and Marcy's escort, who had been moving separately but close together, were accosted by four Kiowa braves, painted and dressed to the nines in war costume and armed with rifles, lances, bows, and buffalo shields. There was a short parley and then the Kiowas were invited to sit down and eat. They were on their way to Chihuahua, they said, to steal Mexican mules and horses. They would be gone a long time—even a year or more. Captain Marcy was "spellbound" by the pantomime as Black Beaver and the Kiowas sat straight, conversing in gestures and hand signs.

[31] "Report of Exploration and Survey of a Route from Fort Smith, Arkansas, to Santa Fe, New Mexico." 31 Cong. 1 sess., *House Exec. Doc. 45.*

Two weeks later: the columns again are in evening camp. From his position on a rocky eminence (now out of the Panhandle and into eastern New Mexico), Simpson makes notes on the scene below. In golden slanting light the officers' tents are pitched on one side of the tributary creek or dry wash. On the other side, on high ground selected by Dillard, the emigrants are settling in for the night. A corral of the wagons has been made to protect the mules and horses—a few of the number having been run off on recent nights by Comanches. The corral is made this way, Simpson notes: the lead wagon has been halted on the level plain; the second wagon is driven up to the left and rear of the first; the third wagon halts to the right and rear of the second, front and rear wheels touching—and so on until an enclosure is made in the form of an ellipse. The animals will graze free until dusk and then be turned into the corral. Right now, emigrants and troops alike are scrounging through the sage scrub for fire kindlings.

Down there somewhere among all of the moving figures is the "Arkansas young lady" named Mary, bound for California with the others—with husband or parents we'll not know—but possessed, be sure, of charm. Three weeks back, on an evening like this, Simpson had climbed to the top of another hill, resembling "an Indian lodge" in its curious formation. Others joined him as he exuberantly planted a flag: Marcy, Lieutenant Harrison, and Dr. Julian Rogers, attached to the troops as physician and bone-setter. Without argument they agreed with Simpson that the hill must be named Rock of Mary.

Rock of Mary, or Mary's Rock, Simpson soon would do better naming a mountain. And what more do we know of Mary—tonight, or in the days and nights later in California? Nothing. Mary is lost to us, and so is the Mary's Rock whose name her winsomeness gave to that curious hill with a flag on its top. Of Lieutenant Harrison we know a bit more. On the return to Fort Smith, while scouting a ravine off the main trail, he was met and led off by Indians, probably Comanches, and was killed. He was scalped first; the troops later found his stripped and mangled body sprawled down among the rocks.

Two days west of Cerro Tucumcari, on June 19, Captain Marcy met in full force the Indians who had been lurking behind the train and for whom he had presents and a reminder of their treaty promises. On this day the train was "lain by," resting the animals, mending wagon gear, and giving the Comanches of Is-sa-kiep's band an opportunity to come in and trade.[32]

One by one or in pairs they rode up to the encampment, until by noon they numbered some fifty or sixty warriors. Simpson noted, as Is-sa-kiep and a few others met with Marcy in his tent, that the Comanches were mounted variously on mustangs or ponies or full-sized American horses and Mexican mules. The presents were distributed, and in return, to display his momentary good faith, Is-sa-kiep restored to an emigrant named Murray a horse stolen from him a few nights previously. Another of the emigrants, a Dr. Bledsoe, wandered away during the council and came back in the afternoon to report that he had come upon the Comanche camp a few miles distant. He counted the village as one hundred lodges, and said he found there "several captive Mexican boys and a very good looking young Mexican woman, also captive among them."

Several days more over the rolling, bare plains, now with occasional glimpses of mesa formations, and the train raised the hazy outline of the Sangre de Cristos. Presently, after the Gallinas was crossed, the ground ahead tilted upward. And then, approaching Anton Chico on the Pecos, Simpson in a few moments counted more sheep than he had seen before in his life. Together, in two flocks or herds, they numbered six thousand—the sight of them, to his astonished gaze, a reminder of how far he had traveled from his native New Jersey. The sheep, of course, belonged to people of this Mexican settlement; and at Anton Chico, "delighted to see houses and cultivated fields" again—

---

[32] *Ibid.* The account here is Simpson's, who translated Is-sa-kiep's name as Wolf Shoulder. In the 1835 treaty the Comanche chief's name appears as Ishacoly, or The Wolf.

the first since Edwards' trading post—Captain Marcy decided to lay over for a day to rest the horses.

Santa Fe was near, a few days ahead at most, and all hands welcomed their first real chance in weeks to relax. The occupants of this village, furthermore, appeared to be friendly. Marcy tells of attending a fandango held by the villagers that night to celebrate St. John's Day. We may believe that the Captain found the dance lively, the music loud and gay, and some of the girls attractive. Whether Simpson was there also we cannot be sure, for he makes no mention of it.

It is possible that we may read too much into his silence; to avoid injustice let us presume that Simpson did attend the fandango and enjoyed the dancing as much as any of the others. A point remains, however, and it should be mentioned now, that the author of the Navaho journal reveals himself as a complex individual. He possessed an inquisitive, intelligent, informed mind. He was gifted with a degree of sensitive perception and had an ability to communicate his observations in an engaging manner—all quite rare among army officers of his time. On the young side of middle age, speculatively bookish, he had surprising energies and endurance. His inquisitiveness, coupled with an instinct to probe deeper than was expected of him, led him to efforts that younger officers in his position would have avoided.

His journal of the Navaho campaign is the second and most interesting of the three western journals that distinguish him. And yet he profoundly disliked very nearly everything he saw, felt, and tasted in the West. He writes that he could not contrast the "general nakedness" and the "sickening-colored aspect" of the Southwest with his native green valleys "without a sensation of loathing." In his two references to the food of the country, Pueblo Indian and Mexican, we find him nauseated. He tells us again and again of the scrub cedar and artemisia that withered his soul, but he tells us nothing of the purple aster and golden jimmyweed that carpeted many of the high valleys he passed through. His descriptions of nature are nearly all in terms of black and white. Could he have been color blind?

And yet, paradoxically, the only events that lift him from the obscurity of a long career as a builder of roads and supervisor of harbor improvements are the achievements resulting from his brief three and one-half years in the West.

He could be brilliantly perceptive in some matters and almost totally myopic in others. While still a junior officer, he could advise the colonels and generals where military posts or forts should be built to protect this western territory—and that is where they were built. While accompanying Captain Marcy to Santa Fe, he saw the need for, and in his report later advocated, a military post on Tucumcari Creek. In that vicinity Fort Bascom was built later and proved useful (1863–70) in discouraging raids by Navahos, Kiowas, and Comanches. As we will see presently, he selected the site for a garrison of dragoons at Cebolleta; and he was instrumental in choosing the site of Fort Union, which for years guarded the lower end of the Santa Fe Trail.

From the perspective of time, we know that Simpson was right and acted wisely in the selection of these posts. We know also that a conservative side of his nature caused him to oppose as impractical and visionary an east-west railroad built on a line approximating the Canadian River route which he and Marcy now explored. To his mind, he wrote, "the time has not yet come when this or any other railroad can be built over this continent."[33] Captain Marcy differed with him and advised the construction of a railroad on this route, and in time it was built.

Conservative he was, but the fandangos of Anton Chico and Santa Fe later apparently did not disturb him, nor did the powder and paint and the *cigarritos* and low-cut blouses of the *señoritas* move him to pious comment on this territory's moral standards. Other visiting Americans of his time professed to be shocked or even disgusted by all of this, but not Simpson. And yet, as several passages in his Navaho journal will demonstrate, he remained close to his strict upbringing in the Episcopal church.

Of his father, J. N. Simpson, and his mother, we know almost nothing except that they "were honored residents of his native

[33] *Ibid.*

city, and devout Christians."[34] At his birth, March 9, 1813, in New Brunswick, New Jersey, he was named by his mother "James Hervey" after an Episcopal clergyman then noted in England. If she hoped that this infant would enter the ministry, she was disappointed, although an elder brother, Theodore William, does appear to have tended that way, during the Civil War serving as hospital chaplain of volunteers.[35]

Brother Theodore received an appointment to West Point in 1824 but for some reason, perhaps theological, decided not to attend. Four years later, a prodigy at the age of fifteen, James Hervey Simpson was recommended for appointment to the Academy by former Secretary of the Navy Samuel L. Southard and a New Jersey congressman named Lewis Condict. He reported to West Point in September, 1828—an intellectual and serious boy finding himself suddenly among men. We have no description of his appearance then or later, nothing more, in fact, than an antebellum steel engraving that portrays a dismayingly mousy-looking man, bearded and high-domed, probably short in stature, and with a bemused expression that suggests a thinker or a poet, but scarcely a warrior. If the portrait is a true likeness and not a libel, then we may account his appearance as another paradox.

A classmate at West Point was Randolph Marcy, with whom we have left him for the moment at Anton Chico. They graduated together in 1832, Marcy drawing assignment to an infantry unit and much later advancing to inspector general of the United States Army. Simpson's career for the next seventeen years, while it may have satisfied him, shifted him about the Atlantic seaboard and in the Great Lakes region, almost always in duties that are without much interest and frankly make dull reading.

His first commission on graduation from West Point was as a second lieutenant with the Third Artillery assigned to Fort Preble, Maine, on recruiting duty. He was there for one year.

[34] C. C. Andrews (ed.), "History of St. Paul, Minnesota," 141.
[35] National Archives, War Records. Record Group 94, Academy Papers, 297–1824.

In 1833–34 he was at Fort Monroe, Virginia, and in 1835 at Fort King, Florida; the following year found him on commissary duty at Charleston, South Carolina. In 1837–38 his prospects brightened: he was promoted to first lieutenant (as we find him in 1849), and served as aide-de-camp to Brigadier General Eustis during the Seminole War and the action at Locha-Hatchee.

Simpson was twenty-five years old when his military career finally took direction, with his transfer from artillery to the newly reorganized Corps of Topographical Engineers. From Florida's Everglades he went, as an assistant engineer, to the construction of harbor improvements along the east shore of Lake Erie. In the years immediately following, he was engaged in building roads in Florida, the improvement of Erie Harbor, Pennsylvania, and surveying the northwestern lakes. The war with Mexico was of distant concern to him: at the start of the conflict he was working on harbor improvements, and at the end—as we first found him—he was in Michigan.

On that June evening of the fandango at Anton Chico, then, the author of the Navaho journal was removed by only three months from his lighthouse in Monroe. This abrupt change was not sought by Simpson and probably was unwelcome to him. Among other things, it meant a prolonged separation from his wife of only a few years, the former Jane Champlin of Buffalo, New York, the daughter of a onetime commodore in the United States Navy. Much that he found in the Southwest distressed him, but neither in the Fort Smith–Santa Fe report nor in his Navaho journal will we find any evidence that the young engineer of harbors and lighthouses was out of his element. On the contrary, the Navaho journal demonstrates again and again his lively, informed curiosity—a curiosity informed by a considerable amount of advance reading—that led him to stray far and often enough from Colonel Washington's single-minded objective to produce a work of lastingly fresh interest. His enthusiasms of discovery more than offset his nausea induced by native food and his loathing of the landscape, induced by homesickness.

From Anton Chico, Captain Marcy led his troops and train

of emigrants northwesterly into the Galisteo region and then to Santa Fe, arriving there on the afternoon of June 28 after covering a distance of 819.5 miles. John Dillard's people found shelter in the town as they could, Marcy and Simpson reporting with the troops to Colonel Washington and taking quarters at Fort Marcy. Several days later, as Dillard's train was outfitting for the next stage of its journey, Simpson received new instructions. The emigrants were to proceed to California without escort. Captain Marcy and his command would return to Fort Smith, and Simpson would remain at Santa Fe, attached until further notice to Colonel Washington's staff and subject to his orders.

The Colonel might have wished that he had Marcy's infantry and dragoons at his disposal, as well. He was finding it difficult, with the few troops allowed him, to contain the depredations by hostile tribes surrounding his garrisons. In a report foreshadowing his late summer expedition against the Navahos he remarked: "Within the last three weeks several of the inhabitants have been murdered . . . and a considerable quantity of their stock run off. In these outrages, which had been confined to the Eutaws and Apaches, the Navajoes and Comanches appear also to have been recently engaged. From their numbers and formidable character, greatly increased exertions have become necessary to suppress them."[36]

This was the state of things when, on July 22, James S. Calhoun arrived in the capital with the unpromising commission as first Indian agent to New Mexico Territory. His appointment by President Zachary Taylor was dated April 7 and, as forwarded to him by Indian Commissioner William Medill, stipulated an annual salary of $1,500 plus $2,300 more for expenses and contingencies. Within a week of his arrival, though handicapped by no previous knowledge of the Indians in his charge, he showed a thorough awareness of his thorny situation.

"At present," he advised Commissioner Medill, "it is the opinion of Col. Washington . . . that any attempt to conciliate the

[36] Washington to Jones, July 7, 1849. 31 Cong., 1 sess., *House Exec. Doc. 5,* Part I.

tribes who have caused the recent and present troubles in this territory, would have a very serious tendency. The Indians presuming upon their knowledge of safe retreats in the mountains, and our entire ignorance of all avenews, except established military roads and well known trails, are not to be subjected to just restraints until they are properly chastised. When they shall feel themselves so chastised, they will sue for peace."[37]

Calhoun must be numbered among the relatively few Americans who, in the public service of their country, met oppressive challenge with surprising capacities of wisdom, courage, and integrity. His appearance in the Southwest coincided with a period of most virulent eruptions and sorest need. As accidental as the circumstances that drew Simpson and the Kern brothers together, Calhoun's arrival was fortuitously happy: it was a man of his patient enduring fiber that this rough new territory demanded. Let him be numbered also among those men in public life whose services have been generally misunderstood or gone unrecognized.

His early background is obscure. He was born in either 1802 or 1803; and while a granddaughter placed this event near Abbeville, South Carolina, he himself claimed to be a native of Georgia. A "rabid" Whig, he said he was, first engaged in a shipping business and later as a captain of Georgia volunteers in the war with Mexico. He came out of that war a lieutenant colonel commanding a battalion of Georgia mounted volunteers. There are important gaps in what we know about him. His political activities before and after the war, even more than his useful military record, must have brought him closely to the attention of the war leader and new president, also a southerner and a fellow Whig. Annie Heloise Abel, who collected his official letters while he was Indian agent and then civil governor of New Mexico,

[37] Calhoun to Medill, July 29, 1849. Calhoun, *Official Correspondence*. This valuable source book, edited by Annie Heloise Abel and long out of print, documents an important era of southwestern history. All following references to Calhoun, whether factual statements, direct quotations, or opinions of my own, are based on these letters or later correspondence relating to Calhoun found in the Indian Records division of the National Archives.

thought there was much more to his appointment than his modest office might indicate.

Calhoun's appointment was mainly political, she writes, and he "had practically nothing to say about the remarkable Indian civilization of the southwest. He seems not to have been even remotely interested, scientifically. His letters are all strangely lacking in references to scenery, to archaeological remains, to interesting Indian customs, or to evidences of previous Spanish occupation. . . . Calhoun was most certainly sent to Santa Fe for a purpose but what the real purpose was does not appear. Somewhere, no doubt, and very probably in the *confidential* files of Interior, War, or State department, there are papers that hold the secret."[38]

Possibly so. And it is true that in the large collection of his correspondence we find him matter-of-fact, with no inclination, apparently, to the diversions he might have found in the scenery and ethnology that surrounded him. Perhaps he lacked the time. His letters tell us nothing of the mythology or religious rites of the Pueblo Indians, but they do tell specifically how and why the Zuñis appealed for arms against the raiding Navahos—and what he did about it. His letters do not once mention the name of Don Juan de Oñate, the colonizer of New Spain, but do reflect Calhoun's surprising (for a Georgian) abhorrence of the Mexican-Indian slave system and his determination to end it. There is nothing in the correspondence describing rain and sunlight sweeping the mountains and valleys of the Río Grande, but there are letters detailing the nasty habits of some of the vagabond

[38] Calhoun, *Official Correspondence.* President Taylor indeed had veiled reasons for sending Calhoun to New Mexico, according to historian H. H. Bancroft, who writes (1889, pp 446–47n.) that upon Calhoun's arrival, "he declared that he had secret instructions from the govt. at Wash. to induce the people to form a state govt. For a time the plan received but little support, but in the course of the summer and fall an excitement was raised, and both parties, state and territorial, published addresses to the people, the former being headed by Calhoun, Alvarez, and Pillans, and the latter by St. Vrain, Houghton, Beaubien, and others."

traders—and what Calhoun proposed to do about them. The letters tell us nothing of ancient ruins, but they document the peaceful aspirations or murderous proclivities of his Indian charges and, later on, the blind arrogance of a military commander whose behavior conceivably hastened Calhoun's early death. For the patient matter-of-factness of his correspondence, Calhoun's letters are richly self-revealing and a mine of information about this emerging territory and its savage or half-savage or desperately struggling population.

If Calhoun came to Santa Fe with powers or influence granted confidentially by the Whig administration in Washington, he used them so carefully that, even when he needed help the most, they were never apparent. Working easily or in great strain with three military commanders, first as Indian agent and then as Indian superintendent and civil governor, he could co-operate and lead at the same time. As Indian agent under Colonel Washington, he was co-operative, while obliged to learn a great deal very quickly. Later, as we shall see, as governor, he tried his best to work in harmony with Colonel Edwin Vose Sumner, never overstepping the prerogatives of his office, until his health snapped.

And so we find him, in early August, 1849, freshly arrived in Santa Fe. Lieutenant Simpson was there and waiting, rested after a month's inactivity at Fort Marcy. Richard and Edward Kern were there, down from Taos long enough to have become acquainted with Simpson and to have enlisted his friendship and interest in their abilities as artists and cartographers. Henry Linn Dodge was not there, but at Jemez, and John Chapman with his militia was at Abiquiu, when Colonel Washington—unknown to any of them—made the following report to the army's adjutant general in Washington: "From the repeated depredations committed on the settlements of New Mexico by the Navajoe Indians, and which have lately been attended by the murder of some of the inhabitants, it has become necessary to make a campaign against them. Accordingly I expect, in a few days, to set out with a sufficient force to insure the most favorable results—one of which will probably be to lay the foundation of a lasting peace."[39]

The activity of the fort, in the last days before the middle of August, centered in the commissary and quartermaster's quarters and around the forge of the blacksmith's shop, where the sound of hammer on iron must have dinned interminably. Before the orders were posted, the troops were alerted to readiness; and while they waited, they had long hours to speculate on the Colonel's plans. Nearly the entire strength of Fort Marcy's garrison —infantry, dragoons, and artillery—sat in quarters and waited. If we are right in believing that only by rumor they knew what Colonel Washington planned, there was evidence on all sides of what was coming.

From stables to the rear the horses and mules of the post were led out for shoeing, and the fort's wheelwright and harness maker were only less busy than the blacksmith and his assistants. Across the bare quadrangle of the parade ground, enclosed by the officers' quarters and troops' barracks, a dozen or more heavy army wagons were drawn up in rank and left standing with shafts down. Close by, covered with tarpaulins against blowing little twisters of sand, stood the waiting guns—one six-pound field gun, and three twelve-pound mountain howitzers.

As Simpson will refer frequently in his journal to these field pieces, they deserve a moment's consideration. The most awkward of the four and the gun that caused greatest difficulty in the rough places on the trail was the six-pounder. This weapon had to be dragged on its carriage. Its ponderous weight centered on its bronze barrel, too long (six and one-half feet) and heavy to be lashed to a mule's back. A viameter, measuring the expedition's daily progress, was attached to one of the wheels, these of tough white oak and standing about shoulder-high to a very tall man.

On the morning of the departure the three mountain howitzers

[39] Washington to Jones, August 5, 1849. 31 Cong., 1 sess., *House Exec. Doc. 5,* Part I.

were unlimbered and packed on mules—stubby bronze barrel and carriage shafts, or prolonges, on the back of one mule; wheels and carriage on another; the lunette and trail plate projecting rearward over the mule's tail. Ammunition chests for the three guns were also packed on mules, two in tandem over the animal's back, secured below by wide belly straps of leather and over the top by heavy rope. The chests were made of poplar braced with corner irons. There was room in such a chest, in addition to the ammunition, for a portable forge, anvil, and smith's tools. Ammunition for the howitzers was of three varieties: shells, spherical case shot, and canisters—the latter filled with musket balls. The charge for each was the same—eight ounces of gunpowder. This half-pound charge would hurl a 6.9-pound shell about one mile. The total weight of each howitzer, including carriage, was about 550 pounds.

Colonel Washington's plans for transport, as we will see, were modified drastically on the march from Santo Domingo Pueblo to Jemez. In crossing the intervening mesa, ascending by the sandy dry wash of Borrego Canyon, and coming down on the other side off Chamisa Mesa, the drag and braking of the heavy wagons proved so difficult that the wagons were discarded, with much of the superfluous baggage they carried, at Jemez.

Records of the expedition do not preserve the supply lists of Fort Marcy's quartermaster. For this reason we know only the quantity of the rations carried (thirty days' rations for five hundred men), and that tents for the entire command were taken in the wagons as far as Jemez. Here Colonel Washington "disencumbered the troops of tents and other heavy baggage" and transferred the lightened equipment to a pack train of mules. We may only guess, then, with a few hints from Simpson's journal, of the number of mules required (seventy-five to one hundred?) and the equipment they carried in addition to rations. twelve tents, perhaps, for the Colonel and officers of his staff, Agent Calhoun, his assistants, and some of the civilians; several hundred pounds of rope and chain and an equal weight of tools, such as axes, picks, and shovels; possibly a score of lanterns and enough oil to light them for thirty nights; a chest of medical supplies; and, possibly, extra rounds of small-arms ammunition. The command carried no water, except in canteens, and, of course, no forage for the animals: these would be as the country provided, and in this August and September, in this normally sunburned country, the country's provision, except on a few occasions, was adequate. The commissary department may have sent along a stove for the officers' mess. If this is so, and if a stove and its cook lasted beyond Jemez, Simpson gives no indication whatever. We may strongly suspect that some provision for these amenities lasted out the expedition. Beyond this may be added another half-ton or so of possibles and imponderables, these perhaps including a supply of treaty goods that may or may not have been given to the Navahos at Canyon de Chelly.

Let us add to this the very delicate weight of Simpson's thermometers and sextant and the small burden of the Kern brothers' drawing materials—of which the firms of Santa Fe then offered an unsatisfactory supply—and we about have it. Otherwise, marching ahead or to the side of the mule pack train, the troops, militia, and Indian scouts would carry the weight of the command's equipment for 587.11 miles in their hands or on their shoulders and backs.

With only a few replacements, the troops now at Fort Marcy were the same as the original raw, unruly recruits of General Kearny's Army of the West. The difference now was that they were seasoned, disciplined veterans, and plowboys no longer. Their arms, personal equipment, and uniforms were the same, if less new, than they carried into the war with Mexico. Field uniforms of the infantry and artillery units basically were similar —crush caps, black-visored and dark blue; short jackets of dark blue; trousers of gray wool, falling straight or rumpled to the boot tops. The trim of the uniforms varied with the units, collar and trouser stripes of the infantry being white; of the artillery, red; and of the dragoons, gold.

Colonel Washington and his staff were distinguished in appearance from the troops mainly by the longer cut of their jackets, reaching to six inches above the knee, and the light blue of their trousers. Their brass-buckled belts were wider than those of the troops and of white cloth instead of black or buff leather. Otherwise, there remained only the officers' rank and unit distinctions of brass and gold braid.

In following the troops in good weather or bad, but usually over rough terrain, we might remember other details of interest. The four companies of the Third Infantry were encumbered with very accurate Model 1841 muzzle-loading percussion-lock rifles, shoulder packs, and belts weighted with two cartridge tins, each containing twenty spherical bullets. Troops of the two companies of Second Artillery, marching on foot (their officers mounted), also were armed with the infantry rifle, nicknamed "Yerger" for Jäger. Besides being very accurate, this rifle had great shocking power, and it weighed a bit under ten pounds, the troops at the end of a day swearing it was more like thirty.

The orders moving this force into the field were posted on August 14. On the morning of August 16, quite early and with no fanfare or notice by the townspeople, ranks were formed, and then passed through the main gate of Fort Marcy. Possibly a few barking dogs provided musical escort as the troops skirted the empty plaza and marched southward out of the adobe capital.

Regular Army Officers, Officers of Volunteer Militia,
Civilians, Guides and Scouts, and Pueblo
and Mexican Volunteers
Who Accompanied the
Navaho Expedition of Summer, 1849

ARMY OFFICERS

Alexander, Brevet Lieutenant Colonel Edmund Brooke, commander of Companies D, F, G, and H, Third Infantry, from Fort Marcy garrison, Santa Fe (123 privates and non-commissioned officers). Illness compelled his return to Santa Fe after the command reached Jemez Pueblo. A native of Virginia, Alexander was graduated from West Point Military Academy in 1823. He saw frontier duty (1824–29) at Council Bluffs, Iowa; Green Bay, Wisconsin; and Detroit. From 1831–40 he served at Fort Towson, Indian Territory, and Fort Smith, Arkansas. In the war with Mexico he was brevetted lieutenant colonel for gallant conduct in the battles of Contreras and Churubusco. Prior to this expedition he was commander of Fort Marcy. Afterwards he saw more service in the West—at Fort Union, New Mexico; Fort Laramie, Dakota Territory; and Fort Kearny, Nebraska. He served with Union forces in the Civil War and was brevetted brigadier general in 1865.

Brent, Captain Thomas Lee, assistant quartermaster for the Fort Marcy garrison, and for this expedition. A Virginian, Brent was graduated from West Point in 1835, transferring the next year from the Sixth Infantry to the Fourth Artillery. He served in the war with Mexico, being brevetted captain in 1847 for gallant service in the battle of Buena Vista. Captain Brent accompanied the troops only to Jemez Pueblo and then returned to Fort Marcy. He died at Fort Leavenworth in 1858.

Brower, Second Lieutenant Charles B., commander of Company F, Third Infantry. A native of New York State, Brower enlisted in 1846 as a second lieutenant with the First New York Volunteers. Upon his transfer to the regular army in December, 1847, he was given the same commission with the Third Infantry. Following this expedition he was assigned, in August, 1851, to the new military post at Cebolleta, New Mexico, established upon Simpson's recommendation. (In the 1850 printing of Simpson's journal, Brower's name appears as Brown, although Simpson used the correct spelling in his manuscript.)

Dickerson, Second Lieutenant John H., attached to the First Artillery. He served the expedition as acting assistant adjutant general. As a youth, Dickerson moved from his native Ohio to Indiana. He was graduated from West Point in 1847, in time to see action in the war with Mexico. After this expedition he served in Florida in campaigns against the Seminoles (1850–53), was on quartermaster duty with the Utah Expedition (1857–58) against the Mormons, led by Brigadier General Albert Sidney Johnston. In the Civil War, Dickerson was chief quartermaster of the Department of Ohio. He was twenty-seven years old when, at the time of this narrative, he signed Colonel Washington's treaty with the Navahos as a witness.

Edwards, Assistant Army Surgeon Lewis A., appointed assistant army surgeon in August, 1846. Edwards was a native of the District of Columbia. His name first appears on the Fort Marcy muster roll in July, 1849. He returned to Santa Fe after the command had gone as far as Jemez Pueblo. During the Civil War, Edwards served with the Union Army. He was appointed a full colonel in March, 1865.

Hammond, Assistant Army Surgeon John Fox, a South Carolinian, Hammond was appointed assistant army surgeon in February, 1847. He was stationed at Fort Marcy in May, 1849, and after this expedition was assigned to the military post at Cebolleta. He served with Union forces in the Civil War and was promoted to the rank of colonel in December, 1882. (In the 1850 printing of Simpson's journal, the surgeon appears as J. H. Hammond.)

Jackson, Second Lieutenant Andrew, commander of Company G, Third Infantry. A Virginian, he was commissioned as a second lieutenant with the Third Infantry in December, 1847. In 1855 he was promoted to first lieutenant. The only officer accompanying the 1849 expedition who fought on the side of the Confederate Army in the Civil War, Jackson served (1861–65) as a lieutenant colonel with the Fifth South Carolina Infantry.

Kendrick, Brevet Major Henry Lane, commander of Companies B and D, Second Artillery (55 privates and non-commissioned officers). Graduated from West Point in 1835, Kendrick, a New Hampshire man, was brevetted major in the war with Mexico for his part in the defense of Pueblo, Mexico. Later, from Jefferson Barracks, Missouri, he led an artillery battalion from Fort Leavenworth to Santa Fe, arriving in time to join this expedition. Simpson and Kendrick shared an interest in geology, and there is reason to believe that Kendrick's knowledge of the subject proved useful to Simpson on many occasions before the command returned to Santa Fe. In 1851 he accompanied Colonel E. V. Sumner's abortive Navaho campaign and in the same year commanded the military escort for Captain Lorenzo Sitgreaves' expedition from Zuñi Pueblo to Camp Yuma. As commander of Fort Defiance (1852–57), he saw further action against the Navahos. From 1857–80 he was a professor of chemistry, mineralogy, and geology at West Point. Major Kendrick was about thirty-six years old at the time of the 1849 expedition and was one of those who signed the Navaho treaty.

Nones, Second Lieutenant Jefferson H., commander of Company D, Second Artillery. From his native Maryland, Nones enlisted and served as a midshipman in the U.S. Navy (1840–46) before transferring to the army in December, 1847. He was one of those who signed the 1849 Navaho treaty. Nones resigned from the army in March, 1856.

Peck, Brevet Major John J., commander of Company B, Second

Artillery. Appointed from Manlius, New York, Peck was graduated from West Point in 1843. He served in the military occupation of Texas (1845–46) and in the war with Mexico (1846–48). He was brevetted captain for his conduct in the battles of Contreras and Churubusco, and brevetted major after the battle of Molino del Rey. Twenty-eight years old at the time of this expedition, Major Peck commanded Union forces in North Carolina during the Civil War (1863–64) and Union troops stationed on the Canadian border in 1864–65.

Simpson, First Lieutenant James Hervey, an officer in the Corps of Topographical Engineers and author of this journal of the 1849 Navaho Expedition. Simpson was thirty-six years old at the time. His name appears last among those who signed the Navaho treaty.

Sykes, Brevet Captain George, commander of Company D, Third Infantry. A native of Dover, Delaware, Sykes was graduated from West Point in 1842. He served in the Florida war with the Seminoles, took part in the military occupation of Texas (1845–46), and fought in the war with Mexico (1846–48), being brevetted captain for gallant conduct in the battle of Cerro Gordo. After the expedition of 1849 he served at Fort Union (1852–55), engaged in campaigns against the Apaches, and engaged in the Navaho campaign of 1859 while serving at Fort Defiance. Skyes fought with Union forces through the Civil War, being brevetted a brigadier general for gallant conduct in the battle at Gettysburg. Returning to the Southwest, he commanded a regiment at Fort Sumner, New Mexico, in 1866–67.

Ward, Brevet First Lieutenant James N., acting assistant quartermaster, attached to Third Infantry. A Kentuckian, Ward as a youth moved to Georgia. After graduating from West Point in 1845, he was first stationed at Fort Smith, Arkansas. In the war with Mexico he was brevetted first lieutenant for action in the battle of Cerro Gordo. Ward was twenty-six years old at the time of the 1849 expedition and was one of the signers of the Navaho treaty. Afterward, he was stationed at Las Vegas, New Mexico

(1850), accompanied Sumner's 1851 Navaho expedition, served in Texas in 1853, and at Fort Union in 1853–54. Ward was promoted to captain in 1857, but his career ended abruptly with his death the following year.

Washington, Brevet Lieutenant Colonel John Macrae, commander of the Ninth Military Department, Santa Fe, military governor of New Mexico, and leader of the 1849 Navaho expedition. Colonel Washington was fifty-three years old at the time. His name appears first among the signers of the Navaho treaty.

Williamson, First Lieutenant Andrew J., commander of Company H, Third Infantry. From his native Virginia, Williamson moved to Ohio and was graduated from West Point in 1842. He served in the military occupation of Texas (1845–46), and the war with Mexico (1846–47). Upon his return from this expedition, he was stationed at Albuquerque (1849–50), and resigned from the army in 1851.

Wirtz, Assistant Army Surgeon Horace Raquet, a Pennsylvanian, Wirtz was appointed assistant army surgeon in December, 1846. Shortly before this expedition he served with Major Benjamin Lloyd Beall's dragoons at Taos. Afterward, he served with the Union Army in the Civil War, and was brevetted lieutenant colonel in 1865. He served later at Fort Whipple, Arizona, and died in 1874.

Officers of Volunteer Militia

Chapman, Captain John, commander of New Mexico Mounted Volunteers. With his company of Mexican militia, Chapman joined the expedition August 23, on the day's march west of San Ysidro. Three days later, twenty of his original company of eighty-three men had deserted. Chapman's origins are obscure. He volunteered, and was mustered in with his company at Santa Fe for six months' service, March 23, 1849. At the time of this expedition, he was thirty-one years old. Afterward, he was a captain of Santa Fe Guards of Mounted Volunteers, serving in campaigns against the Southern Utes and Jicarilla Apaches. Curiously, his name is not mentioned by Simpson after his company joined the expedition.

Dodge, Captain Henry Linn, commander of a company of New Mexico Volunteer Infantry. One of the signers of the Navaho treaty, Dodge and fifty of his Mexican "foot volunteers" joined Colonel Washington's command at Jemez Pueblo, where they had been stationed since April, 1849. One of the ablest officers attached to the command, Dodge was then thirty-two years old.

Torez, First Lieutenant Lorenzo, one of the junior officers in Captain Dodge's company, Torez enlisted at Santa Fe on March 23, 1849, and was mustered out September 23, the end of his six-months' enlistment and the day Colonel Washington's party returned to the capital. The spelling of his name here is the same as used by Agent Calhoun in his report of the expedition and also his copy of the 1849 Navaho treaty, which Torez signed as a witness. (In the 1850 printing of Simpson's journal, the lieutenant's name appears as Tores. It turns up as Lorenzo Force in the treaty copy printed in Kappler's official *Laws and Treaties.*)

CIVILIANS

Bird, W(illiam?), a civilian assistant to Simpson, whom he accompanied from Fort Smith to Santa Fe, and then on this expedition. Bird emerges only briefly, as a cook in the Inscription Rock episode. Bird assured his own footnote to this chronicle, however, when he carved his last name and first initial and the year on El Morro's south face, sixteen inches to the left of R. H. Kern's more hurried of two 1849 inscriptions.

Calhoun, James S., first Indian agent appointed to New Mexico Territory and one of the ablest ever sent out from Washington. Later named civil governor of New Mexico, his useful career was cut short by his death in 1852.

Champlin, Thomas A. P., a native of Buffalo, New York, and brother-in-law of Lieutenant Simpson. On this expedition, as well as the earlier survey of a route from Fort Smith to Santa Fe, Simpson is content to identify him merely as his assistant.

Choice, Cyrus, veteran of the war with Mexico. General Choice accompanied the expedition as an aide to Agent Calhoun. He was one of those who signed the Navaho treaty. In late January, 1850, he was named as first agent—at Abiquiu—for the Wiminuche and Capote Utes. He died the following September.

Collins, James L., Spanish interpreter assigned to Colonel Washington. Collins also was one of those who signed the treaty as witness. He was among the first Americans to reach Santa Fe, traveling the Santa Fe Trail in 1827 and at least twice more before 1843, when he settled there. After this expedition Collins became editor of the Santa Fe *Weekly Gazette,* and superintendent of Indian affairs for New Mexico (1857–63).

Conklin, James, a resident of Santa Fe, and possibly—because of his knowledge of the Navaho language—an Indian trader. Neither Calhoun nor Colonel Washington mentions him, but Simpson identified Conklin as the expedition's interpreter when the troops encountered Narbona and his band of Navahos on August 31. Conklin (whose name was spelled as "Conkling" in the 1850 printing of Simpson's journal) appears as one of the witnesses to the treaty.

Jones, John G., an aide to Agent Calhoun. He, too, appears as witness to the treaty.

Kern, Edward M., artist, topographer, and cartographer, veteran of John Charles Frémont's third expedition to California in 1845, and ill-fated fourth expedition of 1848–49. His map illustrates the route followed by Colonel Washington's command. At the time of this expedition, aged twenty-five, he was an assistant to Lieutenant Simpson.

Kern, Richard H., artist and Simpson's "second" assistant who became his mainstay on this expedition. He joined the command at Jemez Pueblo on August 19. He was twenty-eight years old and, like his brother Edward, a native of Philadelphia. He appears as witness to the treaty.

Lewis, ——, a trader to the Navahos. He guided Simpson to the pueblo ruins and Spanish inscriptions at El Morro. Nothing further has been learned of Lewis, who never troubled to leave his name on Inscription Rock.

Love, William E., an aide to Agent Calhoun, his father-in-law. He also signed the treaty.

GUIDES AND SCOUTS

Beheale, Hosea (Hosteen), of Santa Ana Pueblo, but probably a Navaho. Calhoun remarked of him that he was "selected Captain to command all the Indians engaged in the expedition. This excellent man is without official position in the pueblo to which he belongs, and there are but few who have such a decided influence over these people generally."

Carravahal, Mexican guide who joined the expedition August 23 at San Ysidro. According to New Mexico family notes of Fray Angelico Chávez, Carravahal was probably descended from Juan de Vitoria Carvajal, who came to New Mexico "as an Alférez [ensign, or second lieutenant] under Oñate in 1598." Bancroft (1889, p. 125) lists "Estévan Carabajal" as one of Oñate's associates in the conquest of New Mexico. A native of the village of San Ysidro, Carravahal obviously was thoroughly familiar with all of the Navaho country between this place and Canyon de Chelly. No clue is given to his age, but one imagines him, at this time, as being in middle age. It was he who named for Simpson the great *anasazi* ruins of Chaco Canyon—names in common use ever since. Unlike the more engaging Hosta, he was far more reliable as guide and informant. He has sometimes been confused with the Navaho, Caravajal, a leader of the *Diné Ana'aii,* or Enemy Navahos, who lived at this time in the vicinity of Cubero, New Mexico.

Chávez, Mariano, war captain of San Felipe Pueblo and one of six leaders of the fifty-four Pueblo volunteers comprising the Mounted Indian Militia. Agent Calhoun gave his name the phonetic spelling of Chavis. All of the Indian militia joined the expedition at Jemez Pueblo.

Hosta, Francisco, civil governor of Jemez Pueblo and a friendly and imaginative fabricator of tall tales, which the usually perceptive Lieutenant Simpson was inclined to believe. Past middle age at this time, Hosta also served as guide for William Henry Jackson when the noted Western photographer visited Chaco Canyon in the spring of 1877. Although he is memorialized by a prominent butte bearing his name, between Thoreau and Crownpoint, New Mexico, Hosta is no longer remembered in his own village. Antonio Sando, governor of Jemez in 1961, said he had never heard of Hosta, could tell nothing of him. Calhoun spelled his name variously as Francisco Sosto and Francisco Josto. The latter spelling appears in both Calhoun and Kappler versions of the Navaho treaty, which Hosta signed as witness.

Quandiego, civil governor of Santo Domingo Pueblo and a leader of the Indian Militia.

Salvadore, war captain of Santa Ana Pueblo and a leader of the Indian Militia.

Sandoval, Antonio, Navaho chief of the *Diné Ana'aii,* living in the region of Cebolleta, and attached to this expedition as guide, scout, and occasional but unofficial interpreter. This outcast leader of a band of outlaws had the dubious distinction of signing both 1846 and 1849 Navaho treaties—but only as leader of an outlaw band and witness in 1849 for the Americans. Sandoval guided other forays against his people, but was mistrusted by the Americans who hired his services. In March, 1851, he returned from a raid upon the Navahos, bringing eighteen Mexican captives, a quantity of stolen stock, "and several scalps." The following month he appealed to Agent Calhoun for guns and ammunition to arm his band and asked to join any new operation against the Navahos that might be impending. Sandoval's penchant for scalps is interesting, as Navahos did not customarily scalp their foes. This Navaho counterpart of Benedict Arnold at least was consistent. At the outbreak of warfare with the tribe in summer, 1858, Sandoval led some of his renegade people into the ranks of Captain Blas Lucero's New Mexican and Zuñi scouts, who served with army forces led by Colonel D. S. Miles. Five years later, when the first of the beaten Navahos were being forced into internment at Bosque Redondo, Sandoval submissively volunteered to go into captivity and with his Cebolleta followers was first to go off to Fort Sumner, his band reaching there in September, 1863. Descendants of these *Diné Ana'aii* in recent times have been known as Cañoncito Navahos, living on allotments about twenty miles west of Albuquerque.

PUEBLO VOLUNTEER MOUNTED MILITIA

Members of six pueblos, these Indian volunteers served bravely and faithfully, winning greatest respect of the regular army officers for their performance during the dangerous crossing of Washington Pass.

From Jemez Pueblo: Francisco Asti, Jose Paublin, Jesus Bernal, Jose Ambrosia, Lorenzo Yankin, Miguel Naso, Juan Domingo, Jose Antonio, San Juanito, Juan de Jesus.

From Santa Ana Pueblo: Jose Vigil, Salvadore Andres, Jose de la Luc, Jose Romero, Armijo Navajo, Garcia Juanico, Manuel Armijo, Manuel Rincon, Manana Chavez, Tapon.

From San Felipe Pueblo: Rafael Antonio Garcia, Jose Santiago, Jose Sandoval, Lorenzo Duran, Jose Domingo, Jose Miguel, Juan Lucerio, Jose Ancihuo, Jose Valencia, Jose Santos.

From Zia Pueblo: Francisco Miguelito, Francisco Siha, Jose Antonio Siha, Jose Sepreano, Francisco Mariano.

From Santo Domingo Pueblo: Juan Diego Corrio, Bentura Corrio, Juan Pedro Aguile, Jose Santos, Pedro Corrio, Jose Cilla, Tomas Corrio, Ancelmo Aguila, Jose Vista, Jose Antonio, Francisco Garcia, Jose Baublista, Juan Jose, Jose Lucero.

From Cochiti Pueblo: Ballasa Atencio, Cristoval Archuvicia, Francisco Augustin, Augustin Toro, Roque de Antonio.

NAVAHO EXPEDITION

---

*Headquarters 9th Military Department
Santa Fe, New Mexico, August 14, 1849.*

I. The colonel commanding intending to make a movement against the Navaho Indians, the following troops will rendezvous at Jemez, subject to further orders: Four companies of the 3d Infantry, under the command of Brevet Lieutenant-Colonel Alexander, 3d Infantry; two companies of the 2d Artillery, under command of Brevet Major Kendrick, 2d Artillery; Captain Ker's company, (K), 2d Dragoons; and Captain Chapman's mounted company of volunteers. The infantry and artillery commands will move from Santa Fe on the morning of the 16th instant; and Captains Ker and Chapman will move with their companies and be at Jemez on the 19th instant. The artillery command will take one six-pounder gun and three mountain howitzers, in addition to their other guns.

II. The quartermaster's department will provide pack mules and packs for the transportation of the necessary baggage of the command, and for thirty days rations for five hundred men; and the commissary department will furnish the necessary subsistence stores.

III. Lieutenant Simpson, Topographical Engineers, will accompany the expedition, making such a survey of the country as the movements of the troops will permit.

IV. Assistant Surgeon Hammond will leave the general hospital in charge of a citizen physician, until the return of Assistant Surgeon Edwards, and proceed with the command on the 16th instant.

By order of Lieutenant-Colonel Washington.

JOHN H. DICKERSON,
Lieutenant, and A.A.A. General.

The Journal

Santa Fe, August 15—Today, in consequence of information having reached headquarters of the concentration of the Utahs near Albiquin [Abiquiu], Orders No. 32 have been so far modified that Captain Ker's company of dragoons, now stationed at Albuquerque, and Captain Chapman's company of mounted volunteers, now stationed at the *Placer,* instead of moving on Jemez, are to proceed to Albiquin, and, in conjunction with Major Grier's company of dragoons and Captain Valdez's company of mounted volunteers, the whole under command of Brevet Lieutenant-Colonel Beall, effect, if possible, a peace with the Utahs in that quarter, or, failing in this, prosecute a war against them. Effecting a peace, Captains Ker and Chapman, with their companies, are to join the main command under Colonel Washington at Chelly. Not accomplishing a peace amicably, or by force of arms, Colonel Washington will, after accomplishing his objects with the Navahos, join the troops in the Utah country.

First camp, August 16—The preparations being in a sufficient state of forwardness, the portion of the troops referred to in Orders No. 32 stationed at Santa Fe took up the line of march this morning, their destination being Jemez, *via* Santo Domingo. These troops consist of two companies of the 2d Artillery ("B," commanded by Brevet Major John J. Peck; "D," by 2d Lieutenant J. H. Nones; the battalion by Brevet Major H. L. Kendrick), and four companies of the 3d Infantry ("D," commanded by Brevet Captain George Sykes; "F," by 2d Lieutenant C. B. Brow-

5

er; "G," by 2d Lieutenant Andrew Jackson; and "H," by 1st Lieutenant A. J. Williamson; the battalion by Brevet Lieutenant-Colonel E. B. Alexander)—the whole aggregating (fifty-five of artillery, and one hundred and twenty [-three] of infantry) an effective force of one hundred and seventy [-eight] men, under the command of Brevet Lieutenant-Colonel John M. Washington, 3d Artillery, commandant of the 9th Military Department, and governor of New Mexico. The officers of the staff are 1st Lieutenant J. H. Simpson, Corps Topographical Engineers; Brevet 1st Lieutenant James N. Ward, 3d Infantry, acting assistant quartermaster and commissary; 2d Lieutenant John H. Dickerson, 1st Artillery, acting assistant adjutant general; and Assistant Surgeon J. F. Hammond. Lieutenant Simpson has with him, to assist him in his duties, Mr. Edward M. Kern, of Philadelphia, and Mr. Thomas A. P. Champlin, of Buffalo. In addition to the officers mentioned, James S. Calhoun, Esq., of Georgia, Indian agent, goes out with a small party of assistants to effect, in connexion with the colonel commanding, a proper treaty with the Navahos; and Mr. James L. Collins accompanies Colonel Washington, as Spanish interpreter.

Wagon transportation is furnished to the troops as far as Jemez, and then pack animals are to be resorted to.

The road taken by the artillery was the usual one to Santo Domingo, *via* Agua Fria (a small collection of *ranchos*—farms—six miles from Santa Fe), and thence along the Rio de Santa Fe, on its east side, to Sieneguilla, a distance of 16.02 miles, where they encamped. The general course was east of south.

The infantry and my own party, having taken a more eastern route—that usually traveled by wagons to Algadones—after having marched about the same distance, sixteen miles, are encamped two miles to the east of the artillery, on a small tributary of the Rio de Santa Fe.

The face of the country today has been generally level—a few *arroyos* (dry beds of streams) intersecting it at intervals, and the famous Placer or Gold Mountain, and the Sandia Mountain, with some intermediate conical mounds, forming, to our front, the chief features of the landscape.[1] Saving a very narrow and interrupted margin bordering the Rio de Santa Fe between Agua Fria and Santa Fe, and which was cultivated in corn, the country has exhibited one extended barren waste, with nought to diversify it but a few dwarf or bush cedars, sparsely scattered.

At Sieneguilla—a village composed of one Roman Catholic church and a few scattered ranchos—good grass and water are found, and sufficient fuel.

At this place, Captain Ker, with his command, has also encamped, on his way to Albiquin. It was the intention of Colonel Washington, after reaching Santo Domingo, to make a night march upon the Utahs about Albiquin, and thus, effecting a junction with Lieutenant-Colonel Beall's command, strike the enemy a blow when he might be least expecting it; but Captain Ker's force being unexpectedly in advance of such a movement, it is abandoned.

Second camp, August 17—The infantry, as also my own party, joined the artillery, in the cañon of the Rio de Santa Fe, just after the latter had left their camp. The general course today was slightly south of west, the road threading the cañon of the Rio de Santa Fe to its mouth, a distance of six miles; thence across the valley of the margin of the Rio Grande del Norte, seven miles, to the *Pueblo de Santo Domingo;* and thence by ford across the Rio Grande to our camping ground, directly opposite Santo Domingo —the whole march having been 14.85 miles. Through the cañon, the road, on account of rocks and boulders, and for a mile and a half before reaching Santo Domingo, on account of sand hills, is rough, the remaining portion is level and good.

The cañon of the Rio de Santa Fe is quite interesting. Varying in depth from one hundred to one hundred and fifty feet, the Rio de Santa Fe trickling through it, its mesa heights on either

[1] Placer (Gold) Mountain, still pocked with working shafts, lies south of Galisteo Creek and southeast of Santo Domingo Pueblo, within the boundaries of the old Spanish Ortiz Mine Grant. The mountain is figured on E. M. Kern's map of this expedition and on the John Parke–R. H. Kern Map of the Territory of New Mexico, 1851.

side are crowned by overlying basaltic trap. This trap shows eminently, in particular localities, the blackening, scoriaceous effect of fire; and in some places is to be seen underlying it an earthy formation of an ashy character, and in others a reddish porphyritic rock in beds slightly dipping towards the east. At the mouth of the cañon, on its north side, is a well-defined ash-colored formation presenting, with striking and pleasing effect, the appearance of the façade of a highly finished piece of Grecian architecture. This object cannot fail to attract the notice of the traveler.

Debouching from the cañon, an extended plain—upon which I saw some fifty head of cattle grazing—stretches westward about six miles to the Rio Grande; the Jemez Mountains appear on the further side of the river, quartering to your right; an extended mesa shows itself also beyond the river to your front; and the Sandia Mountain lifts itself high and sublime to your left. Not a tree is to be seen until you can look down upon the Rio Grande, and then the cottonwood is noticed sparsely skirting its banks. The bed of the Rio Galisteo, which we crossed just before entering Santo Domingo, indicated only here and there that it was even moistened with water.

Santo Domingo, which lies directly on the Rio Grande, is a pueblo or Indian town, containing about eight hundred inhabitants. It is laid out in streets running perpendicularly to the Rio Grande. The houses are constructed of *adobes;* are two stories in height, the upper one set retreatingly on the lower, so as to make the superior covering or ceiling of the lower answer for a terrace or platform for the upper; and have roofs which are nearly flat.[2]

[2] Simpson's description of Santo Domingo is taken nearly verbatim from notes made by Richard Kern and preserved now as a fragment in the collection of Kern papers at the Huntington Library (FS 134). Kern was following the main command by one day, leaving Santa Fe August 17 and reaching Santo Domingo on the following afternoon. In his diary of the expedition, Kern found the Río Grande Valley "beautiful and fertile . . . dotted by the shanties of the Indians"—meaning the outlying farm huts—"with rude carettas lying about. . . . It is harvest time & the Indians are carrying their wheat in bundles on their heads to the thrashing place and singing their wild songs—in the foreground wagons, spainards mules & americans."

These roofs are made first of transverse logs, which pitch very slightly outward, and are sustained at their ends by the side walls of the building; on these, a layer of slabs or brush is laid longitudinally; a layer of bark or straw is then laid on these; and covering the whole is a layer of mud of six or more inches in thickness. The height of the stories is about eight or nine feet. The lower stories have very small windows, and no doors; the lights of the windows, wherever there were any, being of selenite—the crystallized foliated form of gypsum. The mode of access to the building is by exterior ladders, which may be seen leaning against every house.[3]

In the west end of the town is an *estuffa* [kiva] or public building in which the people hold their religious and political meetings. The structure, which is built of adobes, is circular in plan, about nine feet in elevation, and thirty-five feet in diameter, and, with no doors or windows laterally, has a small trap-door in the terrace or flat roof by which admission is gained. Directly below the opening, and detached from the wall, is a fireplace, its height being about three feet—the opening referred to serving as a vent to the smoke.

The men, I notice, wear generally nothing but a shirt and a breechcloth; the women, a dark-colored blanket covering one shoulder and drawn under the other, a girdle confining the

[3] Modern Santo Domingo is almost entirely a village of one-story adobe buildings. Governor Rafael Lovato, who in 1961 lived in one of the pueblo's ten or twelve remaining two-story dwellings at the southwest corner of the pueblo, told me that the village Simpson describes lay immediately west of the present Santo Domingo, occupying a now flat cultivated field. Lovato said that almost all of the old village was washed away by the flooding Río Grande before he was born—or sometime before 1910. Other authorities say this flood occurred in 1886. Leslie White ("The Pueblo of San Felipe," *American Anthropological Association Memoirs*, No. 38 [1932], 12–13, 15, 17, 25) traces the Domingo people from Frijoles Canyon to the Potrero de la Cañada Quemada, on the west side of the Río Grande, to two successive pueblo (now ruin) sites east and north of the present pueblo, both known as *Gipuy*. Here they remained through the sixteenth century. Gipuy almost certainly was one of the seven Quirix (Keresan) villages visited by Coronado in 1540. Gaspar Castaño de Sosa found them in the second village of Gipuy, close to the site of the present village, in 1591, and named the pueblo Santo Domingo.

9

blanket about the waist, and their arms being left free and bare. This appears to be their *ordinary summer dress*. The children run naked.

At the house of the governor I noticed a woman, probably his wife, going through the process of baking a very thin species of corn cake, called, according to Gregg, *guayave*. She was hovering over a fire, upon which lay a flat stone. Near her was a bowl of thin corn paste, into which she thrust her fingers; allowing then the paste to drip sparingly upon the stone, with two or three wipes from the palm of her hand she would spread it entirely and uniformly over the stone. This was no sooner done than she peeled it off as fit for use, and the process was again and again repeated until a sufficient quantity was obtained—the necessarily rapid character of the process causing the perspiration to roll from her face in streams. The woman, noticing the interest I took in the operation, handed me a sheet of the food to eat. Like the Mexican *tortilla*, although I was exceedingly hungry, it did not fail to leave at the stomach a slight sensation of nausea. When folded and rolled together, it does not look unlike (particularly that made from the blue corn) a "hornet's nest"—a name by which it is sometimes called.[4]

The Rio Grande, at the ford, is about three hundred yards wide, is between three and four feet deep, and is full of bars. Its bottom, in spots, is of quicksand character—two of the wagons stalling on this account.

The soil today, excepting a very limited area upon the Rio Santa Fe, at Sieneguilla, and for a breadth of about a mile along the Rio Grande, is probably worthless for cultivation, and of but very slight, if of any, value for grazing purposes.

Our camping ground, which is near some cornfields, is a fine one—the Rio Grande, besides furnishing us with water to drink, affording us a refreshing bath; and the grass in the vicinity being good, and wood sufficiently near.

[4] This corn cake, or bread, thin as tissue paper and rolled into cylinders about nine inches in length, is common to most of the Pueblos. Among the Hopi it is known as *piki*. The bread is crisp and flaky; most people find its taste pleasantly bland.

A series of astronomical observations make the latitude of this camp 35° 30′ 56″; its longitude, 106° 29′ 45″.

Third camp, Jemez, August 18—Not being able last evening, on account of the strong wind, to get satisfactory astronomical observations, I obtained some this morning before daylight.

Our route today, to Jemez, a distance of 26.60 miles, was generally in a northwesterly direction and, besides being exceedingly heavy on account of sand, and rough and uneven on account of sand hills and arroyos, did not furnish us a drop of water throughout its whole extent.

For the first nine miles it was up a heavy sandy arroyo, at the fourth mile of which there was a short steep hill to ascend, and at the ninth a rather long and steep one—which surmounted, brought us to a piece of tableland of about three miles in breadth, whence could be seen, almost due west about thirty-five miles off, the remarkable peak called *Cerro de la Cabeza*. This tableland traversed, we reached the brow of the valley of the Rio de Jemez, whence, looking down upon and across the valley, a confused mass of sedimentary hills and mesa heights appeared to sight—the escarpment walls of the mesa being generally of a well-defined stratified character, and of sensible dip towards the south. To our right, and on *our* side of the Rio de Jemez, were mesa heights crowned with basaltic trap apparently fifty feet thick. From the brow of the valley down to the Rio de Jemez, the road is very heavy and rough, on account of sand hills and arroyos.

Four miles from our last camp, I noticed on the route an outcrop of silicious limestone containing, sparsely, some particles of felspar. Near this spot, observing a plateau or mesa from two hundred to three hundred feet high, which promised a fine view of the country we had been traversing, I ascended, to scan the landscape. As I anticipated, a noble view extended itself before me. There lay, far off towards the northeast, the Santa Fe Mountains; to the southeast, the Placer Mountain and Sandia Mountain; intervening between them, and just discoverable, lying beyond the gleaming waters of the Rio Grande, the little town of Santo Domingo; to the north and northwest, stretching far away, were the Jemez Mountains; to the south, mesa formations crowned with basaltic trap; and everywhere else, sparsely scattered over mountain and plain, the dwarf cedar.

The Pueblo of Jemez, as its prefix indicates, is an *Indian* town of probably between four and five hundred inhabitants, and, like the Pueblo of Santo Domingo, is built upon two or three parallel streets, the houses being of adobe construction and having second stories disposed retreatingly on the first, to which access is had by ladders.[5] I notice here, on the outskirts of the village, the usual accompaniment of Mexican and pueblo towns, the ragged-looking picketed goat enclosure—it giving to the suburbs an unsightly appearance. About the premises are probably a dozen of acres covered with apricot and peach trees. An infantry company of Mexican volunteers, under command of Captain Henry L. Dodge, is stationed at this place.

The Rio de Jemez, upon which the pueblo lies, is an affluent of the Rio Grande, varies from thirty to fifty feet in breadth, is

[5] Jemez, according to Bandelier, is the Spanish form of the Keresan word *Ha'-mish*, or *Hae'-mish*, meaning "Jemez people." Sometime after 1880 most of the second-story habitations noted by Simpson were reduced to single-story, until in 1950 Stanley Stubbs (*Bird's-Eye View of the Pueblos*, 61) found only eighteen remaining two-story rooms. When the pueblo was originally built is uncertain, but probably the dwellings were laid out, generally on an east-west axis, in the late 1500's. Jemez occupation of the valley, however, goes back much farther. Hewett ("Antiquities of the Jemez Plateau, New Mexico," 45), commenting on many ruin sites of the region, notes that "the Jemez pueblos were first visited by the Spaniards under Francisco de Barrionuevo in 1541. Oñate, in 1598, saw eight villages, and [three] others were mentioned to him. Bandelier says that at the time of his visits in 1880–1885 the Jemez gave him the names of seventeen of the old pueblos. He believes that the numerous small villages were gradually consolidated into two, and finally into one—the present pueblo." Simpson's estimate of the pueblo's population in 1849 is conservative and probably correct. Fr. Leo, Franciscan superior of the pueblo's San Diego Mission in 1961, said that a predecessor, Fr. Barnabas, "counted less than seven hundred" villagers in 1902. Fr. Leo added at the time of our interview that thirteen hundred persons were living at Jemez. He observed that the older people of the pueblo spoke Spanish and their own Tewan language, whereas the younger people spoke either Jemez or English. Stubbs (59) says that Jemez is the last remaining Tewa-speaking pueblo.

of a rapid current, and tends southwardly. Its bed is a commixture of red sand and gravel. Patches of good corn and wheat skirt it here and there along its banks, and the extent of cultivable land bordering it may be estimated at about a mile in breadth. Its waters are palatable; good grass is found along it, and wood exists in the vicinity. Our encamping ground, which is just to the north of the town, has, therefore, all the requisites to make it a good one.[6]

The soil along the route today, excepting the narrow margin along the Rio de Jemez already mentioned, is utterly worthless for cultivation.

The latitude of this camp, by astronomical observation, is 35° 36' 7"; its longitude, 106° 51' 15".

Third camp, Jemez, August 19—The wagon attached to headquarters breaking down yesterday, on account of the rough state of the road, it did not reach us early enough in the evening to have our tents pitched. The consequence was, that the colonel commanding and his staff bivouacked for the night—a change which we found quite agreeable.

The troops will remain here for a day or two until the assistant quartermaster, Captain Brent, can perfect his arrangements for a change from wagon to pack-mule transportation, and also for the purpose of giving time for the concentration of the Pueblo and Mexican force, which is to join us at this point.

This afternoon, a dance—called, in the language of the Jemez Indians, *Lou-pel-lay,* or the green-corn dance—having been reported as being about to be enacted in the village, several persons from camp (among them my assistant, Mr. E. M. Kern, from whom I get my information), went down to witness it. In order the better to see the performance, they took a position on one of the houses in the principal street. When the performers first appeared, all of whom were men, they came in a line, slowly walking, and bending and stooping as they approached. They

[6] Like all other Puebloans, the Jemez people were, and remain, predominantly a farming people. The command's camp ground is now a broad cornfield bordered by a few cottonwood trees.

were dressed in a kilt of blanket, the upper portion of their bodies being naked, and painted dark red. Their legs and arms, which were also bare, were variously striped with red, white and blue colors; and around their arms, above the elbow, they wore a green band decked with sprigs of piñon. A necklace of the same description was worn around the neck. Their heads were decorated with feathers. In one hand they carried a dry gourd, containing some grains of corn, with which they produced a rattling kind of music; in the other, a string, from which were hung several tortillas. At the knee were fastened small shells of the ground turtle and antelope's feet; and dangling from the back, at the waist, depended a fox skin. The musicians were habited in the common costume of the village, and made their music in a sitting posture. Their instruments consisted each of half a gourd, placed before them, with the convex side up; upon this they placed with the left hand a smooth stick, and with their right drew forwards and backwards upon it, in a sawing manner, a notched one. This produced a sound much like that of grinding corn upon a metate (a slightly concave stone).

The movements in the dance differed but slightly from those of Indians generally.

The party were accompanied by three elders of the town, whose business it was to make a short speech in front of the different houses, and at particular times join in the singing and dancing, the occupants of each awaiting their arrival in front of their respective dwellings.

My second assistant, Mr. R. H. Kern, brother to my first assistant, Mr. E. M. Kern, joined me from Taos this afternoon.[7]

Third camp, Jemez, August 20—During the past night we had

[7] Simpson refers to Richard Kern's previous residence in Taos. Richard left Santa Fe one day following the departure of the main command. Evidently he was accompanying Captain Brent, the quartermaster, because he notes in his diary leaving the capital "with the pack animals." As always during the first day or two on the trail the animals were frisky: "Many of the mules being wild much trouble ensued and we did not reach camp [at Sieneguilla, where the troops camped the day before] until quarter after one oclk."

an unusually heavy rain, attended with sharp thunder and lightning.

This morning, after breakfast, Major Kendrick, Assistant Surgeons Edwards and Hammond, Mr. E. M. Kern, and myself left camp for *Los Ojos Calientes,* (the Hot Springs), said to be twelve miles above in the valley of the Rio de Jemez. The lieutenant-governor of Jemez accompanied us as guide. Our course, which lay directly up the valley called the Cañon of San Diego, was slightly east of north. Soon after leaving camp we passed some red-colored argillaceous rocks, the gorge which we threaded being coincident with the line of strike.

Two miles from camp we came to a Mexican settlement, which continued sparsely scattered along the river for about five miles. The most populous portion of it, called *Cañoncito,* we found to be about three miles from camp, at the mouth of the *Cañon de Guadalupe.* Here I saw, within a hundred yards of the village, a small gray wolf shying off very reluctantly from us.

For a distance of six or seven miles the bottom of the Cañon de San Diego is pretty well cultivated—corn, wheat, and peppers being the chief product of the soil. The corn, which looked well, greatly predominated.

Beyond the settlements, the ruins of old adobe buildings were ever and anon to be seen, which, according to our guide, were once inhabited by Mexicans who had deserted them from fear of the Navahos.[8]

Nine miles up the cañon we found an old copper-smelting furnace, which looked as if it had been abandoned for some considerable period. It is quite small, is built of stone, and has

[8] The Jemez people first, and their Mexican neighbors later, had cause to fear Navaho raids. Van Valkenburgh, who elsewhere tells of early Navaho settlement immediately to the northwest of Jemez, observes: "Navajo raids almost depopulated the Jemez in the latter part of the 16th century, as well as difficulties with the Spanish. During the 17th century a number of Jemez people fled the Jemez Valley and settled at the Laguna de San José (not to be confused with Laguna Pueblo) a few miles north of present Cuba, New Mexico. Some joined the Navajos and became the first group of the *ma-ii deeshgiizhnii diné e* [clan] of the Navajo."

arched ovens traversing each other at right angles, each oven being furnished with a stone grating. We picked up some fragments of copper ore (probably green malachite) which lay scattered around.[9]

Twelve miles from Jemez, we came to Los Ojos Calientes. Here, desiring to make some examinations, and it being our purpose to regale ourselves with the eatables we had brought with us, we unsaddled our horses and turned them loose to graze.

On examination, we found the springs to be situated within the compass of a few feet of each other, some of them boiling up immediately from the bed of a small bifurcated branch of the Rio de Jemez.[10] The principal one, which is in the branch mentioned, issues from a small knoll or heap of boulder stones, which seem to partake both of a calcareous and basaltic character, the vent not being more than a foot above the bed from which it springs. The volume of water which issues from it may be estimated at about a gallon and a half per minute. This spring, as well as all the other principal ones, shows a limited accumulation of crystalline deposit about its mouth, which, on account of its fine-grained character and hardness, may probably come under the head of travertine. The complexion of the deposit is white with a shade of greenish yellow.

We put into the jagged cup or bowl of the fountain some eggs and raw venison, both of which were cooked in about twenty minutes. The time required to do this would doubtless have been

[9] Until very recent years the shaft was operated, sporadically, under various names, but most lastingly as the Spanish Queen Mine. The now abandoned shaft is found low on the east slope of the Jemez River canyon. Below the timbered mouth of the shaft are an old adobe ruin and concrete foundations of buildings erected—and left to disintegrate—long after Simpson's visit. At the base of the workings is a slag heap of lumps and nuggets of a by-product resembling obsidian, the rest studded with bright green shards of copper base.

[10] The springs are situated forty yards east of the Jemez River—here, at an altitude of 6,200 feet, normally a clear, shallow stream. An odor of sulphur drenches the air, pungent contrast to the visual beauty of chemical encrustations resembling ice but hued in jeweled yellows, greens, and blues. The temperature of the waters is said to range between 154° and 186°, the principal gases or by-products being chlorine, acid carbonate, and sodium.

much less had the bowl been sufficiently concave to have admitted a more perfect immersion of the articles and the fixture of a cover, by which the heat lost through evaporation could have been retained. As it was, upon an immersion by Major Kendrick of a thermometer, Dr. Edwards assisting him, the highest point to which the mercury would rise was 169°.

These springs are said, in diseases of a cutaneous or rheumatic kind, to possess powers of a highly curative character; and it is doubtless on this account that the arbors which we noticed near the main springs are placed over some basins, scooped out from the ground, into which the hot water finds its way.

Observing, about a third of a mile above the springs, the ruins [of a Catholic mission], we saddled up for the purpose of visiting them. On reaching the spot we found them to be the remains of an old Roman Catholic church, in dimensions about fifty feet front by one hundred and twenty deep. The tower, which was octagonal in form, and which rose up from the middle of the rear end of the building, was still standing, as were also the greater portion of the walls of the main building. The height of the tower I estimated at thirty feet. The thickness of the walls of the main edifice at base measured six feet.[11]

[11] Simpson may have noticed, but here does not mention, that surrounding the mission ruins are the crumbled walls of *Giusewa*, one of the early Jemez pueblos. This ancient village of one and two stories had been occupied for some years before the Franciscans, sometime between 1617 and 1621–22, directed Indian laborers to build the church in the very center of their pueblo. In modern times the pueblo and mission have been cleared and stabilized, but thus far not excavated. Hewett (47–48), like Simpson, finds the mission ruin the most imposing feature of the site, and remarks: "The tower and upper parts are of the impure friable limestone of the promontory against which the foundations are built . . . the adobe mortar has been made from the debris of ancient house sites and is full of fragments of pottery, obsidian chips, and charcoal." Hewett then quotes Bandelier as saying the pueblo once "formed several hollow quadrangles at least two stories high. It contained about eight hundred inhabitants. . . . Ginsewa [Giusewa] is an historical pueblo. It first appears under the name of Guimzique in 1626. It seems that it was abandoned in 1622, on account of the persistent hostility of the Navajos, who had succeeded in scattering the Jemez tribes. In 1627 Fray Martin de Arvide obtained permission from his superior, the custodian Fray Alonzo de Benevides, to attempt to gather the tribe again in its old home. The

It getting late, we were obliged to hasten our return to camp —a drenching rain, which had in the meantime sprung up, adding not a little to our alacrity. A spring, however, which we unexpectedly met with on our route, tempting us by its cool appearance, we could not resist the desire to alight and try its waters, which we found not less grateful than they were unexpected.

The cottonwood, the cedar, and pine, the latter of dwarfish growth, and all rather sparsely scattered, constitute the *sylva* of the valley. The wild currant we found growing in great luxuriance and perfection about the old church.

Third camp, Jemez, August 21—This afternoon Captain Dodge, the brothers Kern, and myself visited the Roman Catholic church of the village—the governor of the town, Hosta, procuring for us the keys, and acting as *cicerone*. The church, an adobe structure some one hundred by twenty-eight feet in plan, appeared very old, and was evidently wasting away under the combined influence of neglect and moisture.[12] The swallows, as is to be noticed in the Roman Catholic church at Santa Fe, seemed to be perfectly at home within it, and now, as in the church mentioned, brought home to me the appositeness of those beautiful remarks of the sweet psalmist of Israel to be found in Psalms, 84th, 3d. A pilaster and arch arrangement, with crosses at intervals, characterized the side walls; and a number of paintings, all daubs excepting the central one, the wall back of the chancel. Hosta informed us that this central piece was a representation of San Diego bearing the cross. At present it is considerably defaced, but the touches of a genuine artist are yet visible upon it.

efforts of the monk were successful, and the Jemez Indians settled in two of their former pueblos—at Ginsewa and at Amoxiumqua." Giusewa was abandoned forever following the Pueblo Revolt in 1680.

12 Fr. Leo said that since Spanish colonial times Jemez has had three successive Franciscan missions. The one described here by Simpson was torn down and replaced in 1887 or 1888 by the church now standing. Neither Fr. Leo nor Fr. Angelico Chávez, his predecessor at Jemez, could give me any information about the church Simpson visited with Hosta. However, according to Fr. Chávez, the first church "on the western edge of the pueblo, of which bare traces can be seen on the way to the present Franciscan friary, was described by Fr. Dominguez in 1776."

None but a true son of the muse could have thrown into the countenance the expression of beautiful sadness with which it is radiant. In addition to the objects of garniture already mentioned, I noticed upon a projecting piece of the side pulpit a human skull and some bones, and in a side room, to which I could only peep in, some images and pictures.

Finishing our examination at the church, we visited the estuffas of the town, of which there are two.[13] Both are one story high and, like the one noticed at Santo Domingo, have no doors or windows laterally, and are only accessible from above, through the flat roof. They differ from it, however, in being rectangular—the one we measured being twenty by twenty-seven feet in the clear, and seven and a half feet high. On the walls were representations of plants, birds, and animals—the turkey, the deer, the wolf, the fox, and the dog [coyote], being plainly depicted; none of them, however, approaching to exactness, except the deer, the outline of which showed a good eye for proportions.

Upon questioning Hosta in relation to the object of these estuffas, he informed us that they were after the custom of Montezuma, and for that reason they were not allowed to give them up. He also called them the churches of Montezuma.[14] In the spring,

[13] An informant who is a member of the Jemez tribe told me that Jemez Pueblo has six kivas, two of them apart from the village. All, presumably, were in use before 1849. The kivas Simpson describes belonged, respectively, to the Turquoise moiety (the winter people), and the Pumpkin moiety (the summer people). In addition to these, each of the moieties has an underground rectangular kiva, their use carefully restricted and their location, even their existence, concealed from outsiders. Besides these four, according to my informant, there is a Snake clan kiva located about a mile from the pueblo and a Bear clan kiva about two and one-half miles distant. The Turquoise moiety has, or until recently had, seven clans; the Pumpkin moiety comprises nine clans, including those of the Pecos inhabitants.

[14] Simpson's reading of Prescott and Humboldt before starting on this expedition led him to believe that the Aztec Indians had origins in the country he was now seeing or was about to enter. His preconceptions on this point made him too receptive to Hosta's imaginative stories about Montezuma. Commenting upon this in a personal letter, Fr. Chávez said that "the Montezuma legend is an importation into the pueblos, either by the Spanish colonists or the Mexican Indians brought along as servants. Early Americans heard the Pueblos talk of it, and accepted it as a genuine prehistoric tradition."

he says, they go there to chant to him to send them rain, and in the fall they sing to him to obtain any good thing they may want. He further remarked—(and I give what follows to show the superstition of these people, for he narrated it as if he thought it might be true)—he further remarked, there was a tradition among his people that Montezuma, whenever in his travels he stopped for the night, would make a house in one hour; and that he would plant corn one night, and the next morning it would be fit to be plucked. He went on further to inform us that they worshipped the sun, moon, and fire. The moon he called the captain of the night. The sun, however, when he rises, he remarked, puts away all the children of the night, and therefore he is the great captain.

To the question of the object of the paintings upon the walls of the estuffa, he said they were *por bonito,* (for ornament). The circles represent the sun and moon; the semicircles, clouds; and the barbed zigzag line, the forked, destructive lightning. The emblem of good lightning he represented in pencil upon my notebook as terminating more bluntly, thus:

The two human figures with trumpets to their mouths he represents as the adjutants of Montezuma, who are sounding a call to him for rain.[15]

[15] The Jemez kiva paintings illustrated in Simpson's journal and referred to or depicted by others later are discussed at length by Watson Smith (*Kiva Mural Decorations at Awatovi and Kawaika-a,* 84–88). "The paintings," Smith says, " . . . appear to be faithful drawings by R. H. Kern, and they deserve some commentary, although Simpson apparently elicited no explanation of their ceremonial significance, and may perhaps have been unsuspecting of that feature since he seems to have accepted gullibly the evasion of the crafty Hosta that they were merely *por bonito.*" Smith adds that the "two human figures with trumpets" that Hosta said were "adjutants of Montezuma" probably in truth were less exalted flute players. Richard Kern also was deceived by the Montezuma legend, but not by the musical instruments. "Two men," he noted in his diary, "are on the house top blowing flutes that the surrounding clouds may give out rain." After Simp-

Before the conquest, he says, according to tradition the Jemez Indians were fighting with all the other tribes—those of San Felipe, Santa Ana, and Santo Domingo. At length a Spanish priest appeared among them very mysteriously. This priest, whenever he celebrated mass, made it a condition of his acceptance of them that they should every previous Saturday bring him wood. And it was his habit whenever he wanted anything, such as skins or blankets, to take them. The people at length getting enraged at such treatment, determined to kill him. He, hearing of it, however, disappeared as mysteriously as he had come. They then looked for his tracks, but the snow having covered them up, they concluded he must have gone down the *Ojo Caliente!* (one of the hot springs I have already described).

son, the next reference to the kiva paintings was a brief note by Garrick Mallery ("Sign Language among North American Indians," 373; Figs. 188, 189; Pl. 184) illustrating the "destructive" and the "good" lightning from photographs taken by William Henry Jackson, probably on his visit to Jemez in 1877. Mallery also reproduced Kern's illustration of "Montezuma's adjutants." Lieutenant John G. Bourke ("Bourke on the Southwest" [ed. by Lansing B. Bloom], *New Mexico Historical Review*, Vol. III [1938], 228) visited two painted kivas at Jemez in November, 1881. He made no drawings of the murals, but his description of the figures—human, animal, and symbolic—would seem to correspond in part to Kern's illustrations. In 1899–1900, while employed as a government Indian farmer at Jemez, Albert B. Reagan was permitted to enter two of the pueblo's kivas and make drawings of the wall paintings and ceremonial masks. Again, according to Watson Smith, a distinct similarity is found between Reagan's drawings and those of Kern, made fifty years earlier. This is of interest because, while kiva walls usually are freshly recoated with adobe plaster about every six years, there is indication here that the symbols and figures of 1849, or many of them, were painted afresh on the walls at least through 1900. Reagan wrote extensively on the Jemez ceremonials, illustrating his work with drawings. Elsie Clews Parsons, of this assemblage (other than Smith) the only trained ethnologist, wrote of the kiva murals ("The Pueblo of Jemez." Department of Archaeology, Phillips Academy, *Papers of the Southwestern Expedition*, No. 3 [1925], 13; Pl. 3) without personally having seen them. Her informants were members of the pueblo, and her drawings, supplied by "a townsman," are similar in some details to the drawings by Kern and Reagan. Other brief references to these murals are given by Adolph F. Bandelier ("Final Report of Investigations among the Indians of the Southwestern United States." Cambridge, Archaeological Institute of America, *Papers, American Series*, Vols. 2–3, Part I [1890–92], 300), and Lucy W. W. Wilson ("Hand Sign of Avanyu," *American Anthropologist*, Vol. 20, No. 3 [1918], 319; Fig. 29).

He further told us that, when living upon the mesa between the cañons of Guadalupe and San Diego, there came another *padre* among them, whom, whilst on his way to receive the confessions of a sick man, they killed. That, upon another occasion, whilst engaged in their dances, they were told that the Spaniards were below, but they did not believe it and continued dancing. The consequence was that one night, after a dance, and when they had retired for the night, the Spaniards came upon them with all their force, and they, having nothing but their arrows and knives to defend themselves with, closed in with one another and began to throw each other over the precipice of the mesa. Just at this time there appeared in the direction of the Cañon de Guadalupe *Nuestra Senora de Guadalupe* (Our Lady of Guadalupe), and in the direction of the Cañon de San Diego the Saint of that name! The Indians, noticing this, fled—some to Sandia, some to Isleta, and some settling here at Jemez. All, however, have since come to live at the last mentioned place.[16]

The Pecos Indians, he went on further to inform us, were the only people that speak the same language they do; that during one of the revolutions of the country, when he was quite a youth,

[16] Hosta's recital, recorded by Simpson without apparent reservation, is a humorous mixture of part truth and obvious blarney. Between 1617, when Fr. Zarate Salmeron was appointed head of Franciscan activities in New Mexico and took up residence among the Jemez people, and the Pueblo Revolt of 1680, Indians and Spaniards were frequently embroiled in violent conflict. Of the two Franciscan priests at Jemez at the time of the revolt, one escaped and the other, Fr. Juan de Jesus Maria, was killed with an arrow. Hosta's mesa pueblo between the canyons de Guadalupe and San Diego is not imaginary, even if the saintly apparitions are. Antonio Sando, governor of Jemez in 1961, pointed out to me the high butte some ten miles to the north and west, to the summit of which he said some of the Jemez people fled after the revolt. The pueblo they built, now in ruins, was occupied "many years," with access over a steep trail on the eastern slope. The name of the pueblo was *Astialaqua*, or High View Above the Water. Van Valkenburgh notes that after the revolt, other "groups of Jemez people fled to the Navajo country. One group went [as] far as the White Mountain Apache country [in southeastern Arizona], then moved northward to live with the Hopis on First Mesa. After some years, a drought (1730–34) drove them eastward to the Canyon de Chelly where they met with other *ma'ii deeshgiizhnii* who had previously joined the Navajos."

this tribe, being very much harassed by the Spaniards (Mexicans), asked permission of the people of Jemez to come and live among them. They not only granted them permission to do this, but sent out persons to help them get in their crops and bring them and their property to their new abode. When they arrived, they gave them houses and fields.[17] The old man and his daughter, who at the time were tending the sacred fire at Pecos, the enemy [Mexicans], he says, seized and beat [the old man]—the daughter at length being carried away captive and the old man escaping by the way of Galisteo to Jemez. This was the reason of the fire of Montezuma ceasing. He went on to state that the Pecos and Jemez Indians, though they speak the same language, differ somewhat in their religious customs. In relation, however, to Montezuma, the different Pueblo Indians, although speaking different languages, have the same belief.

Yesterday, in getting some information from a Jemez Indian, I asked him whether they now looked upon God and the sun as the same being. He said they did. The question was then put, whether they still worshipped the sun, as God, with contrition of heart. His reply was, "Why not? He governs the world!" From this Indian I also learned that they worship the sun with most pleasure in the morning, and that they have priests to administer their own religion which they like better than the Roman Catholic, which he says has been forced upon them, and which they do not understand. He said they were all the children of Montezuma, and a tradition had been current among them that they were to be delivered by a people who would come from the East; that in consequence of the good treatment they were receiving from the Americans, they were beginning to believe that that people had come; that General Kearny had told them they would

---

[17] Also of Tewan stock, the Pecos people once numbered some two thousand. Their pueblo, twenty-four miles southeast of Santa Fe, was built about 1348. In the period 1720–50 the pueblo was decimated in wars with the Comanches and Jicarilla Apaches. A smallpox epidemic in 1768 cut the survivors to 180; "mountain fever," or typhoid, reduced the remainder to 104 in 1805. When Pecos Pueblo was finally abandoned in 1838, it is said there were only seventeen survivors able to travel across the mountains to new homes at Jemez.

believe this more and more, because they would continue to be treated well by the Americans, and they were finding it so.

From Hosta I learn there are now living among his people only fifteen Pecos Indians, seven being male adults, seven female, and one a little girl. One Pecos male adult, he says, is living at Cuesta, one [woman] at Santo Domingo, and one in the Cañon of Pecos. These eighteen, he states, are all that are now living of this people.

Hosta is one of the finest looking and most intelligent Pueblo Indians I have seen, and on account of his vivacity and offhand graciousness, is quite a favorite among us.

Fourth camp, August 22—The arrangement for transportation by pack mules being complete, and the Pueblo levies, 55 [actually 54, in addition to six headmen] in number, having joined us, the command also having been increased by Captain Dodge's company of Mexican volunteer infantry, the whole force took up its line of march today for the *Cañon of Chelly*.[18] At the same time, Brevet Lieutenant-Colonel Alexander, on account of indisposition, and Assistant Quartermaster Brent and Assistant Surgeon Edwards, on account of the theater of their duties being at that post, returned to Santa Fe. Our route lay directly down the valley of the Rio de Jemez, the stream of which we crossed just above San Ysidro, a small Mexican settlement about three miles below Jemez. Three miles more brought us to our present camping ground, where we find good water, tolerable pasturage, and wood in the vicinity.[19] The valley, as far as San Ysidro, is hemmed in by secondary mountains and within this extent is but slightly cultivated.

At San Ysidro I called to see Señor Francisco Sandoval, the

[18] The orthography of this word I get from Señor Donaciano Vigil, secretary of the province, who informs me that it is of Indian origin. Its pronunciation is chay-e.—Simpson's note.

More recently, authorities have agreed that the name is a Spanish adaptation of the original Navaho *tséyi'*, meaning "in between the rocks."

[19] The command's fourth camp was in a wide valley of strongly alkaline flats, on the north side of the Río Salado. The valley here is enclosed to the north by the foothills of the Jemez range, and on the south by high mesas of richly-hued pink, gray, and yellow sandstone.

proprietor of the copper furnace we saw two days since up the Cañon de San Diego. He informs me that the mine near this furnace was worked until about three years since; that one man could get from it ten *arrobas* [250 pounds] of rich ore per day, and that gold was found in association with it. He further stated that he had now cached near the furnace twenty-three arrobas of pure copper.

Several times today on the march a beautiful humming bird, the first I have seen since I left the States, has been hovering about me. The last time it paid me a visit I was seated under a tent, where it lit for a moment within a foot or two of my person and then disappeared, not to be seen again.

The length of the march today has been only 5.78 miles—it having been deemed prudent, on the first day's trial with the packs, to go but a short distance.

Fifth camp, August 23—The troops decamped at 8 o'clock this morning—a Mexican, by name Carravahal, whose residence is at San Ysidro, accompanying them as guide. Our course lay generally for the day north of west, and for the first fourteen miles directly up the Cañon de Peñasca—low mountains of a ridgy, primary character skirting it on the right, and mesa heights of some 300 or 400 feet elevation bordering it on the left.[20] The formation of these latter is generally an ash-colored sandstone, alternating with a red argillaceous rock. A mile further and we were upon the high land dividing the waters of the Rio de Jemez from those of the Rio Puerco—an extensive prospect of the valley of the latter, with the accessories of some high isolated mountain peaks, bursting unexpectedly upon us from this point. Among the peaks are to be noticed the Cerro de la Cabeza, the summit of which was an object of interest on our march from the Rio Grande to Jemez.[21] This head mountain, I perceived, resembled very much

[20] The canyon derives its name from Peñasco Arroyo, angling into the Jemez range and, at the arroyo's mouth and at the foot of Red Mesa, the Peñasco Springs—these and others in the vicinity similar to the hot springs Simpson visited above Jemez.

[21] The route taken by the troops this day, and for the next four days, was a trail evidently well known to Indians traveling between the San Juan and Puerco

in contour, though much higher, Cerro Tucumcari, a prominent landmark about 160 miles east of the Rio Grande, on the Fort Smith route. This mountain I described in my report of that route as resembling very much in shape the dome of the Capitol at Washington; and Cerro de la Cabeza, though not so good a representation, yet cannot fail to suggest to the traveler a like resemblance.

The top of the high land referred to being reached, the road commences descending towards the Rio Puerco, two miles further bringing us to the Rio de Chacoli, a small affluent of the Puerco, upon which we are encamped.[22]

Two miles from our last camp, and directly on the route, are several springs of a mineral character, the taste of the water sensibly indicating the presence of soda (probably sulphate of soda), nitre, and some ferruginous matter. One of these springs has made for itself a basin of an elliptical shape, which is several feet in diameter and raised about three feet above the argillaceous soil from which it flows. The incrustation about the mouth of the spring appears to be of a calcareous character, and colored with iron. These springs, on account of my having left the road to examine a geological formation, I did not see; and for the

---

valleys and Jemez. Long after this, the trail was rutted with the wheels of wagons carrying freight for the Hyde Exploring Expedition from Albuquerque to Pueblo Bonito. The vantage point Simpson describes was the top of a rugged switchback pass out of Warm Springs Valley and into the Puerco Valley, and to travelers from the Río Grande, afforded the first view of Cabezon Peak. Captain Dutton, reporting on his geological survey of the region, wrote in 1884–85 ("Mount Taylor and the Zuñi Plateau," 175) that "the topographers of the survey who have ascended the Cabazon find its summit to be 2,160 feet above the valley bottom. Its diameter is about 1,400 feet." Modern geological survey maps show the elevation of the plain at Cabezon's base to be about 6,300 feet.

[22] The camp site at the head of the stream or arroyo that Simpson refers to as the Río de Chacoli is figured on E. M. Kern's accompanying map as lying within the "Valle de Chacoli." The Parke-Kern map of 1851 shows neither Chacoli river nor valley, nor is either found in any later text or on any other map. In any case, the troops were encamped within gunshot of Chamisa Vega Spring, near the headwaters of the Río Salado. Richard Kern, in his diary, refers to this place as the "Chacalina valley" and observes that the region was "formerly cultivated by the Navajoes when they were at peace with the Spaniards."

information I have given I am indebted to Majors Kendrick and Peck.

In the vicinity of the springs, cropping out from the base of the mesa, forming the south wall of the cañon, I noticed large beds of earthy gypsum and sulphate of lime; and constituting the superior strata of the mesa was a formation, some eighty feet thick, composed of an alternation of crystallized fibrous gypsum and thin layers of argillaceous shale. At the foot of the escarpment I picked up what appeared to be, from its taste and appearance, common salt.

About nine miles from our last camp, in the cañon, thrown together promiscuously, are some huge specimens of conglomerate boulders, one of them in magnitude probably not being short of twenty-five by twenty-five feet, or containing over fifteen thousand cubic feet. And near our present camp there is to be seen cropping out of a side hill a red argillaceous rock, in appearance very much like that from which the Indians living on the headwaters of the Mississippi make their pipes.[23]

It is observable that the overlaying basaltic formation which I have already, in my journal, noticed as beginning at Sieneguilla, on the Rio de Santa Fe, and extending westward as far as the valley of the Rio de Jemez, has not been seen today on either side of the route. The valley, then, of the Rio de Jemez may be considered as the limit of this formation westward.

The march today has been 16.27 miles. The first half of the road was tolerably good, the last half very rough—the tongue

[23] Catlinite: a red claystone once quarried by Sioux and neighboring tribes, in Pipestone County, southwestern Minnesota. Prized by all Indians, the easily cut red steatite was named for George Catlin, the American artist and writer who in the 1830's brought it to the attention of mineralogists. The stone, Catlin wrote (*North American Indians*, Vol. I, 36) "is found but in the hands of the savage, and every tribe and nearly every individual in the tribe has his pipe made of it." Hodge writes (*Handbook of American Indians North of Mexico*, Vol. I, 219) that "white traders began the manufacture of pipes from the pipestone many years ago, and according to [F.V.] Hayden these were used by the fur companies in trade with the Indians of the n. w. . . . In 1866 Hayden stated that in the two years just passed the Northwestern Fur Company had manufactured nearly 2,000 pipes and traded them with the tribes of the upper Missouri."

of the six-pounder's limber having been broken on account of it. Not a particle of cultivable soil did we meet with until we reached the valley of the Rio de Chacoli, where we find it rich and mellow. The *sylva* has been generally the dwarf cedar, sparsely scattered; and some pines were observable on the last portion of the route.

Our camping ground furnished good grazing, tolerable water, and a sufficiency of wood. The water, however, cannot be depended upon except in the wet season.

There have joined us today some eighty Mexican mounted militia.[24] Our force, then, as now constituted, consists of fifty-five men of the regular artillery, one hundred and twenty [-three] of the regular infantry, fifty of Mexican volunteer infantry, fifty [-four] of the Pueblo or Indian mounted militia, and eighty [-three] of Mexican mounted militia—in all aggregating, with the employes of the quartermaster's and subsistence departments, about four hundred men. The longitude of this camp, by observation, is 107° 3′ 15″.

Sixth camp, August 24—We had some fine showers of rain last evening and during the night.

Seven men belonging to the Mexican mounted militia are reported to have deserted last evening.

The troops resumed the march at 8 A.M.—our course for the day being generally northwest. One and a half miles from camp we crossed the Rio de Chacoli, a running stream, four feet in breadth and a few inches in depth with banks six feet high, which had to be cut down to give passage to the artillery. This creek traversed, the route lay up a very shallow valley for about three and a half miles, when we got on the brow of the immediate valley of the Rio Puerco—this valley being hemmed in on its west side by heights with tableau tops and precipitous escarpment walls. The Rio Puerco, as far as visible, runs a course west of south and is slightly fringed with the cottonwood. Cerro de la Cabeza and other mountain peaks to the south and west show well from this point. Close by the route, on its right, just before

24 These militia were commanded by Captain John Chapman.

reaching the bed of the Puerco, is an old circular stone corral about thirty feet in width, and three in height, laid in mud mortar.[25]

The Rio Puerco, which, from its great length upon the maps we had conjectured to be a flowing stream of some importance, we found to contain water only here and there, in pools—the fluid being a greenish, sickening color, and brackish to the taste. The width of its bottom, which is a commixture of clay and gravel, is about one hundred feet. Its banks, between twenty and thirty feet high, are vertical and had to be graded down to allow the artillery and pack animals to cross them.[26] The six-pounder had to be unlimbered and dragged up on the west side by men at the prolonges. A mule, with one of the howitzers packed on his back, in attempting to traverse the bed of the river lost his footing and capsized—the howitzer, on account of its great weight, naturally seeking the lowest place, and the legs of the poor animal correspondingly tending upwards. The sight, it may well be conceived, partook both of the painful and the ludicrous.

The valley of the Rio de Chacoli and that of the Puerco, both of which, on account of the slight elevation of the dividing ridge, may be considered as but one, and which embraces a breadth of about six miles, is, to all appearances, quite a rich body of land, and, if not ordinarily too dry, must be susceptible to productive cultivation. It differs from the other cultivated soil we have passed over in being argillaceous instead of felspatic.

A mile beyond the Rio Puerco we entered the Cañon de la Copa (Cup Cañon), so called on account of the cup or vaselike

[25] The troops were now entering the southeast corner of the very old Navaho country. The stone corral may have belonged to a Mexican herder of sheep or horses, but more likely it was Navaho and, if so, first sign of the *Diné* mentioned by Simpson. Between the Puerco Valley and Torreon, twenty-seven miles to the northeast, the troops could not have failed to have passed within sight of Navaho hogans, but curiously Simpson makes no reference to them.

[26] This is the Río Puerco of the East. The depth of the arroyo cut by the stream is interesting, in view of what Simpson later reports of the Río Chaco's being a surface stream. Arroyos of both Chaco and Puerco in 1961 had reached depths of forty feet. Richard Kern notes that the Puerco was "a miserable dirty & little stream of brackish water lined with high cut soil banks & cotton woods."

appearance of some of the sandstone rocks forming its walls. In the left-hand or south escarpment wall of the cañon may be seen some well-defined and beautiful stratification, its dip being slightly *from* the valley of the Puerco, or westward. The breadth of the cañon is about one hundred and fifty yards. Among the escarpment rocks I noticed some seams of a perfectly white saline pulverulent substance which, from its taste, I should judge to be soda. We also found, in the same locality, in some crevices and also attached to the rock, a dark pitchy substance agglutinated with the excrement of birds, and of animals of the rat species.

Near these rocks are several deep and narrow arroyos, which required to be worked to make them practicable for the passage of the artillery.

About half a mile further, just as we emerged from the cañon, noticing on the right of the road what appeared to be bituminous coal, I examined it and found it to be veritably such, though of an impure, slaty character. It exists in beds a foot thick, which are in some instances overlaid by yellowish sandstone, and then again by calcareous rock. I noticed in some instances, superposing the coal, loose, disintegrated masses or fragments of what appeared to be a species of jasper, the evidences of igneous influence being quite apparent from its baked and blackened aspect. The coal, when fractured, occasionally discovers resinous particles of a beautiful iridescent character, the reflections being those of the garnet.

Getting out of the Cañon de la Copa, the country becomes very much broken by low hills of a mound or mesa shape, some of them, on account of the symmetry of their form, creating a degree of interest.

From twelve to fifteen miles off, on our left, have appeared all day a chain of pretty high mountains, some of them ridgy and some of mesa shape.[27]

After a march of 13.27 miles, falling upon an insignificant

[27] More like twenty miles distant, and slightly more to the north than he indicates, Simpson saw the south and eastern escarpments of Chacra Mesa.

tributary of the Rio Puerco, which drains the valley called *Cañada de Piedra de Lumbre,* we have encamped—the pasturage about our camp being but tolerable, the water (of a high clay color) barely endurable, and fuel being found in the vicinity.[28] The water, however, can only be depended upon during the wet season.

The face of the country today, as usual, has presented pine and cedar of a dwarf growth, very thinly scattered; and the artemisia [sagebrush] has been seen everywhere. The soil, excepting the valley of the Rio Puerco, for purposes of cultivation may be considered as worthless. Astronomical observations put this camp in latitude 35° 46′ 13″.

Seventh camp, August 25—Three more of the Mexican mounted militia are reported to have deserted yesterday.

The troops took up the line of march at 7 A.M. Our general course for the day has been about northwest. At the start our route lay through a shallow valley—a succession of them, bounded by tableau or rounded hills, crossing each other in every direction and causing the country to have a broken appearance. A mile or two from camp, looking back, an imposing view of Cerro de la Cabeza presented itself to us. There was nothing about it to detract from its towering sublimity; and as the morning sun threw its golden light upon its eastern slope, leaving all other portions in a softened twilight shade, I thought I had never seen anything more beautiful, and at the same time grand.

Four miles on the route, to the left of the road upon a little hillock, another and more extensive view of the country bursts upon you. To the south, some twenty miles off, lay an extensive range of mountains of a mesa and ridgy character; intermingled with these and diversifying the scene were Cerro de la Cabeza and a dozen other peaks, one of them quite sharp; to the east

[28] This sixth camp, in high rolling sagebrush country, found only the tip of Cabezon Peak visible, now far to the south. Probably the troops made their small night fires on the summit, rather than in the depression of Piédra de Lumbre.

and northeast were still to be seen, stretching from north to south some forty to fifty miles off, the Jemez Mountains; and everywhere else a broken country made up of low swelling hills, isolated cones and mesa heights, sprinkled with pine and cedar of a scrub growth, and with the artemisia, in connexion with an everywhere-prevailing dirty yellowish arenaceous soil, completed the picture.[29]

As we proceeded on, the country stretched out more prairie-like and rolling, furnishing an extensive range of view on every hand. Six miles from our last camp we met some very dirty, clay-colored water, in pools, the permanency of which, however, cannot be depended on. A mile and a half further, we traversed about one-third of a mile of what appeared to be a good argilla-ceous soil. Four miles from this a very beautifully-shaped tableau mound appears, ranging directly in front of our course. After a march of thirteen and a half miles, coming upon an arroyo containing some water of a highly-charged clay character, as scanty in quantity as unpalatable to the taste; and, the guide who had been sent in advance not returning in time to give the colonel commanding the information needed in respect to water to make it prudent for him to go any further for the day, the order was given to encamp.

The valley through which the arroyo runs is called the *Cañon de Torrijon;* and I notice a few cottonwoods skirting the arroyo. The pasturage about camp is but tolerable.[30]

[29] Since leaving Santo Domingo, the troops had been steadily ascending toward the Continental Divide, and would soon cross it. Simpson's "little hillock" itself is unimposing, but because of its elevation—close to 7,000 feet—affords an unusual view. Perhaps even more unusual is Simpson's accuracy in reckoning airline distances. The mountain range he mentions as twenty miles to the south is the northern extension of the San Mateo mountains. Simpson could see, though he did not name them all, the east brow of Chacra Mesa, seven miles due west; Cabezon Peak, twelve miles south-southeast; Sandia Peak, fifty-four miles to the southeast; and the summit of the mountain he later would name—Mt. Taylor—forty-five miles to the southwest.

[30] The troops were camped on Torreon Arroyo. The region then, as now, was a stronghold of the eastern Navahos, and it is impossible to explain why Simpson fails to remark their presence.

INTERIOR OF QUARTERMASTER'S CORRAL,
HEADQUARTERS, DEPARTMENT OF NEW MEXICO, SANTA FE.
The view is looking south to southwest toward the center of town.

COLONEL JOHN M. WASHINGTON
From a portrait made some years before the 1849 expedition.

The soil today, excepting the very narrow belt already alluded to, is worthless. The road was pretty good.

About sundown, Major Kendrick and myself took a stroll about a mile from camp in a northwest course, to a tableau mound where we found, horizontally disposed, an outcrop of bituminous coal of an indifferent character.

The latitude of this camp, by astronomical observations, is 35° 50′ 31″; its longitude, 107° 23′ 45″.

Eighth camp, August 26—The nights and mornings at the last two camps have been quite cold. This is doubtless owing to our great elevation. We have been ascending more or less ever since we left the Rio Grande. Indeed, from the appearance of the Jemez Mountains and other indications, it is not at all unlikely that the country we have been traveling over today is considerably higher, atmospherically, than Santa Fe.[31] But this point, it is to be regretted, I cannot determine, for the want of a barometer, with which it was impossible to supply myself on setting out upon the expedition. Major Emory, in his report, speaks of the absence of dew along the Rio Gila, and on that account, of his scarcely ever finding it necessary to wipe his horizon-glass.[32] I, on the contrary, find it so heavy in this region as to make it necessary to wipe mine often.

The troops decamped at 7 A.M.—the weather, as it generally has been, being beautiful, clear, and pleasant. Our general course during the day was northwest, and for the first seven miles the route was gradually ascending.

Just after leaving camp, we passed, to the right of the road, the beautifully-shaped mound referred to yesterday. Four miles from camp, on the right of the road, is an oblong mound or hill about fifty feet high, exhibiting very strikingly the gradual effect of igneous action upon matter in proportion to its proximity to the source of heat. Highly scoriaceous rocks protruded here and

[31] Geographically, there is no appreciable difference in altitude between the Torreon region and Santa Fe, both near 7,000 feet.
[32] Lieutenant William Hemsley Emory, "Notes of a Military Reconnoissance from Fort Leavenworth, in Missouri, to San Diego, in California . . . 1846–47."

there through argillaceous rocks, burnt to different degrees of calcination; and a dirty yellowish friable sandstone rock crops out all around from underneath the mass. This is the first scoriaceous or lava rock I have noticed since I left the valley of the Jemez. From the mound just adverted to, Cerro de la Cabeza and the Jemez Mountains could still be seen to our rear.

A mile and a half further on the route we came to a locality where coal crops out of the soil. Near this locality is a very shallow depression or basin caused by the washing of the rains. In this basin we found some beautiful specimens of petrified wood —in two instances the trunks of the trees still standing erect and *in situ*. One of these trunks was two feet high by two in diameter, and the other three feet high by two and a half in diameter. In another instance a trunk of a tree, in its petrified state, had fallen over and split open, the parts lying together as if they had just been cleft with an axe. Do not these petrifactions show that this country was once better timbered than it now is? All the *sylva* we now find—except the cottonwood occasionally to be seen on the water-courses—is a scrub growth of cedar and pine.

Prescott, in his *History of the Conquest of Mexico,* speaking of the absence of forest trees in southern Mexico at the present period, remarks: "In the time of the Aztecs, the table land was thickly covered with larch, oak, cyprus, and the other forest trees—the extraordinary dimensions of some of which, remaining to the present day, show that the curse of barrenness in later times is chargeable more on man than nature."[33]

If by this remark this favorite author means to say that the curse of barrenness may be chargeable to the wickedness of the people who inhabit it, I can assent to it; but if, on the contrary, his idea is that its inhabitants had caused it by their own spontaneous agency (positive or negative), either by acts of devasta-

[33] Volume 1, page 9—See Isaiah, chapter 24; also, Psalms, chapter 107, verses 33 and 34, in which the Hebrew word, which in the text is rendered "barrenness," is also, according to the marginal reference, convertible into *saltiness;* and it is not a little remarkable that the cause of the barrenness of the soil in Old as well as New Mexico is, in a very considerable degree, if not mainly, owing to this same condition of the earth—its saltiness.—Simpson's note.

tion or neglect of culture, I do not perceive that a sufficient
motive could be assigned to the former; and the history of rich,
uncultivated lands in other portions of the world does not, in
my judgment, justify the belief of the latter.

Seven miles from our last camp, we reached the highest point
of the land dividing the tributaries of the Gulf of Mexico from
those of the Pacific [the Continental Divide]. This land, on all
the maps I have seen, is represented as being either of a ridgy,
primary character, or of a mesa or tableau character, its lateral
walls in the latter case being represented steep and deep. On
some maps it is designated as the *Sierra de los Mimbres,* or in
others as the *Sierra Madre.*

The highest point of land just referred to reached, we commenced gradually descending its western slope—three miles
more bringing us to the Rio Chaco, a tributary of the Rio San
Juan; and five miles more to a point whence could be seen in
the distance, on a slight elevation, a conspicuous ruin called, according to some of the Pueblo Indians with us, *Pueblo de Montezuma,* and according to the Mexicans, *Pueblo Colorado.* Hosta
calls it *Pueblo de Ratones;* Sandoval, the friendly Navaho chief
with us, *Pueblo Grande;* and Carravahal, our Mexican guide,
who probably knows more about it than anyone else, *Pueblo
Pintado.*[34]

34 And Pintado it would remain. One wonders at Simpson's choice, since Carravahal could not have learned the name Pueblo Pintado (Painted Village) from
its ancient occupants, who left it abandoned forever by or before the middle of
the twelfth century. Simpson possibly found Pintado more pleasant to the ear,
and more appropriate, than Montezuma's Pueblo, Red Pueblo, Hosta's Pueblo
of Rats, or Sandoval's Great Pueblo. As to the recurrence here of the Monte-
zuma-Aztec legend, Lansing Bloom (in Hewett's *Chaco Canyon,* 145) observes
that "the Montezuma legend is certainly an anachronism, and the tradition of the
origin of the Aztlans, whatever historic fact may underlie it, cannot be connected with the pueblo ruins of the San Juan drainage. . . ." Pueblo Pintado is
the easternmost of the great Chaco pueblos, separated from them by ten miles
but, since 1907, included with them as part of Chaco Canyon National Monument. The trader Josiah Gregg, five years before Simpson's visit to the Chaco,
wrote (*Commerce of the Prairies,* 197–98) of "the ruins of Pueblo Bonito, in
the direction of Navajo, on the borders of the Cordilleras" and evidently confused Bonito with Pintado; he was writing from hearsay, not from personal observation.

After having marched 21.45 miles, coming to a spring of good water in a ravine to the left of the road, about a mile from the ruins, in the vicinity of which we found fuel and good grazing, we encamped.[35]

The superior rock today was argillo-arenaceous; the soil the same; the route smooth and good. About a dozen hares, half a dozen doves, and one curlew, are all the game I have seen since I left Santa Fe. A wolf is seen occasionally. Today I saw four, two of them very large.

After partaking of some refreshments I started off, with high expectations—my assistants, the Messrs. Kern, accompanying me—to examine the ruins of Pueblo Pintado. We found them to more than answer our expectations. Forming one structure, and built of tabular pieces of hard, fine-grained compact gray sandstone (a material entirely unknown in the present architecture of New Mexico), to which the atmosphere has imparted a reddish tinge, the layers or beds being not thicker than three inches, and sometimes as thin as one-fourth of an inch, it discovers in the masonry a combination of science and art which can only be referred to a higher stage of civilization and refinement than is discoverable in the works of Mexicans or Pueblos of the present day. Indeed, so beautifully diminutive and true are the details of the structure as to cause it, at a little distance, to have all the appearance of a magnificent piece of mosaic work.

In the outer face of the building there are no signs of mortar, the intervals between the beds being chinked with stones of the minutest thinness. The filling and backing are done in rubble masonry, the mortar presenting no indications of the presence of lime. The thickness of the main wall at base is within an inch or two of three feet; higher up, it is less—diminishing every story by retreating jogs on the inside, from bottom to top. Its elevation at its present highest point is between twenty-five and thirty feet, the series of floor beams indicating that there must have been originally three stories.

[35] The encampment was on high ground wooded with piñon and juniper, the ravine referred to being the head of a fork of the north branch of Chaco Canyon.

The ground plan, including the court, in exterior development is about 403 feet. On the ground floor, exclusive of the outbuildings, are fifty-four apartments, some of them as small as five feet square, and the largest about twelve by six feet. These rooms communicate with each other by very small doors, some of them as contracted as two and a half by two and a half feet; and in the case of the inner suite, the doors communicating with the interior court are as small as three and a half by two feet. The principal rooms, or those most in use, were, on account of their having larger doors and windows, most probably those of the second story. The system of flooring seems to have been large transverse unhewn beams, six inches in diameter, laid transversely from wall to wall, and then a number of smaller ones, about three inches in diameter, laid longitudinally upon them. What was placed on these does not appear, but most probably it was brush, bark, or slabs, covered with a layer of mud mortar. The beams show no signs of the saw or axe; on the contrary, they appear to have been hacked off by means of some very imperfect instrument.[36] On the west face of the structure, the windows, which are only in the second story, are three feet two inches by two feet two inches. On the north side they are only in the second and third stories and are as small as fourteen by fourteen inches. At different points about the premises were three circular apartments sunk in the ground, the walls being of masonry. These apartments the Pueblo Indians call estuffas, or places where the people held their political and religious meetings.

[36] Imperfect indeed, in terms of modern tools. Pintado's builders with amazing patience cut and trimmed hundreds of large trees with stone axes and with stone mauls faced the stones used in the massive walls. Never excavated, the true size of Pintado has not been determined, but it corresponds to Pueblo del Arroyo, Tsin Kletzin, and Kin Biniola in the Chaco group. Only Bonito, Chetro Ketl, Pueblo Alto, and Peñasco Blanco are larger. Reginald Fisher (in Hewett's *Chaco Canyon*, 159) estimated the population of the Pintado group at eight hundred, the population of the four larger pueblos at from one thousand to twelve hundred. Richard Kern made detailed notes in his diary of wall and room measurements. Where Simpson observed only three kivas, Kern found four, in the court or plaza, each about twenty-four feet in diameter. In the southwest quarter of the ruin he noted also the presence of a great kiva fifty-four feet in diameter.

The site of the ruins is a knoll, some twenty or thirty feet above the surrounding plain—the Rio Chaco coursing by it two or three hundred yards distant, and no wood being visible within the circuit of a mile.

The quarry from which the material was obtained to build the structure seems to have been just back of our camp.

Hosta says this pueblo was built by Montezuma and his people when they were on their way from the north towards the south; that after living here and in the vicinity for a while, they dispersed, some of them going east and settling on the Rio Grande, and others south into Old Mexico.[37]

The captain of the Mexican mounted militia informs me that twenty of his men have deserted since they joined us on the 23d. The latitude of this camp is found to be 35° 56′ 27″; its longitude, 107° 46′.

[37] Hosta is romancing again. Tree-ring dates from Pintado are not available, but would correspond approximately to known dates from several other Chaco ruins. Pintado's first rooms may have been built about 1000 A.D., and the pueblo possibly was completed during the next one hundred years. Aztec history begins in 1168 A.D. with arrival of migratory tribes in the valley of Anáhuac, Mexico. Montezuma I ruled from 1440–69 and his grandson, Montezuma II, from 1503 until his death in 1520. A professor, Oscar Loew, was equally receptive to the Montezuma legend when Hosta guided him to Pintado in 1874. "Hosti," Loew wrote ("Report of the Ruins of New Mexico," 1095–96), "a very kind, intelligent old Indian, denies that these ruins [of the San Juan drainage] were the result of Spanish wars, remarking that, the rain falling less and less, these people emigrated to the southward long before the Spaniards arrived in the country, being led by Montezuma, a powerful man, who was born in Pecos, and had settled with the Pueblos on the Rio San Juan." Van Valkenburgh tells the following clan development legend relating to Pueblo Pintado: "Fourteen years after the *Hashk'ann hadzohi dine'e,* Expanding Yucca Fruit People, came to join the nuclear Navajo clans, the tribe moved to Pueblo Pintado. It was deserted then. They spread out and camped there at night. Their many camp fires attracted the attention of some wanderers on Chacra Mesa. On the next morning, the strangers came down to see who the numerous people were who had made the camp fires. When asked from whence they came, the wanderers said that they came from *nahoobáh* [in the vicinity of Atarque, New Mexico, thirty-five miles south of Zuñi]. . . . They had been driven from their country by enemies. The Navajos called them *nahoobaanii dine'e* and the *dził na'oozłii dine'e,* People who Encircled [a Navaho clan from the vicinity of Huerfano Mesa, thirty-five miles to the north]. These people then became members of the Navajo tribe."

Ninth camp, August 27—Not finishing our examinations at the ruins of Pueblo Pintado yesterday afternoon, we again visited them early this morning. On digging about the base of the exterior wall we find that for at least two feet (the depth our time would permit us to go), the same kind of masonry obtains below as above, except that it appears more compact. We could find no signs of the genuine arch about the premises, the lintels of the doors and windows being generally either a number of pieces of wood laid horizontally side by side, a single stone slab laid in this manner, or occasionally a series of smaller ones so placed horizontally upon each other, whilst presenting the form of a sharp angle, in vertical longitudinal section, they would support the weight of the fabric above. Fragments of pottery lay scattered around, the colors showing taste in their selection and in the style of their arrangement, and being still quite bright. We would gladly, had time permitted, have remained longer to dig among the rubbish of the past; but the troops having already got some miles in advance of us, we were reluctantly obliged to quit.[38]

Two miles over a slightly rolling country, our general course being still northwest, brought us to the commencement of the Cañon de Chaco, its width here being about two hundred

[38] Between the troops' campsite and Pueblo Pintado are ruins of three small pueblos. Had Simpson been allowed more time, he might have examined and mentioned them—he could scarcely have failed to see them—as well as eleven other separate small sites ranged in an arc to the north-northeast of Pintado and situated between that pueblo and the Chaco Wash. Each of the smaller ruins was a one-story habitation of perhaps eight to twenty rooms. The largest of the group, centered in the arc, was important enough to have a single plaza or court. Trash mounds associated with these secondary sites are all located to the southeast. Pottery sherds, found scattered in great profusion over the ruins, are of the same types associated with Pueblo Pintado. From this superficial evidence one might conclude that Pintado was occupied contemporaneously with some fourteen closely associated smaller pueblos for a period of perhaps 150 years. Directly north of Pintado, beyond these small pueblo sites and on sand flats close to the Chaco Wash, earlier sherds of plain, coarse grayware indicate the presence of Developmental Pueblo or Modified Basketmaker sites of 900 A.D. or before.

yards.[39] Friable sandstone rocks, massive above, stratified below, constitute its enclosing walls. Four miles further, on the right side of the cañon, is a habitation excavated in the rocks, its front wall being of stone and masonry. The height of the apartment is four feet; dimensions in plan, fourteen by fourteen feet; and size of doorway, two by two feet. Alongside of it is another small apartment, also excavated in the rocks.[40]

Bituminous coal again makes its appearance, nine miles from our last camp, cropping out from sandstone rocks. A mile further, on the left-hand side of the road, is a stone and mortar enclosure, elliptical in shape, sixteen by eight feet in plan, and having two equal compartments. About a mile further are to be seen a number of very large sandstone boulders, which have tumbled from the rocks above, some of them containing probably as much as fifteen thousand cubic feet. In some instances I noticed rocks of the same kind *in situ*, and just ready to tumble down. On several of these boulders were found a number of hieroglyphics.

Thirteen miles from our last camp we came to another old ruin, called by Carravahal *Pueblo Weje-gi*, built, like Pueblo Pintado, of very thin tabular pieces of compact sandstone. The circuit of the structure, including the court, was near seven hundred feet. The number of apartments on the ground floor, judging from what was distinguishable, was probably ninety-nine. The present elevation of the exterior wall is about twenty-five

[39] The troops were following the north or main branch of the Chaco Wash, beginning their entrance into Chaco Canyon. The words *Chusca, Chaca, Chacat, Chacra,* and *Chaco* are all old. Each may be, or probably is, the Spanish variant of Navaho words that might be pronounced in many ways. Certainly to be considered is the previously unpublished speculation of Tietjens, who in 1929 left these notes with the Chaco custodian: "*Chaco: Tsékhò:* Navajo name for a canyon, literally *tsé* (rock), *khò* (opening); *Charco:* New Mexican Spanish for a pool in a stream, a mud hole, or contemporary puddles caused by rain; *Chacra:* ... derived from Navajo *Tsékay.*"

[40] Between this point and Pueblo Wijiji, Simpson would see—but not record—other small cliff dwellings, none of more than a few rooms, built into the north face of the canyon. Builders of the cliff rooms probably came to the canyon late in its period of *anasazi* occupation. They may have come from the region of Mesa Verde, to the northwest. They were not Chaco people, and remained only a short time.

feet. The great mass of rubbish below, however, shows that it must have been higher.[41]

The view from these ruins, both up and down the cañon, is fine. Rocks piled upon rocks present themselves on either side and in such order as to give the idea of two parallel architectural façades, converging at either extremity, at a remote distance. Another and more splendid view burst upon us as we turned an angle of the cañon, just before reaching camp. The chief object in the landscape was *Mesa Fachada,* a circular mound with tableau top, rising abruptly midway in the cañon to a height of from three hundred to four hundred feet.[42] The combination of this striking and beautiful object with the clear sky beyond, against which it was relieved, in connexion with lesser mounds at its base, the serried tents of the command, the busy scene of moving men and animals in the vicinity, and the curling smoke from the camp fires, which made up a picture which it has been seldom my lot to witness.[43]

[41] Carravahal's name for the pueblo, spelled different ways, is derived from the Navaho. Van Valkenburgh offers three Navaho variants: Turquoise House, *(Khindotlizih)*; Greasewood House, *(Kin doot-'izhi)*; and Black Greasewood, *(Diwozhiishzhiin).* The last appears phonetically closest to Wijiji, and probably is the word Carravahal was approximating. Diagonally across the canyon and situated close to the south rim, clearly visible from Wijiji, are eight refuge sites. These circular one-room dwellings are believed to have been built and occupied after the Pueblo Revolt of 1680 by Pueblo refugees from the Río Grande. The rooms are about ten feet in diameter and appear to have been carelessly put together with little or no adobe mortar. Only a few pottery sherds are found here, and these, of plain gray, mulberry red, and thick, glazed white, are unrelated to Chaco types.

[42] Carravahal again appears to have been Simpson's informant. Fahada actually is a large butte, with numerous small *anasazi* sites found at its base and several refuge dwellings built on a narrow ledge half way to the summit. Navahos, according to Van Valkenburgh, refer to Fahada as "*Tsedighili* [or] *tsedighin,* both meaning holy rock. It is one of the important stopping places in the story of the Male Shooting Chant of the Navajos."

[43] Only one hundred yards or so east of the camp lay the ruins of a small pueblo (Bc 236) which, when excavated in 1958 by Zorro A. Bradley, apparently showed an unusually early occupancy by people of the Mesa Verde culture. An interesting feature of the ruin, and not common to the Chaco, is a circular firepit adjacent to the pueblo, five feet, one inch in diameter, four feet,

The distance traveled today was 14.86 miles. The road was tolerably good. Scrub cedars, very thinly scattered, were to be seen on the heights; and the artemisia characterised the *flora*. Some patches of good gramma grass could occasionally be seen along the Rio Chaco. The country, as usual, on account, doubtless, of constant drought, presented one wide expanse of barren waste. Frequently since we left the Puerco the soil has given indications of containing all the earthy elements of fertility, but the refreshing shower has been wanting to make it productive. The Rio Chaco, near our camp, has a width of eight feet and a depth of one and a half.[44] Its waters, which are of a rich clay

nine inches deep, lined with small rocks and its interior wall plastered with adobe.

Unlike troops who followed them to the Chaco, the soldiers of Colonel Washington's command left no names, initials, or dates carved on the rocks near this encampment. Nine years later a small detachment of Company E, Mounted Rifles, pursued a raiding band of Navahos into the Chaco and camped a few miles west down the canyon. On the cliff face behind Pueblo Chetro Ketl may be found the date—October 30, 1858—and three of the soldiers' names— T(homas) O'Connor, C(harles) Behler, and S. E. Stamt (or Stamf). These troops were part of the garrison at Fort Garland, Colorado. Again, during a minor brush with Navahos, a troop of Company K, Third Infantry, left signs of their passage —the date, November 7, 1858, carved in a large talus rock one-quarter mile east of Chetro Ketl. With the date can be traced the figure of an officer, mounted and wearing a sabre, and the names of four soldiers—E. H. Bradley, J(ulius) Windsbecker, Smyth Maynes, and John Mortell.

[44] Related to Simpson's offhand observation that the Chaco was a small surface stream may lie an answer to the *anasazi* abandonment of Chaco Canyon between 1150–1250 A.D. In 1924–25 geologist Kirk Bryan made extensive tests in the Chaco that led him to conclude that arroyo-cutting and resultant lowering of the water table forced the ancient farming people to move away. The Chaco, Bryan believes, never was a constantly flowing stream. From about 700 A.D., therefore, the earliest pithouse residents depended upon rains to divert water from an occasional surface stream to floodwater their crops. Erosion may have started with heavy deforestation of the region, but, in any case, late in the Chaco's classic Pueblo III period an arroyo cut to a depth of about nine feet below the canyon floor ("The Geology of Chaco Canyon, New Mexico" [ed. by Neil M. Judd], *Smithsonian Miscellaneous Collections*, Vol. 122, No. 7, Bryan, 61). This lowering of the Chaco's bed made floodwater farming impossible. Groups of the canyon's large population had no choice but to abandon their homes. With the passage of years, after Chaco's pueblos stood emptied and silent, the ancient arroyo not only was refilled with silt, but the canyon floor rose six

color, can only be relied upon with certainty during the wet season.

August 28—This morning, the route of the command deviating from the Cañon of Chaco, in which were represented to be some more ruins of an interesting character, I obtained permission from the colonel commanding to visit them—it being my intention to join the command upon the Chaco, which it was said the troops would strike again before halting for the night. I took with me Mr. R. H. Kern and the guide, Carravahal, seven mounted Mexicans accompanying us as an escort. Mr. E. M. Kern was directed to continue with the troops and keep up the topography of the route.[45]

Proceeding down the cañon one and a half miles (its general course northwest by west), we came to an old ruined structure, called by Carravahal *Pueblo Una Vida*. The circuit of this pueblo we found on measurement to be nine hundred and ninety-four feet. The structure has been built, like those I have already described, of very thin tabular fine-grained sandstone—the highest present elevation of the main walls being about fifteen feet. Two stories are now discoverable, but the mass of debris at the base of the walls certainly shows that there must originally have been more. The remains of four circular estuffas are still apparent.[46]

feet with new accumulations of sand and dirt. The Río Chaco, when it ran with rain or melting snow, again flowed on the surface. Thus Simpson found and reported it in August, 1849. Bryan notes (60) that when William Henry Jackson visited Chaco Canyon in 1877, the stream bed was sixteen feet deep in an arroyo that was sixty to one hundred feet broad. On the testimony of old Navahos of the region, Bryan says that the Chaco's second channel-cutting probably started about 1860–70.

[45] Richard Kern's diary entry for August 28 has the party include, besides Simpson and himself, Carravahal, Dr. Hammond, James Collins, and "an escort of 8 Mexicans."

[46] There is no known Navaho name for this ruin. Van Valkenburgh believes the Spanish name (One Life) refers to the living stump of a tree once growing in the ruin. W. H. Jackson in 1877 found the L-shaped ground plan of Una Vida similar to that of Pintado. Within Una Vida's main court he observed ("Report on the Ancient Ruins," 437) "the remains of the largest *estufa* found in any of the eleven great ruins. The inside measurement from wall to wall is 60.2

A mile further down the cañon we came to another pueblo in ruins, called by Carravahal *Hungo Pavie*, which he interprets as Crooked Nose. These ruins show the same nicety in the details of their masonry as those I have already described. The ground plan shows an extent of exterior development of eight hundred and seventy-two feet, and a number of rooms upon the ground floor equal to seventy-two. The structure shows the existence of but one circular estuffa, and this is placed in the body of the north portion of the building, midway from either extremity. This estuffa differs from the others we have seen in having a number of interior counterforts.[47]

The main walls of the building are at base two and three-quarter feet through, and at this time show a height of about thirty feet. The ends of the floor beams, which are still visible, plainly showing that there was originally, at least, a vertical series of four floors, there must then also have been originally at least a series of four stories of rooms; and as the debris at the base of the walls is very great, it is reasonable to infer that there may have been even more. The floor beams, which are round, in transverse section, and eleven inches in diameter, as well as the windows, which are as small as twelve by thirteen inches, have been arranged horizontally with great precision and regularity. Pottery, as usual, was found scattered about the premises.

Continuing down the cañon one and three-quarter miles further, we came to another extensive structure in ruins, the name

feet. . . ." Three or four Navaho stone hogans which he found in Una Vida's court were photographed by Victor Mindeleff about 1885. Apparently they had not been built when Simpson and Jackson saw the ruin. Excavation of portions of Una Vida was started by Gordon Vivian in 1960.

[47] The names supplied by Carravahal remain unchanged—and of uncertain derivation. Generally it is believed that Hungo Pavie (or Hungopavie) is a Hopi name. The kiva observed by Simpson and described more extensively by William H. Jackson ("Report on the Ancient Ruins," 438) appears to have been an unusual "tower kiva" found at two outlying sites but elswhere in the canyon only at Chetro Ketl. Jackson also refers to "a great circular depression" he observed in the court, just within the south wall. Excavation probably would reveal this to be one of the great kivas common to Chaco's largest pueblos. They are similar also to the great kivas of Casa Rinconada and Kin Nahasbas, standing alone in the canyon and not recorded by Simpson.

of which, according to the guide, is *Pueblo Chettro Kettle,* or, as he interprets it, the Rain Pueblo. These ruins have an extent of exterior circuit, inclusive of the court, of about thirteen hundred feet. The material of which the structure has been made, as also the style of the masonry, is the same as that of the ruined pueblos I have already described—the stone a sandstone, and the beams pine and cedar. The number of stories at present discoverable is four—there having been originally a series of windows (four and a half by three and a half feet) in the first story, which are now walled up. The number of rooms on the first floor, all of which were distinguishable excepting those in the west wing, must have been as many as one hundred and twenty-four. The circular estuffas, of which there are six in number, have a greater depth than any we have seen, and differ from them also in exhibiting more stories, one of them showing certainly two, and possibily three, the lowest one appearing to be almost covered up with debris.[48]

In the northwest corner of these ruins we found a room in an almost perfect state of preservation. This room is fourteen by seven and a half feet in plan, and ten feet in elevation. It has an outside doorway, three and a half feet high by two and a quarter wide, and one at its west end leading into the adjoining room, two feet wide, and at present, on account of rubbish, only two and a half feet high.

The stone walls still have their plaster upon them, in a toler-

[48] Since 1849, Carravahal's name for Chetro Ketl has remained unexplained. Some architectural features of the pueblo and its associated talus site suggest influences imported to the Chaco from Mexico or Central America. If such influences there were, they go too deep into prehistory to account for Carravahal's foreign-sounding Chetro Ketl. Van Valkenburgh notes that the Navaho place name *Tsebida' t'ini' ani* (Covered Hole) refers not to the pueblo, but to large round holes or cists carved out of the canyon wall back of the ruin. Hewett (191–93) and Florence Hawley ("The Significance of the Dated Prehistory of Chetro Ketl," 21–30), from the evidence of available tree-ring dates, estimate the period of Chetro Ketl's construction from 945 to 1116 A.D. Chetro Ketl was partially excavated under Hewett's direction in 1919–21 and 1929–33. As a result of this work, Hewett reports on the pueblo's tower kivas (101–106) but in terms scarcely more conclusive than the description offered by Simpson here, or by Jackson (439).

able state of preservation. On the south wall is a recess or niche, three feet two inches high by four feet five inches wide by four feet deep. Its position and size naturally suggested the idea that it might have been a fireplace; but if so, the smoke must have returned to the room, as there was no chimney outlet for it. In addition to this large recess, there were three smaller ones in the same wall. The ceiling showed two main beams, laid transversely; on these, longitudinally, were a number of smaller ones in juxtaposition, the ends being tied together by a species of wooden fibre, and the interstices chinked in with small stones; on these again, transversely, in close contact, was a kind of lathing of the odor and appearance of cedar—all in a good state of preservation. Depending from the beams were several short pieces of rope, a specimen of which I got. The floor of the room is covered with rubbish. A large quantity of pottery lay strewed about the ruins.

Two hundred yards further down the cañon, in its north wall, are to be seen, about twelve feet from the ground, upon the same level within a number of feet of each other, three horizontal perforations, each about two feet in diameter and having smaller ones between them on the same line of level. Besides these perforations, there were other small ones arranged in a vertical line from the ground to one of the larger ones. What the object of these perforations may have been it is difficult to devine unless, indeed, back of the larger ones and extending from one to the other, is an excavation which may answer as a hiding place— the small orifices on the same level serving for light and ventilation, and those extending from the ground to one of the large ones as means of ascent. And this conjecture agrees with the statements made by one of the Mexicans with me, that it was a *casa* (house).[49]

---

[49] Small house units of one and two stories were built against the cliffs, here as elsewhere through the canyon. Often in such cases the heavier roof beams were anchored into round holes pecked out of the cliff with stone tools. The horizontal series of large and small "perforations" Simpson describes probably were anchor holes for roof timbers in association with the cists mentioned above.

It is to be regretted, however, that the want of the proper appliances to insert in the holes as steps for ascent, together with the necessity of hurrying on to the other labors of the day, did not permit us to satisfy our minds upon this point. Below the perforations on the face of the rock were a number of hieroglyphics.

Two or three hundred yards down the cañon we met another old pueblo in ruins, called *Pueblo Bonito*. This pueblo, though not so beautiful in the arrangement of the details of its masonry as Pueblo Pintado, is yet superior to it in point of preservation. The circuit of its walls is about thirteen hundred feet. Its present elevation shows that it has had at least four stories of apartments. The number of rooms on the ground floor at present discernible is one hundred and thirty-nine. In this enumeration, however, are not included the apartments which are not distinguishable in the east portion of the pueblo, and which would probably swell the number to about two hundred. There, then, having been at least four stories of rooms, and supposing the horizontal depth of the edifice to have been uniform from top to bottom, or in other words, not of a retreating terrace form on the court side, it is not unreasonable to infer that the original number of rooms was as many as eight hundred. But, as the latter supposition (as will be shown presently) is probably the most tenable, there must be a reduction from this number of one range of rooms for every story after the first; and this would lessen the number to six hundred and forty-one.[50]

[50] Counting the rooms of Bonito has challenged many who followed Simpson to Chaco Canyon. Jackson, with nine days at his disposal, made a partial estimate and then wisely gave up (441–42). Formed much like a misshapen half-moon, its arc facing the north canyon wall, Bonito was built over a period of several centuries. Excavation of the ruin has failed to provide terminal dates of its construction or any certainty that occupation was continuous. A series of tree-ring dates secured by Harold S. Gladwin relate only to one phase of Bonito's history—1026 to 1105 A.D.; otherwise, the latest known cutting date is 1130 A.D. Pithouse remains, however, of possibly 700 A.D. have been found under later walls; and masonry and pottery types indicate that in possible evolution from Developmental Pueblo through classic Pueblo III, Bonito emerged gradually from a small unit-type structure which now lies partially visible in the north

The number of estuffas is four—the largest being sixty feet in diameter, showing two stories in height and having a present depth of twelve feet. All of these estuffas are, as in the case of the others I have seen, cylindrical in shape and nicely walled up with thin tabular stone.[51] Among the ruins are several rooms in a very good state of preservation—one of them (near the northwest corner of the north range) being walled up with alternate beds of large and small stones, the regularity of the combination producing a very pleasing effect.[52] The ceiling of this room is also more tasteful than central mass of rooms. New wall junctures and changing masonry forms show successive stages of additions to the original central unit, the additions spreading to left and right but arcing in to maintain a half moon plan. The last period of construction, in the early to middle twelfth century, reflected an invasion of people from the Mesa Verde region. After Simpson and Jackson, others reported visiting the Chaco; but the first scientific excavation of Pueblo Bonito awaited Richard Wetherill and George Pepper who, for the Hyde Exploring Expedition (1896–99), excavated 198 rooms and 7 kivas. By government order in 1900 further work by the HEE was forbidden, and excavation at Bonito was suspended until Neil Judd, sponsored by the National Geographic Society in 1921–27, uncovered an additional 151 rooms and 26 kivas. Aspects of Pueblo Bonito archaeology may be found in the published reports of Pepper and Judd; the work of the Hyde Expedition is related in Frank McNitt's biography of Richard Wetherill. Van Valkenburgh says that the old Navaho name for Pueblo Bonito (Beautiful Village) is Tsebiyah'anii'ahi, Propped Rock. This is a reference to a massive wedge of stone which separated from the north cliff face in ancient times and threatened to demolish the pueblo. Bonito's occupants built a stone retaining wall at the base of the balancing cliff, and more effective methods were employed in modern times. The wedge of rock stood until 1941, when it fell, burying a part of Bonito's northeast wing.

[51] Simpson overestimates by eight feet the size of one of Bonito's three great kivas and otherwise falls short in his count. Jackson reports "at least" twenty-one kivas, while later excavation shows a total of thirty-six kivas and traces of several more. The great kiva mentioned by Simpson is described and diagrammed in R. Gordon Vivian's "The Great Kivas of Chaco Canyon" (66–70).

[52] Either this or an adjoining room is referred to by Jackson (442): "In one of these, a small room in the outer tier of the north side, which we entered by a small hole which had been broken through the exterior wall, we found the names of Lieutenant Simpson, Mr. R. H. Keen, and one or two others, with the date, August 27 [28], 1849, scratched into the soft plastering which covered the walls, the impression appearing as plainly as if done but a few days previously." This room is one of three that Wetherill used in 1896 as storerooms and for a photographic darkroom.

"Northwest View of the Ruins of the Pueblo Pintado
in the Valley of the Río Chaco."
By R. H. Kern, August 26, 1849.

"Narbona, Head Chief of the Navahos."
By R. H. Kern, August 31, 1849.

NATIONAL ARCHIVES

any we have seen—the transverse beams being smaller and more numerous, and the longitudinal pieces which rest upon them only about an inch in diameter and beautifully regular. These latter have somewhat the appearance of barked willow. The room has a doorway at each end and one at the side, each of them leading into adjacent apartments. The light is let in by a window, two feet by eight inches, on the north side.

There was among the ruins another room which, on account of the lateness of the hour and the consequent despatch of our examination, escaped our scrutiny. This room having been represented by Assistant Surgeon J. F. Hammond and Mr. J. L. Collins (both of whom started from camp with us) as being more perfect in its details than any of the others we had visited, and as indicating the use of *smooth* plank in the flooring, I requested the former to furnish me with a description of it. This description, thanks to the courtesy of the doctor, will be found in the appendix.

Besides the ruins of the main structure, there were some others lying just to the northeast of the pueblo, along the wall of the cañon.

A few hundred yards further down the cañon we fell in with another pueblo in ruins, called by the guide *Pueblo del Arroyo*, the circuit of which was about one thousand feet.[53] The day, however, being far gone and the camp of the command doubtless many miles in advance of us, we were obliged reluctantly to forego the critical examination of these ruins which we would have been pleased to give them.

About a quarter of a mile further we came to another small ruined edifice; and half a mile further to still another—the style

[53] Jackson correctly observes that the pueblo is "so named probably because it is on the verge of the deep arroyo which traverses the middle of the cañon" and adds that the ruin "was given only a passing glance by Simpson, but it well repays more careful inspection. It is of the rectangular form, but with the open space or court facing a few degrees north of east. The west wall is 268 feet long and the two wings 125 and 135 feet respectively; their ends connected by a narrow and low semicircular wall." Unremarked by either Simpson or Jackson, bonded to the pueblo's west wall are the considerably later remains of a circular

and construction of each being the same as of those already described, except that the stones of the walls were a little larger.[54]

All the ruins we have seen today, up to this point, have been on the north side of the cañon and within a few feet of its escarpment wall, the sandstone rocks composing it being magnificently amorphous and running up to a height of about one hundred feet. Two miles further down the cañon, but on its left or south bank, we came to another pueblo in ruins, called by the guide *Pueblo de Peñasca Blanca,* the circuit of which I ascertained to be approximately one thousand seven hundred feet. This is the largest pueblo in plan we have seen, and differs from others in the arrangement of the stones composing its walls.[55] The walls of the other pueblos were all of one uniform character in the several beds composing it; but in this there is a regular alternation of large and small stones, the effect of which is both unique and beautiful. The largest stones, which are about one foot in length and one half a foot in thickness, form but a single bed, and then, alternating with these, are three or four beds of very small

---

tri-walled structure not typical of Chaco architecture. The archaeology of the Del Arroyo group may be found in Vivian's "Hubbard Site" and Judd's "Pueblo del Arroyo." Van Valkenburgh says the Navaho name for Del Arroyo is *Ta baakini,* House Beside the Wash.

[54] These ruins, respectively, are Kin Kletso (Yellow House) and Casa Chiquita, the latter situated at the point where Rincon del Camino enters the Chaco from the north. Late in its history, Yellow House was occupied by people from the Mesa Verde region. In a report of his excavation at this ruin, done in association with Tom Mathews, Vivian gives a tree-ring date of 1178 A.D.—latest yet found in the Chaco pueblos. Casa Chiquita has not been excavated.

[55] Aside from superfical tests (George H. Pepper, "Pueblo Bonito," 385), no work has been done at Peñasco Blanco (White Bluff), and it remains relatively unknown among the Chaco's largest sites. Jackson (445) observes that "next to the Pueblo Bonito this is the largest in exterior dimensions of all the ruins . . . unlike all the others . . . being an almost perfect ellipse." Jackson measures interior dimensions of a court as being 346 by 269 feet, noting: " . . . add to this the depth of the buildings surrounding it and we have a total exterior diameter of 499 by 363 feet with a circuit of 1,200 feet." On an elevation slightly south and east of the pueblo, overlooking it, I have found surface remains of an extensive pithouse village. Van Valkenburgh says the Navaho name for the ruin is *Taala-kin,* House on the Point.

stones, each about an inch in thickness.[56] The general plan of the structure also differs from the others in approximating the form of a circle. The number of rooms at present discoverable upon the first floor is one hundred and twelve, and the existing walls show that there have been at least three stories of apartments. The number of circular estuffas we counted was seven.[57]

The question now arises, as we have seen all the ruins in this quarter, What was the form of these buildings?—I mean as regards the continuity or non-continuity of its front and rear walls. Were these walls one plain surface from bottom to top, as in the United States, or were they interrupted each story by a terrace, as is the case with the modern pueblo buildings in New Mexico?

The front or exterior walls were evidently one plain surface from bottom to top; because, whenever we found them in their integrity, which we did for as many as four stories in height, we always noticed them to be uninterruptedly plain.

The rear walls, however, were, in no instance that I recollect of, found to extend higher than the commencement of the second story; and the partition walls were, if my memory is not at fault, correspondingly step-like in their respective altitudes. The idea, then, at once unfolds itself, that in elevation the inner wall must have been a series of retreating surfaces or, what would make this necessary, each story on the inner or court side must have been terraced. This idea also gathers strength from the fact that we saw no indications of any internal mode of ascent from story to story, and therefore that some exterior mode must have been resorted to—such as, probably, ladders, which the terrace form of the several stories would make very convenient. Again,

[56] Simpson here describes the so-called Superior Type III banded masonry, and errs in saying it is unique to Peñasco Blanco. Truly handsome in its best form, superior banded masonry is found at Bonito, Chetro Ketl, Wijiji, and—in small wall sections—even at Yellow House and Little Alto, a small ruin on the mesa north of Bonito. Inferior types are seen in other Chaco ruins and can be found as far afield as on the La Plata River and in Nutria Canyon, above Zuñi. Hawley ("Tseh-So," 88; Fig. 3) places this type of Chaco masonry, in association with tree-ring dates, at 1062–1090 A.D.

[57] Jackson also reports seven kivas, but concludes that "The great height of the debris would indicate at least four stories in the outside tier."

the terrace form of the stories would best conduce to light and ventilation for the interior range of apartments. The idea, then, which Mr. R. H. Kern was the first to suggest—that these pueblos were terraced on their inner or court side—is not without strong grounds of probability; and it is in consequence with this idea that, in his *restoration* of the Pueblo Hungo Pavie, he has given it the form exhibited in the drawing.[58]

It is a curious fact that in no single instance did we find in these ruins either a chimney or a fireplace, unless, indeed, the recesses described as existing in some of the rooms were used as fireplaces, which their slight height, as well as deprivation of chimney flues, would scarcely authorize.[59] Neither were there any indications of the use of iron about the premises.

In regard to the position of the several structures in respect to the four true cardinal points of the heavens, it deviated in every instance more or less from them; but in no instance was the variation from the *magnetic* cardinal points more than five degrees, except in the case of the Pueblo Una Vida, where it was as great as fifteen degrees east. The magnetic variation of the needle from the true pole being, at these localities, about thirteen and a half degrees east, the deviation from the four *true* cardinal points, in the case of the Pueblo Una Vida, would then be as much as twenty-eight and a half degrees. In the case, however, of all the other pueblos, it was but a very few degrees.

[58] Unwittingly, Mr. Kern has fallen one story short of the number the ruins exhibited. In their restored state, four stories should appear.—Simpson's note.

[59] Chimneys, as Simpson had in mind, do not exist in Chaco pueblos; fireplaces, or firepits, are found in all stages of occupation, and invariably in association with kivas (as well as in some rooms). They were needed: Chaco winter nights touch zero or below. At Shabik'eschee Village, a late Basketmaker site on the south mesa east of Wijiji, Frank Roberts in 1927 excavated seventeen pithouse dwellings and one kiva. All had firepits, usually located centrally in the floor of the room. At the Three-C site near Fahada, a Developmental Pueblo ruin, Vivian in 1939 excavated nine rooms and two kivas. He found firepits in six rooms and in each kiva. When the University of New Mexico excavated the early Bc-50 site (Tseh-So) near Casa Rinconada in 1936, firepits were found in three of the small pueblo's twenty-one rooms. While excavating Pueblo Bonito, Judd found fifty-nine firepits in forty-eight of the pueblo's more than three hundred ground-floor rooms.

In regard to the origin of these remains, there is nothing that I can learn conclusive in relation to it. Hosta, one of the most intelligent Pueblo Indians I have seen, says, as I have before remarked, that they were built by Montezuma and his people, when on their way from the north to the region of the Rio Grande and to Old Mexico. Sandoval, a very intelligent Navaho chief, also says they were built by Montezuma, but further states that the Navahos and all the other Indians were once but one people, and lived in the vicinity of the Silver Mountain; that this mountain is about one hundred miles north of the Chaco ruins; that the Pueblo Indians separated from them (the Navahos) and built towns on the Rio Grande and its tributaries, but that "their house continues to be the hut made of bushes." Nothing more satisfactory than this have I been able to get from either Indians or Mexicans.[60]

On Colton's map of North America, however, I notice that Humboldt is made to locate the residence of the Aztecs, in the twelfth century, between the thirty-sixth and thirty-seventh parallels of north latitude, and the one hundred and ninth and one hundred and twelfth meridians of west longitude; but upon what ground the great explorer has based this hypothesis, I know not, for I have not his works at hand to consult. This thing, however, is certain: the ruins I have described were found upon the Rio Chaco; they were evidently, from the similarity of their style and mode of construction, of a common origin; they discover in the materials of which they are composed, as well as in the grandeur of their design and superiority of their workman-

[60] Arrival of the Navahos in the Southwest is still tentatively placed in the fourteenth century, although Clyde Kluckhohn and Dorothea Leighton (3-4)—and others—believe their advent might be as early as 1000 A.D. Edward Hall, however, gives a tree-ring date of 1540 A.D. for the first known Navaho dwelling, this in Governador Canyon, north of the Chaco. Sandoval's Silver (La Plata) Mountains, in southwestern Colorado, figure as a sacred place name in early Navaho mythology, but—Sandoval to the contrary—Navaho origin stories do not make the *Diné* one with the Pueblos, whose ancestors reached the Southwest many centuries earlier. The builders of Chaco's ruins were a cultural mixture of Basketmaker-Pueblo types who migrated to the canyon from several directions over a long period of time.

ship, a condition of architectural excellence beyond the power of the Indians or New Mexicans of the present day to exhibit; and they are all situated between the thirty-sixth and thirty-seventh parallels of north latitude, and near the one hundred and eighth degree of west longitude. It is, then, not at all improbable that they are the identical ruins to which Humboldt has referred.[61]

But it may be said, "It is true these remains discover a race of men superior to the natives of New Mexico of the present day; but where are the evidences of the very high stage of civilization to which the Aztecs are said by historians to have attained in Anahuac? Where are the evidences of a mechanical knowledge equal to that which must have been exercised in the construction of the temple of Xochicalco, the palaces of Tezcotzinco, and the colossal calendar stone in the capital."[62] But, waiving the question whether these remains are not of Toltec rather than of Aztec origin, or of an origin yet more remote, is it at all an impossible thing that a people who could show the ingenuity and skill which the ruins of Chaco attest could also, self-instructed, by the time of the Spanish conquest, or within the space of three centuries (the interval between the twelfth and fifteenth centuries) have made such advances in the mechanic arts as to be equal to the work in question? And still further, is it not very likely that, as history bases the advanced state of the arts among the Aztecs of Anahuac more upon the superior attainments of their predecessors, the Toltecs, and their contemporaries, the Tezcucans,[63] than upon their own spontaneous, self-instructed efforts—is it not very likely, I say, that under such favorable auspices, the Aztecs could have attained to the degree of proficiency ascribed to them? The foregoing facts and reflections, it is true, do not with certainty *fix* an Aztec origin to the ruins of the Chaco;

[61] Alexander von Humboldt, *Vues des Cordillères et Monuments des Peuples Indigènes de l'Amerique.*

[62] Prescott, *History of the Conquest of Mexico,* Vol. I, pp. 142, 182–85; Vol. II, Ap., Part I, note 73.—Simpson's note.

[63] *Ibid.,* Vol. III, pp. 215–16, 414.—Simpson's note.

but they go to show that, as far as is known, there is nothing to invalidate the hypothesis, but, on the contrary, a great deal to make it probable.

Gregg, in his excellent work upon New Mexico, entitled *Commerce of the Prairies*,[64] speaking of one of the Chaco ruins, Pueblo Bonito, remarks (most probably from information derived from others) that it resembles so much those of *Casas Grandes* as to make it probable that they were originally built by the same people; and, as he seems to adopt the idea of the historian Clavigero, that these latter *are* of Aztec origin, the inference is that he also attributes the former to the same source. Wislizenus, on the contrary, in his interesting *Memoir of a Tour to Northern Mexico in 1846 and 1847*,[65] says (he professes only to speak from report) that the ruins of Casas Grandes are "built of *adobes* and wood squared," and have "a gallery of wood and staircase from the outside." If, then, the information derived by Wislizenus be correct, these ruins cannot be said to resemble those of the Chaco, for the latter are built *entirely of stone*, and, besides, do not discover the *slightest evidences* of ever having had exterior "galleries" or staircases. It is most probable, then, that they are not both the same, or of Aztec origin; but as, with Mr. Gallatin, I am inclined to doubt the Aztec origin of the former, or those of Casas Grandes, so am I equally strong in the opinion that those of the latter, the Chaco ruins, are of that origin.

Major Emory also, in his letter to Mr. Gallatin (to be found in appendix No. 1 of his "Reconnaissance in New Mexico"), speaking of the ruins on the Rio Gila, says: "My own impression is, that the many ruins we saw on the Gila might well be attributed to Indians of the races we saw in New Mexico, and on the Gila itself. I mean by the last the Pimos, who might easily have lost the art of building *adobe* or mud houses." It would then seem to be very probable that not only were the ruins of the Chaco of Aztec origin, but, as far as has been at present discovered, it is

[64] Vol. I, pp. 283–85.—Simpson's note.
[65] Page 59.—Simpson's note.

not at all unlikely that they, instead of those on or near the Gila, constituted the last resting place of this people before entering upon the conquest of Anahuac.

The great historian Robertson, it is said, has stated (I have not his works near me to verify the fact) that "there is not in all the extent of New Spain any monument or vestige of a building more ancient than the conquest; that the temple of *Cholula* is nothing but a mound of solid earth, without any facing, or any steps, covered with grass and shrubs; and that the houses of the people of Mexico are mere huts, built with turf or branches of trees, like those of the rudest Indians."[66] However applicable this may be to the ancient remains said to have been found in New Spain—and I have no reason, from my reading, to believe it so— it certainly cannot be predicated of those discovered on the Rio Chaco.

But to proceed with the journal of our route: the last ruins passed, we obtained from the same eminence on which they are situated a fine view of the *Tumecha* Mountains, some forty miles off to the west, and their apparent range very nearly perpendicular to our course, and the waters of the Chaco, glittering under the rays of an opposite and declining sun, coursing their way as far as they could be seen towards them.

Already it was 5 o'clock P.M., and no signs of the camp of the troops were visible. Thirteen miles more were made by us—the darkness of the night having come upon us—and still the camp was not in view. Just at this moment a strange horse neighed directly in front of us. I felt assured that we had at last reached the camp. An exclamation of joy from me was the natural consequence; and I cried out loud enough to get a response from it, if such it was. All, however, was as silent as death. The thought then flashed upon me, we have perchance got into a Navaho snare, and I prepared my firearms accordingly. The sergeant, however, soon ascertained that the horse was an American one, and had a lariat upon him. This at once gave me the idea that

[66] See Museum of Foreign Literature and Science, Philadelphia, Vol. VII, p. 166.—Simpson's note.

the camp, if not just at hand, could not be far off. I therefore again gave the word, "Forward." We had, however, not gone more than fifty yards before I heard a voice calling out, within but a few yards of me, "Simpson! Simpson! Come over here."

Over an intermediate stream I went, and who should I find stretched out for a night's repose but Doctor Hammond! It appears that the doctor and Mr. Collins, both of whom had preceded us from the ruins in search of camp, had, up to this point, not fallen in with it; and the former believing that it would be better to wait where he was for the troops, and the latter that it was preferable to strike off south from the river in search of them, they had both acted correspondingly—the doctor spreading out his horse blanket and overcoat as a pallet for the night, and Mr. Collins taking off with him the two or three Pueblo Indians they had had in company with them. Of course, this accidental meeting was congratulatory on both sides; and particularly fortunate was it for the doctor that he was awake to hail us as we were passing, for had it been otherwise his horse, which one of the escort was taking away with him, would have been found missing in the morning and he, consequently, in rather a helpless plight.

Judging from the information given me by the guide that the country admitted of the command striking the Chaco about two miles lower down (which it will be recollected I was told before leaving camp they would do before encamping), the doctor consenting to accompany us, we pushed on that distance, but only to be again disappointed. The consequence was, that we were obliged to come to a halt and bivouac for the night. Not anticipating anything of this kind when we left the troops, neither Mr. Kern, the doctor, nor myself had brought with us any provisions or bed clothing. The Mexicans, however, kindly shared their *atole* (a sort of thin mush) with us; and, clubbing our horse blankets and overcoats together, our saddles serving as pillows, we prepared for ourselves a tolerably comfortable bed.

The whole distance traveled today was about twenty-three

miles; and, considering the amount of labor we accomplished at the ruins, we look upon our day's work as being considerable.

The soil in the Cañon de Chaco, though now very arid, seems to possess the elements of fertility; and, probably, when the ruined pueblos along it were instinct with life, it was cultivated. The water of the Rio Chaco has been gradually increasing in volume in proportion as we descended. The *flora and sylva* have been, as usual, the artemisia and a stunted growth of cedar, the latter here and there sparsely disposed on the table lands.

Eleventh camp, August 29—All had a good night of it, notwithstanding our untoward circumstances. The Mexicans again, from their little stock, furnished us with a sufficiency to cause us to feel that we had a breakfast. Believing that we were in advance of the troops and that, therefore, they would meet us, I determined to wait for them where we were.

Between 10 and 11 o'clock A.M., Carravahal, who had gone with my reconnoitring glass up the neighboring mesa height to look out for the command, giving a shout, we were at once convinced that some person or persons were approaching. And sure enough, not many minutes elapsed before we noticed Mr. Collins coming down the cañon with a party of fifteen Indians.[67] He had come to look us up, and supply us with something to eat. Last night, after a hard ride, he had fallen in with the main camp, some ten miles south from the river. Sandoval, the Navaho guide with the command, it appeared, had either honestly changed his mind about striking the Rio Chaco, or his intentions had unwittingly been misinterpreted, or he had in view something sinister.

But, be this as it may, we again started off to find the troops at their next camp—our course continuing to be, for the first ten miles, as yesterday, northwest by west, and immediately down the cañon. Having proceeded five and a half miles, we passed a mound, which, the Indians perceiving, they rushed towards

[67] Simpson's party had camped a mile or two east of the present Tsaya Trading Post (built in the 1870's). The Navahos he encountered here may have been from the region of Juan's Lake, a fertile farming valley several miles to the southeast.

in a mass to provide themselves with some of the red paint which crops out near its summit. It was not many minutes before they came dashing upon us again, their faces totally coated with paint, and with them a Mexican, having not only his face but the sleeves of his shirt of a deep red color; and soon after I noticed not only this fellow's entire clothing, but even his mule's head, of this barbarous complexion—the object being, doubtless, to give him the ferocious bloody look which, in his soul probably, he felt he could testify in no other way.

About this locality were some fresh foot tracks visible, supposed to be those of Navaho spies who had been dogging us. A mile further, we came to a hemispherical mound, fifteen feet high and of about fifty feet base. At the base, coal crops out. Immediately above is a blue rock, apparently argillo-calcareous, two feet thick, blackened as if by fire. Above this and forming the chief covering is a grayish-white pulverulent mass, intermingled with fragments of red argillaceous rock, also showing marks of heat; and immediately at the apex, or summit, are fragments of the same kind of rock, highly scoriaceous. Is it not reasonable to presume that here has been a slight upheave from below, attended with fusion—indeed, a volcano on a small scale?

Leaving the cañon at a point about ten miles from our place of bivouac, we struck a general course south of west—the country for the next ten miles being a barren waste of broken hills and arid plains, and some of the hills being so steep as to require us to lead our horses down them, and even then at the risk of their limbs—the soil of the plains presenting very much the levity and color of ashes and looking, if possible, more under a *curse* than the generality of that we have passed over. This distance traversed, we got in the midst of a most singular profusion and confusion of deep, rugged ravines and high sandstone rocks of almost every shape and character imaginable. Here were at once to be seen domes, pillars, turrets, pinnacles, spires, castles, vases, tables, pitched roofs, and a number of other objects of a well-defined figurative character.

At length, reaching the brow of the Tumecha valley, much

to our joy we could see in a direction south of west the camp of the troops some seven or eight miles off, the tents appearing at times like white specks, and cheering us by the cheerful blue smoke with which they were canopied. The intermediate plain, of an ash-colored, herbless, forbidding character, rapidly traversed, it was not long before we were entering camp, much to the gratification of our comrades who, it appeared, had felt no little anxiety on our account, and greatly to our own satisfaction.[68]

Our day's travel has been about twenty-nine miles. The water at this camp, of a highly alkaline character, is obtained from dug pits. Wood of a shrub or bush character is used for fuel. There being no grass near, fodder is obtained from the green cornfields of the Navahos in the vicinity.

Mr. E. M. Kern having been directed, on my diverging from the route of the troops, to keep up the topography of the country through which they would pass, the following is his journal for the two days we have been separated:

"*Tenth camp, August 28*—Raised camp at 7 o'clock. General course west. About nine miles from our camp of last night, on our left, about three miles distant, appeared the ruins of an old pueblo.[69] The mesa that formed the left side of the Cañon de Chaco turns off square opposite the Mesa Fachada and runs in a southerly direction, leaving on our left a plain, slightly broken by gullies and isolated hills.

[68] The troops were camped near Badger Springs, present site of the Naschiti Trading Post (built in 1880–81). Richard Kern's diary offers interesting sidelights on this reunion with the main command. "When near camp," he wrote, "saw a large band of Indians to the north—Our valiant escort [of Mexican militia] brandished their arms & shouted most valiantly—One fellow in particular who had painted his face, hands, shirt & every part of his clothing as well as his mule, red, seemed particularly brave & to have centered in himself all the courage of Santa Anna & the sublime Mexican Republic—When within a mile of camp a large band of Indians appeared to be coming between us & it & we came in at a round gallop—Found the Navajoes around & in camp—Three had been captured by the command & we had taken corn from their fields for our animals—Water got by digging & very much the taste of a 'bad egg.' "

[69] The ruin Kern refers to is Kin Klizhin (Black House), a tower kiva dominating a small cluster of rooms.

"The road today has been very interesting on account of the curious sandstone formations, having much the appearance of a large ruined city. These places rendered the road somewhat difficult. Camped tonight at some pools of water, sufficient for the camp. Petrified wood along the river. Made 24.50 miles.

"*Eleventh camp, August 29*—Moved at 7 o'clock. The artillery, at about three-fourths of a mile, turned a short distance to the left to avoid a bad ascent of the mesa. The country of the same character as of yesterday, but road better. A few uninteresting ruins of old houses in the rocks.[70] Broken bluffs on the right. Camped at some Indian wells. Made 14.60 miles. No vegetation to speak of for the past two days."

Astronomical observations give for the latitude of this camp 36° 04' 35"; for the longitude, 108° 39' 30".

Twelfth camp, August 30—Several Navaho men and women were yesterday afternoon and this morning in our last camp. They said the troops had come over sooner than they had ex-

---

[70] E. M. Kern's ruins once formed a small *anasazi* farming community that was possibly a western outpost of Chaco Canyon. Situated to the southwest of the present White Rock Trading Post, the dwellings lie within a cove formed by sandstone cliffs, sand slopes, and talus. A distinguishing feature of the site is a large one- or two-room habitation covering the top of a plug of rock that stands apart from the cliff, about forty feet high. Access to this elevated dwelling was by hand and toe holds cut into the east face of the rock. Near the base of the structure is a kiva some twenty feet in diameter and built within a rectangular block of masonry that includes two rooms forming the west side. Enclosing the front or south side are traces of a court. Fifty feet above the cove, on the rim of the ledge to the east, are ruins of two large rooms, the walls twenty inches thick at the base. Masonry of the kiva unit is similar to Neil M. Judd's Pueblo Bonito Type IV ("The Material Culture of Pueblo Bonito," 20), dated by Hawley at 1100–16 A.D. Pottery sherds, notably scarce, are similar to the black-on-white hatchure and corrugated ware of Chaco's classic period. Associated with the *anasazi* dwellings are four circular stone hogans, now roofless, built in a row along the base of cliff forming the cove's west side. Gordon Vivian has estimated that hogans of this type might date from about 1800, although these presumably were not present when the troops passed by in 1849. Before reaching the site, the command passed numerous smaller ruins, recognizable only as low mounds littered with broken pottery. The relationship of this site to the Chaco community might be very similar to that of the Kin Ya'ah group near Crownpoint, about equally distant from the canyon to the southeast.

pected; that their people were yet living on their cornfields near by; and that they had collected some fifteen horses and mules and a number of sheep, to deliver up, according to the requirements which the colonel commanding had made of them, through Brevet Major [William N.] Grier some weeks previous, at Jemez; that they would conform to the treaty which Colonel Nuby had made with them; did not want to fight, &c.[71]

The women I noticed wore blankets, leggins, and moccasins —the blankets being confined about the waist by a girdle. They bestrode their horses *à la mode des hommes*. One of them, on horseback, had a child at her breast confined on its back to a board, the upper portion canopied by a frame of willow-work to protect its head from the weather.

The troops decamped this morning at seven—their course, which was up the valley of the Tumecha, being generally about northwest. Having proceeded five and a half miles, a most splendid view of the peaks of the Ojos Calientes (Warm Springs) presented itself to our front.[72] These splendid peaks first appeared to view yesterday, from the brow of the Tumecha valley. Two miles further, another body of Navahos appeared in front of us about a mile distant, who, as we approached, discovered

[71] Simpson here refers to Colonel Edward W. B. Newby, who, in the Mexican War, commanded Company D, Illinois Volunteer Infantry. In 1847–48, Colonel Newby was in command of the Ninth Military Department of New Mexico, at Santa Fe. In May, 1848, he led an expedition against the Navahos and at that time made the treaty Simpson mentions (see Appendix D). Newby was mustered out of service October 16, 1848. The Navahos who met Colonel Washington at Badger Springs had a grievance and soon would have occasion for stronger feeling against the troops. Simpson omits mention of this in his report, but the Indians' cause for suspicion and hostility is noted by Richard Kern: "Had talk with Some Navajoe Chiefs—all talk—they said if we were friends why did we take their corn, and they had nothing [to do] but submit although it was hard—Disavowed all connexion with those [eastern Navahos] beyond the Mountains—Would not promise to meet us at Ché [Canyon de Chelly] but agreed to come in council tomorrow at 12 oclk & make peace—[Colonel Washington?] sent off a large force to seize enough corn for our animals."

[72] The reference is to Bennett's Peak, so named some years later for Major Frank Tracy Bennett, Ninth Cavalry, who served as agent to the Navahos at Fort Defiance in 1869–71 and again in 1880–81.

themselves to be mounted. Soon the Pueblo Indians, who were in the advance, were scampering off to commingle with them; and, dressed as they all were in their costumes, they formed quite an interesting and formidable group. Several of the Navahos, I noticed, wore helmet-shaped caps which were in some instances heightened in picturesque effect by being set off with a bunch of eagles' feathers.

One of them, I observed, had hair approaching to red and looked, as was observed by several, very much like a white man painted. Another man, who was quite old and of very large frame, had a grave and contemplative countenance not unlike, as many of the officers remarked (I hope the comparison will be pardoned), that of General Washington. Some of them were almost naked—one of them entirely so, excepting his breech-cloth, his whole person at the same time looking ghastly on account of a kind of whitewash with which it was covered.

Colonel Washington and his staff having remained among the group sufficiently long to enable the main body of the troops to come up, the word was given by him, "Tell Sandoval to direct these people to go forward!" Soon I could see the whole body of Indians (Pueblos and Navahos) moving in a cloud of dust in advance of us. A dark, portentous cloud was hovering at the time over the Tumecha mountains beyond, the forked lightning ever and anon darting vividly athwart it; the beautiful peaks of the Ojos Calientes lay quartering to the right; and in the rear could be seen the main command—first the packs, then the infantry, and last the artillery (which, on account of some obstacle, had for the moment got behind), coming forward.

Fifteen miles on our route, we came to a hill about fifty feet high, up which the artillery was drawn with some difficulty. Six miles further brought us to the Rio Tumecha (a primary or secondary tributary of the San Juan), upon which we are now encamped.[73]

[73] Simpson's phrasing suggests that the artillery pieces had been limbered and prepared for action. The troops were camped on Tuntsa (Big Tree) Wash, a tributary of the Chaco which in turn enters the San Juan River at Shiprock. Ac-

The peaks of the Ojos Calientes, as we approached them today, appeared very much like ships under full sail—two of them
looking very rakish, and the other more upright as if moved by
a gentle breeze.

We passed along the route some very extensive and luxuriant
cornfields, the plant looking finer than any I have seen in this
country; and what makes it more remarkable, at least in this
part of the world, is, there were no evidences of a resort having
been had to irrigation. The soil was arenaceous and light, the
ears of the plant springing low down from the stalk and looking
sometimes as if they came directly from the soil.[74] Colonel Washington informs me that the latter is probably owing to the deep
planting, which the Navahos practice more than other Indians.[75]
They plant as deep as a foot or a foot and a half, and he has been
assured that they never fail in their crops. This kind of planting,
however, I suppose can only be successful in light, porous soils.

The water in the Rio Tumecha we find amply sufficient and
good, and doubtless its constancy may be relied on.[76] The pasture

---

cording to Simpson's astronomical observations, camp was made on a high penin-
sula of land less than one mile south and west of the present Two Gray Hills
Trading Post.

[74] On the high tableland approaches to this camp and in its immediate vicinity
are the crumbled walls of an extensive *anasazi* farming community, the ground
for several miles littered with pottery sherds, manos, and broken metates. The
extent of the one-story ruins suggests a population that may once have exceeded
five hundred. Conjecturally, their farm lands lay in the valleys separating three
fingerlike peninsulas of now treeless land that extend eastward from the Chuska
foothills. Farming would have been practical in these valleys by tapping the
moisture carried off in four principal washes—the Blue Shale, the Crumbled
House, the Tuntsa, and the Tse-nush-chee (Round Red Rock) Wash, all joining to form the main Tuntsa, or Captain Tom's Wash.

[75] Deep planting of corn seed did not originate with the Navahos, but was
borrowed by them from the Hopis. The practice is as common now as in the
past, based on the principle of finding moisture or seepage in runoff areas, even
below surface sand. Such plants seldom grow higher than three or four feet, the
broad leaves forming an umbrella of shade to conserve moisture at the deep
roots. Corn ears from such plants grow close to the ground and may reach more
than a foot in length.

[76] Tuntsa Wash is normally dry. The thunderstorm Simpson previously men-

along the stream, however, is but scant, and therefore the corn-fields of the Navahos in the vicinity have to be drawn upon. It having been represented that the Navahos would resist the troops in cutting the corn, Captain Dodge, with a command, was sent to enforce the order.

This afternoon several of the head men of the Navaho tribe have been in camp, and had a talk with Colonel Washington and the Indian agent, Mr. Calhoun—the object of these gentlemen being to inform them that the troops were there in accordance with the determination made known to them some weeks since at Jemez; that, if they did not comply with the treaty made with them by Colonel Nuby, which required that they should give up all Mexican captives, all murderers of Mexicans who had secreted themselves among them, and all Mexican stock they had driven off since the establishment of the government of the United States over them, the United States would send among them a body of troops to enforce it. The result of the conference was that the chiefs present promised to send word out to all the other chiefs who, they said, would be in camp tomorrow at noon, to hold a council with the United States, and have matters settled.

The latitude of this camp, by observation, is 36° 12′ 59″; the longitude, 108° 50′ 45″.

Thirteenth camp, August 31—Today about noon, at our last camp, three Navaho chiefs appeared in council—Narbona, José Largo, and Archulette—when something like the following collo-quy took place, the interpreter, Mr. Conklin, of Santa Fe, de-livering the several points *seriatim*, as they were expressed by Colonel Washington and Mr. Calhoun:

Colonel Washington: Tell them that I wish them to go to Chelly, so that a treaty may be made with the whole nation.

Tell them the treaty I wish to make with them is to establish the conditions they promised yesterday to comply with.

Tell them the treaty I propose to make with them will be based

tions probably accounts for its running. Furthermore, August and September are the wet months in this region, especially in the mountains.

65

upon the demands I have already made; and the object, in addition, will be a permanent peace.

Mr. Calhoun: Tell them they are lawfully in the jurisdiction of the United States, and they must respect that jurisdiction.

Interpreter: They say they understand it.

Mr. Calhoun: Tell them that after the treaty is made, their friends will be the friends of the United States, and their enemies the enemies of the United States.

Tell them when any difficulty occurs between them and any other nation, by appealing to the United States they may get redress.

Are they willing to be at peace with all the friends of the United States?

Interpreter: They say they are willing.

Mr. Calhoun: Tell them that by the treaty which it is proposed to make with them, all trade between themselves and other nations will be recognized as under regulations to be prescribed by the United States.

Colonel Washington: And the object of this is to prevent their being imposed upon by bad men.

Interpreter: They understand it, and are content.

Mr. Calhoun: Tell them if any wrong is done them by a citizen of the United States, or by a Mexican, he or they shall be punished by the United States, as if the wrong had been done by a citizen of the United States, and on a citizen of the United States.

Interpreter: They say they understand it, and it is all right.

Mr. Calhoun: That the people of the United States shall go in and out of their country without molestation, under such regulations as shall be prescribed by the United States.

Interpreter: They, very well.

Mr. Calhoun: Tell them that, by this treaty, the government of the United States are to be recognized as having the right to establish military posts in their country wherever they may think it necessary, in order to [assure] the protection of them and their rights.

That the government of the United States claim the right to have their boundaries fixed and marked, so as to prevent any misunderstanding on this point between them and their neighbors.

Interpreter: They say they are very glad.

Mr. Calhoun: For and in consideration of all this, and a faithful performance of the treaty, the government of the United States will, from time to time, make them presents, such as axes, hoes, and other farming utensils, blankets, &c.

Interpreter: They say it is all right.

The several points of the proposed treaty having been explained to the chiefs to their satisfaction, Narbona, the head chief, and José Largo, both very aged—the former about eighty and the latter about seventy—voluntarily signed powers of attorney, by which full authority was granted to Armijo and Pedro José, two younger chiefs, to act for them at Chelly in the proposed council, in the same manner and to the same extent as they would do were they present.

The council breaking up, Sandoval harangued some two or three hundred Navahos ranged before him on horseback—the object, as it occurred to me, being to explain to them the views and purposes of the government of the United States. Sandoval himself habited in his gorgeously-colored dress, and all the Navahos as gorgeously decked in red, blue, and white, with rifle erect in hand, the spectacle was very imposing. But soon I perceived there was likely to be some more serious work than mere talking. It appears that it was ascertained very satisfactorily that there was then among the horses in the possession of the Navahos present one which belonged to a Mexican, a member of Colonel Washington's command. The colonel, particularly as the possessor of it acknowledged it to be stolen, demanded its immediate restoration. The Navahos demurred. He then told them that unless they restored it immediately they would be fired into. They replied that the man in whose possession the horse was had fled. Colonel Washington then directed Lieutenant Torez to seize one in reprisal.

The Navahos, immediately perceiving it, scampered off at the top of their speed. The guard present were then ordered to fire upon them—the result of which was that their head chief, Narbona, was shot dead on the spot, and six others (as the Navahos subsequently told us) were mortally wounded. Major Peck also threw among them, very handsomely—much to their terror, when they were afar off and thought they could with safety relax their flight—a couple of round shot.[77]

[77] Richard Kern's diary for this day adds interesting details: "Navajoes crowding around us in great numbers—Council met—Agreed to the terms & some agreed to meet us at Ché in person & the two old chiefs Narbona (head chief) & José Largo by deputy and gave power of attorney to others—The council was dissolved, when a Spaniard [one of the Mexican militia] said a horse had been stolen from him some time ago—the horse was among the Navajoes & he could identify him—The Col. ordered the horse to be given up—The Mexican advanced to get him, when Narbona said Something in Navajoe & the horseman rode off—Col. W. gave the word to fire—the guard did so & at the first shot the Indians broke & fled up a ravine to the N[orth]. The six pounder was fired 3 times at them, and a force sent in pursuit—Narbona the head chief was shot in 4 or 5 places & Scalped." E. M. Kern's biographer, Robert Hine, relates (77) that both of the Kerns "were later furious with themselves" because, in the excitement, they had failed to secure Narbona's head for their scientist friend and associate at the Philadelphia Academy of Natural Sciences, Samuel George Morton. The most comprehensive account of Narbona's death appears in Calhoun's letter of October 1, 1849, to Commissioner Medill: "As an earnest of their intentions, [the Navahos] delivered to us one hundred and thirty sheep, and some four or five mules and horses. This accomplished, orders were given to prepare to resume our march. In the mean time, the Indians were all permitted to descend from the heights, and to occupy a level space, commencing within fifty paces of the Governor's Quarters—The Actings and doings of the parties were duly explained to them by a long and noisy harangue from a Navajo. They were further informed that a certain horse, which was pointed out to them, was the property of a Pueblo Indian then present, and that the horse must be delivered to the proper owner at once. The fact of having stolen the horse was not denied, but a statute of limitation was suggested by the reply, that the horse had been rode back to the country from where the animal was taken, and that, that was the time to have claimed him, and ended by the enquiry why he was not then claimed—This conversation was reported to Governor Washington in the presence of several Chiefs, who were distinctly notified by him that he required the immediate delivery of the horse—The Chiefs, among them the Senior Chief [Narbona] on the east side of the before-mentioned mountain range, left the Governor's tent, as was supposed, to instruct their people what they should do. The Governor having waited a sufficient length of time without the return of a single Chief, or any report from them, ordered a small detachment of the guard to proceed to the crowd, with instructions to the officer of the guard to demand the immediate surrender of the horse, and walked out, in person, to superintend the execution of the order—The demand not producing the desired effect, Lieut. Torez, the

These people evidently gave signs of being tricky and unreliable, and probably never will be chastened into perfect subjection *until troops are stationed immediately among them.*

They had, previous to the affray, during the day, brought in about one hundred head of sheep and four horses and mules; and immediately after it, some thirty or forty more head of sheep were driven in by the troops.

It is to be regretted that in the hurry-skurry movement of the enemy some of the pack animals, which were at the time ready to accompany the troops to the next camping ground, should have been frightened off.

Immediately after the affair alluded to, at about 5 P.M., the command resumed the line of march. We had not proceeded more than a mile before a Navaho appeared ahead of us, as if anxious to hold a parley. Mr. Conklin was sent forward to see what he wanted. He said he wished to talk to the commanding officer. Colonel Washington told him to come forward. He did so; and, with tears in his eyes (I do not know how easily these fellows may cry), he said he did not wish to live any longer among these people; that he wanted peace; that he was related to Sandoval and wished to convey his mother to Sandoval's people, among whom he desired to live. The colonel told him to go home and keep the peace, that he was at liberty to convey away his mother.

Our march this afternoon was only 4.32 miles. The soil of the valley we have been threading for the last two days, it occurs to me, is (a great deal of it) good, and could doubtless be cultivated much more extensively than it is.

officer of the guard, was directed by the Governor to seize the horse and his rider, and to bring them before him. The moment the guard was ordered forward, every Navajo Indian in the crowd, supposed to number from three to four hundred, all mounted and armed, and their arms in their hands, wheeled, and put the spur to their horses; upon which, the Governor ordered the guard to fire. The Senior Chief, Narbone, was left lifeless upon the ground, and several others were found dead in the vicinity. The Indians did not attempt to fire until their own and our forces were scattered, when feeble efforts to kill and cut off small parties were unsuccessfully made. Except the killing of a few horses, and the loss of a few mules, we sustained no injury."

General Character of the Country Traversed
East of the Sierra de Tumecha

And now, as we shall commence the ascent tomorrow of the Sierra de Tumecha, which traversed, according to the report of one of the guides, is to introduce us into a more fertile region, the opportunity seems to be a favorable one for summing up, in *one general view*, the several characteristics of the country we have been passing through since we left Santa Fe.

The geological features of the country have been, from Santa Fe to the Rio Jemez, an intermixture of primary and secondary mountains and mesa or table heights—the latter for the most part being overlaid with basaltic trap. From the valley of the Rio de Jemez to where we now are (or to the Sierra de Tumecha), the formation is entirely of a secondary character, the superior rocks being generally finely (in contradistinction to coarse-grained) argillo-arenaceous—in a few localities exposing outcrops of massive gypsum, selenitic gypsum being found pervading, but sparingly, and bituminous coal, but of an impure, slaty character, characterizing almost continuously this whole section. And, commensurate with this section, arroyos, cañons, mesas with their well-defined crests and escarpments; plateau and hemispherical mounds, intermitting dirty, clay-colored rills dignified with the name of *rios*, and an all-pervading dull, yellow, dirty, buff-colored soil—have, in their respective magnitudes and relations, characterized the face of the landscape.

In regard to the fertility or productive qualities of the soil for the whole area traversed this side of Santa Fe, saving the inconsiderable exceptions which have from time to time been noted in my journal, the country is one extended *naked, barren waste*, sparsely covered with cedar and pine of a scrub growth, and thickly sprinkled with the wild sage, or artemisia, the color of the domestic sage, suggesting very appropriately the dead, lifeless color of the wild.

Our camp for the night is on a very small rill of good water in the vicinity of some cornfields, whence, on account of the absence of pasture we are obliged to draw our forage.[78]

A party of Mexicans and Pueblo Indians who, under the command of Major Kendrick, assisted by Captain Dodge, left camp this morning to reconnoitre the pass of the Tumecha mountains, are still out; and some fears are entertained lest, on account of their being ignorant of the affray this afternoon, they may be surprised and possibly be taken at a disadvantage. Sandoval and a party of Mexicans started off this evening to meet them and direct them to camp.

Fourteenth camp, September 1—Major Kenderick got in with a portion of his party late last evening, the horses of the Pueblo Indians being too much broken down to permit them to return with him. We all have some apprehension lest their ignorance of our present relations with the Navahos may unwittingly lead them to give the enemy an advantage over them.

Major Kendrick reports that the Navaho guide who accompanied him was called aside on the way by another Navaho, and doubtless informed of the affair of yesterday. He thinks he must have been made acquainted with it; for on two occasions he endeavored to lead the major and his command aside to give battle to a bear which, he said, another Navaho had at bay, aside of the route. The major, however, was not to be diverted from his course; and probably it is very well he was not for, the guide making his escape soon after, the chances were that his object was to lead them into an ambush.

The major knew nothing of the commencement of hostilities till he arrived in camp. And, what liked to have proved a very serious affair, he and his party last night, whilst approaching the camp, were fired upon by the Mexican picket guard. Captain Dodge was so near one of these valiant fellows as to become unhorsed by his animal suddenly starting aside from the flash of

---

[78] This camp was in the Chuska foothills, a mile or two north and slightly east of the present Toadlena Trading Post.

the fellow's musket; and, what was still more unacceptable, a ball came whizzing by him nearer than he had ever had one before; and, to cap the climax, he afterwards learned that the shot had been made by one of his own company who happened to be on guard! A soldier was also thrown from his horse for the same cause; and the guide, Carravahal, had his arm grazed by a ball. This vigilant Mexican guard, it seems, had mistaken the major and his party for a body of the enemy! Twice last evening they gave a false alarm!

The troops decamped at 7 A.M.—our course west of south, and the route commencing the ascent of the Tumecha mountains. One mile and a half from camp we came to a very steep hill, probably about seventy or eighty feet high. The artillery, to overcome this, had to be unlimbered, and all hands were required at the bricoles. The slope of the hill approaching quite nearly the vertical, it would seem that no obstacle, no matter how steep, can obstruct the passage of artillery where, with adequate human power and sufficiently strong bricoles, there is present in the officers commanding (as there was here) the necessary energy to secure success. A mile further, we crossed an arroyo coming in from the mountain, from the banks of which bituminous coal, apparently of an excellent quality, exists in beds of from two to three feet in thickness, with argillaceous shale intervening.

About 10 o'clock the command was cheered with the sight of Hosta and Sandoval, returning with the Pueblo Indians, who had not been able to get into camp last night. They were received with cheers and Hosta—the handsome, magnanimous Hosta, apparently unconscious of anything distinguishing about him —was greeted with a most cordial welcome. They reported that three of their mules had been stolen by the enemy, but no attack had been made upon them.

Scarcely had the Pueblos joined us before a couple of the enemy showed themselves, a great distance off to our front and, in the *peculiar far-reaching tone* of the Swiss mountain peasant, in which the Navahos seem to be proficient, they made known to us that they wished to have a talk with Sandoval. Sandoval, with Mr. Collins, approaching them, one of them said it was to be regretted that, for so trifling a thing as a horse, so much damage had been done; that by it they had lost one of their greatest warriors (Narbona); that the people wanted peace; and that they would come in today or tomorrow to obtain it. He further remarked that in the affair of yesterday he had had a relative shot in the thigh, who might probably die from the wound.

The road today up the slope of the Sierra de Tumecha has been very rocky. A few Navaho huts have been seen. These huts are of conical shape, about eight feet high, eighteen feet in diameter at base, and constructed of poles which, laid against each other at the apex, are spread out to the required diameter at the base, the whole being covered with bark or brush and mud. Yellow pine, about eighty feet high and twelve feet in circumference at the trunk, as also some scrub oak—the first we have seen—grow along the route.[79]

Flankers were thrown out today on either side to flush any way-layers that might be along the route. Our day's march has been about ten miles. Our encampment is near a pond of excellent water, margined with fine grass, and being shaded by some noble pines, and a very pretty wide-spreading oak adding its variety to the landscape; the combination makes up the most refreshing picture we have seen during the expedition.

This camp is found to be in latitude 36° 7′ 42″; in longitude, 108° 54′ 15″.

Fifteenth camp, September 2—A sentinel fired during the night at an Indian, as he says, prowling about camp on horseback. The troops resumed the march at 7 A.M.—the general course west of south. Three miles on the route we passed on our

[79] A typographical error: Douglas firs at this altitude grow up to two and one-half feet in diameter. The hogans Simpson refers to would be of the old "forked stick" type, starting, like the Plains Indian tipi, from a tripod formation, with the completed structure built of juniper logs stripped of their long, papery shags of bark, the whole thickly plastered on the exterior with adobe mud.

right a fine pond of water, bordered by a margin of good grass. A mile further brought us to a small streamlet which, taking its rise in the pass of the mountain, flows eastwardly, doubtless to join the Rio de Tumecha. At this stream the troops were commanded to halt, in order to make the proper preparations for a successful passage through the gorge or gate of the mountain.

Major Kendrick who, day before yesterday, with a party had reconnoitred the pass, having represented it as being very difficult, both on account of the obstacles in the way to the passage of artillery and the commanding heights on either side of it, it was believed that here, if anywhere, the enemy would, in a body, make a stand to dispute our advance. The artillery were accordingly placed in a position to cover the passage of our troops; and forty Pueblos, under their elected chief *Ow-te-wa*, Captain Dodge voluntarily offering to lead them, were pushed forward in advance, with directions to scale and take post on the heights to the right of the defile. I had noticed with my reconnoitring glass several of the enemy upon the heights to the left of the defile, and it was not at all improbable that they were strongly posted on the still more commanding heights on the right. The Pueblo Indians having gallantly gained the heights and met no enemy, a preconcerted signal, the firing of a rifle, was given to inform the commanding colonel of the fact.[80] The infantry were then ordered to move forward, a portion of them being at the same time directed to scour the more accessible heights commanding the pass on the left. Soon after, the whole command was put in motion—the packs in the center and the artillery bringing up the rear.

The pass at the most dangerous point we found extraordinarily formidable. On the north side is a wall of trap capped with sandstone, running perpendicularly up from the bottom of the defile

[80] Richard Kern's diary notes this episode: "Skirmishers thrown out on either side—White oak & flowers increasing—Stopped at the Gate of the Mountain & stationed the Cannon so as to bear on it—This being the most dangerous place & where a fight was expected, Capt. Dodge was Sent ahead to seize on a point that commanded the road—He fired the signal agreed on, and we moved on."

to a height of about six hundred feet; and, in addition to this, there are two others, but further removed. On the left side is another height of probably about three hundred feet. The width of the pass at this point is probably not more than fifty feet and barely furnishes a passage-way (a sidling one at this) for the artillery. This, the most difficult portion of the pass, is probably about three hundred yards long. Colonel Washington informs me it is the most formidable defile he has ever seen. The artillery were three hours in getting through it. In honor of the colonel commanding I have, on my map, called it Pass Washington.[81]

The narrow portion of the pass got through, it immediately expands into one of about a quarter of a mile in breadth and which, for this country, is of extraordinary beauty. The soil here is of a very rich quality. The pines are tall and large, the grass luxuriant, and the surface of the ground, which is sweetly undulating, is covered with a profusion of the most beautiful and delicate flowers—the wild rose, the first I have seen during the expedition, being among them. A stream of pure, wholesome water, trickling along through this scene, westward, adds its beauty to the picture. It is in the midst of a landscape like this, about three-fourths of a mile from the narrowest portion of the gorge, we are encamped.

The rocks about the pass are at base a dark green trap, overlaid by sandstone. A late work, entitled *Doniphan's Expedition,*

[81] While serving as special agent to the Navahos in 1872, Thomas Varker Keam recommended that a road be built from Fort Defiance "via Navajo [Washington] Pass to the Tunicha valley" as a necessary step toward establishing a sub-agency at present Shiprock. Van Valkenburgh notes that until the 1940's the defile Simpson named for Colonel Washington often was "shown erroneously as Cottonwood Pass by some geographers." All modern maps name the pass correctly. Van Valkenburgh adds: "Old Navajos tell that while the Navajo warriors skirted the flanks of the soldiers, they stopped at a spring near the summit. The soldiers failed to notice a Navajo camp just back of a small rise. After walling up the spring (the stones still stand), the soldiers passed on to the west. This incident gave the spring significance and today it has certain minor importance as a shrine. Fragments of white shell, turquoise, abalone shell, and jet are cast into this spring as offerings for rain."

represents the Sierra de Tumecha as "the grandest of mountains, consisting of large masses of granite piled on granite, and penetrating into the region of clouds and permanent snows."[82] In crossing the ridge we discovered no granite, and neither remotely, when observing the heights from the plains, nor when near by them, could we perceive the slightest indications of snow.

It is observable that troops attempting to pass the defile from the *east* side of the mountain will find a subordinate eminence, to the west of the point where it was stated the battery was established to cover the movement, upon which a battery could be placed which would be in effective range of the heights commanding the pass on either side.

Captain Dodge informs me that before the Pueblos reached the heights they were ordered to scale, they halted on the way to receive from their chiefs some medicine from the medicine-bags which each of them carried about his person. This they rubbed upon their heart, as they said, to make it big and brave; and they also rubbed it on other parts of their bodies, and upon their rifles, for the same purpose.

The distance marched today is estimated at six miles. For the past two days, on account of the roughness of the route and consequent fear of damage, the viameter has been detached from the wheel of the six-pounder. It was quite apparent that the route we have come is practicable for wagons only *as far as the east base of these mountains.*

A very pretty stone, between the jasper and chalcedony, has been found strewed over the ground at this and our last encampment. A grizzly bear, it is reported, has been seen near our present camp. The whole command has been in the most buoyant

[82] Page 179—Simpson's note.

A work of imagination, the book was written in 1847 by John T. Hughes, a private in Company C, First Missouri Mounted Volunteers, attached to Doniphan's command in the Mexican War. Hughes vividly described many wonders he never saw.

spirits ever since we commenced the ascent of the Sierra de Tumecha—the air, the water, and the scenery all doubtlessly contributing their joint influence.

Sixteenth camp, September 3—Carravahal representing that there yet remained a very narrow and difficult defile to pass through before we should be entirely extricated from the natural defiles of the route, I was ordered this morning by the colonel commanding in advance (thirty Pueblos and Lieutenant Torez accompanying me), to reconnoitre the defile. After getting about half a mile from the camp, we entered a gorge which, for about a mile, we found very narrow and commanded by heights on either side. These heights, however, are easily accessible and can be swept by troops thrown out as flankers. The narrowest portion of the gorge extends only for about one-third of a mile. The artillery were detained here, on account of obstacles, three-quarters of an hour, and also slightly in crossing the Rio Negro, which they did twice subsequently. This stream, which is the one spoken of as passing through our camp of yesterday and taking its rise in the pass, is a beautiful mountain brook and, coursing generally south of west, probably runs into the Cañon de Chelly.[83]

The gorge we found today, as yesterday, surpassingly beautiful. Primary mountain heights extend on either hand for the first three miles, and then the secondary commence. Four miles further, the gorge expands indefinitely to the right and left, the greatest elevation of the heights on either side being probably about eight hundred feet.

The soil of the valley of the Rio Negro is exceedingly rich. Among the *sylva,* I noticed towering pines and firs, also the oak, the aspen, and the willow; and bordering the stream was a great variety of shrubbery, the hop vine, loaded with its fruit, being in-

[83] The stream is shown but not named on maps of the period soon following, including Captain J. N. Macomb's map of 1860. For more than fifty years the stream has been known as Crystal Wash, and it does, as Simpson supposed, flow into the head of Canyon de Chelly.

tertwined among them. Flowers of rich profusion, and of every hue and delicacy, were also constantly before the eye—upwards of ninety varieties having been picked up since we entered the gorge yesterday. Indeed, we are all in hopes that, yesterday and today, we have been having an earnest of what we may yet behold in this part of the world—a rich, well-timbered, and sufficiently watered country, *a thing I have not seen since I left the confines of the United States.*

Our march today is estimated at twelve miles, and we are encamped upon the Sieneguilla Chiquita (Little Meadow), near the Rio Negro, a locality which furnishes good water and grass; and near at hand is an abundance of the artemisia, which answers very well for fuel.[84]

Carravahal informs me that the governor of New Mexico, some years since, attempted to make his way into the Navaho country through the pass we have been threading, and was driven back.

Gregg also, in his *Commerce of the Prairies,* probably refers to the same pass in the following passage:

"Towards the close of 1835, a volunteer corps, which most of the leading men in New Mexico joined, was raised for the purpose of carrying war into the territory of the Navajoes. The latter, hearing of their approach, and anxious no doubt to save them the trouble of so long a journey, mustered a select band of their warriors, who went forth to intercept the invaders in a mountain pass, where they lay concealed in an ambuscade. The valiant corps, utterly unconscious of the reception that awaited them, soon came jogging along, in scattered groups, indulging in every kind of boisterous mirth; when the war-whoop, loud and shrill, followed by several shots, threw them all into a state of speechless consternation. Some tumbled off their horses with fright; others fired their muskets at random; a terrific panic had seized everybody; and some minutes elapsed before they could recover

[84] At this point the command was camped in a high mountain meadow slightly west of the present Crystal Trading Post (a trading site since 1877).

their senses sufficiently to betake themselves to their heels. Two or three persons were killed in this ridiculous engagement—the most conspicuous of whom was a Captain Hinófos, who commanded the regular troops."[85]

Hosta today has been treating us again with some more of his traditionary lore. The French (so he says) once attempted to subdue the aboriginal Mexicans, and failed. The Spaniards then came, and succeeded. The latter began to brag of their guns, by which they had accomplished the conquest. Montezuma, hearing of it, said they had no reason to do this, for he could bring a bigger gun than they could. "Why, what can your gun do?" remarked he to the Spaniards. "It can make a hole through a tree," was the reply. "Well," says Montezuma, "mine can split a tree from top to bottom. Now, show me what yours can do?" So the Spaniards shot at a tree and made a hole in it. Montezuma, seeing this, called down his thunder from the clouds and shivered it from top to bottom!

A series of astronomical observations make the latitude of this camp 36° 2' 7"; its longitude, 109° 5' 45".

Seventeenth camp, September 4—The weather, during the nights, ever since we left the Puerco, has been quite cold; during the day, on the contrary, it has been generally pleasantly warm—occasionally very warm.

[85] Pages 288–89.—Simpson's note.
Max Moorhead, editor of the 1954 edition, identifies (200–201) the troop commander as "Captain Blas Hinojos, of the Santa Fe company." In 1834, Hinojos, as *commandante principal,* was leader of the Mexican republic's small military force in New Mexico. This mountain engagement even today remains important to the Navahos. Captain Dodge related one version of it in 1856: "In my late visits to different parts of [the Navaho] country . . . they have taken great pleasure in pointing out to me one of their mountain passes in which they say they put to rout one thousand Mexicans and Pueblos. That they kill[ed] a great many of them among whom was the three captains in command, to wit—Captain Inanhos & the father of Don Tomas [and] Baca the rich man of Peña Blanco, and forced Salvador, the captain of Jemez Pueblo to jump off a precipice and kill himself." Dodge to Governor Meriwether, June 13, 1856. National Archives, Indian Records. New Mexico Superintendency, 1856–57, Letters Received, Micro. roll 548.

Four Navahos had a talk with Sandoval outside the line of sentinels this morning. Subsequently, four more came to the conference. They all, however, being unimportant men, nothing came out of it.

Our route today, more winding than usual, has been generally west of north. The distance marched was 13.43 miles. For the first half of the distance, the *Sierra Rayada* was immediately on our left; and throughout the whole of it, the *Sierra de Sieneguilla* was immediately on our right. These mountains are of a basaltic trap character, in some instances resembling very much the palisades on the Hudson River.[86] This trap is apparently the effect of protrusion rather than of overflow, and is more irregular in its outlines than that I have already noticed as characterizing the country west of the Rio de Jemez.

At about six miles from our last camp, immediately on the right of the road, I observed a well-marked dike of trap rock, its course being north of east and it leaning slightly towards the north. It exhibits itself in an outcrop of detached blades, some of them being from thirty to forty feet above the plain, and about three feet thick. The soil from which it projects is of a reddish argillaceous character. This outcrop, it is obvious, must have been the effect of protrusion from below, and at a time when there were rocks against it to prevent an overflow; and these adjacent formations must since have been either decomposed or have sunk.

About a half mile further, we crossed a shallow stream of very good water, running southwestwardly, good grazing being apparent along it. Seven and a half miles from our last camp, we passed on our left a very rich field of wheat, the stalks averaging five and a half feet high, the heads very full, and the grains plump and large. A mile and a half further, another streamlet comes in

---

[86] Simpson's *Sierra Rayada* is known to Navahos as Sonsela Mountain, or Sonsela Buttes. In his later years, Chee Dodge owned a home at the south foot of the mountain. The *Sierra Sieneguilla* is a lower extension of the Chuska range, at one point indeed resembling, in height and form, the Hudson River Palisades. Instead of brown, however, the rock here is somber gray.

from the northeast and crosses the route.[87] I noticed, also, in the vicinity of this stream, some good grazing.

Ten miles from our last camp, we met a very steep rocky ascent of about fifty feet in altitude, where the men had to assist at the guns. A mile further brought us to the *Sieneguilla de Juanita* (Little John's Meadow), the soil of which, of considerable area and of a rich mellow calcareo-argillaceous character, looks as if it might produce well. I noticed, also, a great deal of horse ordure lying about, it indicating that the Sieneguilla is a favorite resort for these animals. Running through the Sieneguilla, in a southerly direction and probably in the Cañon de Chelly, is the *Rio de Juanito*, a stream of a sandy bottom, fifty feet wide and of a few inches in depth, upon which we are encamped.[88] The water of this stream, which is probably constant, is good, and the neighborhood furnishes proper grass and fuel.

The *sylva* today has been the large yellow pine and the piñon —willows fringing, in places, the streams. Signs of large droves of sheep have been noticed. Prairie dog towns, and rattlesnakes, their concomitants, though not so common as on the great plains intermediate between the United States and this country, are occasionally to be met with. Just before reaching camp we crossed a well-beaten Navaho trail, running north and south.

It is very interesting to see the picket-guard, composed entirely of Pueblos, gathered around the commanding officer's tent every evening, to receive from him their instructions for the night. Habited as they are, with their blankets thrown around them, their *white* turbans (assumed to distinguish them from the enemy, who generally wear *red*) encircling their heads, their

[87] The first shallow stream is known as *Toh delh Wlith* (Whisky) Creek, which, on crossing, gave the troops a view of broad valleys that even today are known as the Wheatfields. The second stream Simpson mentions is Wheatfield Creek. Both streams, like the Crystal Wash, enter Canyon de Chelly.

[88] The Spanish names Simpson supplies suggest that Carravahal, again, is his informant. The troops were camped on Tsaile (or Sehili) Creek, which flows into de Chelly's Canyon del Muerto. Immediately to their south and surprisingly not mentioned by Simpson was plug-topped Tsaile Peak, a towering landmark visible for miles.

rifles lying in their arms, or their bows and quivers slung to their backs, their attitude that of respectful attention, they present a group of a very interesting character. These people possess a great deal of native ease and dignity; and in their calm, reflective countenances I think I can perceive a latent energy and power, which it requires only a proper political and social condition to develop and make useful.

Some more Navahos (uninfluential men) have had a talk this afternoon with Sandoval, outside the line of sentinels. The word is, as usual, that they want peace; but the official persons, the chiefs, not presenting themselves to obtain it, the colonel commanding is determined to push on to Chelly, the heart of their country, and dictate the terms there. Besides, according to his original design, he is anxious to meet Captain Ker, who, with his command, from information obtained from a chief at the last council, he is disposed to think must have pushed on to that place.

The resulting latitude of this camp, from a series of observations, is 36° 10′ 36″; the longitude, 109° 12′ 15″.

Eighteenth camp, September 5—This morning a party composed of Colonel Washington, Mr. Calhoun, Mr. Collins, Major Kendrick, Lieutenant Dickerson, the two brothers Kern, and myself, visited the head of the renowned Cañon of Chelly, lying southwest about five miles distant from our last camp. This cañon has been for a long time of distinguished reputation among the Mexicans, on account of its great depth and impregnability—the latter being not more due to its inaccessibility than to the fort which it is said to contain. This fort, according to Carravahal, is so high as to require fifteen ladders to scale it, seven of which, as he says, on one occasion he ascended, but not being permitted to go higher he did not see the top of it.[89]

[89] Instead of de Chelly, which is the central and major canyon of this group, Colonel Washington's party was exploring the head of Canyon del Muerto. Carravahal's reference to a Navaho fort, which was to puzzle Simpson later, may have been to a small ruin, but more likely was to Massacre Cave, from which this north branch canyon derived its name. Massacre Cave will be mentioned again when Simpson tries and fails to find something resembling a fort.

On reaching the cañon, we found it to more than meet our expectations—so deep did it appear, so precipitous its rocks, and so beautiful and regular the stratification. Its probable depth I estimate at about eight hundred feet. At its bottom a stream of water could be seen winding its way along it, the great depth causing it to appear like a mere riband.

As far as time would permit an examination, for a depth of about three hundred feet—I could descend no further on account of the wall becoming vertical—the formation appeared to be sandstone, horizontally stratified with drift conglomerate. At this depth I found protruding horizontally from the wall, its end only sticking out, a petrified tree of about a foot in diameter, a fragment of which I broke off as a specimen. How did this tree get there? I also picked up at this point, upon the shelf on which I was standing, a species of iron ore, probably red hematite. The colonel commanding returning to camp, after a cursory look at the cañon in order to put the troops in motion for the day's march, I had not the time necessary to make the full examination which I would have liked. I saw, however, enough to assure me that this cañon is not more worthy of the attention of the lover of nature than it is of the mineralogist and geologist. The whole party returned to camp greatly pleased with this offset excursion, and promise themselves still greater delight when, on their reaching the mouth of the cañon, they will have more time to examine it.

In consequence of the excursion this morning, the troops did not move till about 9. Our course for the day was generally west of north. Two and a half miles from our last camp we passed on our right a cylindrical mass of trap rock protruding from the summit of the mountain ridge, the outcrop being probably as much as one hundred and fifty feet high. This singular landmark was seen yesterday before reaching camp. Two and a half miles further can be seen, also, immediately on the right of the road, a dike of trap rock ranging very nearly east and west, its eastern terminus of the form of a semi-conical abutment, about five hundred feet in protrusion from the plain below. A portion of this dike is perfectly columnar in its details.

Five and a half miles on our route, we reached the brow of a valley running generally north and south, it being apparently hemmed in at the north, nearest to us, by a range of secondary mountains, and further off by mesa heights. The former are of rounded form and, on account of their white ground being sprinkled with the evergreen cedar, have a motley aspect. The latter present a beautiful façade-like appearance and are of a deep red color. The intervening valley, on account of the copse-like character of its *sylva*, in contrast with the barren wastes which we traversed on the east side of the Tumecha ridge, was very refreshing to us.[90]

Having marched 7.39 miles, we came to the creek upon which we are encamped.[91] This creek is a clear stream of good water, ten feet wide by half a foot deep, coursing west of south over a clean and pebbly bottom and presenting here and there rapids and cascades as delightful to the eye as they are rare in the country. Upon its margin we find a sufficiency of grass for our animals.

The road today has been generally good, there having been but two steep hills, which detained the artillery but a short while. The soil has been of an argillaceous character, and in the valleys always appeared to be fertile; the timber, which has been pine and cedar, of a large growth; a few large oaks were also seen. The artemisia, as usual, has been the chief and almost the only plant, especially upon the uplands.

Twenty-five Mexicans were sent out this afternoon to examine, with Carravahal, the river ahead for a few miles. They had not proceeded, however, more than a mile when, seeing three or four of the enemy, their hearts failed them and they returned to

[90] Emerging from the high trees and mountain meadows, the troops were on rolling, open plateau, olive green in a covering of sagebrush. Simpson's "beautiful . . . deep red" formations were Los Gigantes Buttes, twenty miles airline to the north and in their way quite as breath-taking as de Chelly's deep gorges. From this same vantage point Simpson saw the long top levels of Black Mountain and the basalt thumb of Agathla Peak, sixty miles distant to the northwest.

[91] Having rounded the head of Canyon del Muerto, the troops were camped near the head of Sheep Dip Creek.

camp. Some Pueblos were then added to the party and the whole put under the charge of Lieutenant Torez. The party returned at about dusk, and report the road good for eight miles, excepting one steep hill which, however, Lieutenant Torez thinks practicable.

Nineteenth camp, Chelly, September 6—The troops decamped at 6 this morning—an hour earlier than usual, on account of an anticipated long march without water. Our route, though curving considerably towards the north, has been generally a little south of west.

At the respective distances of six and a half, twelve, thirteen, thirteen and a half, sixteen and a half, sixteen and three-quarters, and eighteen miles, we crossed some deep rocky arroyos, the first detaining the artillery three-quarters of an hour, the fourth three-quarters of an hour, and the last an hour.[92] The artillery today have been obliged to work harder than they have done any day since they started on the expedition. They, however, appear to be equal to any emergency and, though detained, at times necessarily on account of difficulties, they are always sure to be getting along in due time. The infantry, under Captain Sykes, from the commencement of the march have constantly preserved a compact, effective form, and have ever appeared as a *unit*, to be wielded by their leaders with precision and power.

The country today has been rolling—almost, indeed, broken—belts and clusters of trees, and sometimes solitary ones, diversifying its face. Piñon, yellow pine, and cedar have been the *sylva* —acres of the latter occasionally being dead, the cause not obvious. The artemisia has been the chief *flora*. The cactus, which hitherto has been seen but seldom, today was more prevalent.

When two miles on our route, looking back, a fine view pre-

[92] The geography of Canyon de Chelly, which resembles nothing else so much as a three-toed turkey track moving east, confused Edward Kern completely. Ruggedness of the terrain is more than sufficient excuse. His map of the canyon, therefore, is thoroughly disoriented. It was down the northern rim of Muerto that the troops marched all of this day. Near the end, beneath scrub cover of sagebrush, the rocks and soil turned to deepening hues of red.

sented itself, made up of mountains, beautifully variant in outline, prominent peaks here and there in the background and, intermediate between them and myself, the troops—horsemen, footmen, and artillery—their arms glittering under the glancing rays of a morning sun, and a cloud of dust betokening their approach.

A mile and a half further, some beautiful bastion-like rocks appeared, two miles distant on our right, capped with a whitish amorphous formation. Fifteen miles from our last camp, on our right, we noticed two very singular mesa formations, one of them looking like a high square fort, and discovering, by the daylight which could be seen through it, the appearance of a tunnel running horizontally through and through.

Though not expecting to find water along the way, thirteen and a half miles from our last camp we met some, in deep pools, in a rocky arroyo which we crossed. Here may be seen some singular-shaped basins and arches, all the effect of the erosive influence of water upon sandstone formation.

Innumerable signs of stock, principally of sheep, have been seen along the route; and the road we have been traveling looks as if it might be one of the great thoroughfares of the nation.

One of the pack animals today falling too far in rear of the main body of the command, the soldier in charge, seeing a Navaho near and at the same time a dust in rear as if made by a host of the enemy approaching, thought that discretion was the better part of valor and, leaving his pack, fled. The force in rear, however, proving to be the Mexican cavalry, and Lieutenant Dickerson happening at the time to be with them, he directed a chase after the Navaho, who by this time had got possession of the pack animal and was appropriating the contents of its pack to himself. Lieutenant Dickerson informs me that he got five distinct shots at the fellow with his revolver and, though he was not able to bring him to a surrender, was, nevertheless, successful in causing him to leave the animal and his pack.

It was somewhat exciting to observe, as we approached the

valley of Chelly, the huts of the enemy, one after another, springing up into smoke and flame, and their owners scampering off
in flight.[93]

Just after dark, after crossing an extensive *down* or sand drift,
we reached our camping ground in the valley of Chelly; and
much to our disappointment, after a hard day's march of 26.45
miles, we are obliged to spend the night without water. The cornfields among which we are encamped furnish, however, an abundance of forage for the animals and fine roasting ears for the men;
but the great beverage of the soldier in his marches—coffee—will,
in most instances, have to be dispensed with.[94]

Nineteenth camp, Chelly, September 7—The fires of our camp
were all, yesterday, at dark, from motives of military expediency,
extinguished—a phenomenon which doubtless was not without
its moral effect upon the enemy, who are hovering around us.

This morning a couple of Navahos—one of them a chief—were
brought into camp by Sandoval, both of them embracing Colonel
Washington and Mr. Calhoun, apparently with a great deal of
good will. The chief, whose name is Mariano Martinez—habited
as he was in a sky-blue blanket greatcoat, apparently of Ameri-

[93] If Simpson knew who set the hogans on fire, he chose not to say. Richard
Kern probably was not among the skirmishers and troops leading the advance,
but in his diary says that the hogans were set afire by the Navahos themselves:
"[We] came in sight of Cheille just before sun down; the Indians were around
us in small parties, & as we descended into the valley, the Sand hills began to be
covered with them—About 20 of [them] were a mile ahead of the command &
were the first to enter the cornfields—Several houses had been fired by them
as signals, before the command appeared in sight." Such action would be un-
characteristic of Navahos—or any other Indians—and Kern probably was mistaken. It is more likely that the hogans were burned at Colonel Washington's
order.

[94] The command was camped in a wide valley well to the west of the mouth
of the canyon, on the northeast bank of the Chinle Wash as it bends to the north.
Disregarding convenient supplies of wood, water, and forage, Washington
proceeded far enough away from the hilly approaches to the canyon to find a
defensible, sandy flatland. Simpson's longitudinal readings from this point to
Zuñi Pueblo were faulty, placing the command some ten miles too far to the
west. Near the site of this camp Lorenzo Hubbell built a two-story trading
post about 1900.

can manufacture and not unlike my own; a tarpaulin hat of rather narrow brim and semi-spherical crown; buckskin leggins and moccasins; bow and quiver slung about him; a pouch and knife at his side; and possessing a sombre cast of countenance which seemed to indicate energy and perseverance combined—appeared like a man who had naturally risen up by virtue of the energy of his character and, from the effects of a marauding life upon a civilized community, had become impressed with the jacobin look which he at the time discovered. The conversation which passed between these chiefs and the colonel commanding was as follows:

Colonel Washington: Who is this man? (referring to Martinez.)

Interpreter: He is the principal chief of the Navahos.

Colonel Washington: Tell him when a chief wishes to talk with me, by making known his intentions by a white flag, he will be conducted safely into camp; but that everybody else must keep a mile off, or else be liable to be shot.

Are he and his people desirous of peace?

Interpreter: He says they are.

Colonel Washington: Tell them if they are they can easily obtain it by complying with the terms of the treaty which they have made, and that the sooner they do comply with them the better it will be for them, as less of their property will be wasted and destroyed.

Interpreter: His reply is that they will bring in all they have stolen, and comply with the treaty.

Colonel Washington: Mr. Collins, where is the list of the property to be restored under the treaty?

Mr. Collins: Here it is sir.

Colonel Washington: Add to it that which has been stolen from us on the march.

Mr. Collins: Here it is, sir, with the additions made.

Colonel Washington: Tell the chief the stolen property which the nation is required to restore is 1,070 head of sheep, 34 head of mules, 19 head of horses, and 78 head of cattle.

Interpreter: The cattle, the chief says, he knows nothing about; the Apaches must have stolen *them*.

Colonel Washington: Tell him that if this should afterwards prove to be true, the cattle will be paid for.

Interpreter: He says if he cannot bring in the same cattle, he will bring in others to supply their place.

Colonel Washington: When can the chiefs collect here to make a treaty with me?

Interpreter: He says the day after tomorrow.

Colonel Washington: Tell him that will do; and that when the treaty is made with them, all the property the troops have taken, they will be compensated for. And there was one more thing he would say: that if they now entered into a treaty with him in good faith, it would result in blessings upon him and his people; but if they did not, it would result in their destruction.

Interpreter: The chief replies that his people will do all he has promised.

Colonel Washington: Tell him the talk is good.

The conference ended, the chief and his attendant, *à la mode Mexicaine* again embraced Colonel Washington and Mr. Calhoun very impressively, and apparently with much *endearment*.[95]

Today, by digging several pits five feet deep in the arroyo of the valley, a sufficient supply of good water has been obtained for the camp.

The latitude of this camp, by a series of astronomical observations, is found to be 36° 9′ 4″; its longitude, 109° 42′ 30″.

Nineteenth camp, Chelly, September 8—Early this morning a Mexican captive, of about 30 years of age, came into camp to see the colonel commanding. He represented that he was stolen by the Navahos seventeen years ago, and that he did not now wish to be restored to his people again. Indeed, he did not as much as ask about his friends who, I am informed, are now living at Santa Fe—from the vicinity of which he was stolen whilst tending sheep. He is a very active, intelligent-looking fellow, and speaks

---

[95] Richard Kern's only comment on this meeting is his diary entry that "The head chief Mariano Martins & a brother of Narbona came in—They said they wanted peace & agreed to comply with the terms."

like a native born Navaho—having all their characteristics in dress, conversation, and manners.[96]

Agreeably to the orders of the colonel commanding, I left camp at 7½ o'clock this morning to make a *reconnaissance* of the renowned Cañon of Chelly. In addition to my assistants, the two Kerns and Mr. Champlin, there were in company an escort of about 60 men—Brevet Major Kendrick being in command, assisted by Captain Dodge. Lieutenants Ward, Dickerson, Jackson, and Brower, as also Assistant Surgeon Hammond and Mr. Collins, accompanied the party. Our course for nearly two miles, as far as the mouth of the cañon, was east of south, and up the valley of Chelly. The soil of this valley, which is generally very sandy, is in spots quite fertile—on an average a belt of probably half a mile in breadth being planted in corn. The cane, also, I noticed growing very luxuriantly in places. The whole breadth of this valley is about three miles.

Reaching the mouth of the Cañon of Chelly, we turned to the left to go up it. Its escarpment walls at the mouth we found low. Its bottom, which in places is as little as one hundred and fifty feet wide, though generally as wide as three or four hundred feet, is a heavy sand. The escarpment walls, which are a red amorphous sandstone, are rather friable and show imperfect seams of stratification—the dip being slight and towards the west.

Proceeding up the cañon, the walls gradually attain a higher altitude till, at about three miles from the mouth, they begin to assume a stupendous appearance. Almost perfectly vertical, they look as if they had been chiselled by the hand of art; and occasion-

---

[96] Josea Ignacio Anañe, one of four Mexican captives the Navahos offered to surrender. Calhoun *(Official Correspondence)* says that Anañe was captured "when quite a boy, by a roving band of Navajoes, at Tuckalotoe [Tecolote]. His parents then lived at Santa Fe, where he supposed they now reside. He is the fortunate possessor of two wives and three children, living at Mecina Gorda (Big Oak), north of Cheille two and a half days travel. He was originally sold to an Indian named Waro, to whom he yet belongs. I do not think he is under many restraints, for he prefers most decidedly to remain with the Navajoes. . . ." Tecolote is a small Mexican trading center settled in 1824 on Tecolote Creek, eleven miles south of Las Vegas, New Mexico.

ally cizous marks, apparently the effect of the rotary attrition of contiguous masses, could be seen on their faces.

At the point mentioned we followed up a left-hand branch of the cañon—this branch being from one hundred and fifty to two hundred yards wide, and the enclosing walls continuing stupendous.[97] Two or three patches of corn, intermingled with melons, pumpkins, and squashes, were met with on the way.

Half a mile up this branch we turned to the right, up a secondary branch, the width of which was rather narrow. This branch shows rocks, probably as high as three hundred feet, almost perfectly vertical, and in some instances not discovering a seam in their faces from top to bottom. About half a mile up this branch, in the right-hand escarpment wall, is a hemispherical cave canopied by some stupendous rocks, a small, cool acceptable spring being sheltered by it. A few yards further, this branch terminates in an almost vertical wall, affording no pathway for the ascent or descent of troops. At the head of this branch I noticed two or three hackberry trees, and also the *stramonium*, the first plant of the kind we have seen.

Retracing our steps to the primary branch we had left, we followed it up to its head, which we found but two or three hundred yards above the fork—the side walls still continuing stupendous, and some fine caves being visible here and there within them. I also noticed here some small habitations, made up of natural overhanging rock and artificial walls laid in stone and mortar—the latter forming the front portion of the dwelling.

Having got as far up the lateral branches as we could go, and not yet having seen the *famous* fort, we began to believe that in all probability it would turn out to be a fable. But still we did not know what the main cañon might yet unfold, and so we returned to explore it above the point or fork at which we had left it. Starting from this point our general course lay about southeast by east. Half a mile further, or three and a half miles from the mouth of the cañon, on its left escarpment, I noticed a

[97] Simpson's party was in Cottonwood Canyon, a small spur reached before the main dividing point of the gorge.

shelving-place where troops (but not pack animals) could ascend and descend. Less than a mile further I observed, upon a shelf in the left-hand wall, some fifty feet above the bottom of the cañon—unapproachable except by ladders, the wall below being nearly vertical—a small pueblo ruin of a style and structure similar, to all appearances, to that found in the ruins on the Chaco. I also noticed in it a circular wall which, in all probability, has been an estuffa.[98]

The width of the cañon at this point is probably from two to three hundred yards, the bottom continuing sandy and level. And, what appears to be singular, the sides of the lateral walls are not only as vertical as natural walls can well be conceived to be, but they are perfectly free from a talus of debris, the usual concomitant of rocks of this description. Does this not point to a crack or natural fissure as having given origin to the cañon, rather than to aqueous agents, which at least at the present period, show an utter inadequacy as a producing cause?

About five miles from the mouth, we passed another collection of uninhabited houses, perched on a shelf in the left-hand wall. Near this place, in the bed of the cañon, I noticed the ordinary Navaho hut and close by it a peach orchard. A mile further, observing several Navahos high above us on the verge of the north wall, shouting and gesticulating as if they were glad to see us, what was our astonishment when they commenced tripping down the almost vertical wall before them as nimbly and dexterously as minuet-dancers! Indeed, the force of gravity and their descent upon a steep inclined plane made such a kind of performance absolutely necessary to insure their equilibrium. All seemed to allow that this was one of the most wonderful feats they had ever witnessed.

Seven miles from the mouth, we fell in with some considerable pueblo ruins. These ruins are on the left or north side of the cañon, a portion of them being situated at the foot of the escarpment wall, and the other portion some fifty feet above the bed of the cañon.[99] The wall in front of this latter portion being vertical,

[98] The small ruin Simpson describes is in the vicinity of Antelope Point.

access to it could only have been obtained by means of ladders. The front of these ruins measures one hundred and forty-five feet, and their depth forty-five. The style of structure is similar to that of the pueblos found on the Chaco—the building material being of small thin sandstones from two to four inches thick, imbedded in mud mortar and chinked in the façade with smaller stones. The present height of its walls is about eighteen feet. Its rooms are exceedingly small, and the windows only a foot square. One circular estuffa was all that was visible.

Half a mile above these ruins, in a re-entering angle of the cañon, on its left side, are a peach orchard and some Navaho lodges. Proceeding still further up the cañon, the walls, which yet preserve their red sandstone character but which have increased in the magnificence of their proportions, at intervals present façades hundreds of feet in length and three or four hundred in height, and which are beautifully smooth and vertical. These walls look as if they had been erected by the hand of art—the blocks of stone composing them not unfrequently discovering a length in the wall of hundreds of feet and a thickness of as much as ten feet, and laid with as much precision, and showing as handsome and well-pointed and regular horizontal joints as can be seen in the custom-house of the city of New York.

About eight miles from the mouth of the cañon a small rill, which below this point had lost itself in the sandy bottom of the

[99] The party was now in the canyon's central gorge (Canyon de Chelly proper), and here gazing at White House ruin. There is believed to be some relationship between the ancient puebloans of the Tsegi Canyon—Marsh Pass region and the builders of White House. Harold Gladwin (*History of the Ancient Southwest*, 220) says White House has supplied a good series of tree-ring dates from 1066 to 1080. There is evidence that long after the site was abandoned, Hopi Indians occupied White House briefly during the Spanish colonial period. A three-storied pueblo once rose to within ladder reach of a small cliff dwelling above it. The outer wall of the central cliff house, above a band of yellow, retains a kaolin or gypsum base plaster that is distinctly white—hence the ruin's name. In this plaster visitors after Simpson left their names. Among them: V(ictor) Mindeleff (no date, but perhaps in 1884, a year when the ledgers of trader Lorenzo Hubbell show Mindeleff outfitting at Ganado for an exploring trip through this region); J. W. Ellison, Sept. 20, 1884; and A. W. Conway, Santa Fe, Sept. 24, 1873.

cañon, appears above ground; and about five hundred yards further, on the right-hand side, is a lateral cañon in which we saw another peach orchard.

Having ascended the cañon nine and a half miles, the horses of the Pueblos in company with us not being strong enough for a further exploration, there being no prospect of our seeing the much-talked-of *presidio* or fort of the Navahos, which had all along been represented to us as being near the mouth of the cañon, and the *reconnaissance* having already been conducted further than Colonel Washington had anticipated would be necessary, the expedition returned to camp highly delighted with what they had seen.[100] We found, however, the further we ascended it the greater became the altitude of its enclosing walls —this altitude, at our point of returning being (as I ascertained by an indirect measurement) five hundred and two feet. The length of the cañon is probably about twenty-five miles. Its average width, as far as we ascended it, may be estimated at two hundred yards.

Both in going up and returning through the cañon, groups of Navahos and single persons were seen by us, high above our heads, gazing upon us from its walls. A fellow upon horseback, relieved as he was sharply against the sky and scanning us from his elevation, appeared particularly picturesque. Whenever we met them in the cañon, they appeared very friendly—the princi-

100 Simpson's party had progressed to Wild Cherry Canyon, about one-third the distance to the head of Canyon de Chelly. Near the juncture of Canyon de Chelly and Canyon del Muerto, and situated in the southeast of the latter, is a small ruin called Navajo Fortress. Conceivably—but improbably—this could be the "fort" Carravahal had mentioned and which Simpson failed to find. Almost certainly the Mexican guide was referring to Massacre Cave in Canyon del Muerto, about sixteen miles above the canyon mouth. After one of their periodic raids on Zuñi Pueblo, a band of Navahos late in 1804 or early in 1805 was followed back to de Chelly by a troop of Mexican cavalry. The Navaho warriors scattered after hiding their women, children, and old people in a cave in the canyon's north cliff. All might have gone well had not one of the old Navaho women called out a taunting insult as the Mexican troops filed past below. For the next hour or so the soldiers poured musket balls into the cave, their fire directly or by deflection killing all of the Navahos who were trapped there. After this episode de Chelly's northern gorge came to be called Canyon del Muerto.

pal chief, Martinez, joining and accompanying us in our exploration, and the proprietors of the peach orchards bringing out blanket-loads of the fruit (at best but of ordinary quality) for distribution among the troops. Indeed, the chief admonished his people, as they stood gazing upon us from the heights above, to go to their homes and give us no trouble.

I noticed the cross, the usual emblem of the Roman Catholic faith, stuck up but in one instance in the cañon; and this is the only one I have seen in the Navaho country.

Should it ever be necessary to send troops up this cañon, no obstruction would be found to prevent the passage of artillery along its bottom. And should it at the same time, which is not at all unlikely, be necessary that a force should skirt the heights above to drive off assailants from that quarter, the south bank should be preferred because less interrupted by lateral branch cañons.

The mystery of the Cañon of Chelly is now, in all probability, solved. This cañon is, indeed, a wonderful exhibition of nature and will always command the admiration of its votaries, as it will the attention of geologists. But the hitherto-entertained notion that it contained a high insulated plateau fort near its mouth, to which the Navahos resorted in times of danger, is exploded. That they may have had heights upon the side walls of the cañon, to scale which would require a series of *fourteen ladders,* is indeed probable, for it would require more than this number to surmount the height we measured.

I did expect, in ascending the cañon, to find that the Navahos had other and better habitations than the conical pole, brush, and mud lodge which, up to this time, we had only seen. But none other than these, excepting ruined ones, the origin of which they say they know nothing about, did we notice. Indeed, a Mexican who is a member of the command and who was a captive among them, says that they have no other habitation. In the summer, he informs us, they live wherever the cornfields and stock are. In the winter they take to the mountains, where they can get plenty of wood. As yet we have not met a single village of them

—it appearing to be their habit to live scatteringly, wherever they can find a spot to plant corn or graze stock. The necessity of living more densely, probably, has not heretofore existed, from the feeling which they doubtless have had up to this period that the inaccessibility of their country was a sufficient barrier to the intrusion of an enemy.

It seems anomalous to me that a nation living in such miserably constructed mud lodges should, at the same time, be capable of making, probably, the best blankets in the world!

Gregg, in introducing his remarks relative to their skill in this kind of manufacture, holds the following language: "They (the Navahos) reside in the main range of the Cordilleras, one hundred and fifty to two hundred miles west of Santa Fe, on the waters of Rio Colorado of California, not far from the region, according to historians, from whence the Aztecs emigrated to Mexico; and there are many reasons to suppose them direct descendants from the remnant, which remained in the north, of this celebrated nation of antiquity. Although they live in rude *jacales*, somewhat resembling the wigwams of the Pawnees, yet, from time immemorial, they have excelled all others in their original manufactures; and, as well as the Moquies, they are still distinguished for some exquisite styles of cotton textures, and display considerable ingenuity in embroidering with feathers, the skins of animals, according to their primitive practice. They now, also, manufacture a singular species of blanket, known as the Sarape Navajo, which is of so close and dense a texture that it will frequently hold water almost equal to gum-elastic cloth. It is therefore highly prized for protection against the rains. Some of the finer qualities are often sold among the Mexicans as high as fifty or sixty dollars each."[101]

As regards the hypothesis which Gregg advances in the above, that the Navahos are the direct descendants of the Aztecs, it is possible they may be. But if, as is likely, and as Gregg also supposes, this ancient people once inhabited the pueblos, now in

101 *Commerce of the Prairies*, Vol. I, pp. 285–86.—Simpson's note. (Moorhead edition, 198–99.)

"Mariano Martínez, Chief of the Navaho Indians."
By R. H. Kern, September 8, 1849.

"RESTORATION OF THE PUEBLO OF
HUNGO PAVIE (CROOKED NOSE), CHACO CANYON."
By R. H. Kern, August 28, 1849.

ruins, on the Chaco, how is it that they have retrograded in civilization in respect to their habitations, when they have preserved it in their manufactures?

I know of but two ways to account for it. Either the Navahos are descended from a cognate stock, *prior* to that which built the Chaco pueblos, which stock lived as the Navahos do now in lodges—and this agrees with the tradition given by Sandoval[102] —or, in process of time, the cultivable and pastoral portion of the country becoming more and more reduced in area and scattered in locality, the people of necessity became correspondingly scattered and locomotive, and thus gradually adopted the habitation most suitable for such a state of things—the lodge they now inhabit.

In regard to the manufacture of *cotton* fabrics, in which, according to Gregg, they excel, we observed no evidences at all of this species of manufacture among them, nor any signs of the domestic culture of the plant from which, rather than from a foreign source, they would be most likely to draw the raw material.[103]

In regard to the manufacture of *plumage,* or feather-work, they certainly display a greater fondness for decorations of this sort than any Indians we have seen; but, though they exhibit taste in the selection and disposition of this kind of ornament about their persons, I saw no exhibition of it in the way of embroidery.

In respect to the population of the Navaho nation, it has been impossible for me to arrive at anything like an approximation of it. Indeed, if the few we have seen bear a proper proportion to the whole number contained in the country, the extent of this population has been greatly exaggerated. But I prefer to believe that, as a nation, they live much scattered and that those whose

[102] *Ante,* August 28—Discussion of the origin of the Chaco ruins.—Simpson's note.

[103] Since writing the above, on inquiry I learn from Señor Vigil, secretary of the province, that the Navahos (he has been in their country) formerly manufactured a few cotton fabrics from the raw material, which they were in the habit of importing from Santa Fe and other places; but that this species of manufacture has now almost, if not entirely, ceased.—Simpson's note.

precincts we have passed have studiously avoided us. All things considered, then, I would estimate the population from eight thousand to ten thousand souls: this last number is Gregg's estimate.[104]

As regards their stock, so far as I could observe, and from what the reclaimed Mexican captive before referred to has told me, I should say that it consisted mainly of sheep and horses—mules and cattle forming but an inconsiderable portion of it. We have as yet, however, not fallen upon a drove of either of these animals —which the Mexican explains by saying that they have, the better to conceal them from the troops, been driven to the mountains. Innumberable signs of sheep, however, have been seen by us. Their horses, though generally better than those to be seen among the New Mexicans, and capable of long and rapid journeys under the saddle, are not, in my judgment, near as fine as what I have seen among the Comanches; and in all these cases they are far inferior to our own, in point of bulk and power.

Nineteenth camp, Chelly, September 9—Today the two chiefs, Mariano Martinez and Chapaton, the latter the chief of the San Juan Navahos, have been in, on the part of the nation, to deliver up some of the captives, stock, and other property required to be delivered according to the treaty made by Colonel Nuby, and also to enter into a more comprehensive and complete treaty.[105]

[104] Gregg (Moorhead edition, 198) in 1834-44 wrote: "The *Navajoes* are supposed to number about 10,000 souls. . . ." Governor Charles Bent, writing to Commissioner Medill on November 10, 1846 (*Official Correspondence*), said that the Navahos "are variously estimated at from 1000 to 2000 families or from 7000 to 14000 souls."

[105] Calhoun (*Official Correspondence*) said that "at the appointed time, the Head Chief [Martinez] with the second, appeared and announced their readiness and their full authority, to redeem the pledge of the Head Chief; at the same time, bringing forward 104 Sheep, 4 mules & horses, and delivering four Captives." Josea Anañe was one of the four, but was permitted to remain behind with his two Navaho wives and three children. The other captives were "Anto Josea, about 10 years old, taken from Jemez where his parents now live. . . . He was well treated. . . . Teodosia Gonzales, twelve years of age, was taken about six years ago, from a corral near the Rio Grande. . . . He was well treated," and "Marceito, eighteen years of age, [who] was taken from Socorro. . . . He has evidently been a captive many years, as he has entirely forgotten his native

A large portion of this property not being immediately available, as they said, on account of the distance whence it had to be brought, the colonel commanding, with their consent, appointed a limited period—thirty days—in which all that yet remained outstanding was to be delivered up at Jemez. The murderer of a citizen of Jemez was, as soon as he could be apprehended, to be turned over to the governor at Santa Fe.

The parties there entered into a treaty, by which the government of the United States assumed the paternal control it has been in the habit of exercising over the tribes of Indians within or bordering upon its domain; and the Navaho nation, on its part, through its head chiefs, Martinez and Chapaton, who represented that what they did was binding on the whole nation, gave their full and unequivocal assent to all its terms. Particular care was taken, both by the colonel commanding and the Indian commissioner, to make the chiefs comprehend the full import of the treaty to which they were invited to give their assent. And, to be certain that all was done that could be done to insure this, each and every officer present was appealed to to know whether he considered the treaty had been sufficiently explained; to which they all without exception responded in the affirmative.[106]

All that could be accomplished by the expedition, then, may be considered as having been accomplished. A full and complete treaty had been made with the Navahos, by which they have put themselves under the jurisdiction and control of the government of the United States, in the same manner and to the same extent as the tribes bordering the United States. The portion of the captives and stolen property near enough to be made available have been given up, and the remainder has been promised to be restored within a determinate period. Added to this, what is of

tongue. The novelty of a home, as explained to him, seemed to excite him somewhat."

[106] The full text of the treaty appears in Appendix E. Van Valkenburgh and McPhee, evidently on the word of Navaho informants, say the treaty council was held "on the crest of the small knoll between the Thunderbird Ranch [formerly Sam Day's trading post] and the mouth of the Canyon de Chelly."

no inconsiderable value, the troops have been enabled to penetrate into the very heart of their country, and thus a geographical knowledge has been obtained which cannot but be of the highest value in any future military demonstration it may be necessary to make.

It is true the Navahos may fail to comply with the terms of the treaty. But whether they comply or not, the fact still remains the same, that a treaty *covering the whole ground* of their fealty (the former covered but a few points), as well in the general as the particular, was necessary in order to satisfy the public mind, as well as testify to the whole world that should any future coercion become necessary, it would be but a just retribution and, in a manner, their own act.

In the afternoon, after the treaty was concluded, quite a number of Navaho warriors, at least a hundred, came within the vicinity of the camp to trade with the troops, seemingly happy that so peaceful a termination had been given to affairs. They were generally armed with bows and lances, and carried also shields. Very few of them had rifles. In some instances they were handsomely dressed, an appendage of eagle feathers to their helmet-shaped cap adding not a little to the picturesqueness of their appearance.[107]

[107] Navaho bows were short, backed with sinew, and powerful; arrows were steel-tipped. Shields of this period, according to Willard Hill ("Navaho Warfare"), were "made of buckskin from the hip of a deer, where it is thick. If possible, there were two thicknesses." The shield might be two feet in diameter, attached to the forearm with thongs. Over the shield's top edge might be a wrapping of bright red or yellow cloth; otherwise, eagle feathers might be secured at quill end to the shield rim. War raiment, which would have been worn on this occasion, might have included a heavy buckskin war shirt, poncho style but sewed up the sides, with loose sleeves to the elbow. Buckskin pants were worn baggy—to the knee, if buckskin leggings were worn above the moccasins, otherwise to the ankle and slit on the outside of the leg to below the knee, Spanish fashion. If leggings were worn, they were tied below the knee with woven garters (*janezhi*). As described by Charles A. Amsden (*Navaho Weaving*, 106; Pl. 21), these were nearly always alike: a triangular white figure on a red ground, with green stripes along each edge of the figured central band. The helmets Simpson mentions in fact were caps made from the skinned-out heads of mountain lions or lesser but fierce animals, the ears made to point upward at the top. A few

Their principal articles of traffic consisted of blankets of their peculiar and superior handiwork, dressed skins, and peaches.

The blankets, though not purchasable with money, as it is not used as a tender among them, were sold in some instances for the most trifling article of ornament or clothing—it being their manner, if they saw anything about your dress which they fancied and wanted to buy, to point to it and then to the article for which they were willing to barter it.[108]

There was a Moqui Indian present at the council this morning as a spectator, and a more intelligent, frank-hearted looking fellow I have seldom beheld. Indeed, it occurred to me that he had all the air and manner of a well-bred, vivacious American gentleman, and the only thing Indian in his appearance was his complexion. His people, whom he represents as living three days' travel from this place, have the *reputation* of being quite intelligent and orderly—it being one of the articles of their political as

owl or eagle feathers might be attached at the top, to droop down the back. Footgear, similar to that of the southern Apaches, consisted of plain moccasins, dyed brown or red, the buckskin uppers wrapped across the ankle and tied with a thong. Soles might be of buffalo hide, secured in trade with one of the neighboring Plains tribes, or elkskin, taken in trade or war with enemy Utes. At this time there was no native silverwork, but turquoise beads and pendants, bartered from the Pueblos, were worn, as were occasional Spanish and Mexican gewgaws.

[108] Richard Kern notes that "trading commenced" at once upon the signing of the treaty. The Navahos, interestingly enough, at this time showed no interest in the silver money—American or Mexican—which at least some of the troops carried. Conceivably a few of the soldiers were willing to barter a bit of tobacco, issued to them in limited supply by the quartermaster. Otherwise, as Simpson observes, the soldiers, traveling light and battle-ready, had only personal trinkets to trade. A ring, a musty pipe, a ticking timepiece, a bright silk scarf, an awl, a punch, or any of the small leather-working tools such troops would carry, pocket knives, pocket mirrors—and so on. Otherwise, and most coveted by the Indians, brass buttons pulled from uniform jackets and brass buckles stripped from leather belts and harnesses. Also, conceivably, the oval, U.S.-lettered brass plates affixed to the infantry cartridge boxes, even the leather cartridge boxes themselves. For a few such trinkets the Navahos eagerly exchanged worn objects common to their own lives: brightly woven garter belts, feathered and painted articles of adornment or war—but mainly, as Simpson points out, those Navaho blankets admired by traveling Americans then and ever since. Aside from all of this, there is no evidence that Colonel Washington brought gifts for the chiefs and headmen with whom he treated.

well as religious creed, that they are at liberty under no circumstances to take human life; and in regard to infidelity on the part of their women, their laws are said to be very stringent. These people, I am informed, herd stock, grow corn, and live in pueblos, of which there are, according to the Moqui present at this time, but three. It is reported that originally they had a greater number of towns, but—one or more of them becoming guilty of shedding blood—they were on that account exscinded.[109] Does not this article of their creed, if true, point to a civilized origin? At all events, there is nothing in the features, manners, and general appearance of the Moqui I have seen to belie such an hypothesis, but on the contrary, a great deal to make it probable.[110]

Martinez, the principal Navaho chief, brought in a beautiful mule this morning to present to the colonel commanding. The colonel, however, with the remark that it was neither customary nor proper on the part of public officers to receive such presents, graciously declined it.[111]

[109] Simpson evidently either misunderstood, or later misinterpreted his own notes of this conversation. Instead of three pueblos, his Hopi informant presumably referred to the three mesas on which the Hopis occupied seven pueblos, in addition to an eighth village (Moencopi) farther to the west. In earlier historic, and ancient, times (as now) there were other pueblos; while the Hopis usually were peaceable people, there is nothing in Hopi legend telling of one of their villages having been cast off through the mere shedding of human blood. Richard Kern, in his diary, added that the Hopi "was a fine looking fellow, larger & much better built than any we had met—his countenance was finer & more expressive & his manner also. He remembered old Bill Williams."

[110] It is proper, however, to state that Señor Vigil, who has twice visited these people, says he knows nothing of this peculiar article of their faith. He knows, however, that though they are a docile people, they once were in a defensive war with the Navahos, against whom they used the bow and arrow. I suspect, when the exact truth is known with regard to these people, it will be found that, though inclined to a state of peace, they are not so disinclined to war as not, under coercive circumstances, to stand up, even at the risk of bloodshed, to defend their lives and property.—Simpson's note.

[111] In his position, Colonel Washington could not decline the gift without insulting Martinez. From the moment of the troops' arrival in the canyon, one may be sure, the Navahos were enduring their presence with the best grace possible; rumors of an Apache raid upon Zuñi—which soon caused the command to divert its march in that direction—no doubt were a Navaho ruse to speed the troops' departure.

There having been various contradictory reports among us relative to other American troops having visited Chelly besides Colonel Washington's command, I today inquired of Martinez whether such was the fact. His reply was, that the first American troops that had visited Chelly were those at present there.[112]

The climate of this valley we find much milder during the night than that we have heretofore experienced since leaving Jemez.

Twentieth camp, September 10—Colonel Washington learning yesterday from Chapaton that Captain Ker was not on his way to meet him at this place, as he was led at Tumecha, through information from a chief, to believe might be the case, and a report having been received that the Apaches had within a few days made an attack upon the friendly Pueblo Indians of Zuñi and killed a number of them, the program of operations has accord-

[112] This introduction of American troops to Canyon de Chelly was, for the Navahos, only the beginning of unpleasantness. Colonel E. V. Sumner entered the canyon ("my object was to attack the Indians") in 1851 at the head of four companies of cavalry. Nothing at all came of it, and no one was hurt, except one of the Colonel's orderlies, wounded by a Navaho musket ball "but not dangerously." After this there may have been informal calls by patrols riding up from the new Fort Defiance—nothing of importance, however, until 1858. In September of that year, Lieutenant Colonel D. S. Miles marched against the Navahos at de Chelly with three companies of mounted rifles, two of infantry, and Captain Blas Lucero's Mexican "spies" (guides). Miles found the canyon—its rims defended by armed Navahos—no place to start a fight. A few shots were exchanged, and the troops withdrew from the canyon with Miles' observation that "no command should ever again enter it." ("Report of the Secretary of War, 1857–58.") In the summer of 1859, Captain J. G. Walker led a scouting force from Fort Defiance to the San Juan River and then to Canyon de Chelly. His troops rode back to quarters without clashing with the Indians. On his return, Walker reported that " . . . the Navajos everywhere evinced the most earnest desire for peace . . . there is no doubt that a war made upon them now . . . would fall the heaviest upon the least guilty." (*Ibid.*, 1859–60.) In the same year three parties of Mexican traders ventured up the Kletha Valley to Canyon de Chelly, where they caused trouble by telling the Navahos mischievous stories of the troops' plans to attack them. Possibly there were other patrols, as the Navahos were depredating in other, settled regions. The end for the Navahos came in the winter of 1863–64. Under orders of Colonel Kit Carson, Captain A. H. Pfeiffer and Captain Asa B. Carey, First New Mexico Volunteers, swept the canyon, burning and destroying, and leaving twenty-three Navaho dead. This incident was decisive in the tribe's crushing defeat and subsequent internment on the military reservation at Fort Sumner, New Mexico.

ingly been altered, and our destination is now Santa Fe by the way of Zuñi—the object being to afford this people all the necessary aid which their reported situation demands.

The troops accordingly took up their line of march from Chelly at 7 A.M., the general course for the day being southeast. For the first two miles our route lay up the valley of Chelly, and then turned more eastwardly, it at this point commencing the ascent of a species of mesa, or rather upland. Three miles further, the road approximates within a few yards of the Cañon of Chelly. To this point the road is exceedingly rocky and hilly; but these hills can in all probability be avoided by continuing up the valley of Chelly as far as the opposite point mentioned, and then turning to the left up the mesa. The country at the point referred to begins to be rolling—scrub pine and a species of spruce, thickly interspersed, constituting the *sylva*. Four miles further, a protrusion of trap rock, looking for all the world like the square tower of a church, with windows, could be seen, bearing northeast, some twelve miles off.[113] Eighteen miles from our last camp, we commenced the ascent of the *Sierra de Laguna*, the slope of which wagons would find some difficulty in overcoming unless one more easy could be found—a thing not at all improbable—or some labor be expended. The ascent we found to be two miles long—which accomplished, we were on a plateau, a mile more bringing us to our camp ground for the night where we find an abundance of wood, a sufficiency of pasturage, but no water.

The soil today has been principally of an arid, argillaceous character—the scrub pine and cedar characterizing this portion of the route. Since commencing the ascent of the Sierra de Laguna, scrub oak and yellow pine of a large growth have been the *sylva*. Cacti have been frequently seen. We crossed a number of heavy Navaho trails, and signs of large droves of sheep were observable. The day's march has been 20.50 miles.

Twenty-first camp, September 11—The troops raised camp at a quarter after 6 A.M. and followed, as yesterday, a well-beaten

113 The landmark Simpson describes is Tsaile Peak, distant some twenty-two miles air-line from this point.

trail—the general course for the day continuing about southeast. Having proceeded two and a half miles, one of the guards sent in advance yesterday to find water returning and informing the colonel commanding that there was some in a cañon to the left, about five miles off, a detour to the northeast was made by the troops in order to reach it. The cañon is *said* to be a branch of the Cañon de Chelly, and its banks were so steep as to make it necessary for the animals to be disburdened of their packs to enable them to reach the water at its bottom.[114] The supply we found ample, and it doubtless is constant.

After halting for about an hour, the troops resumed the march, the remaining portion of the day's route continuing slightly more southwardly.

For the first fourteen and a half miles the country is a pine barren, resembling very much in appearance and in the arenaceous character of its soil, the pine barrens of Florida, excepting that the former is more compact. For the remaining portion of the route, it is a rolling prairie, variegated with copses of piñon —the soil being of a reddish color, argillaceous in character and doubtless fertile if sufficiently watered. Five miles before reaching our present camp, a mesa escarpment comes in from the left, and skirts the road on that side for the balance of the way. The walls of this mesa are probably three to four hundred feet in height. Just before reaching camp, a most singular-looking column appears on the left of the road—resembling, when viewed nearby, a vase; when remotely, a statue. It is of sandstone formation and has an altitude of from thirty to forty feet.

Our camp for the night is more pleasant than usual—a small pond or lake, bordered by a margin of green luxuriant grass, being directly in front of us to gladden our sight; and the beautiful stratified walls of the *Cañoncito Bonito*, down which we are to turn tomorrow, adding its beauty to the scene. Some ducks, I notice, are constantly hovering around this spot.

[114] In this forested wilderness Simpson understandably was less than certain of his surroundings; very likely, however, the water was found at the head of Monument Canyon, the southern gorge of the de Chelly group.

The road today has been good. The distance marched is 24.83 miles. Several showers of rain have passed around us.

Astronomical observations put this camp in longitude 109° 15′ 30″.[115]

Twenty-second camp, September 12—Failing, on account of a hazy atmosphere, to get my usual astronomical observations last evening, I succeeded after the exercise of a great deal of patience, to get a few barely tolerable ones after midnight.

The command left this excellent camp ground at 7 A.M.—its general course for the day being a trifle west of south. Immediately on resuming the march, we turned short to the left, or eastwardly, to thread the Cañoncito Bonito (Beautiful Little Cañon). This cañon, which is about a quarter of a mile in length is, on account of its high enclosing walls, and the well-defined character of their stratification, beautiful. The walls, which are nearly vertical, are probably from three to four hundred feet high. Their formation is red friable sandstone—the stratification, which discloses a dip of about ten degrees toward the east, as also the line of clearage, being very distinctly marked. The width of the cañon is about one hundred feet, a small stream finding its way through its bottom. This cañon differs from that of Chelly in the face of its walls not being so smooth, in not presenting as large unstratified masses, and in having a talus of debris at the foot of the walls.

This cañon passed through, the route turned almost due south —following for the remaining portion of the day a succession of wide, shallow, fertile valleys, which are generally bordered on their eastern side by escarpment walls of a white and red sandstone formation.

Just after we debouched from the Cañoncito Bonito, a most singular prospect of detached turret-like rocks appeared skirting the valley just referred to on its eastern side. And down the valley, in a more southerly direction, a trap dike of a striking

[115] Simpson's reading again is faulty. The troops actually were eight to ten miles east of longitude 109° 15′, camped near the head of Beautiful Little Canyon (now called Quartzite Canyon).

character presented itself a short distance to our front.[116] This dike, on examination, I found to present a most interesting exhibition of igneous action and vertical protrusion. Its height above the plain is some three or four hundred feet; its breadth, one hundred and fifty; and its length, about two hundred yards. Its strike is nearly due east. Here can be seen, in the same formation, rocks that have been once perfectly fused and then cooled under pressure, the effect being to make them more dense.

About nine miles from our last camp, on the route, is *Sieneguilla de Maria,* where we found some very cold water and grass of an excellent quality.[117] The supply of water here is probably perennial. Three miles further, some very singular whitish abutment rocks, probably of sandstone, are to be seen on the left, jutting out from among rocks of a sandstone character and red color. The difference in the complexion and shape of the former of these rocks indicates a superior hardness in the formation of which there are prominences. Four miles further, just to the right of the road, appears a beautiful exhibition of horizontal stratification, terminating in one of a bent, semicircular character—the strata (red stone) in the last case being concentric, like the coatings of an onion, and disclosing themselves both by a side and end

[116] On Simpson's approach from the north, this volcanic formation resembles the ruins of some medieval castle or fortress. James Damon, son of the old Fort Defiance trader Anson Damon, who lived within a mile of this place, told me in 1960 that in earlier times one would see piles of sheep bones at the base of this rock, left where sheep were slaughtered in herds by Carson's troops in the 1863–64 Navaho roundup. In the cove formed by the mouth of Cañoncito Bonito, Colonel Sumner in the fall of 1851 established Fort Defiance while engaged in his ineffectual Navaho campaign. When his command reached this point on the march to de Chelly, Sumner left Major Electus Backus with the Third Infantry, a part of his artillery, and his train. Under the Major's supervision an adobe and log fort was built around a rectangular parade ground. The new post was first garrisoned by Company G, First Dragoons; Company K, Second Dragoons; Company B, Second Artillery; and Company F, Third Infantry.

[117] Simpson refers to the yellow-flowered *Cienega Amarilla,* an upland valley settled in the 1880's by Sam Day, Joe Wilkin, John Wyant, Billy Meadows, and other traders. Near here is the St. Michaels Franciscan mission and school, established in 1898. Derivation of Simpson's *Sieneguilla de Maria* is unknown.

view.[118] Eighteen miles from our last camp we crossed a rough, bad place where some little labor would be required to make it practicable for wagons. Two miles further, immediately on the left of the road, are two enormous hemispherical masses of solid sandstone rock, the radius of one of them being about one hundred feet.

After a march of 23.02 miles, reaching a babbling streamlet of excellent water which heads in a spring not far distant, and the vicinity affording fine pasturage and plenty of fuel, we encamped.[119]

The soil today along the route has been of an argillaceous character, and looks as if it might produce well. As usual, pine and cedar of rather a scrub growth have constituted the timber. A deer was killed by a soldier this morning, after running the gauntlet of numerous shots from the command—myself, among the number, throwing away a pistol shot. This is the first deer which has been killed by any of the party. The scarcity of this kind of game may therefore readily be inferred. Indeed, a more wretched country for game of every kind I have never seen than that we have been traversing since we left Santa Fe. A rattlesnake was also killed today, and a wildcat is reported to have been seen. I noticed today for the first time on the march a flock of blackbirds. I have also seen along the route a species of swallow different from any of the kind I have ever before met with. It is peculiar in being, a large portion of it, both on its back and its belly, white. It probably is a bank swallow.

It is reported that there is a wagon route from Cañoncito Bonito to the Pueblo of Jemez, but, as I have no certain knowledge of its existence, and none at all of its location, I cannot even trace it generally on my map.[120]

118 Simpson's analogy is apt. The onionlike formation is located about one mile below the present Hunter's Point Trading Post, at the southern closure of the valley through which the troops had been descending all day.

119 The stream Simpson describes—Black Creek—no longer flows on the surface, but at the bottom of an arroyo eight feet deep. The troops were camped near the head of an open, south-sloping valley.

120 An old Navaho trail did run from Cañoncito Bonito south to the Cienega

The longitude of this camp, by observation, is found to be 109° 18′ 30″.

Twenty-third camp, September 13—In consequence of a settled, steady rain nearly all last night—a thing uncommon in this country—the troops did not raise camp today till about noon. Our route today has been a little east of south, through a narrow valley, skirted on the left by a red sandstone escarpment, and on the right by a height, sloping gently towards the valley.

Two miles on the way, to the right of the road, a cañon comes in from the southwest, exhibiting some red sandstone rocks, beautifully stratified in curves, very similar to those of the cycloid reversed.

Just before reaching camp, we noticed to the left of the road a singular combination of swelling buttresses, vertical piers, and caves, and surmounting the whole a natural sandstone formation having very much the appearance of a tankard. The cover, as well as the handle, was perfect in outline—the latter appearing not a little like the embodiment of William Penn.[121]

A few hundred yards from this, in the direction of our progress, a beautiful view opened upon us, made up of finely stratified and variegated rocks, and a refreshing green valley, interspersed with copses of cedar.

The soil today has been argillaceous, and looks productive. The *sylva* has been largely yellow pine, cedar of a medium size, and a few scrub oaks. The artemisia has been very common. Limestone boulders have been seen today for the first time since

Amarilla and then southeast to Ojo del Oso, through the Wingate Valley eastward to San Mateo (Mt. Taylor). Here the trail divided, the south fork continuing east to Laguna Pueblo and Albuquerque, the north fork to Cabezon Peak and Jemez Pueblo. Mexican traders used this trail frequently. Possibly a sufficient number of Mexican carts or wagons were used in the trade to leave a marked trail. By far the most substantial travel, however, was by horsemen, moving with or without mule or burro trains.

121 The summit formation of red sandstone indeed resembles a pewter tankard with handle and knob-topped lid. Richard Kern also remarks that "this rock resembled an old fashioned Punch mug with lid & handle . . . putting one in mind of wm Penn with his broad brimmed beaver [hat] & inflated by a hearty meal." This whimsical note on the founder of his native state probably was original with Kern and borrowed later from his diary by Simpson.

we left the valley of the Rio de Jemez. Fragments of pottery are found about our present encampment, as they have been about others; and, what seems strange and has occured at other points, is, that you not unfrequently find it in localities where you would not suppose anybody would ever think of having a habitation.

Our encampment tonight appears peculiarly beautiful.[122] The heavens are deeply blue; the stars shine resplendently bright; the bivouac fires mark well the form and extent of the camp; and peacefully ascending can be seen the blue smoke—the whole forming, in combination with the general cheerfulness which pervades all nature, both animate and inanimate, a most pleasing picture. Indeed, this cheerfulness has been a general characteristic of our encampments ever since we began the march.

The water near our camp, which is in small pools, can only be relied on after showers. The grazing is good, and wood abundant.

Some cutting of cedars along the route today would probably be required to make it practicable for wagons.

Twenty-fourth camp, September 14—The march was resumed at 7 o'clock A.M., the course for the day being about southeast. Two miles on the route, we crossed an arroyo, coming in from the north[east], and coursing through a valley half a mile wide, this valley being skirted on either side by mesa heights of red sandstone.[123] The arroyo, I noticed, had a few cotton[wood] trees bordering it. Five miles more brought us to a steep hill, about eighty feet high—ascending which, we got out of the valley we had been traversing since we left camp. Wagons, to overcome this hill, would require a slope of easier ascent than the one we followed; and this could be attained by making a road, half exca-

122 The command was camped in a broad, open valley, about two miles north of present Lupton, Arizona.

123 E. M. Kern's map does not show the arroyo, and from Simpson's reference to it we might gather that the arroyo was not deep or wide enough to make the crossing difficult. Dry then, as it often is now, this nevertheless was the Río Puerco of the West, which today runs in a channel forty feet deep and, at this point, nearly one-quarter of a mile wide. Rains and running water delayed my crossing of the Puerco for more than one week in 1961.

vation and half embankment, along the side of the hill, or, what is very probable, by finding a natural grade at some other locality. Three miles further, another very steep hill, of about one hundred feet in altitude, was surmounted. Here, as at the other hill, a better locality could doubtless be found for a wagon road, or this one be made practicable, as suggested in relation to the other. The ascent of this hill accomplished, we again descended and crossed another valley, and then a succession of shallow ones, until we reached a canebrake pond where, finding a bare sufficiency of water and some good grass, we encamped. The taste of the water, as well as its discoloring effect upon the soil through which it oozes, shows it to be decidedly of a chalybeate [salts of iron] character.

Fragments of painted pottery were seen today for miles strewed along the road.[124]

The soil, for the first two-thirds of the route, has been argillaceous and fertile; the last third was arenaceous and arid. The *sylva* has been piñon, yellow pine, and cedar. Artemisia, as usual, has been very common. Nodules of compact limestone are found on the road eight miles from our last camp, in an argillaceous soil. More labor would be required on the route today to make it practicable for wagons than upon any portion since we left Chelly; but still it can be done without a very considerable expenditure of labor.

Our march today, though but 12.08 miles, has been, on account of the heat, more exhausting to the men than any day's march we have had.

I find this camp, by astronomical observation, to be in latitude 35° 11′ 56″, and longitude 109° 6′ 45″.[125]

[124] The Puerco Valley and the country immediately to the north and south of the wash is richly covered with *anasazi* ruins, late Basketmaker pithouses found in association with pueblo dwellings through Pueblo III (about 760–1200 A.D.). The sherds Simpson found in such profusion included Puerco black-on-red, Houck polychrome, and black-on-white wares of crude stepped designs and diagonal hatchure elements.

[125] The troops were camped on Whitewater Creek, Simpson's reading again placing them ten miles off course to the west.

Twenty-fifth camp, September 15—The troops decamped at 7 o'clock A.M.—the general course for the day being, as yesterday, about southeast. They immediately commenced ascending a hill, which would require a little labor to make it practicable for wagons. Having proceeded four and a half miles, we reached the brow of a long gradual slope, whence an extended prospect of distant mountains, mountain peaks, mesas, and valleys burst upon us, some of these peaks being probably as much as one hundred miles off. Three and a half miles further, we crossed an arroyo, which would require some little labor to make it traversable by wagons. Half a mile further, an old rubble stone wall, without mortar, of an inferior character, was passed on our left. Two miles further, a couple of mesa mounds, with a very singular-looking pinnacle standing isolated between them, were also to be seen on the left.[126]

Thirteen miles from our last camp, we entered the valley of the *Rio del Pescado* (or, as some call the stream, the *Rio de Zuñi*), which we find extensively cultivated in corn. There are indications also of there having been an abundant harvest of wheat. The Pueblo of Zuñi, when first seen, about three miles off, appeared like a low ridge of brownish rocks—not a tree being visible (a general characteristic of Mexican and pueblo towns), to relieve the nakedness of its appearance. We had not more than begun to get sight of the pueblo when we noticed a body of Indians approaching us from it. This party purported to be a deputation, headed by the governor *(cacique)* and *alcalde*, which had come out for the purpose of escorting the governor of New Mexico (Colonel Washington) into town.[127] Their reception of the

[126] These were the Zuñi Buttes, six miles air-line northwest of the pueblo.

[127] The functions of the Zuñi dignitaries who welcomed the command are here a trifle confused. The governor of Zuñi, an elected officer, represented the pueblo in its temporal affairs and relations with non-Indians. His power was not as great as that of the cacique, the religious head of the pueblo whose duty was to look after the spiritual needs of the villagers, as they supplied all or nearly all of his material wants. The cacique set the dates for and was in charge of all important ceremonial events, which could not be held without his approval.

"CHAPATON, CHIEF OF THE SAN JUAN NAVAHOS."
By R. H. Kern, September 8, 1849.

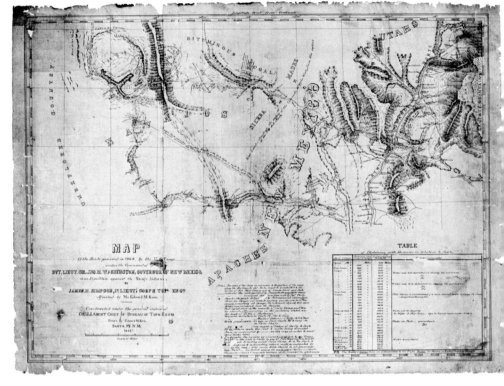

EDWARD M. KERN'S MAP OF THE 1849 NAVAHO EXPEDITION.

governor and his suite was very cordial. The alcalde, I noticed, was habited in the undress frock of the officers of the army, garnished with the white metallic button.

After proceeding in company about a mile, we were unexpectedly saluted, at a preconcerted signal from a chief, with an exhibition of a sham fight, in which men, young and old, and boys entered with great spirit. Guns were fired, dust was thrown in the air, men on foot and on horseback could be seen running hurry-skurry hither and thither, the war-whoop was yelled, and altogether quite an exciting scene was exhibited. Just as we reached the town, quite an interesting scene occurred. All the male inhabitants of the place, including gray-headed old men, the middle-aged, and the youthful portion of the population, came out to see the governor and shake hands with him. It was particularly interesting to see the juvenile portion of the community engaged in this refined act of courtesy. The governor and suite were then conducted to the *casa* of the governor of the pueblo, where bread in every variety of form (loaf, *tortilla*, and *guayave*), watermelons, muskmelons, and peaches, were laid in profusion before us.

Governor Washington took this occasion to make known to the chief men of the pueblo the cause of his coming among them (the report, now found to be false, of the Apaches having killed some of their people), and expressed to them the great satisfaction he felt in seeing their people in so flourishing a condition. He also represented to them the care which the government of the United States had for their welfare. The talk over, the governor and suite, after bidding their hospitable entertainers *adios,* continued their journey a couple of miles further to the camp for the night.

The alcalde's office, like that of the governor, was imposed upon the pueblos by the Spaniards, who in colonial times usually appointed a Spanish cleric or military man to serve as alcalde. The alcalde now functions as a lieutenant or subordinate of the cacique, generally in a religious capacity resolving disputes and preserving order.

Zuñi is a pueblo or Indian town situated on the Rio de Zuñi.[128] This river, at the town, has a bed of about one hundred and fifty yards wide; the stream, however, at the time we saw it, only showed a breadth of about six feet and a depth of a few inches. It is represented as running into the Colorado of the West. The town, like Santo Domingo, is built terrace-shaped—each story, of which there are generally three, being smaller, laterally, so that one story answers in part for the platform of the one above it. It, however, is far more compact than Santo Domingo—its streets being narrow and in places presenting the appearance of tunnels, or covered ways, on account of the houses extending at these places over them. The houses are generally built of stone, plastered with mud. It has a Roman Catholic church, in dimensions about one hundred feet by twenty-seven, built of adobes. A miserable painting of *Nuestra Señora de Guadalupe* and a couple of statues garnish the walls back of the chancel. The walls elsewhere are perfectly bare. This is by far the best-built and neatest-looking pueblo I have yet seen, though, as usual, the ragged picketed sheep and goat pens detract not a little from its appearance. The population of the place, based upon the number the governor has given me of persons capable of bearing arms, I estimate at 2,000. But, judging from the size of the town and the number of its inhabitants I saw, I should not place it

128 Zuñi Pueblo, as Simpson found it, occupied the site of Hálona, one of the original six villages of Cibola subdued by Francisco Vásquez Coronado in July, 1540. The first printed reference to Hálona was in Hernán Gallegos' *Relación* of 1582: "The third pueblo is called Alonagua [Hálona]. It had forty-four three- and four-story houses." Hodge relates how in the Pueblo Revolt of 1680 the mission churches at Hawikuh and Hálona were burned ("History of Hawikuh," 100–101). The friar at Hawikuh escaped, but at Hálona the Zuñis murdered their missionary, Fray Juan de Bal, and fled to the summit of Toaiyalone (Corn) Mesa. Hálona and other Zuñi villages thereafter remained deserted until November, 1692, when Diego de Vargas, during the reconquest of New Mexico, visited Cibola and persuaded the Zuñis to abandon their pueblo on Toaiyalone, return to the valley, and submit to Spanish rule. Old Hálona, situated on the south side of the Zuñi River, was reoccupied and in time rebuilt, spreading out on both sides of the river. By 1849 the Zuñi people were concentrated in this pueblo and several smaller farming villages. Zuñi Pueblo remains today substantially the same village that welcomed Colonel Washington's command.

above 1,200. Gregg, I notice, puts it at between 1,000 and 1,500.[129] And the author of *Doniphan's Expedition* states that it is upwards of 6,000.[130]

These people seem further advanced in the arts of civilization than any Indians I have seen. They have large herds of sheep and horses, and extensively cultivate the soil. Being far off from any mercantile population, they will sell nothing for money, but dispose of their commodities entirely in barter. Some of our command thought, from their apparent closeness in business transactions, they were the most contracted people they had met. But to my mind, in view of the treatment which they represent themselves to have received from a party of California emigrants which had but a week or two previously passed through their town, their conduct discovered only a proper degree of caution—a caution founded on the principles of self-conservation, and which it was wise only to allow to be removed in proportion as they discovered to be different from that party, or, in other words, more worthy of their confidence.

In *Doniphan's Expedition* I notice that this pueblo is represented as having been *discovered* by that expedition; and the author, after calling it "one of the most extraordinary cities in the world," adds, "that perhaps it is the only one now known resembling those of the ancient Aztecs."[131]

As regards the fact of its remaining undiscovered until the expedition of Colonel Doniphan brought it to light, I have only

[129] *Commerce of the Prairies*, 269, note.—Simpson's note. (Moorhead edition, 188.)

[130] In historical notes that he supplied for Matilda Coxe Stevenson's "The Zuñi Indians," Hodge says that in 1798–99 the population of Zuñi was reported at 2,716, but by 1820–21 apparently had dwindled to 1,597.

[131] Doniphan himself did not claim to have discovered Zuñi. After visiting Zuñi on November 25, 1846, he described his impressions of the pueblo in a letter to T. B. Thorpe, editor of the New Orleans *National*. Thorpe in turn wrote a piece for his newspaper, based on Doniphan's information, which Doniphan's imaginative biographer, John Hughes, included in his book (312): "The discovery of this city of the Zuñians will afford the most curious speculations among those who have so long searched in vain for a city of Indians, who possessed the manners and habits of the Aztecs."

to remark that the archives of the State Department of New Mexico show, from 1692, the year when these people were reconquered by the governor and captain-general of the State, Curro Diego de Bargas Zapata [Diego José de Vargas Zapata y Luján Ponce de León y Contreras, or more simply, Diego de Vargas], until the present time they have been a recognized and loyal portion of said territory.[132]

And as respects its claim to be regarded as "one of the most extraordinary cities in the world," and as undoubtedly resembling, and as probably being the only one now known to resemble the cities of the ancient Aztecs, the only marked difference I can perceive between it and the pueblos I have visited in New Mexico is that the town is rather more compactly built, and its streets at some points have the houses built over them. In the

[132] For the following extract from the official journal of Don Diego de Bargas Zapata, now filed among the archives of the State Department at Santa Fe, I am indebted to Mr. Samuel Ellison, the official interpreter for that department. As it fixes the date of the reconquering of Zuñi by New Mexico, and discovers incidentally the previous Spanish Roman Catholic rule which obtained over the pueblo, it will not be without interest. The literal translation furnished me by Mr. Ellison I have freely turned into the following:

"Tuesday, 11th November, 1692: I, the said governor and captain-general, on this day entered the Pueblo of Zuñi [the refugee pueblo on the summit of Toaiyalone] and received the submission of its people. On the same day, the Reverend Fathers Corbera and Banoso baptized two hundred and ninety-four children, male and female. This concluded, I was conducted to a room, and shown an altar, on which were burning two large tallow candles. Removing a piece of ornament, I found the following articles of religious worship; two brass images of Christ, four inches in length, set in wooden crosses; also another image of Christ, eighteen inches long; a portrait of John the Baptist, beautifully executed: one consecrated vase, gilded with gold; a small box with two plates of glass, in which the host is exposed to public view; four chalices, all of silver, and of different patterns; one ancient mass book, very well preserved; one confession book, in the Spanish and Mexican language, &c., &c.

D. Diego de Bargas Zapata, Roque Macbred,
 Lugan Ponce de Leon, Juan de Dios,
Martin de Alday, Cucero de Godoy.
Juan Paiz Hurtada,
"Before me: Alonzo Rail de Aguilar,
   Secretary of State and of War."—Simpson's note.

habits and dress of the people, so far as they exhibited themselves to us, excepting that they appeared to be somewhat more advanced in refinement, I could observe no difference between them and the other pueblos. So that one pueblo seems to have as good a claim to the Aztec descent, as far as appears to be known, as another. And who can say positively, or even with any *satisfactory* basis of hypothecation, that any of them are descended from that remarkable people?[133]

It is true that these people, as did the Aztecs, possess the art of taming birds; and some might reason from this that they are probably, on that account, from the same stock. But the people of *Pueblo of Tesuque* also possess the same art. And Abert says it is an art common to the Pueblos generally.[134] The Tesuques then, as also all the other Pueblos, on the ground mentioned (taming of birds), have equal claims to the same descent. But the languages of the Tesuques and the Zuñis, as will be seen by referring to Appendix B, are radically different. They cannot then have descended from a common stock. In other words, they cannot both be of Aztec origin, though both resemble the Aztecs in the practice mentioned. And so with all the other Pueblos. The different languages they speak are all resolvable (see Appendix B) into six distinct tongues. If, then, either of them is to be regarded as of the Aztec descent, on the ground stated, all the others, on the ground of a radical difference of language, must be thrown out of the pale of that descent. And yet they all alike practice the same Aztec art, from report. The idea has also been entertained that the people of Zuñi "live in

[133] In reasonable annoyance with Doniphan's biographer, Simpson is confronting his own new doubts about the validity of the Aztec legend.

[134] Report of Lt. J. W. Abert of his examination of New Mexico, 1846–47, October 20.—Simpson's note.

On October 20, 1846, Lieutenant Abert was at Laguna Pueblo. In his report (470), he says "The Indians here have numbers of turkeys and chickens. I also saw some tame macaws, that must have come far from the south. The 'Pueblos' have a great fancy for taming birds, and in this respect resemble the ancient Aztecas. But they have lost the art of making the beautiful feather embroidery, spoken of by Clavigero, DeSolis, and others."

houses scooped from the solid rock." The description of their habitations which I have already given will show this to be a fallacy.

The governor of Zuñi paid us a visit this evening, and a very interesting man we found him to be—about six feet high, athletic in structure, uncommonly graceful and energetic in action, fluent in language, and intelligent—in fact, he actually charmed me with his elocution. From him I learned that his people, a long time ago, lived on a high mesa directly in front of our camp, the ruins of which, he says, are still visible; that, according to tradition, the cause of their quitting it for their present location was as follows:

The waters of the valley on one occasion came up higher and higher, until at last they threatened to sweep them all away in the flood. Seeing this, they resorted to this expedient to save themselves: they let down into the waters, from the mesa, a man and a woman who had never known each other, and the result was their immediate subsidence. But why they should go down from a mesa height into a valley to protect themselves from another possible rise of water is not apparent. I, however, give the narration just as it was interpreted to me by the official interpreter. The waters, the chief said, came from the Rio Grande and other rivers, and spouted up all around. If this rise of water is not altogether a fable, I know of no other way to account for it than by supposing it to have been the result of an earthquake.[135] He further represents that they came originally from

---

[135] A devout Episcopalian, Simpson failed to note parallels between this Zuñi myth and the biblical flood of Noah related in the Old Testament. Matilda Coxe Stevenson gives a slightly different and more dependable version (61): "The A'shiwi [Zuñi people] were not destined to remain undisturbed. They were compelled by a great flood to seek refuge on a mesa near by, which they named To'wä yäl' länne from the quantity of corn they carried from the lowlands to the mesa, the corn occupying much room in their houses. . . . Though this tableland stands hundreds of feet above the valley, the waters rose nearly to the summit and caused consternation among the A'shiwi, who feared that the flood would sweep them from the face of the earth. It was finally decided that human sacrifice was necessary to appease the angry waters. Consequently a son and a daughter of the Kia' kwemosi [rain priest of the north] were dressed in their

the setting sun.[136] To the question, whence the origin of the albinos among them, he replied that they were all of pure Zuñi blood (and I have since learned from him, at Santa Fe, that there are *but seven* of them among his people). In regard to the ruins on the Chaco, he says he has seen them but knows nothing of their origin.

Two Navahos came into camp this afternoon and delivered up a captive Mexican boy.[137] They represent they are from *Chusca*, and that their people are collecting the stolen property for the purpose of surrendering it, agreeably to treaty.

The services of the Pueblo Indians being no longer required, they were this evening, after a complimentary notice of their conduct by the colonel commanding, discharged.

The soil today along the route, for the first eight miles, was arenaceous; for the balance of the way it was argillo-arenaceous. For the first ten miles the *sylva* was cedar and piñon; for the balance of the way there was no wood to speak of. The distance marched was 17.45 miles. The road was heavy, but, with some little labor upon the arroyos, can be made practicable for wagons.

Just before reaching Zuñi, we passed the dead body of an In-

most beautiful clothes, adorned with many precious beads, and then cast into the great sea. The waters immediately began to recede, and the youth and maiden were converted into stone. This columnar rock, known as the 'mother rock,' stands for all times as a monument of the peril from which the A'shiwi were happily delivered."

136 Simpson evidently misunderstood the Governor's meaning. Among the Zuñis, according to Stevenson, "the sun is referred to as father, the ancient one. The moon is his sister; the Sun Father has no wife. All peoples are children of the sun." In addition to this father-deity figure, the Zuñis, recognize "A'wonawil'ona, the supreme life-giving bisexual power, who is referred to as He-She, the symbol and initiator of life, and life itself, pervading all space." The Zuñis also perpetuate an origin myth similar to that of other Pueblos insofar as they all believe their people "in the beginning" were born in some dark underworld region beneath the earth's surface. By continuing effort, the A'shiwi progressed upward by stages, until finally they emerged into sunlight upon the earth.

137 Manuel Lucira (or Lucero). According to Calhoun (*Official Correspondence*), the youth was captured two years before while herding sheep. "He is about fourteen years of age, and has been sold several times, and badly treated, by flogging &c."

dian lying perfectly exposed upon the ground. We afterwards learned from the governor of the pueblo that the body was that of a Navaho prisoner, whom they had killed five days since, by direction of a California emigrant.[138] Competent authority, surely!

Twenty-sixth camp, September 16—I left this morning in advance of the troops, to visit the ruins of Old Zuñi spoken of by the governor of the pueblo last evening. To reach the mesa on which they are represented to be situated, I passed a large number of cornfields. On reaching the foot of the mesa, I found the ascent so difficult as not to be able, with the time I had at my disposal, to reach its summit. I therefore struck off diagonally to meet the command, which I noticed had, in the meantime, at the usual hour—7 A.M.—resumed its march. I paused, however, sufficiently long near the mesa to contemplate the figure of a woman seated high up upon a pedestal, from which, with face turned towards the probable locality of the ruins, she presented the appearance of one overcome with grief at the sad picture which lay before her. The formation was probably of sandstone; and it is not at all unlikely that the narrative made by the governor last evening had a great deal to do with the conceit.

The route today, which has been slightly north of east, up the valley of the Rio de Zuñi, after getting a mile and a half from

[138] There may or may not have been a connection between this Navaho's death and the arrival, at about the same time, of a train of emigrants bound for California. The emigrants outraged the Zuñis (and Calhoun later) by commandeering, in the name of the United States, a quantity of food and a number of horses and mules. The dead Navaho was one of a raiding band who unsuccessfully attempted to drive off a flock of Zuñi sheep. Their approach was detected, according to Calhoun, and "a battle ensued, and several Navajoes are said to have been wounded, and one, whose undried flesh was food for Carrion Crows as we passed his remains, was left dead on the field, within half a mile of the village." Hine, Edward Kern's biographer, adds a footnote to the episode (80). To compensate for his failure to secure Narbona's head and entirely in the interest of science, Richard Kern "rode out, like Perseus, brought back the [Navaho's] head and later sent it triumphantly to Morton." Richard Kern's diary entry of the affair is laconic: "Went after supper with Dr. H[ammond] & Tom C[hamplin?]—to procure the head of a Navajoe who had been found near this place trying to steal and was killed by the inhabitants. Succeeded & returned to camp about 10½ oclk."

camp, passed between a couple of low mesas capped with basaltic trap—that on the left being surmounted with the remains of some old and comparatively recent buildings and corral enclosures.[139] These structures have been built of basaltic boulders, coarsely held together with mud mortar. The circuit of the pueblo, in plan, is about five hundred by one hundred feet. I noticed here, for the first time on the march, a beautiful exhibition of lava which had been fixed in its wavy, undulating state by sudden refrigeration. This locality is the commencement, eastward, of the evidences of a basaltic, if not of a comparatively recent volcanic overflow, and on that account was regarded by me with considerable interest. The thickness of the overflow was as much as thirty feet above the soil, and seemed also to extend below it.

A mile and a half further, we crossed the Rio de Zuñi—its bed at this point being about thirty feet wide and very miry. We then threaded a cañon of about three hundred yards in breadth, bounded by mesa walls of sandstone.[140]

Twelve miles from our last camp, we passed, on our left, the ruins of another old pueblo, the plan of which was about three

---

[139] Similar in location and description to the ruins Simpson mentions are a group of ruins identified by J. W. Fewkes in 1891 as Hesh-o-ta-thlu-al-la ("Reconoissance of Ruins in or near the Zuñi Reservation," *Journal of American Ethnology and Archaeology*, Vol. I [1891], 111): "Nearly north of Zuñi, not more than three miles away . . . considerably elevated above the plain . . . are many ruins of stone houses irregularly scattered over several acres of ground. . . . Although this place has been inhabited within the memory of some of the old inhabitants of Zuñi, at present it is deserted, except temporarily in summer."

[140] In crossing to the north side of the Zuñi River, the command, upon emerging onto a wide plain, evidently passed to the north of and failed to see a major ruin probably built after the abandonment of Cibola's six original pueblos (Hawikuh, K'iánawa or Kechipawan, Kwákina, Hálona, Mátsaki, and K'iákima). Sam Chintor, a Zuñi sheepherder, in 1961 identified this site as Hesh-o-ta-lup-ton (Hesh-o-ta: earth pitch or lava; thus, literally, yellow lava rock). The ruin is found on the north bank of the Pescado River at the junction of state highways 32 (Gallup-Zuni) and 53 (Zuni-Grants). Unevenly rectangular, a bit larger in ground plan than the Chaco's Pueblo del Arroyo, the pueblo rose to two stories along its rear north wall, one story in the single tier of rooms on the south side. At approximately the center, the pueblo is bisected into two rectangular plazas. Most of the stone used in the walls is a rough lava rock, which is found in the immediate vicinity.

hundred by four hundred feet.[141] The houses, I noticed, were continuous in structure, originally two stories in height; had been built of flat stones, cemented by mud mortar; and were arranged on the sides of a rectangle, thus making a large interior court. In the center of the court, I noticed what appeared to have been a square estuffa, eighteen by twelve feet in plan, and ten feet in height—its flat roof, or *azotea*, still remaining quite perfect. The floor joists of the houses could still be seen protruding from the walls, in a very good state of preservation; and fireplaces and chimneys were yet apparent. This pueblo, like those on the Chaco, ranges about north and south, but in the details of its masonry it is far inferior; and in the style of its architecture it resembles not a little that of the Mexicans of the present day. Indeed, the evidences are that it is of comparatively modern origin. The courtyard, I noticed, had been recently cut into corrals for stock. Fragments of pottery, as usual, lay scattered around. In *Doniphan's Expedition* I read as follows: "On the head-waters of the *Piscao*, and high up in the mountains, Colonel Doniphan relates that he came to the ruins of an ancient city. Near the ruins are immense beds of citreous deposit and blackened scoriae, presenting the appearance of an immense molten lake in the valleys, and other volcanic remains, with chasms and apertures opening down through this stratum of lava to an unknown depth. This vitreous surface, with its sharp asperities, was exceedingly severe on the feet of the mules and horses, wearing them to the quick in a short time. The figure of the city was that of an exact square, set north and south, so that its four sides corresponded with the four cardinal points. In the centre was a large square, or plaza, which, from its appearance, might have been used for

[141] The Pescado Valley here varies from one to two miles in width, the stream of that name flowing parallel and close to the northern mesa escarpment. Proceeding eastward, the command evidently held to the center of the valley. The ruin Simpson refers to, now in considerably worse state than it was in 1849, is close to the south bank of the Pescado River. It is reached by a dirt road off Highway 53. In offering directions to this site, Sam Chintor said he knew of no Zuñi name for the ruin.

military parade-grounds, and for corraling stock in the night time."[142]

Query? As the ruins I have just described are the only ones we saw on the headwaters of the *Pescado* (which we followed up to its source) approaching the form of a square, are they not the same as those referred to in the above abstract? But we saw nothing of the "extensive molten lake in the valleys, with chasms and apertures opening down through lava to an unknown depth," spoken of as being near the ruins; neither did our animals have their hoofs "worn to the quick in a short time" by traveling over any vitreous surfaces.[143]

But to proceed with my journel: there are about the ruins just adverted to some fine springs, and the waters of the *Rio del Pescado* course directly by it, clear and bubbling. The soil in the vicinity exhibits signs of recent cultivation, and appearances indicate that the valley in this quarter was once yet more extensively cultivated. Two miles further brought us to a couple of noble springs, bubbling up, pure and cold, from the foot of some basaltic rocks. These springs seem to be the main sources of the Rio del Pescado (Rio de Zuñi), and are called *Los Ojos del Pescado*. Near these springs we are encamped.

Within a few yards of us are several heaps of pueblo ruins.[144]

142 The Hughes interpretation of the Doniphan command's journey is fanciful. Quite certainly Doniphan never reported having come to the ruins of "an ancient city." He was a Missourian. Which one of half a dozen pueblo ruins he may have seen is not at all certain. Hesh-o-ta-lup-ton is a possibility because of its position athwart a natural trail and its association with a relatively minor outcropping of lava.

143 Some fifty miles east of this locality, on our route to Laguna, we met *acres* of lava, and extensive fissures; but this was on the headwaters of the Rio San José, a tributary of the Rio Puerco. I never heard, however, that our animals suffered from sore feet.—Simpson's note.

144 The region surrounding Pescado (Fish) Springs was then, and remains, a Zuñi farming community. Since the troops camped here, a cluster of corrals and small stone houses, accommodating some twelve Zuñi families, has made this a year-round settlement. The Zuñi name for Pescado is Héshotatsínakwin, or Place of the Ruins of the Pictographs. Two of the ruins are found on slight elevations immediately east and west of the springs. A third pueblo ruin lies a

Two of them, on examination, I found to be of elliptical shape, and approximating a thousand feet in circuit. The buildings seem to have been chiefly built on the periphery of the ellipsis, leaving a large interior court; but their style and the details of their construction, except that they were built of stone and mud mortar, are not distinguishable in the general mass. The areas of each are now so overgrown with bushes, and so much commingled with mother earth as, except upon critical examination, to be scarcely distinguishable from natural mounds. The usual quantum of pottery lies scattered around.

The governor of Zuñi, who is again on a visit to us, informs us that the ruins I have just described, as also those seen a couple of miles back, are the remains of pueblos which his people formerly inhabited. He has brought to Colonel Washington a finished specimen of the wicker-ware which, both among the Navahos and the Zuñis, I have noticed, in the shape of large bowls and vases. This species of vegetable ware is of so closely compacted a texture as to hold water, and is superior to anything of the kind I have ever seen in the States. The Zuñis give the Coystero Indians [Coyotero Apaches] the credit of making them.

The day's march has been 13.71 miles. The route, which has been of a gradual ascent, excepting for an inconsiderable portion of it, among some basaltic rocks and at the crossing of the Rio de Zuñi—neither of these places presenting any formidable impediments—is excellent for wagons. The soil of the valley, which is of an argillo-arenaceous character, is exceedingly fertile. Scrub cedars have dotted the hills, and the artemisia the valleys.

---

short distance to the north, close to the Pescado River. Bandelier's "Documentary History of the Zuñi Tribe" includes a map indicating the name of one of Pescado's ancient pueblos as Hesh-o-ta-tzi-na. In his diary entry for September 15, Richard Kern quotes the governor of Zuñi as saying that after the ancient flood of Zuñi myth was appeased and had subsided, the Zuñi people left Toaiyalone and "removed into the valley about 13 miles east of their present situation," —in short, to the vicinity of Pescado Springs. Arriving at the springs on September 16, Kern observed that here is "where the Old Pueblo of Zuñi stands—it is nearly level with the ground." The most that should be assumed from this is that at some time in their past, after one of their numerous occupations of Toaiyalone, some of the Zuñi people moved to Pescado Springs.

We have met today, as we did yesterday, a number of Zuñi Indians carrying bags of wheat upon horses and burros to their pueblo. These people seem to have discovered the principle of industrial accumulation, and therefore of social progress, more than any Indians I have seen.

My astronomical observations place this camp in latitude 35° 5′ 12″, and longitude 108° 41′ 45″.

Bivouac, Inscription Rock, September 17—The incidents of to-day have been peculiarly interesting, as the narration of them in their natural order will show:

The troops resumed their march at 7 A.M., the course for the day being generally due east, for the first three or four miles, up the valley of the Rio de Zuñi.[145] This distance traveled, an extended and beautiful view of handsomely-rounded blue hills, or mountain peaks, presents itself to the front, low distant hills being seen on the right, and exhibiting itself a champaign country intermediate.

A couple of miles further, meeting in the road Mr. Lewis, who was waiting for me to offer his services as guide to a rock upon the face of which were, according to his repeated assertions, half an acre of inscriptions, many of them very beautiful, and upon its summit some ruins of a very extraordinary character, I at once fell in with the project, and obtained from the colonel commanding the necessary permission. Taking with me one of my assistants, Mr. R. H. Kern, ever zealous in an enterprise of this kind; the faithful Bird, an employee who had been with me ever since I left Fort Smith—Mr. Lewis being the guide—and a single pack animal loaded with a few articles of bedding, a few cooking utensils, and some provisions—we diverged from the command (see map) [page 128] with the expectation of not again meeting it until we should reach the Pueblo of Laguna, from seventy to eighty miles distant. There were many in the command inclined

---

[145] Actually, the Río Pescado. This stream and the Río Nutria to its north, both heading in the Zuni Mountains, form the headwaters of the Zuni River, joining the Zuni and taking that name in the narrow mouth of the canyon just west of Hesh-o-ta-lup-ton, referred to in note 140.

to the belief that Lewis's representations were all gammon. In regard to the *extent* of the inscriptions, I could not but believe so too; but as respects the fact of there being some tolerable basis for so grandiloquent a description, I could not, reasoning upon general principles of human nature, reject it. Mr. Lewis had been a trader among the Navahos and, according to his statement, has seen these inscriptions in his journeyings to and from their country. And now he was ready to conduct me to the spot. How could I doubt his sincerity? I could not, and my faith was rewarded by the result.[146]

Bearing off slightly to the right from the route of the troops, we traversed for eight miles a country varied, in places, by low mesas, blackened along their crests by outcrops of basalt, and on our left by fantastic white and red sandstone rocks, some of them looking like steamboats, and others presenting very much the appearance of façades of heavy Egyptian architecture. This distance traversed, we came to a quadrangular mass of sandstone rock, of a pearly whitish aspect, from two hundred to two hundred and fifty feet in height, and strikingly peculiar on account of its massive character and the Egyptian style of its natural buttresses and domes. Skirting this stupendous mass of rock, on its left or north side, for about a mile, the guide, just as we had reached its eastern terminus, was noticed to leave us and ascend a low mound or ramp at its base, the better, as it appeared, to scan the face of the rock, which he had scarcely reached before he cried out to us to come up. We immediately went up, and, sure enough, here were inscriptions, and some of them very beautiful; and, although, with those which we afterwards ex-

[146] Simpson's small party and the main command parted company in the vicinity of Ramah, the troops continuing directly toward the Zuni Mountains, Simpson following the southern course of the modern paved road to El Morro. Now a waning farming community situated in a wide green valley, Ramah was occupied by Navahos when Mormon settlers moved in to a place five miles north, about 1876, and called it Cebolla (also written Cibola, Seboyetta, and Savoia). An outbreak of smallpox drove the Mormons away in 1880, but other families of Mormons returned three years later, settling in the valley and naming it Ramah. Some fifty families remain—they, like their fathers, living in harmony with the neighboring Navahos.

amined on the south face of the rock, there could not be said to be half an acre of them, yet the hyperbole was not near as extravagant as I was prepared to find it. The fact then being certain that here were indeed inscriptions of interest, if not of value, one of them dating as far back as 1606, all of them very ancient, and several of them very deeply as well as beautifully engraven, I gave directions for a halt—Bird at once proceeding to get up a meal, and Mr. Kern and myself to the work of making facsimiles of the inscriptions.

These inscriptions are, a part of them, on the north face of the rock, and a part on the south face. Facsimiles of those on the north face, drawn to a given scale, will be found in plates 65, 66, and 67, the order of enumeration being that of their relative position from east to west, and the strength or weakness of the letters in the drawing, as well as the complexion of the rock, being an imitation of them as we found them on the rock. Facsimiles of the inscriptions on the south face will be found in plates 68, 69, 70, 71, 72, 73, and 74.

It will be noticed that the greater portion of these inscriptions are in Spanish, with some little sprinkling of what appeared to be an attempt at Latin, and the remainder in hieroglyphics, doubtless of Indian origin.

The face of the rock, wherever these inscriptions are found, is of a fair plain surface, and vertical in position. The inscriptions, in most instances, have been engraved by persons standing at the base of the rock and are, therefore, generally not higher than a man's head.

The labor of copying the inscriptions having employed us from about noon till near sunset, and there yet being more than enough to keep us at work for the balance of the day, we suspended copying the remainder till the morrow, in order that before dark we might visit the "wonderful ruins" Lewis had assured us we would find on the summit of the rock. So, taking him as our guide, we went around to the south face of the wall, along which we continued until we came to an angle, thus:

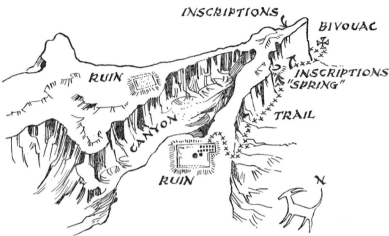

Plan of the Rock

INSCRIPTIONS

BIVOUAC

RUIN

INSCRIPTIONS "SPRING"

TRAIL

CANYON

RUIN

N

where, canopied by some magnificent rocks and shaded by a few pine trees, the whole forming an exquisite picture, we found a cool and capacious spring—an accessory not more grateful to the lover of the beautiful than refreshing to the way-worn traveler.[147] Continuing along the east face of the rear projection or spur of the rock a few yards further, we came to an accessible escarpment, up which we commenced our ascent, the guide taking off his shoes to enable him to accomplish it safely. After slipping several times, with some little apprehension of an absolute slide off, and a pause to take breath, we at last reached the summit, to be regaled with a most extensive and pleasing prospect.

On the north and east lay stretching from northwest to southeast the *Sierra de Zuñi*, richly covered with pine and cedar; to the south could be seen gracefully-swelling mounds and distant peaks, beautifully blue on account of remoteness; to the west

[147] The pool was generally believed to be a spring until, in 1942, heavy rocks fell into it from the cliffs above. On removing the rocks, it was found that the pool was actually a cistern that collected enough runoff of melting snow or rainwater to remain fresh. Immediately south of the pool, cut vertically into the cliff, are hand and toe holds used by the ancient puebloans to reach the water. In addition to this pool, the villagers must have had access to one or more springs.

appeared the horizontal outline of mesa heights, with here and there a break denoting an intervening cañon or valley; and lying between all these objects and my point of view was a circuit of prairie, beautifully tasty on account of solitary and clustered trees, or sombrously dark on account of low mesas and oblong ridges covered with cedars.

This extensive scene sufficiently scanned, we proceeded to examine the ruins which the guide, true to his word, pointed out immediately before us. These ruins present, in plan, a rectangle two hundred and six by three hundred and seven feet, the sides conforming to the four cardinal points. The apartments seem to have been chiefly upon the contour of the rectangle, the heaps of rubbish within the court indicating that here there had been some also. There appear to have been two ranges of rooms on the north side and two on the west. The other two sides are in so ruinous a condition as to make the partition walls indistinguishable. On the north side was found traceable a room seven feet four inches by eight and a half feet, and on the east side, one eight and a half by seven feet.

There was one circular estuffa apparent, thirty-one feet in diameter, just in rear of the middle of the north face. The main walls which, except for a length of about twenty feet, were indistinguishable, appear from this remnant to have been originally well laid—the facing exposing a compact tabular sandstone varying from three to eight inches in thickness, and the backing a rubble kind of masonry cemented with mud mortar. The style of the masonry, though *next*, as far as our observation has extended, to that of the pueblos of Chaco, in the beauty of its details is far inferior. Here, as usual, immense quantities of broken pottery lay scattered around, and of patterns different from any we have hitherto seen.[148] Indeed, it seems to me that to have caused so much broken pottery, there must have been, at some

[148] Simpson errs. Surface sherds found at El Morro—mainly several varieties of polychrome, a plain red, a few black-on-white, and the utility wares—for the most part are of the same types as found at Pescado Springs and the unnamed ruin visited by Simpson the previous day.

time or other, a regular sacking of the place; and this, also, may account for this singular phenomenon being a characteristic of the ancient ruins generally in this country. At all events, we see nothing of this kind around the inhabited pueblos of the present day, in which pottery is still much used; and I can see no reason why, if their inhabitants were of their own accord to desert them, they should go to work and destroy the vessels made of this kind of material.[149]

To the north and west, about three hundred yards distant, a deep cañon intervening, on the summit of the same massive rock upon which the inscriptions are found, we could see another ruined pueblo, in plan and size apparently similar to that I have just described.[150] These ruins, on account of the intervening chasm, and want of time, we were not enabled to visit.

[149] This site was partially excavated by Richard Woodbury, then with Columbia University, in 1954-56. Simpson's speculation over the great quantity of broken pottery led him to a faulty conclusion. Potsherds found at this and other sites through the Southwest were a normal accumulation of time and breakage. Known now as Atsinna, in Zuñi meaning "writing on the rock," the pueblo was occupied during the twelfth and thirteenth centuries. Why this and the neighboring pueblo were deserted is not known, although it is believed that these people moved west to join their kin in one or more of the Zuñi pueblos occupied in historic times. Simpson's measurements are very nearly accurate. The circular kiva he mentions, on excavation by Woodbury, showed all of the features found usually in Pueblo III kivas of the *anasazi*, northward through the Chaco into southwestern Colorado. Directly associated with this kiva to the northeast is a rectangular ceremonial room similar to the rectangular kivas of Zuñi and the Hopi villages, Jemez, and some of the Río Grande pueblos. About fifteen by twenty feet, the subterranean chamber has masonry pilasters in each of its four corners, narrow benches between the pilasters on the east and west sides, and a bench about five feet wide on the south side. A walled room to the north has a bench also, and possibly was a ceremonial storage room used by the clan priests. The floor of the large room is paved with flagstones; centrally located in the floor is a firepit walled with masonry.

[150] This pueblo, also rectangular in plan, is somewhat smaller than the one Simpson describes. The pueblo, like its neighbor, is oriented north to south. It was two stories high on its long north side and possibly the same height in the east and west wings. A central court or plaza was enclosed on the south side by either a tier of rooms or a wall. The pueblo is in very ruinous condition and has not been excavated. From the quantity of sherds found on refuse mounds to the south and west, it is possible that this pueblo was occupied for a shorter period of time than its neighbor.

What could have possessed the occupants of these villages to perch themselves so high up, and in such inaccessible localities, I cannot conceive unless it were, as it probably was, from motives of security and defence.

The idea has been generally entertained, and I notice Gregg gives currency to it, that a portion of the ruins of this country are "at a great distance from any water, so that the inhabitants must have entirely depended upon rain, as is the case with the *Pueblo of Acoma* at the present day."[151]

Near all the ruins I have yet seen in this country, I have most generally found water; and in those cases where there was none, the dry bed of a stream, in convenient proximity, gave sufficient evidence that even here in times past, there was a supply. Besides, there are at the present day Mexican ruins to which the inhabitants now point as having been deserted on account of the creeks near them failing. Such, for instance, is the Mexican village called *Rito* (which we subsequently passed), on the San José—its Roman Catholic church and other buildings conclusively attesting that it had been deserted not many years back.

As regards the inhabitants of Acoma at the present day relying, as Gregg states, for water upon the rains, his information must have been from report; for Abert expressly tells us the contrary. His language is (he is speaking of Acoma and its vicinage), "We had encamped by the side of some holes that the Indians had dug; these, they said, yielded a constant supply of water; and between our camp and the city there was some water that ran along the bed of a stream for a few yards, when it disappeared beneath the sand. This furnished the inhabitants with drinking water."[152] Besides, I doubt very much if in this country the water

[151] *Commerce of the Prairies*, Vol. I, p. 284.—Simpson's note. (Moorhead edition, 198.)

[152] Lt. Abert's Report on New Mexico, 1846–47, Oct. 21.—Simpson's note. Abert, of course, was correct. Rainfall in the Southwest was never sufficient to maintain life in the pueblo villages. Rainwater was used when it collected in pools among the rocks, as at Acoma and Chaco Canyon. Always, however, the main dependence was upon springs—even when some distance removed—and washes that might not run continuously. To the remarks quoted by Simpson above, Abert added (472): "I was obliged to scoop a hollow in the sand

that could be collected from rains by any artificial process would be near sufficient to answer the wants of the people. I doubt it, for the reason that the chief sources of supply to the streams appear not to be from the rains—few and scant—which fall upon the plains, but from the rains which are produced by and break upon the mountains.

But to continue my journal. The shades of evening falling upon us in our labors, we were constrained to retrace our way down to the plain; and it was not long before we were at the base of the rock, hovering over a bivouac fire, eating our suppers and talking over the events of the day—the grim visage of the stupendous mass behind us occasionally fastening our attention by the sublimity of its appearance in the dim twilight.

Twenty-eighth camp, Ojo del Gallo, September 18—The excitement of yesterday's discovery, together with rather a hard pallet and the howling of the wolves, prevented my having as comfortable a night's rest as I would have liked. Often did I gaze, in my restlessness, *au ciel*, to witness the culmination of that beautiful constellation, Orion, the precursor, at this season of the year, of the approach of day; and as often did I find myself obliged to exercise that most difficult of virtues, patience—the sure key, with the proper application of subordinate means, to success.

The dawn of the day at 3 o'clock appearing, we got up for the purpose of hastening breakfast, in order that by daylight we might be ready to continue our labors upon the inscriptions. Besides, finding that, to reach the rock yesterday, our divergence from the route of the troops had been but three miles, and being anxious to join the command tonight, in order that I might keep up the proper succession of astronomical positions (my instru-

---

before I could get my tincup full. The running [spring] water is three-fourths of a mile from the foot of the rock." A dismal chore it must have been to carry water from the springs below to Acoma's high summit. The problem was multiplied a thousand times when a Franciscan mission church was first built on the mesa top in 1629, requiring thousands of gallons of water for the adobe brick and plaster. Echos here of slave labor employed in building the temples of Egypt.

ments being with the troops), I felt desirous to hasten our work so that I might effect the object.

Our breakfast over, the day opening beautifully, and the feathered race regaling us—an unusual treat—with their gay twittering, we hastened to the work of finishing the facsimiles. These completed, and Mr. Kern having engraved as follows upon the rock: "Lt. J. H. Simpson, U.S.A., and R. H. Kern, artist, visited and copied these inscriptions, September 17, 1849," we found ourselves ready by 8 o'clock to commence our journey to overtake the command.[153]

A large number of the hieroglyphics (on the south side of the rock) and many names and dates, are evidently—from the in some cases faint, and in others interrupted or broken, appearance of the inscriptions—gone; and for this cause as well as from an occasional failure in the perfect engravement of a letter, and therefore its assimilation in appearance to others nearly resembling it in form, the facsimiles, though as a whole generally transcriptive of the letters or words intended by the inscribers, in some few instances are doubtlessly variant from the exact orthography intended, and therefore difficult to be deciphered. A *literal* rendering of them into English, so far as I have been able to have it accomplished by the conjoint assistance of Chief Justice J. Houghton, Señor Donaciano Vigil, secretary of the province, and Mr. Samuel Ellison, the official translator, will be found below. I prefer to give them literally, because it is the most faithful mode of translation; and though the sense in some

---

[153] This inscription, the best known of two made at the time, appears on the rock's north face. Three feet to the right is found another inscription: "R. H. Kern/ Aug. 29/ 1851." Nearly two years had passed when Kern, accompanying Lorenzo Sitgreaves from Zuñi to Camp Yuma, noted his second visit to El Morro. Both of these inscriptions are repeated elsewhere. On El Morro's south face, some twenty feet east of the famous 1605 Oñate inscription, and now nine feet above ground, appears this: "Lt. J H Simpson U S A/ &/ R H Kern Artist/Septem 17th & 18th/ 1849." Proceeding to the left, past the pool, one finds on the rock's northeast face: "R H Kern/ 1851." Associated with this inscription are two others: "Dr. S. W. Woodhouse/ Aug. 30th 1851," and "L. Sitgreaves/U S A/ Aug 30 1851." Woodhouse was accompanying the expedition as physician and naturalist.

instances might be given in better English, yet for the sake of accuracy, and because the meaning is apparent under a literal translation, I think it best to present them in this form, beginning with

Plate 65[154]
"Augustin de Hinojos."
"In the year 1641, Bartolome Romelo" [here words not decipherable].
"In the year 1716, upon the 26th day of August, passed by this place Don Feliz Martinez, Governor and Captain General of this kingdom, for the purpose of reducing and uniting Moqui" [a couple of words here not decipherable].
"Licentiate Chaplain Friar Antonio Camargo, Custodiari, and Ecclesiastical Judge."
"Simon de Salas."
"Antonio Nomoya."

Plate 66
"On the 28th day of September, of the year 1737, arrived at this place Batchelor [of Laws] Don Juan Ignacio de Arrasain."
"Passed by this place Diego Belasques."
"On the 28th day of September, of the year 1737, arrived at this place the Illustrious Doctor Don Martin De Liza Cochea, Bishop of Durango, and on the 29th left for Zuñi."[155]
"Joseph Dominguez passed by this place in October, and

[154] In the years since Donaciano Vigil and others assisted Simpson in deciphering Kern's facsimiles, a number of authorities through combined effort have provided more exact readings. The principal inscription of this group now translates as follows: "Year of 1716 on the 26th of August passed by here Don Feliz Martinez, Governor and Captain General of this realm to the reduction and conquest of the Moqui and [in his company?] the Reverend Father Friar Antonio Camargo, Custodian and ecclesiastical judge." Martinez, incidentally, failed in his purpose. After about two months in the Hopi villages, during which his time was spent in quarreling, Martinez returned to Santa Fe. The words in brackets are Simpson's comments.

[155] Vigil's version is close to the modern translation: "28th day of September of 1737, arrived here the illustrious Señor Doctor Don Martin de Elizacochea, Bishop of Durango [Mexico], and on the 29th day went on to Zuñi."

others September 28, with much caution and some apprehension."

"Juan de San Esteban."

"Puilancies."

"The Father Ezquerr."

"Antonio B——," [this name not decipherable].

[Here a word or two not decipherable]. "Don Francisco [a word or two not decipherable] for the impossibility—*Jene*—there to subject; his arm undoubted, and his valor, with the wagons of our Lord the King, a thing which he alone did—*E fecio de Abtosio G*—six hundred and twenty-nine [probably intended for 1629]. *Quesby Eu Acuni Pase y la Felleue.*"

Plate 67

"Juan Garcia de la Revâs, Chief Alcalde, and the first elected of the town of Santa Fe, in the year 1716, on the 26th of August. By the hand of Bartolo Fernandez Moro."

"Augustin de Minojoa."

"Juan Gonzalos, year 1629."

[The characters in the double rectangle seem to be literally a sign *manual*, and may possibly be symbolical of Francisco Manuel, though the double thumb would appear to indicate something more.]

"On the 14th day of July, of the year 1736, passed by this place General Juan Paez Hurtador, Inspector. And in his company Corporal Joseph Armenta, Antonio Sandobal Martines, F. Guapo, Alonzo Barela, Marcus Duran, Francisco Barela, Louis Pacheco, Antonio de Salas, Roque Gomas."

"Vicente de Senorgorta and [name not decipherable] fought on account of these questions," [the remainder not intelligible, except that *lecor*—probably intended for *licor*, liquor—seems to have had something to do with the quarrel].

"Joseph Ramos."

"Diego Nunez Bellido."

"Diego."

"Friar Zapata."

"Bartolome Narrso, Governor and Captain General of the Provinces of New Mexico, for our Lord the King, passed by this place, on his return from the Pueblo of Zuñi, on the 29th of July, of the year 1620, and put them in peace, at their petition, asking the favor to become subjects of his majesty, and anew they gave obedience; all of which they did with free consent, knowing it prudent, as well as very christian [a word or two effaced] to so distinguished and gallant a soldier, indomitable and famed; we love [the remainder effaced].

Plate 68

"Antonio Gon Salez, in the year 1667. [Some characters not decipherable]. Country of Mexico, in the year 1632, folio [some characters not intelligible] Bengoso, by order of Father Liebado Lugan."

Plate 69[156]

"Passed by this place with despatch [a word or two not decipherable] 16th day of April, 1606."

"Cayado, 1727."

"I. Aparela, 1619." [Hieroglyphics not decipherable.]

Plate 70[157]

"Passed by this place Sergeant Major and Captain Juan Archutela, and the traveller Diego Martin Barba and Second Lieutenant Juan Ynes Josano, in the year 1636." [Hieroglyphics not decipherable.]

[156] This, the oldest and most famous inscription, was made by one of Oñate's men on the Governor General's return in 1605 from an expedition, begun the year before, to the Gulf of California (Oñate's "Sea of the South.") In Kern's copy, Oñate's name somehow was overlooked and the date was incorrectly transcribed as 1606. The accepted translation now is: "Passed by here the Governor don Juan de Oñate from the discovery of the Sea of the South on the 16th of April 1605." The two names associated with the Oñate inscription are correctly: "Casados 1727" and "Juan [Jū] Barela." The marks appended to the last name, mistaken by Kern for the date 1619, actually form the Barela paraph, or family seal.

[157] The modern translation: "We passed by here the Sergeant Major and Captain Juan de Archuleta and Adjutant Diego Martin Barba and Ensign [or second lieutenant] Agustin de Ynojos the year of 1636."

Plate 71

"Here served General Don Diego de Bargas, to conquer to Santa Fe, for the royal crown, New Mexico, by his own cost, in the year 1692."[158]

"By this place passed Second Lieutenant Joseph de Payba Basconzelos, in the year in which the council of the kingdom bore the cost, on the 18th of February, in the year 1726."

Plate 72

"In the year 1696 passed D. M." [Hieroglyphics not decipherable.]

Plate 73

"P. Joseph de la Candelaria."

"O. R., March 19, 1836." [These are the only initials with an English date before Mr. Kern engraved ours. The hieroglyphics not decipherable.]

Plate 74

"Pero Vacu [possibly intended for *vaca*—cow] ye Jarde."

"Alma."

"Leo."

"Captain Jude Vubarri, in the year of our Lord 1," [probably meaning 1701. The hieroglyphics, excepting what appears to designate a buffalo, not decipherable.]

The translations of the several inscriptions, so far as it has been possible to have them effected, having now been given, I introduce in this connexion a letter from the secretary of the province (received since the expedition) by which it will be perceived that two of the persons whose names are inscribed—

---

[158] A more exact translation: "Here was the General Don Diego de Vargas, who conquered for our Holy Faith, and for the Royal Crown, all of New Mexico at his own expense, year of 1692." This inscription might rank in interest with that of Oñate for the vain words mark de Vargas' passage to or return from Zuñi. Since the Pueblo Revolt of 1680, the Zuñis had been living on the summit of Toaiyalone, in a state of war with the Spanish authorities. On this journey de Vargas, successfully persuaded the Zuñis to leave Corn Mesa and live in harmony with the Spanish crown and church.

General Don Diego de Bargas, and General Juan Paez Hurtador —have been governors of New Mexico. This letter is also interesting on account of the other historical facts which it divulges. For its translation I am indebted to Chief Justice Houghton:

Santa Fe, October 19, 1849

Sir: The engravings which are sculptured on the rock of Fish spring, near the Pueblo of Zuñi, copies of which you have taken, were made in the epochs to which they refer. I have an indistinct idea of their existence; but although I have passed the place some three times, I never availed myself of the opportunity to observe them. The other signs or characters noticed are traditional remembrances, by means of which the Indians transmit historical accounts of all their remarkable successes. To discover these sets by themselves is very difficult. Some of the Indians make trifling indications which divulge, with a great deal of reserve, something of the history, to persons in whom they have entire confidence.

The people who inhabited this country before its discovery by the Spaniards were superstitious and worshipped the sun.

I would be glad to relate to you, with exactness, events which are passed; but I am deprived of this satisfaction from the want of certain information in regard to the particulars, because some of them occurred a very few years after the conquest made by Juan de Oñate, in the year 1595 [1598], and all records preceding the year 1680 are lost, as the Indians burnt the archives in their insurrection against the conquerors who then occupied the country.

In 1681, Governor Antonio de Otermin received orders from the viceroy to return and conquer. He made his entrance to the Pueblo of Cochiti, encountered resistance and, on account of the small force he brought, retired to El Paso in the same year [actually, 1682]. Gerbaceo de Cruzat y Gongora succeeded him in command [and] also remained established at El Paso.

In the following year, Cruzat made an expedition against New Mexico, took possession of the capital, and extended his conquests a little more effectually, until the following year when, it being impossible for him to sustain himself longer, he returned to El Paso.

In the year 1693, Curro Diego de Bargas Zapata penetrated as far as the Pueblo of Zuñi and, without proceeding further, returned to El Paso.[159] In the year 1695, he obtained the entire pacification of the country.

There were afterwards a succession of governors, among whom are numbered Feliz Martinez, Juan Paez Hurtador, and many others, of whom can be produced exact information by referring to the time of the administration of each, according to the registry in the ancient archives of the government. The short time before your departure does not afford the necessary opportunity to register and give to you an historical relation of these events. This account, therefore, should not be regarded by you as one which should direct your idea entirely, for my limited capacity does not permit me to search into all the particulars necessary; but it may serve you as a guide to direct the history, the events being marked in chronological order.

Should these remarks prove useful to you, and I have a facility of access to the archives, as I have now, I will with pleasure undertake the task of making the relation, and will despatch it to the point you may direct me.

With nothing more, I am, señor, your obedient servant,

DONACIANO VIGIL

Lieut. J. H. Simpson,
Topographical Corps, U.S.A.

But to proceed with our journey. Lewis thinks the road to Laguna by the way of the *Moro* [El Morro], or Inscription Rock, and the Pueblo of Acoma, is better for wagons than that which the troops have taken. He says it has only one bad place, and that can be avoided by making a detour of two miles. Water and grass, according to his representations, are ample along it. Carravahal, however (and a most excellent guide he has proved himself to be), thinks the other the best and, according to the map, it would appear to be quite as direct.

As has been already remarked, by 8 o'clock A.M. we were ready to commence our journey—it being our intention to join the main command, if possible, before night. For the first three

[159] According to the extract from De Bargas's journal already given in a note under the head of the twenty-fifth camp, his conquest of Zuñi bears date Nov. 11, 1692, and in this year corresponds with that inscribed on the rock.— Simpson's note.

miles our route lay east of north when, getting into the road taken by the troops, we immediately turned to the right upon it—our course thence for the day being nearly due east. This road, we find, gives indications of having been considerably more traveled than that passing by the Inscription Rock.[160] A mile and a half more traversed, over a heavy sandy soil, upon which I noticed the flax growing in its wild state, we found ourselves commencing the ascent of the Sierra de Zuñi. This ascent, for a few miles, is quite gradual, the road leading up a beautiful narrow valley, clothed with a rich black loamy soil, and interspersed with large pines. Six and a half miles on the route, I noticed some massive limestone, in large quantities, cropping out from either side of the valley. Some of it is a coarse-grained marble. Two miles further, the ascent becomes quite steep and difficult on account of loose rocks. The route, however, continues practicable for wagons, and no doubt an easier grade could be found, possibly to the right.

A mile further traversed, we found ourselves on the summit of the pass of the *sierra*, from which, bearing north of east, some thirty miles off, we caught sight, for the first time, of one of the finest mountain peaks I have seen in this country. This peak I have, in honor of the President of the United States, called *Mount Taylor*. Erecting itself high above the plain below, an object of vision at a remote distance, standing within the domain which has been so recently the theater of his sagacity and prowess, it exists, not inappropriately, an ever-enduring monument to his patriotism and integrity.[161]

Descending the eastern slope of the Sierra de Zuñi, after a ride of two miles, we reached the *Ojo de Gallinas*, where the still smoking embers of recent fires, in connexion with their relative

[160] Simpson picked up the command's trail in the vicinity of present Tinaja. His route then took him slightly north of the present Paxton Springs Ranch and over the Oso Ridge to his downward approach to the Canyon del Gallo.

[161] Since my return to Santa Fe, I find it can be seen from Fort Marcy and other surrounding heights, the air-line distance being as great as one hundred miles.—Simpson's note.

positions, showed very plainly the *locale* of the last night's encampment of the troops. Finding some good water and grass here, and being considerably fatigued, we gladly halted for an hour to take a lunch and let our animals graze. Resuming our journey, we passed two miles of very hilly pine-barren country—a mile further bringing us to a locality where, immediately on the right of the road, for the first time, some unseemly piles of blackened scoriaceous volcanic rocks make their appearance. Three miles further, in a kind of basin, we met another series of piles of lava debris, covering an area of at least one hundred acres. These piles look like so many irregular heaps of stone coal. A mile further brought us to the entrance of the *Cañon de Gallo,* down which the route continued its course. This cañon, which is a rather narrow one and walled on either side by sandstone rocks some three hundred feet high, is quite interesting, both as an object of vision and because of the blackened volcanic scoriaceous rocks which crop out from its bottom. Did this cañon exist before the development of these volcanic rocks, or was it the result of that development? Is it not possible that the incalescent mass below and the gases generated by the heat, in connexion with the ruptures of the superincumbent sedimentary strata which such a condition of things would be like to produce—I say, is it not possible that such a combination of circumstances could have given rise first to the cañon, and then to the volcanic matter cropping from its bottom?

This cañon is quite rapid in the descent of its bottom—more so than any we have seen. Four miles from its entrance, it is almost choked up with large masses of rock, threading which, however, I subsequently learned, the artillery found little or no difficulty. Three miles further, we debouched from the cañon into the broad, beautiful, and fertile valley of the *Ojo de Gallo.* Bearing thence gradually to the right, four miles further brought us, much to our gratification, just after dark, to the camp of the troops, where we found them all rejoicing in the possession of a fine spring, abundant pasture, and the feelings consequent upon the exhilirating effect of a beautiful and far-extended expanse.[162]

We noticed along the road several rattlesnakes which the troops had killed. One of them was very large.

Our day's travel I estimate at thirty-two miles. The march of the troops yesterday, I learn, was 27.14 miles; today, 18.49 miles. The latitude of this camp, by observation, is 35° 5' 17".

Twenty-ninth camp, near Pueblo of Laguna, September 19— The troops decamped at 8 A.M., the course, as yesterday, continuing for the day nearly due east. The first six miles was directly across the valley of the Gallo, and then down the valley of the *Rio de San José.* The valley of the Gallo is one of the richest I have seen, its soil being a rich black loam. A great deal of

---

[162] The Ojo del Gallo (Rooster Springs), where the troops were camped, was located near the head of the valley of the Gallo and immediately north of the present Spanish-American settlement of San Rafael. The spring in recent years has been dry due to a lowering of the water table by driven wells in the vicinity of Grants. Colonel Washington's command rested a little more than a mile northwest of the site of Old Fort Wingate, whose location was chosen October 22, 1862, on the orders of Brigadier General James H. Carleton, commanding the Department of New Mexico. The adobe and stockade fort was established on this eastern approach to the Wingate Valley to offer protection against the raiding Navahos. The first garrison, composed of Companies B, C, E, and F of the First New Mexico Volunteers, commanded by Lieutenant Colonel Francisco Chavez, arrived in the valley in mid-November and went into winter camp while constructing the fort. According to a contemporary account, the fort was "surrounded by a defensive stockade whose north and west sides are flanked by the enclosure containing the magazine, and the south and east sides by the corral and stables." Specifications for materials included a stockade 4,340 feet long and 8 feet high, 9,317 feet of adobe walls 13 feet high and 2 feet thick, 1,800 feet of adobe walls 8 feet high and 1 foot thick, 1,500 vigas 25 feet long for supporting earth roofs, and 1,000,000 feet of lumber. (National Archives, War Records Division, Fort Wingate File 1251.) During the roundup of the Navaho tribe, Old Fort Wingate was a receiving station on the Navahos' "long march" to Bosque Redondo. Upon the signing of the 1868 Navaho treaty, which placed the tribe permanently on its own reservation, the fort was abandoned and a new Fort Wingate was established July 22, 1868, at Bear Springs (Ojo del Oso). No trace of Old Fort Wingate remains. The ground on which the fort stood crumbling was homesteaded by Manuel Garcia, who sold the property about 1900 to the family of Elfego E. Barela, the present owner. Barela said in 1961 that his father many years before had removed the last of the fort's standing walls while leveling and plowing his fields for crops.

scoriaceous matter, in black angular fragments, lies scattered over the surface of this valley in piles and ridges; and it is doubtless owing to this source that its soil is so fertile; for wherever this igneous product is observable, there have I noticed the soil in proximity to it to be of this character.

Just before entering the valley of the San José, about seven miles from our morning's camp, are hundreds of acres of volcanic rock, a great deal of it exhibiting, with marked distinctness, the undulations of the wave in its oscillatory motion. I endeavored, by the curvature of these waves, to find by a normal or rather an applicable radius, the crater or source of the outflow, but it resulted in nothing satisfactory.[163] I ascended an adjoining hill to overlook the whole field, and found the lava to exist in ridges ranging generally north and south.

This seems to point to a swelling or intumescence of the fluid mass, longitudinally—a partial overflow—and a fixedness of condition, caused by refrigeration, before it could spread laterally to any considerable extent, and subsequently a tumbling in at the sides, from disintegrating causes, and the want of subjacent support.

Near this very large field of volcanic matter the road takes up a long, steep, rocky hill—two miles further bringing us again to the valley of the San José. This hill could probably be avoided by not leaving the valley of the San José at all. Ten miles from our last camp, for about a quarter of a mile, we traversed a sliding rocky hill, where a few picks, crowbars, and spades could, with no great labor, in a short time make it practicable for wagons.

[163] His geological survey of the region in the early 1880's convinced Captain Clarence E. Dutton that the crater of Mount Tayler—as generally supposed—was not the source of the malpais beds which Simpson describes and which extend far to the south and east through the San José Valley to Cubero. Instead, Dutton writes (182) that the malpais beds of the valley regions were caused by volcanic vents in the plain, the basaltic plug of Cabezon and other similar formations to the north by eruptions of Mount Taylor's crater. "We have in this region, therefore, eruptions of two distinct ages: those which built Mount Taylor and the lava caps of the mesas, and those which flooded the valley of the San Jose. The former were probably of the Middle Tertiary age (Miocene?), while the latter belong to modern times."

Along this portion of the route a dense growth of bushes, inter-
twined with vines bearing a most delicious grape—in size that
of our winter grape—skirts the stream, and cheered us with its
luxuriance. The stream here also came tumbling down in a
small but beautiful cascade, the din of its waters not being more
delightful to the ear than its appearance was to the sight. A
mile further, the volcanic rocks which, as far down as this point,
have lain along the valley in scattered oblong heaps, terminate.
About a mile from this, we crossed the San José, at this point a
clear stream fifteen feet wide and one deep, running swiftly over
a gravelly bottom. Willows, I noticed, lined the stream.

The valley thus far has been bounded on its left or north side
by mesas of a sedimentary character, overlaid by basaltic trap;
on the right, or south side, by sedimentary rocks, the superior
formation of which is sandstone.

Three miles from our last crossing of the San José, we crossed
it again—the valley from this point gradually unfolding itself
more uninterruptedly and continuing so down to Laguna, a distance of fourteen miles, within two miles of which we are encamped.[164] All along the valley, for this distance, the land is

164 A wash drawing of Laguna Pueblo by Richard Kern is in the collection of
the Peabody Museum at Harvard. The view is from the south side of the San
José River, looking north across the stream to the steep, rocky hill, across the
upper slopes and summit of which spread the adobe and stone dwellings of the
pueblo. Hodge says that the native name for the Keresan pueblo is Ka-waik',
while Van Valkenburgh notes that the Navahos call the Lagunas To'lan'i', or
Much Water People. In tracing the pueblo's history, Van Valkenburgh adds:
"Laguna, properly Laguna de San José, was established near 1697 on the Rio
San José (then called the Rio Cubero) by rebel Keres Indians, the greater number from the Pueblos of Cochiti, Zia, and possibly Acoma, who fled the wrath
of the Spaniards after the Rebellion of 1680. In the Hodge translation of the
Benevides Memorial presented at the court of King Carlos of Spain in 1630, we
find the footnote: 'It was visited by Governor Don Pedro Rodríguez [Cubero]
on July 4, 1699, when the natives of the new settlement declared their allegiance
and the town was named San José de Laguna, from a lagoon that formerly existed
west of the pueblo, and by that name it has ever since been known.' In the early
1870's Laguna was divided over religious quarrels. The native hierarchy crumbled,
resulting in two factions, the pro-American progressives and the anti-American
conservatives. The conservatives first moved to the town of Mesita. Some went
to Isleta, staying there instead of proceeding to Sandia Pueblo as they original-

cultivated in corn and melons, the luxuriance of their growth attesting the good quality of the soil. I also noticed at different points a number of circular places upon the ground where wheat had been trodden out by horses. This is the usual mode in this country of separating it from the husk. The cultivators of the soil are Pueblo Indians and belong to the villages of *Laguna* and *Acoma*. They were very liberal to us in their donations of musk-melons, of which they seem to have a great abundance. I notice that, to preserve them for winter, they peel them, take out the seeds, and then hang them in the sun to dry. A dry cedar tree covered with them, for this purpose, presented a very singular appearance.

Within about a couple of miles, the San José expands into a small lake, which is the resort of large flocks of cranes.

This day's march, 28.93 miles, has been the most fatiguing one we have had—the artillery not getting in, on account of the horses giving out, until after dark. The regular infantry, whether the march is short or long, uniformly preserve the same compact form and rate of travel and, in this respect, are superior to any troops I have ever served with.

The soil along the route has been arenaceous, and a great deal of it good. No *sylva* to speak of, except near the head of the San José, has been seen in the valley, though scrub cedar has dotted the heights. Bunch and gramma grasses have been seen in patches along the way. The cactus has been quite common.

A flock of two thousand head of sheep was seen by us before reaching camp.

This camp, which observation places in latitude 35° 0′ 49″, has all the requisites of wood, water, and grass.

The alcalde of the Pueblo of Laguna called to pay his respects to Governor Washington this evening, and a very respectable

ly planned. . . . Old Laguna became rapidly depopulated and the former farming communities of Casa Blanca (Seama), Encinal, Paraje, Paquate [or Pojuate, Pajuate, Paguate], and Tsisma became permanent villages." Calhoun reported that the viameter distance from Laguna to Albuquerque was 46.84 miles—almost the same as today by Highway 66.

man he appears to be. He is more at home in American garb than was the alcalde of Zuñi.

Thirtieth camp, September 20—The alcalde of Laguna was again in our camp this morning. He represents to Governor Washington that some persons belonging to the party of California emigrants who passed through his village two or three weeks since, on their way west, tied and forced off one of his people to Zuñi, against his will, and gave him no compensation; that they drove off eight mules belonging to his people, and even tied the governor, because he would not do an impossibility which they wished to exact of him.[165] He also represented that some Mexicans were endeavoring to get from him a pistol which an emigrant had given him in remuneration for his care of him during his illness. Governor Washington told him that he and his people should defend their property, if necessary, even to the taking of life; and that no matter how many were sacrificed in this way, the government would sustain them in it; that this was a rule of the government under which he was now living. He also gave him a paper, calling on all persons to respect the rights of his people.

This morning I preceded the troops a short while for the purpose of visiting the Pueblo of Laguna. The houses of this pueblo, I find, are built like the others—terrace fashion, each story forming by its roof a platform or sill for entrance to that above, and the ascent from story to story—of which there are, in some instances, as many as three—being by ladders upon the outside.

---

[165] Calhoun reported (*Official Correspondence*) that " . . . we encamped in the Valley of Laguna . . . within view of the Pueblo of that name, containing some 400 inhabitants. The outrages committed against these Indians by emigrants to California, *and others,* are as frequent and as flagrant as those mentioned of Zunia. Indeed the last outrage was of an infinitely more aggravated character. Near the hour of 12. m. the day not remembered, the Valley was entered and sheep and other things demanded, to which the Governor of the Village replied, no sheep could be furnished at the hour, as their flocks were regularly, every morning, sent off that they might graze during the day. The emigrants, if such they were, assuming official importance, in their anger, threatened to lynch the Alcalde, tied the Governor and in that condition carried him from his home, Laguna, to Zunia the next Pueblo west."

They are built of stone roughly laid in mortar and, on account of the color of the mortar, with which they are also faced, they present a dirty yellowish clay aspect.[166] They have windows in the basement as well as upper stories; selenite, as usual, answers the purpose of window-lights. The pueblo has one Roman Catholic edifice which, on account of the key not being immediately available, I did not enter.[167] I noticed in its belfry a couple of bells, and on its roof a sort of dial—probably a mock one. Corn in the shuck, after having been boiled, as also strings of red pepper, could be seen hanging up in front of nearly every house to dry. Indeed, the evidences are that these people are quite industrious and thrifty. Their cattle—of which, probably on account of the good pasturage in the vicinity, they seem to have more than any other pueblo—look fine; and their sheep and goat

[166] The idea which has been entertained that this pueblo is situated on a rocky promontory, *inaccessible* to a savage foe, is incorrect, as wagons find no difficulty in getting up to and passing directly through the town. Equally incorrect is the idea that the towns of Pojuate, Cebolleta, Covero, and Moquino are made up of houses *four stories* high, built upon *inaccessible* rocky heights. I have, since the Navaho expedition, made a military reconnaissance of the country in which these towns are situated, and therefore speak from personal observation. It is also a mistake to regard the three last-mentioned towns as Indian pueblos; they are *ordinary* Mexican villages.—Simpson's note.

All of these villages are situated in either the southeast plain or the foothills of Mount Taylor. Paguate, the first of these, was a Laguna farming center that took on permanent status with the addition of dissident conservatives from Laguna Pueblo. Moquino, or Mokino, was a Mexican hamlet a mile and a half north of Paguate, closely situated next to Cebolletita—chosen as a site for a military outpost that served, before Old Fort Wingate, to discourage Navaho raiding parties. Cebolleta, a few miles farther to the north, and Cubero (Covero) in San José Valley, were once notorious as hangouts for Mexican traders dealing in slaves, whisky, and guns. These villages and a fifth Mexican hamlet called Chupidero, below Paguate, were situated on the old Indian trail running northeastward to Cabezon Peak and Jemez Pueblo. They formed also the stamping ground of Colonel Washington's guide Sandoval and his renegade Navahos.

[167] Stanley Stubbs (83–86) explains that " . . . the visual impression of terraced houses is due to their being built up along the rather steep slope of the hill. Photographs taken in 1887 show that there were three-story houses around the plaza. . . . The oldest part of the town is that immediately surrounding the plaza and the section just to the south. The church, built in 1700, is outside the main area"—on the pueblo's high western edge.

folds—which, as usual, encroach upon the circuit of the towns, much to the annoyance of both sight and smell—show also that they are well supplied with this species of stock. I noticed also about the place a number of carts, of the ordinary lumbering Mexican make. The population of the town is probably about eight hundred.[168]

A large portion of the inhabitants are at this time away, gathering *piñones,* an edible fruit of the piñon, the common scrub pine of the country. The dress of these people is like that of the other Pueblo Indians—the women, as usual, having the calves of their legs wrapped or stuffed in such a manner as to give a swelled or dropsical appearance. They, like the Zuñis, regard us with considerable reserve; but how could it be otherwise, when they have been so shamefully treated as they have been recently by persons bearing the name of Americans, like ourselves? Common prudence certainly dictates a proper reserve until they can learn by experience that we are not extortioners like some of our fore-runners; and this they are beginning to learn, for the longer we were among them the more frank and liberal they became.

The troops passing through the pueblo about 11 o'clock, I left the place to accompany them. The course today is south and east and, as yesterday, the road runs along—though not so near— the San José, which it crosses at Laguna. Just as I got out of town, observing a Mexican packer appropriating to himself a watermelon, right in the face of an old woman who was guarding the patch, in my indignation I rushed upon him full tilt, and the consequence was an instantaneous disgorgement. The many signs which the old woman made to express her gratitude amply testified how deeply she felt the slight act of humanity.

Two miles from Laguna, we descended a rocky shelving-place, to get into the valley of the San José. Wagons will find no insuperable difficulty here. This hill descended, and some basaltic

---

[168] Simpson's estimate is more trustworthy than Calhoun's figure of 400. Van Valkenburgh says that the population in 1939 was about 500—long after the departure of the dissident conservatives. Stubbs (83) gives Laguna a population of 2,894 in 1950, this including the newer farming settlements with the old pueblo.

trap passed, lying in a short cañon through which the road runs, the Rio de San José is again crossed—the water, which heretofore has been quite clear, now becoming of a clay color. The river at this point is about twenty feet wide, one deep, and has a muddy bottom. The San José crossed, some old ruins appear, perched upon a mesa some one hundred and thirty feet high, immediately on your right. To clamber up to them, I had no little difficulty; and on reaching them, I found they scarcely compensated me for the exertion. They consisted of a few old stone and mortar structures and some stone corrals, the latter showing signs of having been recently used as sheep-pens. What a barbarous state of things these ruins, which are occasionally seen on almost inaccessible heights, show to have once existed; and how much more glorious their condition now, when the inhabitants can live upon the plains below in comparative ease and quiet, convenient to their fields, water, and stock!

Shortly after passing the ruins, basaltic trap again appears in the valley; and on the left, immediately by the road, gypsum crops out from overlying sandstone. Eight miles from Laguna, an extensive view unfolded itself to our front, of distant blue mountains, mesa heights, tableau and conical mounds—a broad expanse of green valley intervening. Just beyond this point appears, on your left, an almost perfect natural facsimile of a house, with its chimney-top. About a mile further, to our right, on the far side of the Rio San José, could be seen the remains of a Mexican village called Rito, which is represented, and no doubt truthfully to have been deserted on account of the water of the San José failing at this point.[169] This is the village before referred to as illustrating the fact that at the present day, as in more remote periods, towns are deserted on account of the water near them giving out. (*Ante,* September 17.) A few miles beyond this spot, the colonel commanding noticing a very large herd of sheep moving very hastily away from the command as if all were

[169] Deserted in 1849, El Rito was later occupied again as a Mexican farming community, and a few dwellings remain there today. The buildings cluster near the north bank of the San José River.

not right, I rode off to see how the matter stood. I soon discovered, however, that the flock was under Mexican and not Navaho control, and, from my conversation with the *pastor,* became assured that our apprehensions were groundless. It was beautiful to see the young shepherd carrying in his bosom a little lamb; and it at once suggested to me the force and appropriateness of the sentiment to be found in Isaiah (chapter 40, verse 11), expressive of the care of the Saviour for the tender ones of his flock: "He shall feed his flock like a shepherd; he shall gather the lambs with his arm, and carry them in his bosom."

About fifteen miles from Laguna, it being represented by Carravahal that we could get water in the San José, about a mile and a half to the right, we turned off the beaten track to encamp upon the stream. The water of this stream at this point is scarcely an inch in depth and of a bright red color. Its constancy cannot be depended upon. Good bunch grass is found in the vicinity, and wood about half a mile off.

The road today has been generally quite good. Gypsum crops out on the left all along the way for the last six miles. The soil has been argillaceous and, in spots of limited extent, looks as if it might produce pretty well. The *sylva* has been the dwarf cedar, sparsely scattered.

The Mexican mounted militia were discharged this evening, the colonel commanding tendering them his thanks for their services, and strongly reprobating the conduct of those who had deserted the command and whom, he hoped, they would on their return to their homes, hold up to the just ignominy which they deserved.

Thirty-first camp, Atrisco, opposite Albuquerque, September 21—The wolves last night in the vicinity of our camp were more uproarious than usual.

The troops resumed the march at 7 A.M., the course for the day being about north of east. The country today has been generally rolling in the direction of our progress—for the first six or seven miles, mesa heights, with intervening areas of prairie land, being seen on our left. Soon after leaving camp, we could see ahead of us the serrated mountains of the Rio Grande stretching from north to south, looking blue and beautiful, and further to the south a couple of twin peaks lifting themselves high and conspicuously. Between four and five miles on our route, the highest points of the Santa Fe [Sangre de Cristo] Mountains showed themselves for the first time, bearing northeast, the prospect suggesting the pleasing thought that our labors would soon terminate. Eight miles further brought us to the Rio Puerco [of the East], in the bed of which not a drop of water could be seen. The broad bed of this so-called river is about one hundred feet across, the narrower about twenty feet.[170] A few cottonwood trees skirt the banks. Between three and four miles beyond the Puerco, earthy limestone crops out from the soil. Proceeding a few hundred yards further, we reached the summit of a swell of land whence could be seen the broad valley of the Rio Grande, the mountains just back of Albuquerque now showing themselves in all the magnificence of their proportions. Shortly after, much to our relief we met a wagon loaded with barrels of water which had been sent out by Major Howe, from Albuquerque, agreeably to the instructions of the colonel commanding, forwarded by express.[171] The men were exceedingly thirsty, and drank correspondingly.

When within seven miles of the Rio Grande, we caught, much to our delight, the first sight of its glimmering waters. A mile further, we fell in with a couple more of wagons from Albuquerque, loaded with water and forage for the troops. The river, however, being but five or six miles ahead, the order was given to continue forward. Two miles more brought us to where we could see the town of Albuquerque quartering on our left; houses could also

170 Again, because Simpson mentions no difficulty in crossing, as he was careful to do when the artillery had trouble, one assumes that the two channels of the Puerco of the East were close to the surface of the plain. The channels now are forty feet or more in depth.

171 Major Marshall Saxe Howe, Second Dragoons, commanding the military post at Albuquerque. The barrels of water that brought such relief to the thirsty men would have been filled from the muddy Río Grande, the jogging of transportation roiling the silt and making the water tan and gritty.

be seen lying scattered for miles up and down the river, the cottonwood very sparsely dotting its banks. Just at dusk, we were winding our way through the little village of *Atrisco*, situated on the Rio Grande opposite Albuquerque—our camp for the night being to the north of the town, in the midst of a fine plot of pasturage, convenient to the river.[172]

The soil today has been alternately argillaceous and arenaceous. The face of the country presented one expanse of barren waste, thinly sprinkled with dwarf cedar. The last half of the road was, a good portion of it, very heavy on account of sand, and in places quite hilly. The day's march has been 28.33 miles.

We met on the road today three Mexican men on horseback, two of them each with a woman behind him, and the third with a very pretty child in his arms. This is a common mode of traveling among them—the woman, however, most generally sitting in front. These women had their faces plastered with a sort of whitewash, also a very common fashion—the object being, as I am told, to protect them from the weather. Not unfrequently they are covered with a red pigment—but for what purpose, unless for the same reason the whitewash is used, I cannot divine. The fact, however, of their more frequently putting it on in blotches, would seem to point to some other object. But, whatever be the purpose, they in both instances give to the face a frightful and disgusting appearance.

Sad news has reached us tonight. The mail from the States, for which we all have been looking with so much anxiety, is reported to have been cut off by the Navahos, on its way out to us, at *Chelly*. This is a serious disappointment to us all.

Algadones, September 22—The expedition, in its *integrity*, terminated at Atrisco. The different commands, artillery and infantry, are to march independently, each under the head of their respective chiefs, to Santa Fe as soon as practicable. Colonel

---

[172] Atrisco is figured on the E. M. Kern map accompanying Simpson's report and also on the Parke-Kern map of 1851, as well as the Whipple map of 1853–58 and the Anderson map of 1864, but thereafter—so far as cartographers and historians are concerned—drops from sight. Evidently a Mexican farming community in 1849, it has since been absorbed within the limits of Albuquerque.

Washington and staff crossed over to Albuquerque this morning at the ford. The river at this point is probably about three hundred yards wide, the stream rapid, its depth four feet, and its bottom of a somewhat quicksand character. During the higher stages of the water, the river is too deep to be forded; but, though this is the case at the several fords along its course, boats seem never to be resorted to by the Mexicans. Indeed, I have not seen a single one since I have been in the country.

Albuquerque, for a Mexican town, is tolerably well built.[173] Its buildings, like all I have seen inhabited by Mexicans, are of a rigid parallelopipedon shape, constructed of adobes, and arranged generally on the four sides of a rectangle, thus creating an interior court (patio) upon which nearly every one of the apartments opens. There is generally but one exterior or street

[173] Albuquerque was the third villa (Hacienda de Mejía) established after the Spanish conquest of New Mexico, but did not become a town until many years later. Ranches and haciendas of the vicinity were destroyed during the Pueblo Revolt, and the valley remained unoccupied by white settlers until after the reconquest of New Mexico by de Vargas in 1692–93. Adobe dwellings near the river formed the nucleus of a town established in 1706 by Governor Don Francisco Cuervo y Valdés, who increased the size of the village by moving some thirty families to this place from Bernalillo, about eighteen miles upstream. The governor honored his patron saint, Francisco Xavier, and the Duke of Alburquerque, then viceroy of New Spain, by naming the town San Franscio de Alburquerque. Subsequently the name was changed to San Felipe de Alburquerque, honoring King Philip V of Spain, and some time after the American occupation in 1846 the first *r* was omitted from the last name. In the same year of the town's founding, the Church of San Felipe de Neri was built on the north side of the town's plaza. Bells in the tower of this church no doubt were heard by the troops in Colonel Washington's command. Old Albuquerque was frequently subjected to Navaho raids. In 1779, according to Max Moorhead (*New Mexico's Royal Road*, 25–26), the town "was reorganized so that the public buildings enclosed a regular square for better defense." Gregg makes no descriptive reference to Albuquerque, which may indicate how far overshadowed it was in that time by Santa Fe. Hughes, Doniphan's biographer, in his diary entries for September 4–5, 1846, writes (231) that "Albuquerque stretches about 7 or 8 miles up & down the River" and the town "has about 800 inhabitants [and] takes its name from the apricot groves in its vicinity, this fruit being called by the Mexicans, Albuquerque." In estimating the spread of the town, with its outlying farms, and its population, Hughes probably was nearly right. His observations in this case were firsthand, made while his company of fellow Missouri volunteers were camped in the valley on a march from Santa Fe to Socorro.

153

entrance and this is generally quite wide and high, the usual width being six feet and the height seven. They appear to be made thus wide, at least as far as I have been able to discover, to enable the burros and other animals to go through with their packs. They are generally secured by double doors. There are two or three buildings in the town with extensive fronts and *portales* (porches), which look, for this country, very well—one of them being the house formerly occupied by Governor Armijo. There is a military post at this place, garrisoned by a couple of companies of dragoons, the commanding officer being Major M. S. Howe, of the 2d Dragoons. The population of the town and its immediate suburbs is probably about one thousand. Wood for fuel has to be drawn a distance of twenty-five miles.

Colonel Washington and myself, after partaking of the generous hospitality of Major Howe and his lady, left at 2 o'clock for Santa Fe, it being our intention to tarry all night at Algadones, the usual stopping-place for travelers either way between Albuquerque and the former place. Mr. Calhoun and Captain Ker were in company, the latter having kindly provided the vehicle which conveys us hither.[174] On our left was the Rio Grande, and on our right, some eight or nine miles off, the lofty mountains of Albuquerque and Sandia. The valley of the Rio Grande for a number of miles above Albuquerque presents the finest agricultural and pastoral country I have yet seen in New Mexico. The breadth of the valley under cultivation is, probably, not quite a mile. The clemency of the climate—it is some two thousand feet lower in altitude than Santa Fe—is such as to cause the grape and peach, as well as the melon, to grow to perfection. The corn also looks luxuriant and productive.

About six miles from Albuquerque we passed the inconsiderable village of Alameda, the most conspicuous building in it being the Roman Catholic church. Six miles further, we passed by

---

[174] Captain Croghan Ker at this time was stationed at Albuquerque, commanding Company K, Second Dragoons. Under his initial orders, Ker was to have accompanied the Navaho Expedition, but instead at the last minute was directed to join a similar expedition against the Southern Utes, led by Brevet Lieutenant Colonel Benjamin Lloyd Beall, commanding the garrison at Taos.

the pueblo of *Sandia*, a town similar in the style of its buildings to the other pueblo villages—the usual quantum of ladders and ragged-looking sheep and goat pens discovering themselves about the premises.[175] Just after leaving Sandia, within the space of about a mile along the road, are between sixty and seventy piles of stones which are said to designate the locations where as many Navahos fell in a battle which the Pueblo Indians had with that people some years since.

Six miles more brought us to the small village of *Bernalillo*, its vicinage presenting some respectable-looking *rancho* residences, surrounded by well cultivated grounds, which are fenced by adobe walls. Some of these walls are twelve feet high and crowned with the cactus, to prevent their being scaled. Another six miles traversed, we found ourselves at Algadones, our stoppingplace for the night. This miserable-looking village contains about forty houses, and has a population of some two or three hundred souls.[176] Subsistence, such as it is, and forage, can be obtained here. The inn, kept by a Mexican, is far from being such as it should be, either as respects cleanliness or the character of the *cuisine*. Miserable muddy coffee, a stew made of mutton smothered in onions, half-baked tortillas, and a few boiled eggs, constitute the best meal it pretends to furnish. I do not know

[175] Sandia (watermelon) is the Spanish name for the small pueblo known to its Tewan occupants as *Nafiat,* meaning a dusty or sandy place. Van Valkenburgh says the Navahos call the pueblo *Kin Łigaai,* or White House. Sandia is believed to have been one of the valley pueblos of the Province of Tiguex visited by Coronado in 1540. Sandia was abandoned during the Pueblo Revolt, Van Valkenburgh says, "and the people fled to the Hopi country where they are supposed to have built the pueblo of Payupkihe, whose ruins are to be found on Second Mesa about one mile north of Shipaulovi. The Sandia people stayed with the Hopis until 1742 when Fathers Delgado and Pino brought 441 of them back to their old home." In recent years, according to Stanley Stubbs (31), the population has dwindled to 139.

[176] By-passed now by a modern highway, Algadones for years has not supported an inn—good or indifferent. Hughes, in 1846, said the village had one thousand inhabitants, which is very hard to believe. The town derives its name (cotton) from cotton fields once planted in the vicinity, according to *New Mexico: A Guide* (246). An informal survey in 1961 showed the village to have two bars, six stores, thirty-eight houses, three vacant buildings, a church, and a school.

why it is, but I have not yet drunk a cup of coffee or eaten a tortilla of Mexican preparation without its creating in some degree a sensation of nausea at the stomach. There is certainly great room for improvement in the cuisine of this country. The only eatable I have yet partaken of which does not become tainted by their cookery is the egg in its boiled state, and this is doubtless owing to its being protected by the shell.

The road from Albuquerque to Algadones is generally sandy and in some places, on account of it, quite heavy.

Santa Fe, September 23—Having, by a few moments of experience last evening, become convinced that if I lay within doors all night I should not only have a fight with rabid insects, but have also great violence done to my *olfactories*, Lieutenant Ward and myself slept in the wagon, and a pretty comfortable night we have had of it.

We left Algadones for Santa Fe at half past 7 A.M., our general course for the day being about northeast, and we taking the road *via* Delgado's rancho, the usual wagon route between the two places.

Basaltic trap, I noticed, crowned the mesa heights on the west side of the Rio Grande between Algadones and *San Felipe,* the inferior formation appearing to be sandstone, horizontally stratified.

Six miles above Algadones, we passed the Pueblo of San Felipe. This town is situated at the foot of the mesa, on the west side of the Rio Grande, the river contracting at this point to a width of probably less than one hundred yards. This pueblo, like the others, has its two-storied houses, accessible by ladders; but neither it nor Sandia is as purely Indian in the style of its buildings as the other pueblos we have visited. It is, however, rather a neat looking village, the Roman Catholic church, as usual, showing conspicuously. The ruins of what is usually called *Old San Felipe* are plainly visible, perched on the edge of the mesa about a mile above the present town, on the west side of the river. These ruins are generally, I believe, regarded as indeed the remains of Old San Felipe; but a very intelligent Indian residing in the present town of that name has informed me that they are the remains of a people who have long since passed away, and of whom they know nothing.[177]

Half a mile above San Felipe, the road branches off—one branch extending to Santa Fe by the way of Santo Domingo, and the other to the same place by the way of Delgado's rancho. The former branch is, probably, three or four miles shorter than the latter, and is on that account generally preferred for pack animals. The latter, however, is so much the better wagon road as to cause it to be preferred for wheeled vehicles.

[177] Simpson's informant was deliberately misleading him, since the pueblo ruins on the mesa's summit date back only a little beyond the reconquest of New Mexico in 1692–93. Bandelier ("Final Report," Vol. 2, 146) writes that El Rito de los Frijoles once was the home of "that branch of the Queres [Keresans] which now occupies the pueblos on the Rio Grande, Cochiti, Santo Domingo and San Felipe." Leslie White ("The Pueblo of San Felipe," *American Anthropological Association Memoirs*, No. 38 [1932], 7) says that in migrating from Frijoles Canyon, the ancestors of San Felipe and Cochiti Pueblos lived together at a place called *Kuapa* until their village was destroyed, probably by Tewan aggressors. Thereafter, the pueblos of Cochiti and San Felipe were established, both on the west bank of the Río Grande and separated by seven miles. *Katishtya*, the native Keresan name for the latter pueblo, was visited by Coronado in 1540, by Castaña de Sosa in 1591, and by Oñate in 1598. Ralph Twitchell (24n.) says that probably it was de Sosa who gave the pueblo its saint's name, San Felipe. Early in the seventeenth century the first Franciscan church was built here by Fray Cristóbal de Quiñones, who died in 1607 and was buried in the church. The people of San Felipe, Twitchell says, "were active in the revolution of 1680 and helped to murder the frayles at Santo Domingo." Abandoning their pueblo, they fled with the Cochitis and others to the Potrero Viejo [La Cieneguilla, in the Jemez Mountains]. They returned in 1683 but fled again on de Vargas' first *entrada* in 1692. De Vargas found them the following year on the summit of Black Mesa, occupying the pueblo whose ruins Simpson found "plainly visible" in 1849. The present pueblo was built at the foot of the mesa, centering around a large, bare plaza, early in the eighteenth century. Prior to Simpson's arrival, San Felipe was visited by Zebulon Pike (1807), and J. W. Abert and W. H. Emory (1846). Van Valkenburgh notes that the Navahos know this pueblo as *Tsedahkin*, House on the Edge, or *Tseta'kin*, Houses Between the Rocks. Stubbs (71) says that San Felipe "must be included among the most conservative of the present pueblo groups." Conservative, even hostile, I found San Felipe to be on my two visits in 1961. Lieutenant Governor Juan Valencia and the pueblo's other headmen refused to discuss any aspect of Simpson's visit in 1849—as if, in so doing, they might be asked to disclose some carefully guarded secret.

About twenty miles from Algadones, we crossed the Rio Galisteo, the road following it up for some distance. Where we first met it, not a particle of water could be seen in its bed; but at the point where we left it, about half a mile above, it was a running stream. Colonel Washington informs me that in Chihuahua he traversed the bed of a river which was perfectly dry when the head of the column commenced crossing, but within half an hour, before the whole column had passed over, it was scarcely fordable.

Some fine specimens of trap dike are discoverable just after crossing the Rio Galisteo—one of them resembling, as nearly as may be, an artificial wall; another, the dark-colored remains of an old pueblo. About six miles further, we crossed the small affluent of the Rio de Santa Fe, on which Delgado's rancho is situated. Travelers sometimes make this rancho a stopping place for the night between Santa Fe and Albuquerque. Sixteen miles more transversed, at half past three in the afternoon, much to the gratification of the whole party, we reached Santa Fe.

The road from Algadones to Santa Fe is generally very good, the only exception being a few short steep hills.

The face of the country today has presented, with some trifling exceptions—along the Rio Grande, at Delgado's, and between Agua Fria and Santa Fe—one extended barren waste of uncultivable soil.

Santa Fe, September 26—The artillery, under Major Kendrick, reached this place yesterday; the infantry, under Captain Sykes, today.

Character of the Soil from the Eastern Base of the Sierra de Tumecha to Chelly, and Thence to Santa Fe, by the Return Route

It may be thought, from the frequent mention of good land along the route since we left the eastern base of the Tumecha Mountains, on our return trip, that fertility has characterized the country generally through which we have passed since that period. But, lest so erroneous an impression may obtain, I think it proper to observe that for the greater portion of this distance the road has threaded the valleys of the country, and therefore the land has presented itself such as I have described it. The country, it is true, has exhibited a greater extent of cultivable soil than that traversed between Santa Fe and the Tumecha Mountains, but yet, in comparison with the whole area of surface, it should still be considered as but a very *small fractional part*.

The idea I pertinaciously adhered to when in the States, before ever having seen this country, was that besides partaking of the bold characteristics of the primary formations, rocks confusedly piled upon rocks, deep glens, an occasional cascade, green fertile valleys—the usual accompaniments of such characteristics with us in the States—it was also, like the country of the States, generally fertile and covered with verdure.

But never did I have, nor do I believe anybody can have, a full appreciation of the almost universal barrenness which pervades this country, until they come out, as I did, to "search the land," and behold with their own eyes its general nakedness. The primary mountains present none of that wild, rocky, diversified, pleasing aspect which they do in the United States, but, on the contrary, are usually of a rounded form, covered by a dull, lifeless-colored soil, and generally destitute of any other *sylva* than pine and cedar, most frequently of a sparse and dwarfish character. The sedimentary rocks, which, contrary to my preconceived notions, are the prevalent formations of the country, have a crude, half-made-up appearance, sometimes of a dull buff color, sometimes white, sometimes red, and sometimes these alternating and, being almost universally bare of vegetation except that of a sparse, dwarfish, sickening-colored aspect, cannot be regarded as a general thing—at least, not until familiarity reconciles you to the sight—without a sensation of loathing.

The face of the country, for the same reason—the general absence of all verdure, and the dead, dull yellow aspect of its soil—has a tendency to create the same disagreeable sensation. I desire it, therefore, to be borne in mind that when I have in the course of my journal spoken of *fertile* soil, or of *beautiful* prospects, I have spoken *relatively*—that is, in relation or contrast with the other portions of the country in which these exceptions have occurred, *and not in relation to our more favored domain in the States.*

Conclusion

Before concluding my journal, I think it proper to bring to the notice of the department the expediency of having the country examined west of the Pueblo of Zuñi, for the ascertainment of a wagon route from the former point to the Pueblo de los Angeles, or, failing in this, to San Diego.

The route from Santa Fe to Zuñi—a distance of two hundred and four miles—is, with a very slight application of labor, practicable for wagons; and the guide, Carravahal, who has been down the Rio de Zuñi to its junction with the Colorado of the West, says it continues practicable all the way along this tributary to the point mentioned.

Mr. Richard Campbell, of Santa Fe, since my return has informed me that, in 1827, with a party of thirty-five men and a number of pack animals, he traveled from New Mexico to San Diego by the way of Zuñi and the valley of the Rio de Zuñi, and found no difficulty throughout the whole distance.[178] He further states there is no question that a good wagon route, furnishing the proper quantum of wood, water, and grass, can be found in

[178] Richard Campbell arrives late but is one of the most interesting individuals to appear in Simpson's narrative. He is the José Ricardo of Robert Cleland's reckless breed, the Richard Campbell who "reached New Mexico at least as early as 1825." (*This Reckless Breed of Men*, 264.) Cleland finds him, on April 27 of that year, entering "six bales of mixed goods, valued at about 800 pesos, in the National Customs House at Santa Fe. A year later, in company with John Pearson, Julian Green, Lucas Murray, and Ewing Young, he applied for Mexican naturalization, and his name appeared frequently thereafter in New Mexican affairs." A trader or trapper who wished to remain in New Mexico at that time was tolerated only on condition that he become a Mexican citizen. Simpson's informant is not to be confused with Robert Campbell, one of General William H. Ashley's company, who helped to pioneer the Rocky Mountain fur trade (1822–26), and on Ashley's retirement joined William Sublette to form a carrying-outfitting-banking firm in St. Louis to supply the Rocky Mountain Fur Company.

"Pueblo of Zuñi."
By R. H. Kern, September 15, 1849.

"NORTH FACE OF INSCRIPTION ROCK."
By R. H. Kern, September 17, 1849.

this direction, both to San Diego and the Pueblo de los Angeles. He informs me, however, that in order to reach the Rio Colorado, the Rio de Zuñi would have to be diverged from at the falls, within a few miles of its confluence with the Colorado and a valley running southwardly followed down to its junction with the valley of that river.

He has further informed me that above the mouth of the Rio de Zuñi there is a ford, called *El Vado de los Padres* (the Ford of the Fathers), to which a route leads from Zuñi by way of the pueblos of the Moquis. This route, which he represents as much shorter than the other, is, however, on account of the difficulty of crossing the cañon of the river at the ford, only practicable for pack animals.

The Colorado, when he crossed it near the mouth of the Rio de Zuñi, was fordable, but he is of the opinion that it might not always be found so.

It is proper for me, however, in this connexion, to state that I have conversed with two or three trappers, who represent that the Colorado is so deeply cañoned from its mouth upwards as to make a wagon route in the direction proposed impracticable. These persons, however, have at the same time stated that they know nothing personally of the *continuous* existence of this cañon, never having been immediately on the ground. Their representations, then, should not counterbalance the statement of those who have.

I have introduced the above representations, to which I might add those of other persons, corroborative of the statements of Messrs. Carravahal and Campbell, in order that the department, being advised of the true state of the information attainable upon the subject, might take such action and give such instructions in the premises as, in its judgment, it might deem expedient.

By reference to the map, it will readily be seen that a route from Santa Fe to Pueblo de los Angeles, in the direction suggested, running as it would intermediate between the southern detour of Cooke's route and the northern detour of the "Spanish trail" route, or, in other words, as direct as possible, would not only be shorter by probably as much as three hundred miles than either of these routes, but, passing by the pueblos of Laguna and Zuñi, and possibly of the Moquis, situated still further westward, would furnish supplies of subsistence and repairs of outfit for certainly the first two hundred, if not three hundred, miles of the way—*desiderata* certainly not to be disregarded.

Respectfully submitted.

JAMES H. SIMPSON
First Lieutenant, Corps Topographical Engineers

Epilogue

FROM A MILITARY POINT OF VIEW, Colonel Washington's expedition against the Navahos was a qualified success. Others later would do worse. The hardships he encountered at the head of his motley force were real enough, as Simpson relates, but not great. Carravahal's knowledge of the country helped him, as did the loyalty of Henry Dodge's Mexican militia and the Pueblo scouts. The weather helped him, too. This normally was the rainy season that so often fills dry arroyos with muddy torrents and turns to knee-deep gluey mud the flat plains. But this was a dry year; the Puercos east and west were dry, and the country between them and beyond was dry.

The Navahos were hostile, with good reason, but they did not attack. The core of his troops was young but by now seasoned—a good force—but even so, it was no small accomplishment that Colonel Washington maintained for nearly six hundred miles a close line of march without one casualty or serious accident. What is left of good to say may have been more important then than it now appears. His was the first American force to penetrate the Navaho stronghold of Canyon de Chelly and reduce its myths of impregnability. He himself, and with him the several unusual men whom we may now consider further, secured information of the Navaho people and their terrain that would be invaluable to others later.

As a punitive expedition, designed to impress upon the Navahos the power of United States authority, Colonel Washington's campaign was a failure. The Navahos were not impressed. The treaty of Canyon de Chelly was a forced agreement, formally ratified by Congress, but farcical. It was signed only by Martinez and Chapitone, who together could not commit the Navaho people to anything; even they could not have believed in it.

More than once, and with deliberate intent, Colonel Washington revealed to large numbers of the Navahos the two-sided nature of his campaign. The alternatives he offered were death and destruction, or peace. One occasion was the otherwise pointless killing of Narbona and six of his people over the incident of the stolen Mexican pony. A second and disputed incident was the setting afire of Navaho hogans as the column of troops made their already well-heralded approach to the treaty place at the mouth of Canyon de Chelly. We must disagree with Richard Kern's diary entry on this point and say again that on the basis of the evidence and what we know of Indian custom, the hogans almost certainly were not burned by the Navahos, but on Colonel Washington's order. These displays of arbitary force, coupled with the command's raid on the Navahos' Chuska Valley cornfields—from the Navaho point of view—were not the acts of a friendly government, whose friendship and protection Colonel Washington was conditionally offering, but aggressive acts of a hostile invader.

Nevertheless, it would be a mistake to criticize too easily Colonel Washington's conduct. For months before his departure from Santa Fe the Navahos had been raiding and murdering through the Spanish and Pueblo settlements. The younger Navahos especially, and some of their older leaders, were not ready for peace under any form of outside government. From the time that Colonel Washington's troops reached the council ground where Narbona was killed, until they arrived at Zuñi, the troops were surrounded and far outnumbered by armed Navahos. The Navahos' attitude toward these invading *Bilagáana* was not fearful or subservient, but verged from resentful to covertly hostile. In short, the situation which then confronted both sides was nearly impossible, and our sympathies, in Colonel Washington's foredoomed effort, can hardly be more than divided.

Epilogue

Dissident bands of Navahos violated the treaty within twenty-four hours of Colonel Washington's return to the capital. In the vicinity of Sandia Pueblo, while the tracks of the command's passing vanguard were still fresh, a party of Navahos on September 24 killed five Mexicans and rode off with their property. This was the first in a series of Navaho reprisals evidently intended to avenge the death of Narbona and those killed with him. In noting the renewed raids by Navahos, Apaches, and Comanches, Agent Calhoun unintentionally provided one assessment of the recent expedition: "Not a day passes," he reported, "without hearing of some fresh outrage, and the utmost vigilance of the military force in this country is not sufficient to prevent murders and depredations and there are but few so bold as to travel alone ten miles from Santa Fe."[1] He recommended that the Navahos be placed on a reservation, with "their limits circumscribed, and distinctly marked out, and their departure from said limits be under certain prescribed rules, at least for some time to come. Even this arrangement would be utterly ineffective unless enforced by the military arm of the country."

Several days later, within three miles of Santa Fe, another Mexican was found murdered, the body bristling with arrows, two through the chest and sixteen in the back. Calhoun does not identify the Indians who killed the man, but in the same connection noted in his report that "Several Indians from [San] Ildefonso [Pueblo] came to me yesterday, also, saying the Navajoes were impudent, troublesome, and dangerous—and that they were in every nook and corner of the country."

Neither Colonel Washington nor Agent Calhoun could have been surprised, then, when Chapitone failed to surrender—as agreed by the treaty a month before—at Jemez Pueblo on October 10 the additional Mexican captives and stolen property. Chapitone reportedly reached the small pueblo of Paguate, be-

[1] Calhoun to Indian Commissioner William Medill, October 1, 1849. *Official Correspondence.* Reports of the September 24 murders and subsequent depredations are from the same source. Van Valkenburgh and McPhee say that between October 1, 1846, and October 1, 1850, "the Navajos and their Apache cousins had stolen 12,887 mules, 7,000 horses, 31,581 cattle and 453,293 sheep."

low Cebolleta, in good faith intending to carry out the agreement. Informed by Mexican traders at that place that American troops were planning a new expedition against the Navahos, this time with the determination to exterminate The People, Chapitone accompanied a party of Zuñis to Jemez "to ascertain from actual observation whether the reports of the *traders* were true or false."[2] Evidently he found the stories to be false because, after arriving at Jemez, he notified Calhoun and Colonel Washington by messenger that on October 28 or 29 he would be at nearby San Ysidro with the captives and prepared to fulfill the agreement. But that was the end of it. He undoubtedly was deterred by the mounting violence—raids by his people, which were reported, and counterraids by Puebloans and Mexicans, not reported but which certainly occurred.

Lieutenant Simpson, meanwhile, was in the center of much of the trouble, in the vicinity of Cebolleta, in the eastern shadows of Mount Taylor, selecting a site for a new western outpost of dragoons.[3] His journal does not tell us so, but he was at Cebolleta when Chapitone was at Paguate, only a few miles south on the trail to Jemez, and they either met or were aware of the other's close presence. Simpson does not tell us either, but he was there when Navahos "and others unknown" attacked the neighboring Spanish village of Le Bugarito on or about October 5 and killed two residents, left another wounded, and fled with a woman captive.

[2] *Ibid.*, Calhoun to Medill, October 15, 1849. Calhoun says that if Chapitone found the rumors untrue, he had the captives and property "collected together . . . and [was] prepared . . . in every way, to comply with the terms of the late treaty."

[3] Simpson's orders, issued by Colonel Washington at Santa Fe, September 29, 1849: "I. Lieut. Simpson Top. Eng., will proceed to Cibolletta via Albuquerque and make a reconnoissance of the country in the vecinity of that place, and select a suitable Position for a Military Post. II. Major Howe 2nd Dragoons Comdg. at Albuquerque will furnish an escort of one Company of Dragoons to Lieut. Simpson to enable him to make the reconnoissance." On the same day that the order was issued, Simpson wrote Colonel Abert that "The reconnoissance . . . will probably employ me for ten or twelve days. . . . " National Archives, War Records. Record Group 77, Topographical Bureau S, Letters Received, 1845–50, Box 69.

Ten days later a delegation from Zuñi Pueblo, including the cacique, the governor, and the war captain, waited on the Indian agent at Santa Fe. Their request was urgent. They asked, said Calhoun afterward, "for arms and ammunition, and permission to make a war, of extermination, against the Navajoes. The deputation . . . also stated, there were five hundred and fifty-five able-bodied men in their village, and only thirty-two fire arms, and less than twenty rounds, each, for said arms."

The treaty of Canyon de Chelly obviously meant nothing to the warring bands of young Navahos; they would strike whom they pleased, and where and when it pleased them. On November 14 they raided San Ysidro. No one was killed, but from the fields and corrals of the Mexican village the Indians boldly made off with a number of horses, mules, and oxen.

Simpson's proposals to station a company of dragoons at Cebollitita, four or five miles below Cebolleta, were not acted upon immediately. The pressing need for the outpost was clearly recognized in Santa Fe, but Colonel Washington and his successor, Colonel John Munroe, were embarrassed for troops and by a treasury so bare that public officers went for long periods without pay and even emptied their own pockets to maintain the simplest functions of government. Nevertheless, in late summer, 1850, adobe quarters were rented at Cebolleta, and on September 3 the new post was established under the command of Brevet Lieutenant Colonel Daniel T. Chandler. His garrison consisted of twenty-eight men of Company H, Second Dragoons, under Captain William H. Saunders, and thirty-eight men of Company I, Third Infantry, directly under his own orders. The post surgeon was John Fox Hammond, lately of Fort Marcy and a member of Colonel Washington's Navaho expedition. For brave show and martial music the little garrison had two buglers, attached to the dragoons, and a drummer and a fifer, who marched with the infantry.[4]

[4] The post at Cebolleta was established by Orders No. 31, dated Headquarters, Ninth Military Department, Santa Fe, August 20, 1850. National Archives, War Records. Record Group 94, Post Returns, Cibolleta, N. M. Cebolleta was aban-

Post returns for the next twelve months give only hints of what befell these troops. There is no report for example, of a single engagement with enemy Navahos. Surgeon Hammond, however, was busy: he had no troops wounded in battle to care for, but each month the number reporting on sick list was high. The food at the post, we may imagine, was bad; sickness among the soldiers was due to scurvy, influenza, and other natural causes. Some of those who reported sick later died, and there were desertions. And there is a hint, no more, that Colonel Chandler did not drowse in quarters but drove his men hard, on long, wearing marches. At the end of the first month of duty Captain Saunders reported that his dragoons had "31 horses serviceable, 13 unserviceable"; at the end of October, "9 horses serviceable, 34 unserviceable"; and at the end of November, "24 horses serviceable, 38 unserviceable." So it went into the winter, and we may believe that the infantry were as foot-weary and exhausted as the dragoons' horses.

Captain Saunders was one of Cebolleta's casualties. Within a week of the post's establishment he was relieved of duty for drunkenness. Soon after, he was restored to command. He was arrested for drunkenness in December and locked in quarters. In January, during Colonel Chandler's temporary absence, he was in command of the garrison. Upon the Colonel's return, Saunders resigned his commission, but was held on probation with his pledge, "as an officer and gentleman," never to drink again. Captain Saunders several months later was reported dead, with no cause of death given.

The post returns are enlightening, but tell less than we would like to know. They tell nothing of the day in early November, 1850, when—under the noses of Chandler's garrison—Navahos descended on neighboring Mexican ranchos and drove off several thousand head of sheep. The raid was obviously a humiliating test of the garrison's strength.

Colonel Washington's views on the outcome of his expedition,

doned as an army outpost with the garrisoning of Fort Defiance in the fall of 1851.

as yet untroubled by the events just related, were not sanguine. On the day of his return to Santa Fe one of his first acts was to request funds for the payment of his militia so that the two mounted companies, at least, might be persuaded to remain in service. Reporting to the adjutant general in Washington, he said: "The vigilance and activity of our troops in protecting the inhabitants of the Territory against the numerous bands of hostile Indians have been unceasing and with few exceptions their efforts have been successful. The services rendered by the four companies of Volunteers which were mustered in last spring have contributed largely towards this result, and as the time of their engagement draws to a close I am reminded of the necessity of retaining those companies that are mounted a while longer. Not having as yet received a cent of pay and there being no prospect of their receiving any before an appropriation is made by Congress it may be difficult to obtain their consent to continue beyond their present term. I shall endeavor to secure their services for three months more unless sooner discharged and hope that the earliest measures will be taken for their payment."[5]

Here, and later, Colonel Washington emphasized his belief in the superiority of cavalry in any action against the Navahos, Utes, Apaches, and Comanches, who themselves were all well mounted. He continued: "A mounted force is much more efficient to operate against the Indians of this country than any other description of troops. Comparatively, infantry is but of little use. One thousand men well armed and properly mounted would soon put an end to Indian difficulties in this quarter."

Cavalry continued to be the striking force on this frontier

[5] Washington to Major General Roger Jones, September 23, 1849. National Archives, War Records. Record Group 94, AGO, Letters Received, 515–W–1849. The militia's six-month service actually ran out on the day Colonel Washington wrote this letter. The four companies had enlisted the previous March 23—two companies under Captain Henry L. Dodge (eighty-five men) and Captain A. L. Papin (seventy-five men), and two mounted companies under Captain John Chapman (seventy-eight men) and Captain J. M. Valdez (eighty-six men). Washington succeeded only in re-enlisting sixty-nine mounted militia under Valdez for an additional three months. National Archives, War Records. Record Group 94, Muster Rolls, Volunteer Organizations, Box 2550.

until, a few years later, Colonel Edwin Vose Sumner took command of the Ninth Military Department and proposed to revolutionize the tactics of Indian warfare. Sumner's theories on cavalry are chronologically out of order here but so interesting, and in this period were so important to the defense of New Mexico Territory, that a digression from the immediate concerns of Colonel Washington is justified.

Briefly, then. Sumner's first exposure to angry Indians came as early as 1837–38, when in Missouri Territory he led troops through the country of the Osages. At the outbreak of the war with Mexico and before accompanying Doniphan from Santa Fe to Mexico, he was introduced to Navahos and Apaches while scouting the valley of the Río Grande. The war ended, he returned East, but again was summoned to the Southwest in the spring of 1851. Marching from Leavenworth to Santa Fe, where he would take command of the military department and make life miserable for Calhoun, he encountered, near Bent's Old Fort on the Arkansas, an irreverent assemblage of Cheyennes. "As I was marching past," he reported afterward, "several shots were fired towards the rear of my column." Sumner reversed his column, called together the principal men of the Cheyenne village, "and said to them I had come back to meet them, as friends or enimies, it was for them to say which, but they must say it immediately. They at once disclaimed all intention of hostility, and I resumed my march."[6]

Shortly after his arrival at Santa Fe, Colonel Sumner added to his knowledge of Indians when he nearly duplicated Colonel Washington's route of 1849 by leading a punitive expedition against the Navahos as far as Canyon de Chelly. The expedition was not a success, but for two things is notable: while on this campaign, Colonel Sumner selected the site of Fort Defiance, and before his return to Fort Marcy firmly concluded that cavalry, in Indian country, was a nuisance.[7]

[6] Sumner to Major General Roger Jones, October 24, 1851. *Official Correspondence.*

[7] The construction of Fort Defiance is referred to in a previous note. The Nav-

"In all protracted military operations," he explained, "especially against Indians, the main body must be on foot. It is impossible *to make long marches* with Cavalry, *on grass alone,* loaded down as they are with arms, accoutrements and clothing, and have the horses equal to the Indian horses in speed or bottom, when we reach the scene of action, consequently our Cavalry cannot act offensively in the saddle, and their broken down horses are a great embarrassment, requiring a large part of the command to protect them, which could otherwise be used offensively on foot. . . . In Indian expeditions I think there should always be a small body of *very select horse.*"

The new military commander of New Mexico Territory continued: "I would respectfully propose that 4 Companies of dragoons (two of each regiment), now in this Territory may be withdrawn and that the rifle Regiment (dismounted), or a regiment of Infantry, may be sent out in their place . . . I shall feel far more confidence in my ability to carry out the orders I have received, if this change is made. Indeed I would prefer that 4 Companies of horse should be withdrawn, even if they cannot be replaced by any other troops."[8]

Calhoun, who on March 3, 1851, was inaugurated as the first civil governor of the newly-created Territory of New Mexico, was not in a position to overrule Sumner in military matters, but made his own position known in a letter to Secretary of State Daniel Webster: "It is folly to suppose, that *less than two*
aho name for the location is *Tséhootsooi.* Van Valkenburgh and McPhee say this means "Meadows in the rocks (walls)" and add that the garrison knew the fort as "Hell's Gate." The location of the fort, cause for much grumbling among its officer personnel later, drew this comment from Lieutenant John G. Bourke in 1881: "The first thing claiming my attention was the wretched position, in a military point of view, of the Navajo Agency formerly Fort Defiance. It is at the Eastern entrance to the Cañon Bonito and so closely pressed by the vertical walls of the cañon that no defense could be long continued were the Indians to become hostile. Indeed, I had pointed out to me the door in which the wife of an army officer was shot dead by an Indian in the cliffs, at a time when the garrison comprised four companies of regular troops. Several other cases equally bad are on record, but this one impressed me most vividly." "Bourke on the Southwest, VIII," ed. by Lansing B. Bloom.

[8] Sumner to Jones, October 24, 1851. *Official Correspondence.*

mounted regiments, (new) can preserve the quiet of this Territory, and enforce treaty stipulations with our Indians."[9]

Sumner's folly was nipped short—not, however, before the military commander's erratic behavior possibly contributed to Calhoun's illness and early death. Gratefully, in the meantime, Sumner was not yet on the scene, nor was Colonel Washington, if we may now turn back, to be troubled by Sumner's theories.

In reporting on his recent expedition, Colonel Washington accurately gauged the potential threat of the hostile Navahos, and while pointing the need for a military post farther to the west, he actually envisioned (if not precisely in that location) the first plans for what eventually became Colonel Sumner's Fort Defiance. In contrast to Simpson's journal, Colonel Washington's report is a terse, laconic footnote to the expedition and contains but two paragraphs of present interest, the first referring to the death of Narbona: "After marching over a barren, badly watered, and, in many places, rough country for eight days, I arrived in the vicinity of the labores, or cornfields of the Navajoes, at Tuna Cha. Here I first met with the Indians, and on the next day a party of them was fired upon by our troops, which resulted in killing and wounding several of them. Among the dead of the enemy left on the field was Narbona, the head chief of the nation, who had been a scourge to the inhabitants of New Mexico for the last thirty years."[10]

We have no reason to question this, but still might reserve judgment. Narbona was quite possibly a scourge to the settlements, but until now, so far as the present writer has been able to determine, there is only the testimony of Colonel Washington to tell us so. As for the Colonel's summary of his expedition and his conclusions, there remains only this comment at the end of his report: "The estimated number of the Navajoe tribe is from seven to

[9] *Official Correspondence.* Fortunately for the territory, Sumner's ideas did not prevail. Ironically, the military base on the Pecos River where the Navahos, rounded up by Colonel Kit Carson's horse troops, were held in captivity from 1864–68, was named for Colonel Sumner.

[10] Washington to Jones, September 25, 1849. National Archives, War Records. Record Group 94, AGO, Letters Received, 514–W–1849.

ten thousand, of which between two and three thousand are warriors, who are almost invariably well mounted, and generally well armed with guns, lances, and bows and arrows. To secure a firm and durable peace with them, it will be necessary to plant a military post in their country. Tuna Cha [the Chuska Valley] or Sienega Grande [Cienega Amarilla, the valley spreading south from the later site of Fort Defiance] will afford eligible sites for this purpose."

For more reasons than one the Colonel's recommendation gained support. Captain Thomas L. Brent, assistant quartermaster at Fort Marcy, who was charged with subsisting the military department's ever-hungry animals, had this to say: "The expedition made to the Navajo country during the past summer by Lt. Col. Washington . . . has established the existence of much fertile land west of the chain of mountains which separates the waters of the Del Norte from those of the Colorado of the West, and posts established west of this mountain chain on some of the tributaries of the Colorado will most effectually keep in check the Navajos and Eutaws.

"The Navajo Indians raise large quantities both of wheat and corn, and the country on the western slope of the mountains is well timbered and resembles in all its features and productions our Middle States. It is my opinion that Mounted Troops could be foraged more readily and cheaply [there] than in the valley of the Rio Grande, after the first of the year."[11]

On this frontier as elsewhere, the problem of foraging of cavalry horses could be nearly as critical as the strategic position of a fort in relation to a surrounding enemy. The expense and difficulty of providing forage from the valley ranchos of the Río Grande were almost a daily object lesson. Thus, stemming from Colonel Washington's proposal, for the balance of 1850 and through the summer of 1851, there was a steady insistence from the quartermasters at Fort Marcy upon the selection of new posts

[11] Brent to Quartermaster General Thomas S. Jessup, January 31, 1850. National Archives, War Records. Record Group 92, Office of the QM General, Consolidated Correspondence file, 1794–1915, Box 987.

in regions offering an abundant supply of forage. The valley of the Mora and the western slopes of the Chuskas were mentioned repeatedly in reports to Washington. And so the sites of Fort Union and Fort Defiance were chosen, in part, with heed to the importuning of the Fort Marcy quartermasters.

Judged, then, from a military point of view, Colonel Washington's expedition offered no relief from Indian raids and little of immediate material advantage to the civil or military branches of government. Accruing gradually with time, the advantages would derive from lessons learned during the campaign of the Navahos as a raiding enemy and of the vast country dominated by the Navahos. Otherwise, the treaty of Canyon de Chelly was a failure, violated repeatedly before it was ratified; and the expedition, as a punitive campaign, was a failure: the Navahos were not frightened into subjection, but on the contrary were driven to bolder acts of aggression.

If fate had not placed Lieutenant Simpson on Colonel Washington's staff, the expedition would have been comparable to many others—a campaign of measurable but limited value and little lasting interest. Without the presence of this paradoxically gifted man, Colonel Washington and his troops could have trudged from Santa Fe to Canyon de Chelly and Zuñi and back again, and their weary effort would have soon been forgotten. Their effort cannot be forgotten only because of Simpson's journal of the campaign. The journal—and we find it pedantically and repetitiously dry ("the argillaceous soil"), or sometimes lyrical ("the day opening beautifully, and the feathered race regaling us")—is always informative. There has been nothing quite like this, even in the most polished military writing of western exploration. The journal is a deep well of discovery and observation that has been consulted and referred to by nearly everyone who, for any reason, has studied the history or prehistory of the Southwest.

Simpson—this engineer of roads and harbor improvements—abominated the Southwest, as he so grimly confesses. Few writers most ardently attuned to the region have conferred such favor upon it. Alone in Colonel Washington's command, Simpson comprehended what was remarkable in broken walls of ancient stone, the depths and distances of a canyon gorge, and of old names carved on a lonely rock. His record of discovery, fresh and sometimes naive, still illuminates as though for the first time silent places and vanished people of our past.

The vagaries of chance which united them now separated six members of the late expedition, even more strangely shaping the final days of their lives. Of the six, only three were to live more than four years longer, and only one with quiet honors into old age.

Colonel Washington occupied the executive quarters of the Governors Palace for a month after his return and then was succeeded, on October 23, by Brevet Colonel John Munroe. Thereafter through the following March, Washington's and Lieutenant Simpson's names appear together on the muster rolls of Fort Marcy. In April the colonel departed, his orders transferring him to an outer fringe of the world he knew well—to Fort Constitution in New Hampshire. Possibly he was joined there by the family he had left at Warrenton, in his native Virginia. In any event, there he remained, in command of the post, through 1852.

For most of the next year there is no record of his assignment or his whereabouts. We find him again in December, 1853, aboard the steamer *San Francisco,* bound for California with a large contingent of troops of the Third Artillery. In the Gulf Stream, off the capes of the Delaware, the small vessel sailed into the fury of a violent storm. The steamer, which we may surmise was heavily overloaded, managed to stay afloat. But sometime on December 24 the *San Francisco* shipped heavy waves over its decks; several civilians or crew members, 4 officers, and 180 soldiers were swept overboard and all but 2 were drowned. Colonel Washington was among those who perished.

James Calhoun, remaining in Santa Fe, continued in his same duties as Indian agent through the following year. His position was anomalous. His title in theory placed him entirely in control of the destinies of at least 33,450 Indians—about two-thirds of their number then actively hostile. Beyond the dignity the title conferred upon him (this, in the opinion of his wards, not considerable), he had only a few thousand dollars to spend for all "expenses and contingencies," and such force of his own common sense that he could bring to bear upon his problems.

Within a week of his return from the Navaho expedition, as we have seen, he recommended placing the Navahos on a reservation under close military supervision. This he urged again in November, only now, with the Navahos, including reservations for the Utes, Apaches, and Comanches. His proposals were not vindictive and did not end simply with harsh plans for confinement; in his long-range view, if we interpret him correctly, he planned for the means to bring these tribes to a level of harmony with their neighbors. "Extend to them," he urged, "the protection of your laws regulating trade and intercourse . . . establish trading houses, liberally; give to them agricultural implements, for a few years, allow them blacksmiths, and carpenters, and locate among them such agents as will americanize their labor."[12]

Calhoun's proposals now seem quite unremarkable; in 1849 they were regarded as radical. Not in his time would any of these measures be approved, and half a century would pass before all of them would become accepted policy of the Indian Office.

Near the close of 1850, Calhoun was nominated by President Fillmore as governor of New Mexico. His appointment was confirmed by Congress in January, 1851; and he moved into the governor's quarters on March 3, still retaining his duties as Indian agent under the new title of Indian superintendent for the territory.

Calhoun's elevation to the office of governor gave him no more authority in the handling of Indian affairs, but merely increased and intensified his difficulties. While still serving as Indian agent, he had collided again and again with the territory's military

[12] Calhoun to Commissioner Orlando Brown, November 16, 1849. *Official Correspondence.*

JAMES S. CALHOUN

MUSEUM OF NEW MEXICO

COMPANY OFFICERS' QUARTERS, FORT MARCY.
The gun carriages shown here, with ammunition boxes
at the front and rear, are similar to but undoubtedly of
a later period than those used by
Colonel Washington's command.

commander in matters of policy. It was inevitable that this should happen. Working toward the same end but from entirely divergent positions of interest, Calhoun and Munroe clashed over the best means for controlling Indian depredations. Whether in his instructions to his special agents, or in issuing trading permits, or preparing the groundwork for councils or treaties, Calhoun's carefully laid plans often as not ran afoul of Munroe's orders to his troops to restrict communication with certain bands of Indians who, perhaps unknown to Munroe, were now avowing their repentance and eagerness to come to terms. Calhoun's letters of this period testify repeatedly to his inability to avoid misunderstandings and abortive disputes with the military.

Differences between Calhoun and Munroe did not end, nor were they eased when Calhoun became governor. With no control over military operations, Calhoun conducted the affairs of civil government as best he could, crying out meanwhile to officials in Washington that more mounted troops were needed before anything like peace could be brought to the territory. From his point of view, then, the situation became even blacker when Colonel Munroe was relieved of command in the spring of 1851 and replaced by Colonel Sumner. More positive in his ways than Munroe, the new commander also possessed a broad streak of arrogance.

He reached Santa Fe from Fort Leavenworth on July 19. "My first step," he reported later, "was to break up the post at Santa Fe, that sink of vice and of extravagance, and to remove the troops and public property to this place [Fort Union]. . . . I understand that many applications have been made to the government, by the people of Santa Fe, to have the troops ordered back there. I have no hesitation in saying that I believe most of these applications proceed directly or indirectly from those who have hitherto managed to live, in some way, from the extravagant expenditures of the government. I trust their petitions will not be heeded."[13]

[13] Sumner to Jones, October 24, 1851. *Official Correspondence.* Not all of the troops were removed from the capital's evil influence, one company of artillery

Sumner's disapproval of Calhoun's administration soon deepened to the level of personal animosity. On the Colonel's initiative all pretense of co-operation between the military and civil branches of government ended, indeed to the point that Sumner may be suspected of planning deliberately to reduce Governor Calhoun to the stature of a subservient, voiceless puppet.

The military commander did not hesitate in making his contempt for the executive office plain. As governor and Indian superintendent, Calhoun had a right and more than adequate reason to accompany Colonel Sumner's expedition into the Navaho country, but before the command's departure on August 17, Calhoun's request to join Sumner's staff was refused. The Colonel refused also the Governor's request that three newly-appointed Indian agents be permitted to accompany the expedition. Even more: refused this, Calhoun was refused again when he asked that the Colonel furnish military escorts so that his three new agents might proceed in safety to their posts. Nor was that all. Governor Calhoun desired to inspect the Hopi villages, which he had not yet been able to visit, and then proceed to the Gila River country of the Apaches, where there had been frequent incidents of trouble between the Apaches, their Indian neighbors, and vagabond traders. In order to make this difficult journey in safety, Calhoun asked Sumner for an escort. Sumner replied that troops could not be spared for such a purpose—they were needed elsewhere more urgently.

In each instance Colonel Sumner not only undermined the efforts of an able governor, but, for motives of his own, elected to act in disobedience to specific orders. Five months earlier, when notified of his approaching assignment to New Mexico Territory, Sumner was instructed by Secretary of War C. M. Conrad that "In all negotiations and pacific arrangements with the Indians, you will act in concert with the Superintendent of Indian Affairs in New Mexico, whom you will allow to accompany

---

being allowed to remain at Fort Marcy. Construction of Fort Union was started by Sumner's troops in the early fall of 1851, simultaneously with the construction of Forts Defiance, Fillmore (near El Paso), and Conrad (at Valverde).

you in the expeditions into the Indian territory, if he should deem it proper to do so, and to whom you will afford every facility for the discharge of his duties."[14]

One of Calhoun's three new agents, convinced that Sumner's obstructions made his own situation impossible, wrote in disgust to the governor that his presence in the territory was useless and that he wished to return East. Calhoun replied that he had no course but to approve the agent's resignation. In bitter helplessness, he added: "I have no authority to call out the militia, and the Territory is without munitions of War."[15]

Balked by Colonel Sumner even in the normal right of a governor to summon a force of militia, Calhoun—now near the breaking point—on October 1 wrote to Indian Commissioner Luke Lea: "The Military officers and the executive can not harmonize, and I am not certain that the public interests would not be promoted by relieving us all from duty in this Territory."

Calhoun's insistence that it was folly to employ foot soldiers against mounted Indians and that he needed support in his struggles with Sumner eventually gained a hearing. Communication between the territorial capital and Washington required months, but belatedly there came instructions that permitted the Governor to muster in a company of mounted militia and draw upon the quartermaster's depot at Fort Union for necessary arms and equipment. In November, however, Calhoun and Sumner reached a final impasse when the Governor's proposal to send the militia out against raiding Navahos was countered with Sumner's threat to halt and turn back any such "marauding party" of militia with regular troops.

At least partly because of this constant harassment and opposition, Calhoun's health failed; and as winter turned slowly to spring, his condition became worse. No one knew better than he how sick he was. On April 7, with no trace of resentment, he

---

[14] *Official Correspondence.*

[15] Calhoun to Agent E. H. Wingfield, September 17, 1851. *Official Correspondence.* Calhoun's other appointees refused aid by Sumner were John Greiner and A. R. Woolley.

wrote Colonel Sumner that "You are perhaps advised of my weak, feeble, and almost hopeless condition—and I feel that I am speaking almost as a dying man—yet I feel desirous of doing all in my power to promote the public weal. But for my utter inability, I should mount my horse and visit you at your quarters. For the last four weeks I have been unable to stand alone without assistance, and for the same period have been constantly confined to my bed."[16]

Through April the Governor showed no improvement but resolved nevertheless to leave Santa Fe and attempt the long journey home. His intentions were made known to Commissioner Lea by John Greiner, one of Calhoun's Indian agents, who in this emergency was acting as Indian superintendent: "Governor Calhoun although unable to stand alone will leave here for the States on Thursday next. His physicians . . . have strongly advised him to do so—and if the trip across the Plains restores his health, he will at an early date call upon the Department."[17]

The departure was delayed almost a month. On May 31, Greiner again wrote to the Commissioner: "On Wednesday last Governor Calhoun left Fort Union for the States with very little probability of ever reaching there alive—He takes his Coffin in along with him. Mr. [W. E.] Love his Son in Law & Mr. [David V.] Whiting his Private Secretary are in company with him—and should he die on the road will take charge of all his effects. . . . A party of four or five Pueblo Indians from Tesuque accompanies the Governor."[18]

The rough trip by wagon over the Santa Fe Trail was too much for the sick man to endure. Upon reaching Independence, Missouri, Calhoun's secretary informed Commissioner Lea: "You

16 *Official Correspondence.*

17 Greiner to Lea, April 30, 1852. National Archives, Indian Records. New Mexico Superintendency, 1849–53, Letters Received, Micro. Roll 546.

18 *Ibid.* The delegation from Tesuque did reach Washington, apparently in the company of Calhoun's son-in-law Love. Their purpose in making the trip was to straighten out terms of an 1850 treaty. In September, while they were still in Washington, Love informed the acting commissioner of Indian affairs that $4,500 was needed to pay their expenses in the capital and get them home.

have been, no doubt, apprized by this time of the death of H. E. Governor Calhoun, who was on his way to Washington City. His remains have been interred at Kansas [City] Mo. until the body shall decompose sufficiently to enable his friends to take him home and place him along side of his wife and daughter."[19]

If we except only the steel-edged cruelty of earliest Spanish conquest and consequent Pueblo rebellion, the territory of the Southwest neither before nor since has known anything to compare with the unrelieved, stony hardship of the 1850's—the period of transition between Spanish and American rule. At no time in its more than two centuries was the capital at Santa Fe more divided in its allegiances or more exhausted in its resources. Dissension, springing from conflict of authority and ambition and compounded at every turn by poverty—a poverty of money and a poverty of the simplest needed goods—spread out from the capital to tantalize and thwart almost all efforts to reduce the territory to peace. Human values reached basic levels: witness Calhoun's concern to measure out and carry with him his own coffin. Against such uncompromising reality the abilities and weaknesses of men such as Calhoun and Sumner stand in sharp relief and invite a judgment nearly as uncompromising. By his letters, if unconsciously, Calhoun reveals himself as a humanist. But even with patience and fortitude he was unable to hold his ground against the arrogance of Colonel Sumner. And if Sumner emerges here as the stronger of the two, he was manifestly stupid. Fortunately for the territory, he outlasted Calhoun by only a few months, and then was withdrawn to duties elsewhere.

Men of smaller dimensions replaced these two, but in their company, in a relatively minor role, came one unusual man of stature. We have met him before. He was the Missourian, Henry Linn Dodge. His name appears with an identifying reference in scores of books, but by strange neglect he has been allowed to remain virtually unknown, or at best known only as a captain of

[19] *Ibid.* Whiting to Lea, July 5, 1852. In none of the correspondence is the nature of Calhoun's illness disclosed.

militia, a shadowy figure, whose name was taken by a fabled Navaho leader, Henry Chee Dodge.[20]

Among the officers who accompanied Colonel Washington on the Navaho campaign, Henry Dodge alone seemed worthy of mention by Calhoun, who later wrote: "I may be pardoned, I trust, for commending, in terms of decided praise, Henry Linn Dodge. . . . He was at all times efficient and prompt and com-

[20] Henry Chee Dodge (*Adiits'a'ii Sáni*—Old Interpreter) was born in February, 1860, at Fort Defiance, where his Mexican father, Juan Cosinisas, was an interpreter for the army post. His mother was a Navaho of mixed Jemez blood, the oldest daughter of Clah Tsosi (Slim Lefthand). According to Ruth Underhill (*Here Come the Navaho!*, 191–93), Chee's father was ten or eleven years old when captured by a party of Navahos raiding near present Silver City, New Mexico, and thereafter virtually became a member of the Navaho tribe. He was killed by Navahos—perhaps accidentally—in the summer of 1861 while following a raiding party that had stolen his horses in the vicinity of Fort Wingate. During Kit Carson's roundup of the Navahos two years later, Chee's mother fled westward and is believed to have found sanctuary in one of the Hopi villages. The infant Chee was taken in by an aunt, then living near Gray Mountain in Arizona, and with her was soon removed to internment at Fort Sumner. When the Navahos were liberated in 1868, Chee returned with his aunt to Fort Defiance. Shortly after, the aunt married Perry H. Williams, the agency issue clerk and later a trader. Williams and his Navaho wife raised the boy, naming him for Henry Linn Dodge—the middle name Chee (Red) added for good measure. Chee Dodge grew up in the turbulent political atmosphere of the Defiance agency, at the age of twenty-two serving as Navaho interpreter for Agent Galen Eastman. When he was about thirty years old, he joined Stephen E. Aldrich for several years in a trading partnership at the Round Rock Post in Arizona. Thereafter he retired to a ranch seven miles northwest of Crystal, New Mexico, where in the last forty years of his life he accumulated wealth and personal prestige as the principal spokesman for the Navaho tribe. He served as first chairman of the Navajo Tribal Council (1923–28), and was re-elected again for the term of 1942–46. His wealth enabled him to amass a superb collection of Navajo turquoise and silver jewelry, much of it now in the private collection of M. L. Woodard of Gallup, New Mexico. Chee Dodge also had a fondness for diamonds. According to Woodard, William Wurm, a Gallup jeweler now deceased, said that "he bought a number of diamonds for Chee and that he had some of them and other stones cut in Europe. . . . For status reason Navajos have always liked jewelry and Chee bought more expensive pieces in his time than any known Indian. Herman Atkins [Chee's attorney] thinks he got the idea for buying diamonds from C. N. Cotton, Al Arnold, and other *ricos* here at the time." Chee Dodge died January 7, 1947, and was buried at the tribal cemetery near Fort Defiance.

manded the admiration of Governor Washington, as well as others."[21]

Army and Indian Office records fail to account for Henry Dodge during the four years after the return of the expedition and his discharge from volunteer service. Van Valkenburgh, however, says (1941) that "The expedition had given Captain Dodge enough of Indian fighting. He turned to prospecting. . . . In 1851, accompanied by 'Colonel' Hezikiah Johnston, then editor of the *Rio Abajo News,* he led an expedition to the headwaters of the Gila River. Some success favored them, and they made one of the earliest gold strikes in what is now western New Mexico." Nothing would indicate this to be so, but possibly he also found occasion to travel east to visit members of his family, two of whom were United States senators—his father, Henry Dodge of Iowa County, Wisconsin, and a brother, Augustus Caesar Dodge, of Iowa.

The men of this family knew something of warfare. Henry L. Dodge's grandfather Israel Dodge, a native of Connecticut, served as an officer in the American Revolution. As so many others of the time did, the Dodges moved west, Israel's son Henry first appearing in 1827, fighting in the Winnebago War, and then as a colonel of Michigan volunteers from April until July, 1832, leading his troops in the Black Hawk War. He was commissioned as major of U.S. Rangers, and in March, 1833, became the first colonel of the army's first Plains cavalry—the First Dragoons.

Missouri trade with Santa Fe was well into its second decade when Colonel Dodge led his dragoons in 1835 on one of the first military forays by American troops as far west as the Rockies. There were the usual encounters with roving bands of the Plains tribes, as well as several days encamped at William Bent's new fort on the Arkansas, which the colonel commented upon but did not describe in detail in a later report.

Colonel Dodge resigned from the army the following year upon his appointment by President Andrew Jackson, as governor and superintendent of Indian Affairs of Wisconsin Territory.

[21] Calhoun to Commissioner Medill, October 4, 1849. *Official Correspondence.*

These offices he held until 1841. As a Democrat, he was elected that year to serve as delegate to Congress. After two terms, he was again made governor of Wisconsin; and when Wisconsin was admitted to statehood in 1848, he was returned to Washington as a senator, serving until 1857.

As interim treasurer of Santa Fe under Doniphan and later as a captain of militia, Henry Linn Dodge showed more than average competence. Family heritage provided strong strains of courage and good common sense, but otherwise a background of haphazard education. Brother Augustus, later a United States minister to Spain, once was baited in the Senate chamber by a fellow member for his bumbling frontier grammar. Augustus retorted hotly to his more sophisticated critic, but clearly was stung and showed his hurt.

For himself, it could be said that Henry Linn Dodge's letters mark him as only moderately well educated in a society that was then mainly illiterate—as one example, the late Governor Charles Bent's spelling was atrocious and his handwriting almost indecipherable. In any case, to law books and office work, Dodge preferred outdoors life where he might act freely among men— white or Indian it mattered not. Among such companions, or most of them, it also mattered not how he mangled the words and phrases of an official letter, and he was accepted with cheerful respect. What talents he possessed coalesced during the last three years of his life. The start of it came with his last appointment—as agent to the Navahos, in July, 1853.

Dodge replaced Spruce M. Baird of Santa Fe, a former major general in the war with Mexico and after John Greiner the Navahos' second officially designated agent. Practically speaking, however, Dodge was the first Navaho agent who gave that tribe a full measure of attention. Calhoun, all but confined to Santa Fe and as agent to all tribes in the territory, had been unable to do this; Baird, charged with establishing a Navaho agency at Jemez Pueblo, had simply lacked the interest. Baird accomplished little or nothing for the Navahos as long as he was their agent. In the opinion of Governor William Carr Lane, Baird never should have received the appointment, since he "gave little attention to his official duties, and gave the most of his time to his private business—as lawyer, farmer, editor of a newspaper, politician, ec., ec., ec.,"[22]

So we find Dodge again, now aged thirty-six, still dark-haired and of ruddy complexion, not tall but probably stocky, lettered but not bookish, thoroughly familiar with firearms, and with some practical ideas about Indians. His appointment by Governor Lane provided an annual salary of $1,550. Very sensibly, at the same time, the agency was moved from Jemez back into the Navaho country to the quadrangle of log and adobe buildings so isolated and unimpressive and so bravely named Fort Defiance. In addition to his duties as Navaho agent, Dodge's jurisdiction extended also over the affairs of the Hopi villages and the pueblos of Laguna, Acoma, and Zuñi.

Within a short time of his arrival at Defiance and without apparent reason, the Navahos who had been belligerent all but ceased their raids. This lull in hostilities became a truce, which then extended into a peace that continued almost unbroken for nearly three years.

In Santa Fe there was awareness of this, if continuing disbelief. The unorthodox behavior of the agent did nothing to quiet the skeptics. Henry Dodge was derelict in two of the most important traditional functions of an Indian agent: he neglected to write the usual daily or weekly reports, and—even worse—he was rarely to be found in the agency quarters. On the occasions when visiting officials from Santa Fe or Washington did find him at the fort, it was not behind his own desk, but hobnobbing with the officers. But more often he was not there at all. To any callers who came looking for him, he was usually reported off on some nonsensical trip to a distant band of Navahos, or at one of the pueblo villages, or even on a hunting trip through the

[22] Lane to Secretary of Interior Robert McClelland, February 20, 1854. National Archives, Indian Records. New Mexico Superintendency, 1854–55, Letters Received, Micro. Roll 547. Lane briefly succeeded Calhoun as governor (1852–53), and in turn was succeeded by David Meriwether, who took office August 8, 1853, and served until 1856.

Chuskas with a few Indian friends. With the possible exception of Thomas Keam, who as special agent deeply affronted the Indian Office later with the same reprehensible habits, no Navaho agent in the next sixty years traveled as far into the country of his Indian charges or spent as much time among them.

Two months after his appointment as agent Dodge brought a delegation of one hundred Navahos into Santa Fe, causing a small flurry of alarm in the capital as he led them directly to the plaza before the Governors Palace and to an audience the next day with the new governor, David Meriwether. Indians were no strangers to the townspeople, but in this mounted and armed band, led by the head chief Zarcillas Largo, were the most feared chiefs and headmen of the tribe. Their arrival was more stately than threatening, however, and it was noticed that while they carried lances and shields, and some had bows over their backs or rifles across the saddles, all were dressed in their finest raiment of buckskins and soft-hued blankets. It was noticed also, after they went into camp the first night and during the two days and nights that followed, that not one of the delegation became drunk or was even seen to take a drink.[23]

In bringing the leaders of the Navaho tribe directly to the head of the territorial government in Santa Fe, Henry Dodge was attempting a boldly different approach to the same objectives of the military expeditions of Colonel Washington and Colonel Sumner. The council of the Navahos with Governor Meriwether on September 2 was concerned with peace and a mutual exchange of captive prisoners. There is no mention by Meriwether or Dodge of a written agreement resulting from their meeting, and probably there was none. To the Navahos, remembering the treaty signed by Martinez and Chapitone, it could scarcely have mattered. What did matter was the true intent of both sides in the council; on the basis of events later, the Navahos

[23] The "remarkable" sobriety and general good behavior of the delegation during its stay, September 1 through the morning of September 4, is attested to by Meriwether in a letter of September 17, 1853, to Commissioner George W. Manypenny. National Archives, Indian Records. New Mexico Superintendency, 1849–53, Letters Received, Micro. Roll 546.

did want—so far as then possible—an end to hostilities. One of their number, the sub-chief Archuleta (who presumably did not attend the council), resided nearest to the Río Grande settlements and had led frequent raids between this valley and the border of the Ute country on the San Juan. His people and a few other small bands of Navahos would not necessarily be dissuaded from future raiding.

Governor Meriwether presented medals to Zarcillas Largo and other principal chiefs in a ceremony that evening, the Navahos in turn showing their friendship, after dark of night settled over the town, by staging a dance in the plaza. A fiesta atmosphere brightened the capital, lasting through the next day, but Meriwether was unable to share the townspeople's mood of relaxed tension. His uneasiness over the presence of these Navahos leads us to believe that not he, but Henry Dodge, was responsible for initiating the council and also for bringing it to such a happy end. When the chiefs had withdrawn, returning with Dodge to their homes, the governor confessed that his guests had behaved themselves well, but—to his mind—it had been a mistake to bring them to Santa Fe.

"I am inclined to doubt the policy of bringing these Indians into our settlements for many reasons," he wrote to Commissioner George W. Manypenny. "In the first place it is expensive, then it brings them acquainted with our country its roads and settlements which would be a decided advantage in time of hostility. And last though not the least objection which I will mention is that I think it best for both races that they should have as little promiscuous intercourse as possible with each other."[24]

No advocate of segregation, Dodge was too lax—or too busy—to commit his own notions to paper. During his first year as agent the file of his official correspondence consists of exactly one let-

[24] *Ibid.* Dodge failed to share Manypenny's views. Van Valkenburgh (1941) says that not long afterward, and at the time he moved his agency from Fort Defiance to the vicinity of Sheep Springs, Dodge "acquired a Navajo belle for a wife. Her near relationship to the chief Zarcillas Largo, without any doubt played an important part in her husband's congenial relationship with the tribe."

ter of some six lines. And this quite casually asks only that a small part of his salary be credited to a man named Connelly. For one year he had occupied himself, we may gather, by mingling promiscuously with the Navahos on every possible occasion. There is some foundation for believing so: for one year the Navahos had been at peace. Even Archuleta's band had refrained from murder.

One year and a day after the Navaho council in Santa Fe, Governor Meriwether, possibly to his own surprise, reported that the people of the territory had many wrongs in the past to charge to the Navahos, but "under the judicious management of Agent Dodge, who has taken up his adobe among these Indians, we have had but little cause to complain of them during the present year."[25]

Dodge led another delegation of Navaho chiefs to Santa Fe in the spring of 1854. His purpose this time was to appeal on their behalf for agricultural tools. In Meriwether's absence, the acting superintendent of Indian affairs, William S. Messervy, pleaded a total lack of funds to accommodate such a request; but upon Dodge's firm insistence, he finally requisitioned enough tools in the town so that the Navahos were not sent home empty-handed. Afterwards, reporting to Commissioner Manypenny, Messervy pointed out once more that Washington offered almost nothing—beyond the beggarly expenses of a few agents—that would induce the Indian tribes of the territory to ways of peace. The situation, in fact, was so bad, Messervy added, that Governor Meriwether on occasion was forced to meet such emergencies from his own personal funds.

Henry Dodge was in no position to be a philanthropist on his annual salary of $1,550, but he also may have juggled his quarterly installments of income to help the Navahos. There is some evidence of this, if no proof. At Fort Defiance he needed little and lived frugally. But even so, early in 1854, he applied to his father for a loan of one thousand dollars. The senator forwarded the money, and Henry Dodge arranged to repay it within a year,

25 *Ibid.*, Meriwether to Manypenny, September 1, 1854.

the payments to be taken out of his salary beginning the following January.[26] Again, if there is no certainty, it was in Dodge's nature to have found an expensive cause in which the Navahos were in overwhelming need of assistance.

A much sterner side of Dodge's character revealed itself in October of 1854, when a Navaho—evidently without good reason —killed a soldier near Fort Defiance. Dodge started at once in pursuit of the Navaho, accompanied by Lieutenant Getty and twenty-five infantry soldiers. The fugitive was tracked northward to Laguna Negra, through Washington Pass, and down into the Chuska Valley. Near the Ojos Calientes (later named Bennett's Peak) Dodge and his escort came to the hogan of Armijo, the tribe's principal civil chief. Dodge related to Armijo the circumstances of the soldier's murder. The incident, he said, threatened to blow away in one wind all of the good feeling that had been growing between the *Diné* and the *Bilagáana*. The murderer must be found and turned over to the soldiers for punishment, for only in this way could The People and white men live together in peace.

Armijo was conciliatory, agreeing that justice must be done. In the custom of his tribe, he said, the *Bilagáana* would have full satisfaction for the death of the soldier. The Navahos would pay in sheep and horses any fair amount that was demanded. Dodge replied that this would not do. He respected the Navaho custom, but with his people it was different: the person guilty of wrong, not his tribe, should be punished. Back and forth the point was

---

[26] Only one letter relating to the transaction can be found, and this from Henry Dodge's brother, Senator A. C. Dodge, to Commissioner Manypenny, dated January 23, 1855, and reading as follows: " . . . I beg to file the enclosed power of attorney in your office, if it be the appropriate one, and to respectfully ask that you will notify my brother, thro Governor Meriwether, that it has been filed ec. Also that you will as soon as any portion of the salary therein named be due, cause the same to be sent to my father, and thus very much oblige both him and the writer." Filed with this letter is a memorandum dated June 29, 1854, signed by Henry Dodge, permitting his father "to draw $1,000 of [my] salary as Indian Agent as it becomes due, beginning Jan. 1, 1855." National Archives, Indian Records. New Mexico Superintendency, 1854–55, Letters Received, Micro Roll 547.

argued, Armijo at length promising to have the fugitive Navaho brought to his hogan and ready to surrender to the *siláoo*—the soldiers—within seven days.

Before seven days had passed, Dodge later reported, the Navaho fugitive "was delivered to Lieut. Getty badly wounded by an arrow shot in the loins, he having made [a] fight to the last. The man that shot him is a neighbor of Armijo's who says that but for a shield that he [the prisoner] had provided himself with, he would have been killed, that thirty-eight arrows were shot at him, many of which struck the shield in the center."

The wounded prisoner was taken back to Fort Defiance at once, arriving there on November 7. He was identified as the murderer by a sergeant and two soldiers, Dodge reported, whereupon "Major H. L. Kendrick and myself at the urgent request of Armijo . . . and Sarcillo Largo, the war chief, and one hundred other principal men of the nation . . . had him hung until he was *dead, dead, dead.*"[27]

Governor Meriwether forwarded Dodge's report to Commissioner Manypenny, adding his own comment: "The hanging of this Indian in this summary manner, without a legal trial, is to be regretted, but there is no jails or other means of confining such a prisoner in this Territory until next spring when our civil courts are holden, and it became necessary that an example should be made to impress other bad Indians."[28]

Through the remainder of the year the peace of the territory was disturbed only by depredations of the Jicarilla and Mescalero Apaches. The Navahos remained at peace, as did the three divisions of Southern Utes and Gila Apaches. Agents were instructed by Meriwether to distribute corn in moderate quantities

[27] *Ibid.*, Dodge to Meriwether, November 13, 1854. Dodge and his escort had moved swiftly, traveling a distance of more than 120 miles, capturing the Navaho, and returning him to Fort Defiance in eleven days. Bancroft (1889, p. 675) says, "It was known later that they had hanged a Mexican captive instead of the real culprit!" Bancroft is in error, confusing this incident with a well-known episode of 1858.

[28] *Ibid.*, Meriwether to Manypenny, November 30, 1854.

to the peaceable Indians to help them survive the harshest months of winter.

Corn measured out from jute bags at the agencies, handful by handful was all very well. But Dodge felt that more could be done. Unlike the Utes and Jicarillas, by custom roving buffalo hunters, the Navahos—in some areas—showed some desire to raise their own crops, as indeed they had been doing before the arrival of the first Americans. This flickering of interest Dodge determined to encourage by every possible means. Farm tools were not then regularly supplied to Indians of the territory, but from Meriwether in Santa Fe and from military supplies at Defiance, Dodge wheedled or appropriated every spade and hoe and ax that was found standing idle. These, in the spring of 1855, he turned over to the Navahos.

Armijo himself, long envied for his fields of corn in the Chuska Valley, on one visit to the agency watched with interest as soldiers cultivated a farm plot near the fort. After observing their work for some time in silence, he turned to Major Kendrick. The spade and hoe which Agent Dodge had just given to him were gratefully received, he said. They were better, perhaps, than his old planting stick. But could he not have, if only to borrow, the *bee nihwiildlaadi,* the forked-iron stick that the soldiers used, and the animals that pulled it through the ground? Major Kenddick was forced to decline. In this planting season the fort could not spare its plow, nor even one of the three yoke of oxen that the chief requested.

From Taos came word that Kit Carson, in his new role as agent to the Southern Utes, was having more trouble than he alone could handle. In the mountains above Taos the Capote Utes joined with a hungry village of Jicarillas in a campaign of pillage and murder that spread westward into the lower valleys of the San Juan. Large numbers of cattle, horses, and mules were run off, and by late June more than a score of dead were counted by the raided Mexican families. The warring bands were split apart by troops under Colonel Fauntleroy and Carson, the Jicarillas moving off to the Arkansas River and the Capotes, now mingling with the Moaches, driving their stolen herds to the remote plains beyond the foothills of the La Plata Mountains. Here, swaggering with success, the Utes called upon the Navahos—traditionally their enemies—to drop their women's work of farming and join them in an all-out war against the whites.

Navahos loyal to Dodge reported to him in April that a combined force of nearly one thousand Utes and Apaches were encamped southwest of the La Platas. Relaying this information to Meriwether, Dodge wrote: "The Utahs has said to them that we are an easy prey for them, that they had killed eight hundred of our people since the war commenced." As an inducement to the Navahos to join them, the Utes boasted of the great numbers of livestock they had captured, offering to trade even the best animals for almost nothing. "The Navajos replied that they would buy mules and cows if they could see them, and believe that the Utahs have lied with the view of deceiving them. They have begged the Navajos not to plant this year but to join them and drive the Americans from the Territory. The Navajos reply that we are the best friends they have ever had and they will not do any thing to make us enemies. . . . A few days since, five Mexicans came out to [the Utes'] camps from Arbiquiu to sell them corn and . . . they killed them and got the corn for their trouble."[29]

Two weeks later Dodge was able to assure Meriwether that the Navahos would remain at peace. From "Tunicha"—which may be his term for the home he is said to have built for himself near present Sheep Springs, New Mexico—he reported that he had had "the pleasure of receiving one hundred and fifty hoes an twelve axes which I have distruibited to the Navahos of this place & Cañon Blanco." Also, that "The spring has been unusually wet and bids fair to be a good croping year and this Nation have planted four thousand acres of land and cannot be induced to go to war."[30]

[29] *Ibid.*, Dodge to Meriwether, April 17, 1855.
[30] Sheep Springs is located at the eastern foot of Washington Pass, in the

Dodge was in Santa Fe at the end of June, discussing with Governor Meriwether their mutual plans for a new agreement or treaty with the Navahos. The Navahos had made encouraging progress toward peaceful relations with the whites, Dodge felt, but pressures upon them by warring tribes threatened constantly to destroy every gain he had made. A new treaty with the Navahos might help to divide them more solidly from the Utes and Apaches. In the cool gloom of an office in the Governors Palace, Dodge took time to express these views to Commissioner Manypenny.

"At the commencement of this fiscal year," he wrote, "war was raging on our borders with the Apaches and Utahs and every effort that was possible for me to make had to be put forth to prevent the poor, viciously disposed part of the tribe from joining with the enemy. During the year large and petty thefts have been commited upon the property of our citizens and murder perpetrated upon the body of a soldier near Fort Defiance by the party anxious for war. . . ."

Happily, with the co-operation of the majority and the wiser heads of the tribe, the Navahos had remained at peace. Dodge continued: "They had every prospect of peace and contentment for the year to come but for recent depridations commited upon their lives, liberty & property by the Utahs, who it is evident—

Chuska Valley. I have found no direct evidence of Dodge's residence here, but Van Valkenburgh and McPhee, on the basis of Navaho testimony, remark that "He wisely and bravely established his agency near the eastern approach of Washington Pass above Sheep Springs. He created a stone house and started to work with the $5,000 that Congress had appropriated for the Navajos in the year of 1853. He brought George Carter, an ex-soldier and blacksmith to teach the Navajos ironsmithing. He also brought with him the Mexican silversmith, Juan Anea [Anaya], as well as an unknown assistant and interpreter [actually, Juan Anaya was his interpreter] . . . and two Mexican servants." Dodge, they add, was known to the Navahos as "Red Shirt," or *Be'éé'ɫichii*. Only two of Dodge's letters in this file suggest his residence near Sheep Springs—the letter quoted here, of May 2, 1855, and a letter to Manypenny, dated August 2, 1855, from "Navajo Agency, Pass Washington." All of his other agency letters are dated from Fort Defiance. In a letter to Meriwether of June 30, 1855, Dodge named as his employees Juan Anaya, interpreter, at $500 a year; Manuel Gallegos, herder, at $300; and George C. Carter, blacksmith, at $600.

to revenge themselves for a recent defeat recieved from our troops in which they lost many lives [and] all of their horses and camp equipage—attacked the Ranchos of two rich Navijos living on the south side of the Rio San Juan, killing them both, capturing their children, and running off one hundred head of horses. This has produced a panick in all their farming operations for the present and caused the rich to flee to the mountains with their women, children, flocks & herds, where they have concentrated in a body for mutual protection.

"It is impossible to say what will be the result of this war. The Utahs have fine rifles, live by the chase, and are the most war like tribe in New Mexico. The Navijos have but few guns of inferior quality, live by the cultivation of the soil and the produce of their flocks and herds and are not war like, and if this war is persisted in without prompt and efficient aid is recieved by them from our Government, must fall an easy prey to the Utahs.

"A treaty will be made in the early part of next month with them by Gov. D. Meriwether at which Genl. Garland, the commanding officer of this military department has assured me he will be present, & that the Navijos shall have every assistance against their enemies that it is possible for him to give. That a friendly visit to the heart of their country by the Governor and the Genl. commanding the Military arm of our Government in this Territory will have a happy influence upon these people and secure a treaty of limits and friendship which will last for years, I have every reason to believe.

"A liberal and enlightened policy towards this tribe for a few years will fix their destiny as an agricultural, manufacturing, and stock raising community. That these results can be speedily attain by them no person will doubt who is acquainted with their habits of industry, temperance, and ingenuity. . . .

"P. S. I will make monthly reports in future as requested by the department."

On the same day that Dodge steeled himself to the task of penning this letter, Meriwether wrote to the commissioner that "The Navajos are quiet and I expect to start on a visit to their country in a few days, for the purpose of negotiating a treaty with them." If solely on the basis of these two letters and Dodge's evident enthusiasm for the projected treaty and Meriwether's apparent lack of it, we have reason to suspect that it was the agent, not the Governor, who initiated the council. Also it should be mentioned here that until now the Navaho treaty of July, 1855, has remained in obscurity, forgotten or overlooked in written accounts or records of the territory. The treaty, nevertheless, though never ratified by Congress, was of far greater importance to the Navahos and their white neighbors than the treaties of Colonel Washington and Colonel Doniphan—more important because, for the first time, tribal boundaries were proposed and agreed to; because, through Henry Dodge's insistence, specific promises were made by the government to reward the Navahos with needed tools; and because this was the first Navaho treaty signed by truly representative leaders of the tribe in an atmosphere entirely clear of military coercion.

It is a lasting misfortune that Richard Kern or another artist of his talent could not have been present to record the scene in pencil sketches and water color. For the council at Laguna Negra—in the swarm of Indians present, the flash and movement of weapons and people and animals, of camp equipage and of bright-hued costumes—all of this, in a setting of great natural beauty, was one of the overwhelming pictorial moments of the old West in its supreme, barbaric splendor.

Two thousand Navahos, by Dodge's estimate, riding from all directions, gathered at Laguna Negra and went into camp for three days. By day, there was ceaseless motion, a tumult of sound, a pungent odor everywhere of wood smoke and of mutton and corn cakes frying on coals or baking under white-hot ashes; by night, a blackness, a yelping dog, a chanting voice trailing off in distance, a settling stillness. The valley where this great gathering was held stands high in clear mountain air, some twenty-five miles north of Fort Defiance and four miles west of present Crystal, on the western approach to Washington Pass. Black Lake—Laguna Negra—is a sky-mirroring pool fed by springs and flood run-off of Crystal Wash, a jewel centered in lush grasslands that reach out in all directions but south to encircling mountains. Here, in the fall of 1863, Kit Carson sent Captain John Thompson to establish a grazing camp that would subsist the horses of his command during the final roundup and subjugation of the Navaho tribe.

On the first day of the assemblage the council was nearly disrupted before it started when Delgadito (*Chách'osh nez*—Tall Syphilis), who five years before as a renegade had joined in a Mexican attack against the *Diné*, started a blustering demonstration against Governor Meriwether and his escort. Delgadito and his small band of followers were surrounded and jostled aside by cooler heads, among them the young Manuelito, before anyone in the Governor's party was harmed. For a few moments it had seemed that the emotions stirred by Delgadito's actions could have ended in disaster; instead, the swiftness with which the dissident chief was overwhelmed showed the strong desire of most of the Navahos for peace.

When quiet had been restored, Zarcillas Largo, Armijo, and the other principal chiefs gathered in front of Governor Meriwether's tent, a great crowd of warriors pressing in as closely as they could to hear what was said. The Governor observed that of all the tribe's headmen, only Sandoval, now head of a band of about a hundred of the *Diné Ana'aii*, was absent. He noticed, too, that only a few women and children had come with the men to the council ground, and these now remained out of hearing and tending to the horses and camp fires.

"I have come here," Meriwether began, "to meet the Navajos and am glad to see as many present. I am glad the Navajos and the whites have been at peace so long a time, and hope they will remain at peace. I have come to see you to agree upon a country the Navajos and whites may each have, that they may not pasture their flocks on each others' lands. If we have a dividing line so that we know what each others' country is, it will keep us at peace. I will explain the kind of a treaty I desire to make with you; and when I am through I want you to council with each other whether you will agree to such a treaty, and want an answer in the morning."

Meriwether spoke now, as on the two ensuing days, with the aid of two interpreters. Through them, he outlined the treaty proposals, concluding: "These are the propositions I have to make to you, and want you to talk them over, and let me know whether you agree to them, when we meet again in the morning."[31]

Morning brought with it a dramatic surprise. Dodge and Meriwether were notified by the agency interpreter, Juan Anaya, that Zarcillas Largo intended to resign as the tribe's war chief. (Zarcillas Largo was presumably sincere enough at the time and meant to abdicate. The fact is, the Navahos continued to regard him as their principal chief, and did so until his death. This occurred in the spring of 1862, when, according to Van Valkenburgh and McPhee, he "was killed by the Zunis when he walked into an ambush between Klagetoh and Wide Ruins.") The immediate concern was the effect his withdrawal at this critical moment might have upon the council. His successor, if hotheaded, might lead the Navahos back to war.

Zarcillas Largo made his decision known in this way: he sent, Meriwether reported, "a staff of office and medal presented to him by Governor Calhoun with a message, to the effect that he was too old to govern his people, and that he desired to resign his office." Having no alternative, Meriwether agreed to this. He asked that the other head men meet promptly in council and choose one of their number as Largo's successor. Manuelito, then about thirty-seven years old and yet untouched by the thirst for *todilhil*—whisky—which in time ruined him, was the man chosen.

[31] "Notes of a talk between Governor Meriwether and the Chiefs, Head Men, and Captains of the Navajo Indians, held at Laguna Negra, July 16–18, 1855." This and related documents were enclosed by Meriwether in a letter to Commissioner Manypenny on July 27. The actual treaty draft is missing from the file. National Archives, Indian Records. New Mexico Superintendency, 1854–55, Letters Received, Micro. Roll 547.

Any fears that Manuelito might disrupt the peace council were settled in the afternoon, when the chiefs again met with the Governor. The discussion opened harmoniously:

"GOVERNOR: Yesterday I made known the terms of the proposed treaty and I now want to know whether you all agree to [the] terms.

"MANUELITO: We are content with what you have proposed, and will agree to the terms you have mentioned.

"GOVERNOR: I will now have the terms of the treaty reduced to writing, so that we cannot forget what it contains.

"MANUELITO: It is all good."

Gifts of tobacco were distributed. The chiefs sat smoking, as Meriwether's secretary, W. W. H. Davis, transcribed the treaty terms. Manuelito broke the silence, asking one of the interpreters to tell the Governor that the Navahos regretted Delgadito's actions the day before, that "We are sorry our people treated you badly. . . . I was ashamed to show myself." He said this, he explained, as the man chosen to replace Zarcillas Largo—as the new chief of all of the Navahos. Meriwether replied that the previous day's threats were forgotten, that only a few of the younger men had acted badly. Then to an interpreter he said: "Ask those assembled if they are willing that Manuelito shall have the staff of office and medal that Largas delivered to me. Those in favor will hold up their hands." When this was translated, all in the listening circle lifted their hands.

Twice, as Meriwether proceeded to read the treaty terms to them, Manuelito raised objections. He objected first as the interpreter explained the new boundaries of the Navaho country. The *Diné*, he said, "claimed a much larger country . . . that they were in the habit of going to Mount Palonia [the Carrizo Mountains: shown on the Parke-Kern map as *Cerro de la Paloma*] and another mountain, the name of which is forgotten, to worship the spirits of their fathers, and some were loth to give those mountains up." Also, Manuelito said, the proposed southern boundary would prevent his people from continuing to get salt, as they had always done in the past, from the dry salt lake south of Zuñi.

Epilogue

An air of uncertainty moved through the council as Manuelito spoke and became even more noticeable when Meriwether showed the chiefs a copy of the Parke-Kern map, which he and Henry Dodge had used in planning the reservation limits. Markings on the map to the Navahos were merely white man's witchcraft—meaningless. The Governor put the map down. Manuelito was mistaken, he said. The Carrizo Mountains were "within the proposed reservation and [he] said he hoped that this one sacred mountain would be sufficient." Further, while the salt lake below Zuñi was not within the reservation "he would grant them the privilege of gathering salt as they desired" and would pay the tribe in tools and goods for all of the country they relinquished.

The tribe's eastern boundary—and this was of greatest importance— approximated the line of the Continental Divide. On the Parke-Kern map the line was drawn diagonally from the *Cañada del O Amarillo* (Largo Canyon in northwestern New Mexico) to the headwaters of the Zuñi River (below present Gallup, New Mexico).[32] From the standpoint of natural geography the boundary made sense; in terms of the Navaho people it was totally unrealistic. The new diagonal proposed to abolish a large wedge of country held for generations by the Diné, including Lieutenant Simpson's newly-named Mount Taylor, which probably was the second of Manuelito's two sacred mountains. Meriwether later estimated that the proposed reservation contained about seven thousand square miles—no bargain for the Navahos, he admitted to Commissioner Manypenny, as "the entire reservation does not contain over one hundred and twenty five or thirty square miles susceptible of cultivation, and this in small detached portions."

[32] *Ibid.* In his July 27 letter to Manypenny, Meriwether said: "To enable you to understand the eastern boundary of their reservation, refer to Parke's map of New Mexico which I enclosed to you during the last winter, then draw a line from the head of the Armarillo to the head of Zuñi river or creek, which will give you the true position of the ridge which divides the waters of the Rio Grande from those of the the San Juan, which is a well defined boundary, well understood by the Indians."

How clearly the Navahos understood these things at the moment is impossible to say, but after some consultation among themselves Manuelito and the other chiefs said they would accept the boundaries. Not long afterward they disavowed this agreement, and Navahos whose hogans were on the Río Grande side of the eastern limit paid no attention to it.

Manuelito objected a second time as Meriwether finished reading the ninth and final article of the treaty. His objection was to the proposal that the Navahos should be responsible for capturing and surrendering any of their number who committed depredations. Manuelito spoke sombrely of the Navaho recently captured and hanged for killing the Fort Defiance soldier. This incident had been very unpleasant to his people, he said. Navahos "attempting such a thing did so at the risk of their lives, and [they] would rather that the Americans would come and take such men themselves."

Meriwether pressed the point. If Americans went into Navaho country to arrest wrong-doers, he said, "they would not know the guilty or bad men from the innocent and good, and . . . the latter would probably suffer for the bad deeds of the former, and he must insist on this provision."

Once more the chiefs grudgingly gave their assent—and again, in short time the treaty provision proved entirely unworkable. This "policing" proposal was an extension of Articles IV and V of Colonel Washington's treaty with the Navahos, and visionary still by some twenty years.

The treaty of Laguna Negra was signed the following day, July 18. What misgivings or hopes for it were entertained by Henry Dodge we may only conjecture. He apparently believed that the Navahos were satisfied with the boundary limits.[33] Perhaps he put more store than he should have in the relatively

[33] "The country included in the boundary assigned them by the commissioner is amply sufficient for their purposes of stock raising and farming and is larger than they anticipated, which caused them to returne to their homes very much delighted with the liberal treatment." *Ibid.*, Dodge to Manypenny, August 2, 1855.

generous and specific promises of goods to be paid to the tribe—promises fulfilled in part before the council broke up by a lavish distribution of knives, tools, trinkets, and bright bolts of cloth. The treaty otherwise, except for one undetected thorn, contained the usual solemn protestations of the White Father's provisional good will and protection and mutual assurances of everlasting amity and brotherhood.

The thorn in this uneasy bower was lance-sharp. Henry Dodge was soon to feel its point when Manuelito belatedly decided that grazing land ceded for Fort Defiance horses would, after all, continue to be used by Navaho horses and sheep. But for a few months more the issue was not raised.

Through the remainder of the summer Henry Dodge traveled through the Navaho country, visiting "all of their principal planting grounds," reporting that a bountiful harvest was in prospect, and that the Navahos, although skirmishing with Paiutes and Apaches, were still at peace with the whites.

In early August he appealed to Commissioner Manypenny for funds or equipment to provide flour mills for the tribe. "The Navijos are greatly in want of a few or at least two mills," he wrote, "built after the Mexican fashion, which would not cost, including the transportation of the stones from the Riograndy to this point, more than one hundred and fifty dollars each. This would enable them to have flour and meal instead of useing the grain in its entire state."[34] There is nothing to indicate that the mills were supplied.

Among a few of the Navaho men, Dodge noticed, there was a developing talent for a new craft—blacksmithing. With crude tools they made for themselves from scrap metal or obtained in trade from Mexican settlements, these Navahos were producing remarkable results. Again Dodge appealed to the commissioner. "If the treaty [of Laguna Negra] is confirmed," he wrote, "I respectfully suggest . . . that the Navijos may be furnished with four sets of blacksmith tools and one thousand pounds of iron. They have eighteen native blacksmiths who work with the hand

[34] *Ibid.*

bellows and the primative tools used by the Mexicans with which they make all of the bridle bits, rings, buckles &c."[35]

Governor Meriwether evidently was already persuaded of the possibilities in this new Navaho craft, for at the same time, in recommending treaty goods to be purchased for the tribe, he listed five hundred pounds of rod iron, one gross of assorted blacksmith files, five blacksmith's bellows, five anvils, and five sets of blacksmith's tools. Five sets of tools for eighteen blacksmiths? It was not a great deal to ask, but again there is no certainty that the Indian Office complied with the request.

Neither Dodge nor Governor Meriwether has anything to say of ornaments or jewelry made by these first blacksmiths, but certainly, as they refined their craft, their talent turned in that direction. And at this date—1855—the metals used would appear to have been iron, tin, copper, and brass. The beginning of the fine silverwork would wait a few years more. Henry Dodge's famous namesake, Henry Chee Dodge, is offered as an authority on this point by John Adair: "Chee Dodge states that in the early part of the nineteenth century, before the Navajo were rounded up and taken to Fort Sumner, they wore bits of scrap tin and other metal strung on leather. These leather ornaments they wore around their necks or their wrists."[36]

Henry Dodge was earnest in his appeals. He asked, too, that the government establish a school for the Navahos—modest enough, but the first such request for the *Diné* of which there is any record. Further, he asked the Indian Office to send out artisans who could teach the Navahos how to use their tools.

[35] Annual report, Dodge to Manypenny, September 30, 1855. National Archives, Indian Records. New Mexico Superintendency, 1856–57, Letters Received, Micro. Roll 548.

[36] *The Navajo and Pueblo Silversmiths* (43). To this Adair adds (6): "According to Chee [Dodge], Atsidi Sani, who may well have been the first Navajo to work iron, learned the trade from a Mexican . . . about 1853. According to Grey Moustache, Atsidi Sani learned this art twenty years before he first worked silver, which was not until after his return from Fort Sumner. . . . Therefore, he must have learned blacksmithing about 1850. This information checks with Chee's statement."

"They are getting a few plows," he told the commissioner, but "the government should furnish a farmer to teach them—as well as a blacksmith."

Through another winter and into early spring of 1856, Dodge pursued these thoughts of tools and plows and spring crops; he talked often with the chiefs and headmen; and so far as he knew, all was serene. And then the situation changed. Not all at once, but slowly after one unpredictable incident of crazy violence, the peace of nearly three years eroded away.

A raiding band of young Navahos, impatient with the spring planting peace of their elders, swooped down on the little mountain settlement of Peralta, not far from Cebolleta, killed three Mexicans, and ran off a large herd of sheep from the rancho of Antonio José Otero. This raid, in the glorious old tradition, occured on March 27. A few days later Henry Dodge was at the scene. Very quickly he discovered that the episode might have shattering consequences. Leaders in the affair were not the usual youthful wild ones: they were the rich sons of respected tribal leaders who had recently joined a warring camp of Capote Utes. One was a son of the late chief Narbona. Two others were the sons of Archuleta, headman of the unfriendly San Juan Navahos; the remaining two were sons-in-law of Cayatanita, another headman. To capture and punish them would have the same effect as prodding a stick into a hornets' nest.

To make matters worse, there had been no possible justification for the attack. The Mexicans of Peralta had given no offense. As Dodge soon learned, the young Navahos "perpetrated this outrage to revenge the Utahs for the loss of eight horses stolen them." Stolen not by Mexicans, which might have offered cause, but stolen by Navahos.

On his return to the agency Dodge conferred with Major Kendrick. The Navaho leaders who had been most friendly were now cool. They minimized the importance of the raid, declaring that the Mexican Otero lied when he told Dodge that 11,000 sheep had been run off—the number was not more than 4,000. Dodge himself could not be sure. He had seen the trail where the sheep had been driven to the Chuska Valley and knew only that "it was a large flock." As for the treaty agreement requiring them to capture and turn over the murdering young thieves, the Navahos were unanimous in their refusal to comply.

"All of the chiefs and head men of the tribe with whom Major Kendrick and I have conferred with . . . say that it is impossible to give them up," Dodge reported to Santa Fe, "that it would produce a civil war among themselves in which the Utahs would take part on the side of the offenders. . . . It would be madness in the extreme to attempt to effect any thing with the small force at this post at present, as any small party going out to collect sheep or attempt to capture the murderers could be surrounded by a thousand warriors before going twenty five miles."[37]

Among some of the Navahos, Dodge observed a new attitude of defiance. On a recent visit to the Hopi villages he had found Navahos of the region armed with fine new silver-mounted rifles; and when he made some comment about the weapons, the Navahos had made a challenging retort. They had obtained the rifles from the Mormons, they said, in trade for horses. And tauntingly: the Mormons wondered why the Navahos did not drive the Americans away from Fort Defiance. This they reported to Dodge, looking into his eyes as they spoke, watching for his response.

A few leaders of the tribe were ready to compromise. Armijo and Many Horses, son of the chief Ganado Mucho, had rounded up more than a thousand of the stolen sheep and would surrender them presently, but not now; just now it was the lambing season, and they could not be moved. Also, in restitution for the three Mexicans of Peralta who had been murdered, the Navahos would give up "three servants," meaning by this, most likely, three Paiute women or children who would be slaves. The second part of this offer Dodge and Major Kendrick firmly rejected. Instead, they said the Navahos could offer sheep and horses to the families of the murdered men—the livestock to be rounded up

[37] Dodge to Acting Governor W. W. H. Davis, April 19, 1856. National Archives, Indian Records. New Mexico Superintendency, 1856–57, Letters Received, Micro. Roll 548.

and turned over at another council at Laguna Negra on May 31.

At this second gathering at Black Lake there was none of the good feeling that attended the treaty council. Neither side was pleased by the outcome; and Dodge, feeling "quite unwell," was forced by illness to his bed on returning to the agency. Again, the chiefs had refused stubbornly to surrender the murderers, insisting that payment to the Mexicans be made on their own terms. For his loss in the raid the Navahos now returned to Antonio Otero, through the offices of Agent Dodge, 1,400 sheep and 30 horses. Beyond that, "they also tendered Major Kendrick and I their ponies in payment for the three Mexicans killed by them. As we declined receiving them, they were sent to the owner of the sheep [Otero] . . . by a chief . . . Jon Miguel, who speaks Spanish well."[38]

Dodge's hopes for a friendly settlement were further dimmed a few days later when four Navahos were reported to have raided another Mexican settlement. Two of the four were killed, the news of their death causing the Navahos to say they would make no further payment to the Mexicans of Peralta. Even more disturbing was Manuelito's angry refusal to respect the recent treaty agreement reserving grazing land for horses of the Defiance garrison. The agreement was foolish and meant nothing, Manuelito told Dodge—the land "was his when a boy and would remain so until his death. That if Major Kendrick could not do without hay or grass, he had waggons, mules, and soldiers and could go to the Cetitis [Calites Canyon, or Canyon Chenelle, below Hunter's Point and near Colonel Washington's camp 22 in 1849] thirty miles distant for hay."

"Or," wrote Dodge, relaying the war chief's words to Governor Meriwether, the major could "drive him from the grounds that he occupied if he thought his force was sufficient—that he, Manuelito, was a great captain; that he could call around him in less than one day a thousand warriors. Mexicans they had always

---

[38] *Ibid.*, Dodge to Meriwether, June 2, 1856. In his last letter as agent, Dodge notified the Governor on September 30 that the Navahos had paid Otero "2,000 sheep, 52 horses, and 3 servants."

killed and would when they pleased, and the Americans could not prevent it—that they had made several attempts to [do so] but had always failed."

This, and much more. To the effect that Americans were too fond of sleeping, eating, and drinking, and that Americans had white eyes and so could not see the Navahos to catch them. To the effect that his memories of twenty years of warring with Mexicans and Americans were pleasant memories, and that in this time of war his people had become rich and proud.

Dodge said he could give only two reasons that would account for the sudden change in the Navahos' feeling. First was the killing of the two Navahos by Mexicans; second, and probably most important, a rumor that spread through the tribe early in the previous December that Fort Defiance was to be abandoned and its small garrison marched out of the country led the Navahos to think the *Bilagáana* were weak and ready to withdraw.

Reviewing his work as agent during the last three years, Dodge bitterly concluded that his best efforts to help the tribe meant less to them now than their realization that they could return to raiding and thieving with impunity. "They are no fools," he told Meriwether, "and see at a glance . . . that the troops at this place are too few to prevent them killing and stealing. . . . That the dreadful scourge of war should not be visited upon them I have labored and suffered many privations, but I fear to little purpose."

Gloomily, he added this: "I have this moment received information from a Navijo that a war party headed by the son of Jon Largo, a rich man of the tribe who lives at or near the hot springs, [threatens] to *steal* and kill all persons that may be so unfortunate as to fall in their hands."[39]

Dodge's concern was shared by Major Kendrick. Their reports of Manuelito's increasing belligerence stirred Governor Meriwether to action. Within a month the garrison of Fort Defiance was strongly reinforced. The arrival of these troops, instead of the abandonment of the fort, instantly quieted Manuelito's talk

[39] *Ibid.*, Dodge to Meriwether, June 13, 1856.

of white eyes and boozy lethargy. Navaho sheep were removed from the fort's treaty grazing land. The agency interpreters had confused or misstated his true intentions, Manuelito assured Dodge, and only a few Navahos—at most twenty-eight, and these friends of the Capote Utes—had bad hearts. He would comply with the treaty terms made at Laguna Negra, Manuelito promised; and to show his good will, more sheep and horses were turned over to Dodge to be delivered to Antonio Otero. On one point only, the most important point, he refused to give ground. The murderers of the Peralta raid would not be surrendered.

In his view of this suddenly softening attitude Dodge was realistic. His own good feeling for the Navahos was not changed, but he knew that the tribe would not submit willingly, for some years more, to the restraints of peace. "I give it as my opinion," he observed, "founded upon many years of experience with these people, that if a strong fource is consentrated at different points in their country, and that they have to pay the expenses of the war if the offenders are not delivered, they will give any assistence that may be required of them."[40]

Dodge refers again in mid-July to the illness which had persisted since spring and which he found hard to shake off. His reports to Meriwether came with less frequency during the summer, but by late fall he had recovered sufficiently to join Major Kendrick and a small detachment of soldiers on a patrol of the broken and hilly country south of Zuñi. A few Navahos and Zuñis accompanied the troops as scouts, their purpose being to pick up the trail of the Coyotero or Mogollon Apaches who in recent weeks had been raiding against their northern neighbors.

No trace of the enemy Apaches had been seen, and so no more than the usual precautions were taken each night as the troops made camp. Early on the morning of November 19, when the patrol was some thirty miles southwest of Zuñi, Dodge rolled out of his blankets before most of the others were up and, taking his rifle, started ahead on the route he knew the soldiers would follow that day. As already known in the camp, his plan was to

[40] *Ibid.*, Dodge to Meriwether, July 13, 1856.

hunt through the low brush scrub of the valleys and the tree-covered higher elevations until he found a deer. His tracks were encountered from time to time during the early morning, but he still had not rejoined the column when Major Kendrick camped at nightfall near Laguna Sal, the dry lake which for centuries had supplied Indians from the Mogollon Rim to the San Juan with salt.

His abilities as a hunter and woodsman were so well known that Dodge's prolonged absence, even into the early hours of the night, caused no uneasiness. Nevertheless, partly because his soldiers were shivering in the frosty air, and partly to help Dodge in finding the camp, Major Kendrick ordered more wood thrown on one of the campfires. In the gray twilight of the next morning it was found that Dodge was still missing; it was found too, and perhaps ominously, that several horses belonging to the scouts or troops, which had been allowed to graze at large during the night, had been stolen. Major Kendrick for the first time felt immediate concern for Dodge's safety. Plans for the patrol were swiftly changed and, apparently with no thought for recovering the stolen animals, Kendrick instructed the Indian scouts to find Dodge's trail and follow it until they determined definitely what had happened to him.

"About noon on the 21st," Major Kendrick later reported, "the place where he had been taken, evidently by stealth, was discovered, some four or five miles from the camp where he had left us. Armijo, a friendly Navaho chief, & Salvador, the war captain of the Zuñis, at once said his captors were not Coyoteros, but . . . Mogollones, or Gileños. No violence appears to have been used, but after having been taken, it seemed—judging from the signs which were carefully examined by Lieutenant Bonneau & myself—that a conversation was had between them, after which they went off in a south eastern direction.

"This discovery was made forty-eight hours after the Indians had possession of Captain Dodge. All attempts at pursuit, if they had not been otherwise injudicious, would have been useless, as well from the lapse of time as from the snow storm then coming on & which proved so heavy that our guide lost the trail where he was best acquainted with the country.

"A Mexican captive from Galeana in Old Mexico, who made his escape from another party of Apaches, says if no violence was used towards Captain Dodge in the first instance, there probably would be none afterwards; that Mangus Colorado (with whom Captn. D. is acquainted), or his brother will soon learn of his capture & will send for him."[41]

No one believed that the Apaches had killed Dodge. Kendrick, in fact, was so sure of this that he sent an urgent message to Major Van Horn, commanding at Albuquerque, suggesting that the Apaches—probably of the Mogollon band—were holding Dodge for ransom. He asked Van Horn to notify the Apache agent at Fort Thorn, Dr. Michael Steck "as *quickly as possible,* by whom it is presumed Capt. Dodge's liberation can be effected. I have also to ask that this information be at once sent to [the] governor."[42]

Agent Steck, who could report that the Mimbres and Gila Apaches—the latter band under the leadership of Mangas Colorado—were at peace, was pressed into action. From Governor Meriwether came instructions, dated November 25, that Steck should "without delay send out one or more parties of Miembres Apaches or Mangas Colorada's people to communicate with the Mogollon and Gila Apaches, and try if possible to procure the release of Agent Dodge; I think these parties should not consist of more than one or two persons each, and none but trusty men should be sent. You are authorized to pay . . . to those having him in captivity a ransom if necessary to procure his release."

After three weeks in which nothing more was heard, Agent Steck received a discouraging message from Mangas Colorado. Twenty days previously, or soon after Dodge's capture, bands of the Mogollon and Coyotero Apaches were known to be raiding

---

[41] *Ibid.*, Kendrick to Major W. H. Nichols, Assistant Adjutant General, Headquarters, Department of New Mexico, November 25, 1856.

[42] *Ibid.*, Kendrick to Van Horn, November 22, 1856.

through New Mexico, running off large numbers of horses, mules, and sheep, and taking two wagons from the vicinity of Acoma Pueblo. Steck was further informed that these bands would not make peace, but insolently warned that they planned to make new raids on the lower Río Grande. Of the capture or present condition of the agent Henry Dodge, Mangas Colorado could not say—he knew nothing.

On the first day of the new year a Lieutenant A. E. Steen reported on his patrol out of Fort Thorn to the San Diego Crossing of the river. In a sleeping room of the nearby ferry house, as though tossed aside, he found a badly stained manta wrapping sheet and a hat. The floor of the room was stained with blood, and so were a butcher knife and a table knife lying near the manta cloth. A trail of blood led from the room to the river bank and there, face down in the shallow water, Steen found the body of an Indian, a Mimbres Apache well known to those at Fort Thorn as Costates. The man's head had been split open and scalped. This murder and others equally brutal that followed were attributed to either the Coyotero or the Mogollon Apaches.

The fate of Henry Dodge remained uncertain. Even through June, 1857, after a campaign against these and other bands of Apaches was led by Colonel B. L. E. Bonneville, no trace or account of him was reported. The mystery remained unsolved—until late that summer.

James L. Collins, who eight years before was a companion of Dodge's and served as an interpreter during the Navaho campaign, was one of the first to be informed. During the interval following Colonel Washington's expedition Collins had become publisher of the Santa Fe *Weekly Gazette;* more recently, while continuing to operate his newspaper, he had accepted appointment as superintendent of Indian affairs for New Mexico. It was in this new capacity that he received a message in early September, directed to him from Fort Thorn by Agent Steck.

Three of the outlaw Apaches, Steck wrote, had just now come into the agency, whipped and hangdog, begging for peace. They were members of the Coyotero band. A spokesman for the three, identified as Chino Pena, said this band was in camp on the Gila River when attacked by Colonel Bonneville in June. His people were badly punished in that fight, Chino Pena said, and now were sick of war. Grudgingly he assented as Steck accused the Coyoteros of terrorizing the country in recent months by their acts of theft and murder.

Chino Pena admitted, Steck wrote, "that some of their bad men may have been engaged in stealing, and that the murderer of Agent Dodge was in his camp when attacked by Col. Bonneville, and that he was one of the killed."[43] Agent Steck's letter reveals only this much. When Henry Linn Dodge was killed by the Coyoteros and the circumstances of his death are not known.

A warm friendship developed between the Kern brothers and Lieutenant Simpson, beginning during the stress of the Navaho campaign and growing stronger in the months immediately after-

[43] *Ibid.*, Steck to Collins, September 4, 1857. Bonneville's troops attacked the Coyoteros on June 27, thirty-five miles north of Mount Graham. Twenty-four Apaches, including five women, were killed. Twenty-seven prisoners were taken. Bonneville reported that two of his officers and eight men were wounded, but made no mention of Dodge. (Bonneville to Assistant Adjutant General W. A. Nichols, Santa Fe, July 14, 1857, from "Depot on Gila." 35 Cong., 1 sess., *House Exec. Doc.*, Vol. II, Pt. II [1857–58], 136–41.) Van Valkenburgh (1938 and 1941) has Dodge on a hunting trip with Navaho friends when killed and gives the date as November 15, 1856—four days before Dodge disappeared from Major Kendrick's camp. Bancroft (1889, p. 670n.) says Dodge was killed in 1857 by Mogollon Apaches, and then later says Dodge was killed in 1856. The actual date of death remains unknown. Van Valkenburgh adds this: "Owing to the heavy snows, it was not until three months later that the Navajos guided Lieutenants [Josiah Howard] Carlisle and [John W.] Alley and a detachment of dragoons to the scene of Red Shirt's death. Pitifully little of him remained—the coyotes had been at work. Gathering up the few remains and placing them in a sack, the soldiers returned to Fort Defiance. A few days later, Captain Dodge was buried with full military honors in the post cemetery." He adds that Sam Yost, editor of the *Rio Abajo News* of Albuquerque, in 1858 visited the cemetery and later printed this version of the inscription on the headboard of Dodge's grave: "To the memory of H. L. Dodge, aged 45 years. Agent of the Navajos. Killed by the Apache Indians on 15th of November 1856. A portion of his remains rest below this spot." In July, 1963, I found the old cemetery, enclosed by barbed wire, a desolate and forgotten place with only three graves still marked by stones. Dodge's grave was not one of these and could not be positively identified.

ward. From their return to Santa Fe until the day following Christmas, 1849, Richard and Edward Kern remained in the capital on the payroll of the Topographical Corps, under Simpson's guiding eye working on the materials brought back from the expedition. It was in this period of three months that Richard finally completed all of his drawings and Edward made the finished rendering of his map. These, together with the collection of plants and minerals, Simpson kept at hand while writing the manuscript copy of his Navaho journal.

In no hurry to return to Philadelphia, the Kerns lingered on. Richard in March, 1850, accompanied a party of troops under Captain Henry Bethel Judd of the Third Artillery on a patrol down the east bank of the Pecos from its headwaters near Las Vegas to the Bosque Grande, later the site of Fort Sumner. Some weeks later he back-traced the old Spanish *Jornada del Muerto* down the Río Grande to the vicinity of El Paso. Results from these surveys, compiled with knowledge previously gained, formed the basis of the Parke-Kern Map of the Territory of New Mexico. Richard executed the cartography; and when this was finished in July, the map was sent to J. & D. Major, a New York firm of lithographers, for copying and printing.[44] Otherwise, the brothers marked time while waiting for something better—Edward putting in nearly a year as a forage master for the army post at Abiquiu, Richard staying on in Santa Fe as a quartermaster's clerk and storekeeper and as an enumerator in a territorial census survey.

New Mexico had little need of the Kerns' special skills, but

[44] The *Jornada del Muerto* was a ninety-mile stretch of nearly waterless desert north of El Paso from Robledo to Fra Cristobal, avoiding a wide bend in the river and skirting east of the Caballo and Fra Cristobal mountains. The *jornada* was so named when traveled by Oñate's party of colonists, in grim token of extreme hardship, upon their arrival in New Mexico in 1598. Referring to the Pecos and Río Grande surveys, Simpson wrote that Richard had "made a map free of expense to the Topl. Dpt., for the use of the Col. comdg. the 9th Mily. Department, [and] he has been employed for some days back at a small compensation in making a duplicate of it for the use of the bureau." Simpson to Abert, July 4, 1850. National Archives, War Records. Record Group 77, Topographical Bureau S, Letters Received, 1845-50, Box 69.

once more, in the summer of 1851, military assignments offered escape, at the same time requiring them to part company and leave the territory in different directions. Edward was engaged by Captain John Pope to assist him in surveying an easier, more direct route from Santa Fe to Fort Leavenworth. A pencil sketch by Edward shows the point of their departure in August: Barclay's Fort on the Mora River—adobe walls, a round rifle tower, and a guard's room over the main gate giving the structure a small-brother resemblance to the now abandoned Bent's Fort on the Arkansas. Barclay's establishment was soon to be overshadowed by Fort Union, seven miles to the north on Coyote Creek. Besides Edward Kern's drawing we have a pungent description in the words of a contemporary traveler, W. W. H. Davis, who in 1853 " . . . left the fort [Union] in the afternoon, and drove two miles beyond Barclay's Fort, where we encamped for the night. This is a private trading-post, and was built during the war with Mexico. It is a large adobe establishment, and, like the immense caravansaries of the East, serves as an abode for men and animals. From the outside it presents rather a formidable as well as a neat appearance, being pierced with loop-holes and ornamented with battlements. The rooms within were damp and uncomfortable, and all the surroundings looked so gloomy, the hour being twilight, that it reminded me of some old state prison where the good and great of former times have languished away their lives. As we were now in a country abounding with wood, and no danger to be apprehended from the Indians, we built up a large fire at our place of camping, and slept with some degree of comfort."

From Fort Leavenworth, where the charting of the trail ended, they continued to St. Louis, Edward remaining long enough to help Pope complete his notes and a map. The new route they had explored offered better watering places and more forage, but in the years following it was only lightly traveled, most of the wagon trains and stages continuing to use one or another of the several routes of the Santa Fe Trail. Edward, meanwhile, in September was once more home in Philadelphia.

As his brother was traveling east, Richard Kern stayed on briefly in Santa Fe, preparing to go west with an exploring expedition led by Captain Lorenzo Sitgreaves. Although most of the company had assembled in Santa Fe and left there in August, the command would form and officially start from Zuñi Peublo. The first stage of the journey, therefore, back-trailed part of the route Richard had taken two years before with Lieutenant Simpson. One camp was made at Inscription Rock, a place for him of good memories and a place where Richard now might easily have played the role of guide. On a relatively unscarred stretch of El Morro's northeast face, Richard, Captain Sitgreaves, and S. W. Woodhouse, the party's physician and naturalist, carved their names and the date—August 30, 1851. One of the few inscriptions near theirs, of later date perhaps, is the cryptic "Old Punk."

From here in one day's leisurely ride the command moved on to Zuñi, going into camp near the pueblo and remaining for several weeks. The party now included Lieutenant John G. Parke, Antoine Leroux as guide, ten Mexicans and five Americans as packers and *arrieros* (muleteers), and a military escort of thirty men led by Major Kendrick, whom we have met in his duties before and following the present expedition. Among these companions Richard Kern is listed as "draughtsman"—which is good enough; in addition to his sketches and diary notes, he would assist John Parke with astronomical readings and eventually draw the map of the Sitgreaves route. His map would clear up certain military misconceptions of the country's geography; it would not, however, chart a region unknown and unexplored. For some twenty years parts of this central route to California had been followed by occasional adventurers such as the present guide, Leroux, and by Old Bill Williams and Simpson's Santa Fe friend, Richard Campbell.

Members of the expedition, before the journey was done, had their share of snake bite and encounters with Indians—unfriendly Yampais and friendly Mohaves—as well as more than enough of a rough mountain-desert terrain and a diet of mule meat.

Otherwise, for our purposes here, Sitgreaves' general objective of marking out a suitable wagon road north of the familiar Gila River route, is best explained in his orders received from Colonel J. J. Abert: "The river Zuñi is represented on good authority to empty into the Colorado, and it has been partially explored by Lieutenant Simpson to the Pueblo of Zuñi. You will therefore go to that place, which will be, in fact, the commencing point of your exploring labors. From the Pueblo Zuñi you will pursue the Zuñi to its junction with the Colorado, determining its course and character, particularly in reference to its navigable properties, and to the character of its adjacent land and productions. The junction of the Zuñi and Colorado will be accurately determined. You will then pursue the Colorado to its junction with the Gulf of California, taking those observations which will enable you accurately to delineate its course."[45]

Captain Sitgreaves led his command down the Zuñi River on September 24, found that stream did not flow into the Río Colorado, but into the Little Colorado, and at no point in its modest

[45] Captain Lorenzo Sitgreaves, "Report of an expedition Down the Zuñi and Colorado Rivers." Simpson not only inspired the idea of the Sitgreaves expedition, but envisioned its eventual outcome—a direct, short route between Albuquerque and Los Angeles. Simpson first mentioned such a route when, on his return to Santa Fe from the Navaho campaign, he wrote to Colonel Abert, September 28, 1849, in part as follows: "Another matter of interest which has been evolved by the [Navaho] expedition, & which I have come near forgetting, but which probably stands foremost in point of value, is, the belief that we have hit upon a middle route, between the Southern detour made by Col. [Philip St. George] Cook[e], from Santa Fe and the Northern one called the Spanish Trail route, said to be equally long. It is very certain that from Santa Fe to Zuñi, a distance of near two hundred miles & in an almost direct course to the City of the Angels, we traversed a well watered, wooded & pastured route, which, with very little labor, can be made an excellent wagon road. And our guide, Carravahal, informed me that from Zuñi, which stands upon the Rio Zuñi—a tributary of the Colorado, and which has been followed down to its mouth—from Zuñi to the Colorado by the way of the Rio Zuñi the road is equally practicable for wagons and abounds in the necessary quantum of wood, grass & water. If so, and the route can be as favorably extended from the Colorado westward to the Pacific, of which I have very little doubt, there is no question but that a wagon route has been obtained which cannot but shorten the distance to San Francisco, at least from three to four hundred miles, if not more." National Archives, War Records. Record Group 77, Letters Received, Topographical Bureau S, 1845–50, Box 69.

wanderings was navigable by anything much larger than a frog. Kern's map traces the command's route down the Little Colorado to Leroux Creek (named for Antoine) near present Holbrook, Arizona, on past the Grand Falls to Black Falls, and into the moonscape region of cindery black soil and lava that surround the prehistoric walls of Wupatki and its associated ruins. Richard examined a few of the larger sites and conjectured that lack of water had caused the ancient pueblos to be abandoned.

On Leroux's suggestion, no doubt, and to avoid the gorge of the Grand Canyon, the command struck south from Wupatki, circled the San Francisco Mountains to the north, and from Leroux Springs near modern Flagstaff traveled west until the Colorado River was joined, twenty miles north of the thirty-fifth parallel and in the vicinity of present Davis Dam, which forms Mohave Lake. Along the way Richard exercised the prerogatives of an explorer-cartographer, naming landmarks after members of the party. Thus we have the creek and springs named for Antoine Leroux; Kendrick Peak, Sitgreaves Mountain, and Parke Creek, all in the vicinity of the San Francisco Mountains; and—for an old friend—Bill Williams Mountain, rising to the south of present Williams, Arizona.

In skirting to the south of Williams Mountain, the command passed a small creek which stirred memories. It was here, or near here, Leroux told Kern, that he had run into Old Bill—long ago, in 1837—when each on his own had been running trap lines on the mountain streams. The creek, a small branch of the Verde River, therefore is marked as Bill Williams Fork on Kern's map. The name on later maps was confused and finally lost, but survives now as the Bill Williams River—an altogether different proposition. Heading in the Santa Maria Mountains far to the south and west, this stream empties into the Colorado near the present Parker Dam.[46]

[46] Captain A. W. Whipple of the Topographical Corps originated the confusion in 1853–54 with his Preliminary Map . . . for a Pacific Rail Road Route Near the 35th Parallel. In addition to showing "Williams Creek" where Kern placed Bill Williams Fork, Whipple also marked as "Bill Williams Fork" the far distant Bill Williams River and its smaller fork, the Big Sandy. From that time

After meeting with the Colorado, reached through a pass in the Black Mountains, the command worked its way south for more than two hundred miles, riding close to the river's eastern bank and passing through the broken, arid country of the Mohave Indians. On November 30, ending a march of 657 miles, the expedition reached Camp Yuma. There was no purpose in Sitgreaves' continuing to the Gulf of California, since at Camp Yuma he had reached the Gila River and the westward extension of the well-known Gila route to the coast.

If the results of Sitgreaves' expedition were largely negative, the tangential course charted by his command provided useful information. By avoiding his Zuñi River zig and Little Colorado zag, a serviceable central route from Albuquerque to Los Angeles was determined within several years. This followed the now obvious choice of the Wingate Valley and Río Puerco of the West to the San Francisco Mountains, then arching over the Arizona plains to present Kingman and dropping down to Needles and its hot doorway to the great California desert. Otherwise, the principal benefits from Sitgreaves' efforts derive from Richard Kern's map and his drawings—some fifty landscapes and studies of Indians and Arizona flora and fauna.

Sitgreaves himself appears to have taken a sour view of his recent wanderings. In an opening paragraph to his report, which he managed to compress to eighteen pages of lackluster prose, he summed up his two months of travel and adventure with these words: "I can add very little to the information afforded by the [Kern] map, almost the entire country traversed being barren, and without general interest."

Soon after the expedition disbanded at Camp Yuma, Richard arrived "fat and saucy" in San Diego—this expression being the euphemism of a friend, George McKinstry, who encountered him there. As a result of his recent diet of alkali water and jackass steaks, Richard's clothes probably flapped on his usually round frame. His stay in California was limited to a few weeks and a

to the present, other cartographers have accepted the error and failed to identify the creek in Arizona that Kern named for Old Bill.

few new acquaintances—among them, John Sutter—before he boarded a sailing vessel at San Francisco which returned him to Philadelphia in the early part of 1852.

Richard and Edward Kern were to be found during the next year either at home in Philadelphia or in Washington. They both continued to paint, as circumstances allowed, but they were increasingly preoccupied with affairs related to their recent western travels and their efforts to secure assignments to new ventures in exploration. In Congress and the capital's military departments, as elsewhere, there was recognition of the brothers' contributions to the expeditions and reports of Frémont, Simpson, Washington, Pope, and Sitgreaves. Lieutenant Simpson's journal had been so well received by Congress that its first printing as a government document, though running to an extra three thousand copies, was soon exhausted. Public interest was aroused, enhanced by Richard's drawings and Edward's map of the Navaho country, to the point that Simpson arranged for a second edition, to be published privately by a Philadelphia firm in 1852. Again the Kern plates were used, thirty-four of them in color.[47]

From his knowledge of the Río Grande and Upper Pecos valleys and the Zuñi country, Richard prepared a map and an article of seven pages tracing Coronado's exploration in New Mexico, for inclusion in Henry Schoolcraft's revised *Indian Tribes of the United States,* and for later reference by Simpson in writing his "Coronado's March." Also during this period Richard drew attention in Washington as a persuasive advocate of a railroad route to California approximating the route he had so recently explored with Sitgreaves.

---

[47] The private edition was published as the *Journal of a Military Recconnaissance, from Santa Fe, New Mexico, to the Navajo Country in 1849.* Robert Taft, in *Artists and Illustrators of the Old West, 1850–1900* (258), observes that in the private edition the drawings are credited to Richard Kern, but some are recorded as being after sketches by Edward. Of the 1850 government edition, Taft remarks that "although I have not made the matter a point of special study, [the] colored plates must be among the earliest in government reports reproduced by multiple impressions."

Epilogue

Richard had seen enough of the westward migration of 1849 and after, enough of California's golden promise, to be convinced that the tide of westward movement would not soon ebb, but was now only beginning. He could not share Simpson's pessimism that "the time has not yet come" for rails linking East with West. He believed that the time indeed had come for a Pacific railroad. His views on this he expressed in a twenty-four page treatise, an ardent appeal which he placed in the hands of Senator William M. Gwin of California. Senator Gwin read Richard's proposals before the United States Senate on January 17, 1853, and shortly thereafter won an appropriation from Congress for surveying a western rail route. News of this and of Richard's part in it was welcomed in Santa Fe, where the Kerns' old friend, Spruce M. Baird, commented in an editorial for the *Gazette* that Richard Kern "has done us a noble act of kindness for which we trust our citizens will in some appropriate manner express their thanks."[48]

Time would tell the measure of Richard's service. At the moment in Washington, while there was a ground swell of sentiment for a Pacific railroad, there was no unanimity of agreement over the best route. In his report to Senator Gwin, Richard argued against Frémont's Humboldt route to the High Sierras (too much snow) and against the Fort Smith–Canadian–Gila River route as equally impracticable (too little timber for rail ties). He advocated instead a central route, the route taken, with some deviations, in the 1880's by the Atlantic and Pacific Railroad, forerunner of the Atchison, Topeka and Santa Fe.

Richard admitted that this route, too, offered desert obstacles; but it could be traveled in all seasons of the year, and there was ample lumber for ties in the mountains between the Río Grande and the Colorado. There were others, however, who held out for a northern route to San Francisco, following the thirty-eighth parallel.

Edward Kern, meanwhile, in early March of 1853 secured a Navy Department appointment as artist with the North Pacific

[48] Santa Fe *Gazette*, March 26, 1853.

Expedition, sailing in June from Chesapeake Bay aboard the U.S.S. *Vincennes*, a sloop-of-war and the flagship of four sister vessels in the same command. The expedition started out under Commander Cadwalader Ringgold, bound first for the China coast and three years of Pacific charting and exploration.[49] While at sea, Edward busied himself drawing marine specimens and familiarizing himself with the expedition's daguerreotype camera; later, left ashore with ten others at Glazenap Harbor while the *Vincennes* scouted northward into Arctic waters, he sketched the native Chukchis, a Siberian tribe that bore some physical resemblance to the Navahos.

A few days before his brother boarded the *Vincennes* in Chesapeake Bay, Richard traveled overland to St Louis, there in early June joining the survey party of Captain John W. Gunnison. There also, by happy chance, he met Simpson—a cheerful reunion in which Gunnison took part. Under instructions of the Topographical Corps, Gunnison was to retrace Frémont's ill-planned course of 1848–49, but now in summer, and by following the thirty-eighth parallel determine the feasibility of a railroad route from Missouri, near Independence, to Salt Lake City.

Gunnison left Richard in camp at Westport to outfit the expedition while he proceeded to Fort Leavenworth with Lieutenant E. G. Beckwith, his second in command, to pick up an escort of mounted riflemen under Captain R. M. Morris. Others in the party included Frederick Creutzfeldt, a botanist who had been with the Kern brothers on Frémont's last expedition; J. A. Snyder, a youth of eighteen and Richard's assistant topographer; Sheppard Homans, astronomer; Dr. James Schiel, surgeon and geologist; and a small number of muleteers and packers engaged in Westport.

Finally, on June 23, the command moved off to a straggling

---

[49] Hine, in *Edward Kern and American Expansion*, gives a detailed account of the voyage, from Hong Kong (where Ringgold was replaced in command by Lieutenant John Rodger) to the Bonin Islands, the Ryukyus, and the coastal waters of Japan and Siberia. The *Vincennes* recrossed the Pacific to San Francisco and finally, after stops at Hawaii and Tahiti, brought the expedition home in July, 1856.

start in chilling downpours of rain, with Gunnison's gloomy observation that "All is *green,* the men & the business." While the main party followed the Santa Fe Trail, Gunnison took Kern and a small escort on a divergent route swinging to the northwest and following the Kansas River to new Fort Riley, built on the border of the Cheyenne country at the junction of the Smoky Hill and Republican rivers. From here they dropped south again to the Arkansas, rejoining the slower train of the command. On July 29 they looked down into a shallow valley where the river bends south, upon the broken walls of an old landmark—the adobe fort that bore his name and which William Bent had partially burned when he abandoned it four years before. There were ghosts on the river bend, and Gunnison was of no mind to linger.

Seven days later they were winding upward into the forests of the San Juan Mountains, then through the Sangre de Cristo Pass, and down into the San Luis Valley. From Fort Massachusetts their Mormon guide, William Potter, led them northwesterly over Cochetopa Pass to the Grand River—soon to be renamed the Gunnison—and then to the Green River ford on the old Spanish Trail, where they made camp on October 1. Through the warm early days of October the command crossed the Wasatch range, descending to the Sevier River, on the twenty-fourth camping on that stream some eighteen miles above Sevier Lake.

After entering the Sevier Valley, Gunnison had encountered a large band of Paiutes, still smarting from a recent brush with a California emigrant train in which one Indian was killed and two others wounded. While the daily presence of the Indians near his trail was known to Gunnison, he evidently believed there was nothing to fear from them. Possibly he had been informed of the emigrants' attack on the Paiutes; perhaps also he was reassured by word that an agent of Brigham Young had, not long afterward, talked with the injured band and received their promise not to molest the Mormon settlements of this valley.

In any case, on October 25, Gunnison divided his command, sending the main party under Captain Morris scouting northward along the river while he and eleven others descended the stream to explore Sevier Lake. This group, which included Kern, Creutzfeldt, and the guide, Potter, camped that night in the shelter of the riverbank, in wooded bottomland at the head of the lake.

Lieutenant Beckwith, who was with Morris, pieced together and later described what befell the Gunnison party at daybreak on October 26: "The sun had not yet risen, most of the party being at breakfast, when the surrounding quietness and silence of this vast plain was broken by the discharge of a volley of rifles and a shower of arrows . . . mingled with the savage yells of a large band of Pah-Utah Indians almost in the midst of the camp, for, under cover of the thick bushes, they had approached undiscovered to within twenty-five yards of the camp fires. The surprise was complete. At the first discharge, the call to 'seize your arms' had little effect. All was confusion. Captain Gunnison, stepping from his tent, called to his savage murderers that he was their friend; but this had no effect."[50]

Captain Morris first received word of the attack some hours later when one of his corporals, attached to Gunnison's party, stumbled into his camp on foot, collapsing from exhaustion. A second survivor, who had not lost his horse, rode into camp; and two others straggled in later, Morris meanwhile having started for the scene with his remaining escort.

Darkness had settled over the valley when they reached Gunnison's camp. Finding no bodies, Morris began to believe there were other survivors in the vicinity and ordered a fire to be kept burning through the night, as Major Kendrick would do for Henry Dodge in the hills below Zuñi.

In morning twilight a search was made in the willow bushes fringing the river, and here all uncertainty ended. One by one they were found: Richard Kern, with a single musket ball through the chest; Gunnison, pierced with fifteen arrows; Creutzfeldt and Potter; the bald-headed cook, John Bellows; and three privates in Morris' company of riflemen—Caulfield, Liptoote, and

[50] 33 Cong., 2 sess., Sen. *Exec. Doc. 78.*

Mehrteens.[51] All of the bodies had been horribly mutilated, some of them disemboweled and others with the arms cut off at the elbows. There was no thought of removing them: they were buried where they lay.

Long before the news reached Edward, aboard the far-off *Vincennes*, Simpson learned of Richard's death. From his home in St. Paul, Minnesota, their companion of the Navaho campaign wrote a tribute to Richard, now dead at the age of thirty-two, and to Edward, recently "gazetted as artist in the Japan expedition." He wrote, too, of their elder brother, Benjamin (only thirty years old when he was killed), and of their association with Frémont "at the time of his great disaster in the Rocky Mountains." The two younger brothers he commended as "most eminent artists . . . good portrait painters and most excellent topographers." But it was Richard especially he mentioned for his zeal and devotion in assisting him during their days together in New Mexico.

"But both he and Gunnison are gone!" he wrote. "Little did they think when we met together in St. Louis in June last, and talked over the past, and speculated upon the future in respect to the expedition they were just entering on, that so sad a fate awaited them. . . . Kern was all life and animation at the broad prospect before him."[52]

A few broad horizons remained for Edward. Having experienced both, he now knew with certainty that charting the seas

[51] 33 Cong., 1 sess., *House Exec. Doc. 18*. There are several versions of what took place in the moments following the Paiute attack. Evon Z. Vogt, Jr., on the authority of one Charles Kelly of Salt Lake City, gave this account: "The first one to get up in the morning was the cook who was a bald-headed man. As soon as his bald head shone above the tops of the willows, he was filled full of arrows. . . . The terrified shouts of the cook awoke the other members of the party who jumped up and were all filled with arrows except the two who slept in [a] willow patch." Josiah Gibbs, writing in the *Utah Historical Quarterly*, Vol. I (1928), quotes a member of the expedition, Mercer, as saying forty years afterward that Kern was standing beside a campfire and Gunnison was washing in the river, that Kern was killed in the first volley of shots.

[52] The Philadelphia *Daily National Intelligencer*, January 24, 1854. Simpson's letter is signed only with the initial S and is dated December 20, 1853.

appealed more to him than exploring the plains and mountains of the Far West. For two years after the return of the *Vincennes* he remained close to Washington, completing the topographical charts and sketches made during the long months of the North Pacific Expedition. His work inevitably led to his assignment, under Commander John M. Brooke, to a second Pacific survey. The purpose this time was to chart more exactly the reefs, shoals, and islands athwart the main sea channels used by the American sea traders and Navy; to anticipate the dominance of steam vessels by finding suitable harbors that ships could use as coaling depots; and to survey islands and atolls heavy with the white droppings of ocean birds. In guano, it was believed, fortunes might be made: untold numbers of farmers would demand and benefit from the fertilizer. This last, if not offering broad horizons, still in a sense was pioneering.

The U.S.S. *Fenimore Cooper,* a two-master of only ninety-five tons, made its departure from San Francisco on September 26, 1858, bound for Hawaii and Midway (and the guano-rich islands between), and again for the China coast and Japan. It was a voyage that lasted a year and a half. As before, Edward returned to Washington to complete his work for the expedition. But the atmosphere of the capital now was different: Washington was torn with dissensions, each day in fear or anger living under clouds of civil war. Brooke's sympathies were proslavery; when Virginia seceded from the Union, Brooke resigned his commission in the Navy to enlist in the Confederate forces. Charts and drawings for the second Pacific survey were abruptly shelved.

Edward's emotional involvement, perhaps less militant than his late commander's, made him restlessly opposed to a painter's life in a quiet Philadelphia studio. Regardless of past bitterness (in the San Juans one winter it had been hatred), he hailed the return to Washington, as did many others, of a tarnished idol. Frémont had returned, in the uneasy aura of a vindicated national hero, to accept orders as a major general in command of the Western Department of the Army. Which of the two men made the first overture we cannot be sure, but shortly after Frémont's arrival Edward enlisted in the Topographical Corps and accepted Frémont's appointment as a captain and member of his staff.[53] The appointment was irregular, since Frémont through neglect or oversight, failed to enroll Edward's commission with the Adjutant General.

Several weeks later, probably in late July, 1861, Edward reported to Frémont's headquarters in St. Louis. Missouri was then in a seething turmoil of divided loyalties, the Union forces confronted on all sides by guerrilla raiders, who mingled their strikes with the Confederate operations of Sterling Price and Ben McCulloch at Wilson's Creek and Lexington.[54] Edward's services were in immediate demand. For intelligence of Rebel troop movements and military installations, he was sent into the border states of Tennessee and Kentucky, and upon his return performed similar duties in southern Missouri, mapping and sketching Rebel-held terrain.

A moment of crisis came on the morning of August 30 when Frémont, declaring martial law throughout Missouri, issued a proclamation that placed him in direct conflict with President Lincoln's war policies. The proclamation, characteristically

[53] Edward would find himself in colorful company. Among Frémont's guards, helpers, and advisers—as Carl Sandburg notes—"were three Hungarians, General Alexander Asboth, chief of staff, Colonel John Fiala, chief topographical engineer, Major Charles Zagonyi, head of a cavalry battalion; and Italians such as Captain Antonio Cattanco, Captain Ajace Saccippi, and Lieutenant Dominica Occidone. . . . Some of Frémont's foreign aides carried titles queer in St. Louis: 'adlatus to the chief of staff,' 'commander of the bodyguard,' 'military registrator and expeditor.' " (*Abraham Lincoln: The War Years*, I, 340.) Edward, who had no such distinguished title, was subject to Frémont's personal orders, but worked most closely with Captain Charles de Arnaud, a French veteran of the Crimean War. Frémont received his command July 3, 1861, and arrived at his St. Louis headquarters July 25.

[54] Much had happened to Price since he relieved Doniphan at Santa Fe in 1846. A Virginian, more lately removed to Missouri, he had resigned from Congress to serve in the war with Mexico, and in that conflict was credited with the capture of the state of Chihuahua. From 1853 to 1857 he served as governor of Missouri. Ben McCulloch, a Tennessean, followed Davy Crockett to Texas in 1835, was active in Texas politics and in Indian and border warefare. In the war with Mexico he served with a company of Texas Rangers as head of a group of spies and scouts in Mexico.

phrased, arrogated to Frémont the sole administrative command of Missouri. Across the state and dividing it in half he proclaimed a boundary line: Confederate or guerrilla forces caught bearing arms north of the line would be shot. The property of any Missourian bearing arms against the United States would be confiscated, "and their slaves, if any they have, are hereby declared freemen."

Lincoln, who had not been consulted or even advised of the proclamation until it was published in the newspapers, wrote to Frémont on September 2, insisting that the proclamation be modified. "Should you shoot a man," Lincoln said, "according to the proclamation, the Confederates would very certainly shoot our best men in their hands in retaliation; and so, man for man, indefinitely. It is, therefore, my order that you allow no man to be shot under the proclamation without first having my approbation or consent." Lincoln added that "the confiscation of property and the liberation of slaves of traitorous owners will alarm our Southern Union friends and turn them against us; perhaps ruin our rather fair prospect for Kentucky."[55]

As he soon learned, Lincoln was dealing with the same Frémont of old (who in California told General Kearny to go to hell), and an ambitious new Frémont as well (the presidential candidate of the new Republican party in 1856). For Frémont it was a heady moment. He informed the President that he would not change his proclamation by a single phrase. The proclamation touched to the nerve ends issues of vast national political importance, and Frémont knew it. He knew it well enough that he coolly forced Lincoln's patience to the breaking point.

Edward Kern, meanwhile, far removed from these affairs, was off in the field and later, in October, with Frémont's troops marching south on an abortive thrust to liberate Springfield. (Frémont's mind was elsewhere, on larger concerns. In a letter to his wife, he wrote: "My plan is [to capture] New Orleans. . . . I think it can be done gloriously. . . ."[56]) It was in the vicinity of

[55] Sandburg, *Abraham Lincoln: The War Years*, I, 342–43.
[56] *Ibid.*, 349.

Springfield, and with a glorious victory only in visionary prospect, that Frémont was notified of his removal from command.
The message was delivered on November 2, signed with Lincoln's name. Soon afterward Edward shared in his commander's
downfall. Frémont's oversight in the matter of Kern's captaincy
was discovered, the commission was revoked, and Edward suddenly found himself returned to civilian life.

For Edward the horizons had closed in, the days of adventure
were over. The worst years of the war lay ahead, but for him the
war was over, and life itself was over—or nearly so. He returned
to Philadelphia and to a studio on Chestnut Street. All of his
life he had suffered from occasional seizures of epilepsy, and perhaps this contributed to a final illness in the fall of 1863, when
he was one month past his forty-first birthday. When the end
came, the preoccupations of wartime permitted only this brief
notice in the Philadelphia *Public Ledger* of November 28:
"KERN—on the 25th inst., EDWARD M., son of the late John
Kern. The relatives and male friends are respectfully invited to
attend the funeral, from the residence of his brother, John Kern
Jr., on Sunday next at 2 o'clock."

Lieutenant Simpson started writing the Navaho journal during the first week of January, 1850. The work occupied him for
a little more than three months; and as his name appears con-
sistently during this time on the muster rolls of Fort Marcy, we
may presume that his manuscript was written entirely in his barracks quarters occupying one side of the fort's quadrangle. He
wrote with pen and ink on legal-sized sheets of ruled white paper.
He made few erasures, merely scratching out a faulty word or
phrase and writing a correction in the white space above. His
first draft appears to have been the only one he made.[57] On April

[57] The original manuscript is at the National Archives: War Records, Record
Group 77, Office Chief of Engineers, 1789–1877, Case 1, Drawer 4. The work was
evidently edited in the Government Printing Office. Changes were few, mainly
in minor points of style, punctuation, and the spelling of names—in which Simpson was careless. A private edition of the journal was published in 1852 by
Lippincott, Grambo & Co. of Philadelphia.

13 the work was done, Simpson advising Colonel J. J. Abert that he was forwarding his journal, the collection of plant and mineral specimens made on the recent expedition, and the Kern brothers' drawings and map.[58]

There had been interruptions. As early as February, Simpson apparently was advised of an impending survey he might have to make, for he wrote to Colonel Abert saying that "it is all important that I should be supplied with the proper instruments. At present I am without a barometer, and thermometers, and have but one pocket compass that is good for anything." He asked that these instruments be sent to him immediately, as well as "some drawing paper of which I am entirely destitute, and some India ink."[59]

In March the manuscript of his Navaho journal was pushed aside temporarily when, with the coming of spring, he received orders returning him to the field. A survey was to be made for a new military post that would protect travelers on the lower approaches of the Santa Fe Trail. Proximity to the trail naturally was important, but so too was a location offering good water, timber, and pasturage. With a small escort Simpson crisscrossed the trail northward from Wagon Mound to the Ocate and Rayado creeks, the latter a south fork of Cimarron Creek. He was in the vicinity of these streams when a war party of Jicarillas attacked and wiped out a wagon train of eleven men carrying mail from Leavenworth to Santa Fe. Simpson's own party was too small to offer assistance and appears to have only narrowly missed the same fate. In any case, on March 22, Simpson was in the Mexican town of Las Vegas, below Wagon Mound where the mail train was attacked a few days before. From here he advised Colonel Abert of the bloody affair, giving scant details but saying the raid made it imperative to interrupt his survey for the present and return to Santa Fe.

[58] Simpson to Abert, April 13, 1850. National Archives, War Records. Record Group 77, Topographical Bureau S, Letters Received, 1845-50, Box 69.

[59] Ibid., Simpson to Abert, February 7, 1850.

Simpson concluded this letter with a request that he be ordered to duty back in the States. Nearly a year had passed since he had left his young wife in the East; he had accomplished more than required of him in his original orders, and now he was "anxious to return to my family as soon as practicable." His wife had been importuning him to find some means of ending their separation, and others too desired his return. On May 3, Colonel Abert received an undated letter signed by Buffalo's mayor, H. K. Smith, and twenty-seven citizens and members of the Common Council, asking that Simpson be assigned again to duty in or near Buffalo, because "We have the highest opinion . . . of his ability, capacity and talent as an officer . . . we respect him as a man, and we claim him as a citizen of Buffalo."[60] Colonel Abert may have been sympathetic, perhaps even impressed—but he was unmoved. Since the previous June, Lieutenant Simpson had been his chief of Topographical Engineers of the Department of New Mexico, and he would continue in this position so long as the need for his services remained urgent—and just now the need was urgent.

Late in May, Simpson was again in the field, this time with an adequate military escort, and by June 2 was on the headwaters of Cimarron Creek at the crossing of the Bent's Fort route to Santa Fe. He was continuing his survey for the proposed military fort and now would "look further for a site on or near the Ocate." His military escort was necessary he observed, "on account of the last mail party from Leavenworth, ten in number, having all been murdered at the Wagon Mound . . . by Apache Indians, as it is supposed."

Following the first attack by two months, the latest massacre involved the Clay and Hendrickson mail train. The bodies of the ten men had been stripped and left lying near the trail, the mail emptied from the sacks and scattered all about them on the prairie. Their murder was discovered on, or a day or two before, May 20 by two traders who had started out from Las Vegas for

[60] *Ibid.*, Simpson to Abert, March 22, 1850, and Smith and others to Abert, undated.

Independence, but who now turned back, one of them observing that "The company seemed to have been attacked travelling as the mules were in harness, & in running 'round the [wagon] tongue was broken."[61] Barclay, owner of the adobe fort bearing his name on the Mora, who accompanied Lieutenant A. E. Burnside and a troop of soldiers to the scene, identified the arrows found in the bodies as those of Jicarilla Apaches and Utes. Burnside, either forgetting or unaware of the murder of eleven men at the same place in the previous March, reported on May 23 that "The attacking party were evidently in great numbers from the large number of arrows found on the Ground, but the best evidence of it is the small space within which the whole party were killed; so large a party of Americans have never before been entirely destroyed by the Indians of that portion of the Territory, & in fact, ten Americans have heretofore been considered comparatively safe in traveling over the road with proper care."[62]

Evidence of need for a fort in this region was clear enough, had anyone doubted it, and the establishment of Fort Union was the answer. We cannot be sure to what extent Simpson's surveys determined the exact location of the fort. A similar survey was being made at the same time by Major William N. Grier of the First Dragoons; it is conceivable that the findings of both men were considered by Colonel E. V. Sumner the following year when he ordered construction of Fort Union on the Bent's Fort route of the trail. The position was strategic, however, as in this valley above the Mora the Cimarron Cutoff junction with Bent's mountain route at Barclay's Fort was seven miles to the south. Colonel Sumner made Fort Union his headquarters, and for a time it was the central supply depot for all of the garrisons of New Mexico Territory. A constant deterrent to Indian raiders, the fort protected travelers on the Santa Fe Trail within a radius of two hundred miles. In later years, when the danger of Indian attack had subsided, the fort's garrison was reduced, and it became a way station for stagecoaches operating between Santa

---

[61] *Official Correspondence.*
[62] *Ibid.*

Fe and Independence. Troops were withdrawn from the fort in the 1880's, and it was finally abandoned in 1891.

Simpson had been engaged in the fort survey intermittently from March until late June, in the intervals serving as judge advocate in court-martial cases, a duty he performed without great enthusiasm. Time passed drearily for him, and he felt that he had been forgotten. His wife, despairing of his being recalled, wrote to Colonel Abert on July 2: "Since the report came to me that my husband was still to be retained in New Mexico for some time to come, I have made every effort to join him—I have written to all persons, whom I thought were likely to give me any information upon the subject, and also to the gentleman you spoke of at St. Louis, and enclosed your letter to Judge Thompson to him, for which I thank you. I thought by so doing he would be more ready to assist me in my endeavors—but as yet I have been unsuccessful. . . .

"I should have gone on [to Santa Fe] with Major Morris' party early this spring, but I supposed my husband would be engaged during the summer months, upon surveys distant from Santa Fe, and would probably return to the states in the fall. He is not aware that any steps have yet been taken towards my going to him. . . . I would not ask to have him relieved from his duties in New Mexico, but hope it will be consistent with your views to grant his request, and allow him to return *for me* this fall. It would be conferring a *very great favor indeed* upon us, and one for which we would ever hold you in grateful remembrance."[63]

Her appeal, telling so much of what was in her heart, found the Colonel as unrelenting as before. The illness of her husband succeeded, however, where her words had failed. Late in August, Simpson was found to have erysipelas of the throat. Army Surgeon Charles McDougall issued a medical certificate giving him a leave of absence for six months. Within a week Simpson turned

[63] Jane Champlin Simpson to Abert, July 2, 1850. National Archives, War Records. Record Group 77, Topographical Bureau S, Letters Received, 1845–50, Box 69.

over his duties to Lieutenant John G. Parke and departed for his wife's home in Buffalo.

Neither his wife's ties there nor the city's elders were able to hold him for long. Other frontiers were being opened to settlement, country in part still controlled by the Santee and Yanktonai divisions of the Sioux. He was sent in 1851 into the semi-wilderness of the new Territory of Minnesota and there for five years was engaged in surveying and laying out government roads. His work often brought him into contact with backwoods pioneers, just beginning to wrest homestead farmland from the Sioux, and with the Sioux themselves in the lands they still held on the west banks of the Mississippi. He installed his wife in a rented house at the corner of Third and Oak streets in St. Paul, and later— probably after his promotion to a captaincy in March, 1853— built a brick home on College Avenue. Two years more he spent on a coast survey, and then, early in 1858, he received orders to report to General Albert Sidney Johnston in Utah, as chief of his Topographical Engineers.

Johnston's army, after its recent Mormon campaign, was based on Camp Floyd in Cedar Valley, south of Salt Lake City and in the plains west of Utah Lake. Here Simpson saw little activity until August 24, when he was ordered by Johnston to survey a new wagon road from Camp Floyd to Fort Bridger, by way of Timpanogos Canyon and White Clay Creek. On the following day he started out with an infantry escort of twenty men and a Mormon guide, Isaac Bullock. Rounding the north shore of the lake, they dropped down to the Mormon settlement at Provo, a thriving town which Simpson found contained 4,200 inhabitants whose modest homes and stores of adobe were dominated by a tabernacle for secular as well as religious activities. From Provo their route led them north and then easterly across the Wasatch Mountains to Weber River and its tributary, White Clay (or Chalk) Creek. Working their way up that stream, they reached the Bear River divide in the southwest corner of present Wyoming, and then found an easier trail leading through Spring

Valley to Fort Bridger, southern outpost on the California and Oregon trails.

The route Simpson surveyed was shorter and considerably safer than the old army road to Fort Bridger, which lay farther to the north and invited ambush through the narrow gorge of Echo Canyon. A part of his route had previously been improved by Mormons, but before leaving Fort Bridger Simpson arranged for a work party to assure the passage of wagons by clearing the road where he had encountered most difficulty.

The bite of fall weather was in the air when, upon his return to Camp Floyd, Simpson was ordered to explore westward into the Great Basin and if possible, before winter drove him back, discover approaches to a new route to California. His time was already short when he left Camp Floyd on October 19 with a party of laborers and scientists, escorted by dragoons. The country before him was the vast unpopulated plain lying to the south of the Great Salt Lake Desert, a region presenting a series of mountain-range barriers that, one after another, from high pass to valley again, must be crossed.

From Cedar Valley his party almost at once began the ascent of the Oquirrh range. Descending into Rush Valley, he threaded between the West Tintic and Onaqui ranges into the lower reaches of Skull Valley. His course generally was to the southwest, to the vicinity of present Indian Springs and on across arid plains to Short-Cut Pass between the Thomas range and Little Drum Mountains. At this point, faced by a lack of water and threat of early winter storms, he turned back for Camp Floyd.[64] The distance he had traveled was not great—less than two hundred miles—and his survey is important for only two reasons: a landmark and a dawning plan, both of which to this day bear his name. The landmark is the Simpson range, due south of Indian Springs, lost and lonely and godforsaken in a seldom-

[64] Simpson, "Report of Explorations Across the Great Basin." The original manuscript is found in the War Records Division of the National Archives, Record Group 77, Bulky File 66, Box 7.

traveled desert—the only mountain or river in all of the Far West that is named for him. His plan was for a Great Basin route, a practical extension of General Johnston's vaguely conceived notion for a new trans-basin route to California.

During the early days of this winter of 1858–59, Simpson charted a hypothetical wagon road from Camp Floyd (i.e., Salt Lake City) to San Francisco. The country he proposed to travel was then unmapped. His trail would go almost directly across central Utah and Nevada to Genoa, in the eastern foothills of the High Sierras and separated from Sacramento only by those mountains. So sure was he of the distances to be traveled and the feasibility of the route that we may believe that Simpson had access to the experience of others. Jedediah Smith in 1826 crossed the Great Basin, his trail turning diagonally only slightly from the trail Simpson proposed to take. Among the Mormons of his acquaintance there probably were others who knew the desert well and were inclined to give him their knowledge. In any case, Simpson submitted his plan to Secretary of War John B. Floyd, explaining that "It is believed that a direct route from this post to Carson Valley in Utah [now Nevada] can be obtained which would avoid the detour by the Humboldt to the right [north] and that by the Las Vegas and Los Angeles route to the left [south] and that it could be obtained so as to make the distance to San Francisco less than 800 miles . . . 260 miles shorter than the Humboldt River route and 390 miles shorter than the Los Angeles route."[65]

The orders Simpson hoped for were issued late in April, 1859. He was instructed to leave Camp Floyd on May 2 with the purpose of finding "a direct Wagon Route . . . to Genoa in Carson Valley." Early in the morning of the designated day he started into the desert, his party including two lieutenants in the Topographical Corps, J. L. Kirby Smith and Haldiman L. Putnam;

[65] William H. Goetzmann, *Army Exploration in the American West, 1803–1863*, 399–400. Simpson further proposed that another survey be made to establish a wagon road between Camp Floyd, the headwaters of the Arkansas, and Bent's Old Fort on the Santa Fe Trail, thus extending his central route across the entire West, from Fort Leavenworth (or Independence) to San Francisco.

Henry Englemann, the geologist; H. V. A. von Beckh, an artist; a meteorologist; and a taxidermist. His guides were John Reese and a Paiute known as Ute Pete. A military escort of twenty-two men commanded by Lieutenant Alexander Murray of the Tenth Infantry completed the company, which totalled forty-four officers, enlisted men, and civilians.

For ten days Simpson held to a trail only a trifle south of west. Far above him to the north looped the Hastings Cutoff pioneered, west to east in 1846, by Lansford W. Hastings and Jim Clyman. And even farther north of him, still used by the wagon trains out of Missouri, was the old emigrant trail to California, angling down to the Humboldt from Fort Hall. On May 12, Simpson's path crossed that of a predecessor's when he moved through Hastings Pass, at the lower extremity of the East Humboldt Mountains. Thereafter, Simpson cut more diagonally to the southwest, crossing the Lookout Mountains and skirting Carson Lake, where the party encountered for the first time a band of Digger Indians.

Never, Simpson noted, had he seen Indians so destitute or living at so primitive a level. As the Diggers crowded about begging for food, Simpson observed that for them, usually, "two rats make a meal. Like rabbits better than rats, and antelope better than either, but cannot get the latter. Have no guns; use bows and arrows." Dismayed by the barren wasteland in which the Diggers lived and by their naked poverty, Simpson wondered why they didn't move to more promising country. One old fellow shrugged that his desert home was "a good deal better than any other," as it provided "a great many rats."

Dropping south, the party reached the river named for Joseph Walker, Frémont's guide in 1845, and then, turning north again, the Sierra ridges outlined to their left, came to the Pleasant Grove Mail Station. This advance outpost on the mountains' eastern slope furnished them with logs with which they built a raft to ford the Carson River. In the Carson Valley they came to a mining settlement called Chinatown, Simpson observing that it was so-named for its population of fifty Chinese prospectors. As tough and disheveled as any of its kind, the camp boasted whisky at three dollars a gallon, twelve dwellings, and two stores. (At a mountain lake due west of here by several days, though Simpson does not remark it, the Donner party had met disaster thirteen years before.)

The following day, June 12, brought them to trail's end. Genoa had been a Mormon settlement and now had a population of two hundred or less, twenty-eight houses, two stores, two hotels, a telegraph office, and a printing establishment. The Genoese, already advised that their town was to benefit from the trade of a new emigrant road, greeted Simpson's party with a flag-raising and a thirteen-gun salute.

Still snow-streaked, the Sierras in their mellowest season beckoned Simpson on. Because the ultimate end of his road was San Francisco, he felt obliged to go there, but without his escort. Leaving his party at Genoa, he traveled by stagecoach on the Dagget's Trail over the mountains to Placerville. By no coincidence, perhaps, a companion in the coach was Colonel Fred A. Bee, owner of a mail route and of the Placerville and St. Joseph Telegraph Company, whose wires on tree branches and poles followed this trail to Genoa. Before their ride ended, Colonel Bee assured Simpson that his company would extend its services over the new Great Basin route.

Simpson continued to Folsom and thence to Sacramento, there boarding the steamboat *Eclipse* for the final stage of his journey. He remained only briefly in San Francisco, having nothing of importance to do there but send a few messages. His return over the Sierras was a jolting nightmare, his stage driver drunk, the stage careening wildly but somehow holding the trail. Simpson allows us to imagine his farewell to the driver, noting only that he urgently recommended an improvement of the worst sections of the road, for which he said the government should spend at least $30,000.

Leaving Genoa on June 24, Simpson's party retraced the outward road as far as the Kobeh Valley, below and somewhat to the west of Hastings Pass. At this point Simpson followed a southern course through the lower Steptoe and Antelope valleys to White Valley. Within a few miles of Sevier Lake, where Richard Kern had died six years before in the massacre of the Gunnison party, Simpson swung northeastward around the Sevier Desert and so finally back to Camp Floyd. Events of the next few weeks would prove the merit of the Great Basin route; in the meantime, Lieutenant Kirby Smith was sent back with a construction crew to improve the last one hundred miles and to establish road markers to guide the first trains of emigrants who would use it.

With reason, Simpson had faith in the road: in other respects comparable, his northern route to San Francisco was 283 miles shorter than the old trail by way of the Humboldt River, and his southern route shorter by 254 miles—say eight to ten days' traveling time. The Pony Express adopted his northern route within a short time, and the southern route was chosen by the Chorpenning Mail Company and by the Russell, Majors & Waddell outfit for their wagons and cattle, a thousand head of their stock moving west over the road in its first days. Increasing numbers of emigrants also used the southern route, turning off the old California Trail at South Pass and following Simpson's new road from Fort Bridger to Camp Floyd.

Simpson's last tour of western duty was almost over. One task only remained. He was ordered by General Johnston to find "a new pass from the Valley of the Timpanogos River over the Uinta Range of Mountains, into the Green River Valley," and from there proceed eastward to Fort Leavenworth from Fort Bridger. With a party of fifty-four men, he left Camp Floyd on August 9, following the Timpanogos and Coal Creek Canyon to the Uinta Mountain Divide, dropping from there to Potts Fork and to the Duchesne and eastward to the Uinta River. From this point, where he turned off for Fort Bridger, Simpson later reported "it is believed a wagon route can be obtained . . . to Denver City . . . and thus by this route, in connection with my routes across the Great Basin, a more direct route be obtained across the Continent to San Francisco."

Time proved him to be right. What he had in mind perhaps

was a carry-over from Frémont's dream of 1848–49, but in any case a passage of the Rockies near the fortieth parallel. The wagon road he envisioned was built from Camp Floyd to present Ouray, Utah, on the Green River, thence eastward on the White River to the Yampa and Gore's Pass, where the elevation was 9,000 feet. From here the road descended through Middle Park and then over Berthoud Pass to Empire City and Denver. At Denver the route divided, one road going nearly due south to Pueblo, on the Arkansas, the other angling off to the southeast and the headwaters of the Smoky Hill River.[66]

Upon his return home in the year before the outbreak of the Civil War, Simpson was detached from duty in order to prepare his report on the Great Basin survey. By the time his work was completed, the war had started and publication of the report was delayed until 1875. The lapse of fifteen years had nearly the effect of embalming the fruit of Simpson's painstaking labors on the manuscript; when published, the report no longer had the bloom of fresh discovery and observation. Westward expansion had been too swift. Furthermore, many of his observations in 1860 seemed curiously antiquated in 1875—a consequence of Simpson's basic conservatism. As in his Fort Smith–Santa Fe report, he argued earnestly that a railroad was impractical in the "unmitigated desert" and recommended "that the govenment should first build roads and postal routes, then populate the country and develop its resources before attempting to construct a transcontinental railroad." How ironical, then, that the line of the Central Pacific and Union Pacific railroads, completed in 1869, should by-pass his Great Basin route and follow the Humboldt to Carson Valley and California. Strange, too, in 1875 were Simpson's disparaging words about the "photographic apparatus" which he had taken on his Great Basin survey and which he said proved to be a failure. "Indeed," he wrote in the introduc-

---

[66] In modern times this old wagon road is approximated for most of its distance by U.S. Highway 40. This road, as well as Simpson's Fort Bridger road and his Great Basin routes are shown on the U.S. Engineers Department Military Map of the United States, 1869.

tion to his report, "I am informed that in several of the government expeditions, a photographic apparatus has been an accompaniment, and that in every instance, and even with operators of undoubted skill, the enterprise has been attended with failure. The cause lies in some degree in the difficulty in the field . . . but chiefly in the fact that the *camera* is not adapted to *distant* scenery."

It was Simpson's misfortune that these words, written in 1860, would see print in the same year the government purchased a collection of Mathew Brady's Civil War photographs, and five years after William Henry Jackson had stunning success with his wet-plate views of the very country Simpson wrote about, including the Uinta Mountains, Echo Canyon, and Salt Lake City.

So much for Simpson's failings of myopia—they are real enough but irrelevant if considered with his virtues. In intervals amounting to three and one-half years of an otherwise long military career, Simpson explored and mapped more of the Far West than any other officer of the Army's Topographical Corps. Paradoxically, of his three major achievements in the West, the two occasions when he truly blazed new trails produced reports of least historical interest. The Navaho expedition of 1849 charted a region largely unknown, but only indirectly and later, and by others, led to the discovery of what remains the principal transcontinental highway and railroad routes. And yet it was while he was on the Navaho expedition, traveling through country he professed to despise, that the creative chemistry of his senses allowed Simpson to discover or observe and then to communicate a unique experience of lasting interest. The same cannot be said of his workmanlike reports of the Fort Smith–Santa Fe and Great Basin expeditions.[67]

[67] Simpson many times acknowledged his indebtedness to the collaboration of Richard and Edward Kern, both during the Navaho expedition and afterward in the preparation of his journal. With the exception of a few passages borrowed from Richard's diary, the authorship of the journal is entirely his, but Simpson drew stimulus from the Kerns—evident here but lacking in his other two reports. It might be noted that in the appendix to his Great Basin report

The remainder of his career was so far outside the scope of the Navaho expedition that a summary of his later years should serve our purposes here. Of this period, the major phase was his service in the Civil War, beginning in the spring of 1861 when he helped to muster in contingents of Ohio volunteers. From June 20 to August 7 he was chief topographical engineer for the Department of the Shenandoah, resigning that position to accept a colonelcy with a regiment from his native state, the Fourth New Jersey Infantry. He was active in the defense of Washington from early fall, 1861, until the following April, when his regiment joined General George McClellan's Army of the Potomac and engaged in action at West Point and in the Battle of Gaines' Mill, Virginia.

His position during the battle was in a wood, his regiment placed at the center of the Union line. Troops on both his flanks gave way under strong Confederate attack; but Simpson's regiment held its ground, fighting until nightfall, when it was surrounded by a brigade of Texans. As his were the only Union forces remaining on the battlefield and because at this hour of night there was no hope of relief, Simpson surrendered to Lieutenant Colonel Robertson of the Fifth Texas. He was held a prisoner at Richmond, Virginia, from June 28 to August 12, when he was exchanged.

Shortly after his release Simpson resigned his volunteer commission and rejoined the Topographical Corps. In June, 1863, he was appointed a lieutenant colonel in the Corps of Engineers and until December served in the Department of the Ohio, engaged in surveying, constructing and repairing railroads, and erecting temporary defenses. Thereafter, he was in general charge of fortifications in Kentucky, served as engineer agent for the Armies of the West, and as chief engineer of the District of Kentucky until June, 1865.

Simpson was brevetted a brigadier general on March 13, 1865,

Simpson included Edward Kern's previously unpublished report of his explorations of the Humboldt River and Carson and Owen lakes while with Frémont in 1845.

and in the following August was named chief engineer of the Interior Department at Washington. He served in this capacity until the fall of 1867, his duties—perhaps again ironically—giving him the general direction and inspection of the construction of the Union Pacific Railroad, starting westward from Omaha, Nebraska. From that point on, until his final retirement in 1880, he was engaged in river and harbor surveys, mainly in the southern states.

Little is known of his private life, other than that he remained a devout member of the Episcopal Church and twice as a delegate attended Episcopal conventions—in New York in 1874 and in Boston three years later. In 1871, some time after the death of his first wife, he was married to Mrs. Elizabeth Sophia Champlin. Their children were a son, James Hervey Simpson, Jr., a daughter, Marion Suzette, and two adopted daughters, Mary and Minerva.

Correspondence in old army files provides two final bits of information. In June of 1881, when he was in his sixty-eighth year, Simpson made his only known trip outside the United States, sailing for Europe on the White Star liner *Republic*. He returned to his St. Paul home in September, his days of adventure now ended.

At midnight on March 2, 1883, at his residence at 2 Monroe Place, he died. For him, death was comparatively easy; he died in his bed of pneumonia.

Appendices

Santa Fe, October 10, 1849

Sir: In accordance with orders No. 35, current series, issued from headquarters of department No. 9, requiring me to make a reconnaissance of the country in the vicinity of Cebolleta, with a view to the selection of a suitable position for a post in that vicinity, I have the honor to report that I have made the reconnaissance required by said order, and present the following as the result.

The point I would suggest as the most suitable one for the location of a post is the small settlement called Cebolletita, situated two and a quarter miles to the south of, and in the same valley with, Cebolleta, and on the road leading from the Pueblo of Laguna to Cebolleta. My reasons for this selection are involved in the following considerations:

The Navaho nation is the principal one of which the post in question, in its military aspects, is to have relation. Coming from the mountains immediately to the *north* and back of Cebolleta, and passing by Cebolleta and Cebolletita, is an avenue of approach from the Navaho country to the Mexican settlements in that and the neighboring quarter to the east of it. To the *east* of the selected point, I was informed there was another or other avenues of approach. To the *west*, by the way of the valley of the Rio de San José and one of its tributaries, there are two other avenues of descent to be guarded against. Now, as the number of posts to be established is but one, it is obvious that its position should be such as to affect the greatest possible area of country, and that in the most prompt and effective manner. This position, evidently then, should be a central one. This condition is fulfilled in the case in question by locating the post at the place stated —Cebolletita.

The next considerations are, that the locality selected is where the essentials, wood and water, are abundant for the troops, grass abundant for the stock, and corn doubtless to be had in sufficient quantities from that and the neighboring villages.

In regard to the quarters at the point referred to, there are three ranchos upon which buildings are suitable—with some slight repairs, in the case of one—for the quarters of the troops. These buildings belong, respectively, to Juan Chavez, Manuel Chavez, and José Francisco Aragonas; and the order in which they are named is the order of their convenience in respect to wood and water. The first two, I was assured, could be rented; the third, in all probability, if necessary, could be also.

In regard to the facilities of communication, there is a pack-mule route from Cebolletita to Albuquerque, the distance between the two places being represented to be from forty-five to fifty miles. There are also two wagon-roads from Cebolletita to Albuquerque, one by way of the Pueblo de Laguna, which we found pretty good; and the other, a more direct one, by the way of Alamo, said to be the shorter, and equally good. The distance to Albuquerque by the Laguna road is: to Laguna, sixteen miles; thence to Albuquerque, forty-five miles—in all, sixty-one miles.[1]

The valley in which it is proposed to locate the post, I would further remark, besides being the most pleasant one I saw within the circuit of my reconnaissance, is more thickly populated with Mexicans than any in that region.

Another advantage the locality possesses is its proximity to the friendly Navahos—a position which enables them to be reciprocally protected by our troops, and at the same time give that information in relation to their neighbors which might be of the highest importance to us in our relations with them.

I should not fail to report that the escort accompanying me was commanded by Lieutenant John Buford, of the 2d Dragoons, whom I ever found willing and effective in his cooperation with me in the discharge of my duties.

I am, &c.,

J. H. SIMPSON

First Lieutenant, Corps Topographical Engineers
To Lieutenant-Colonel J. M. Washington
Commanding 9th Military Department

[1] Since the establishment of the post at Cebolleta, a pack-mule route has been discovered from that post to Santa Fe by the way of the Pueblo of Jemez, which, doubtless, is from fifteen to twenty miles shorter than by the way of Albuquerque.—Simpson's note.

In the language of the Pueblo In

Name of the object in English.	Santo Domingo, San Felipe, Santa Anna, Silla, Laguna, Pojuate, Acoma, Cochiti. (1.)	San Juan, Santa Clara, S. Aldefonso, Pojuaque, Nambe, Tesuque. (2.)	Taos, Picoris, Sandia, Isleta. (3.)	Jemez, (old Pecos.) (4.)
God	Dios, (Sp.) Montezuma, they say, is synonymous with Dios.	Give no other word than the Span. Dios.	Huam-may-ah .,......	Pay. (Same as for sun.)
Heavens	....	....	....	....
Sun	....	Pah.......	Hoo-len-nah	Pay..............
Moon.......	....	Poy-ye	Pan·nah	Pah-ah.............
Star	She-cat........	A-doy-e-ah .	Hah-he-glan-nah	Woon-bah..........
Cloud	....	....	....	....
Earth..... ..	Hah-ats........	Nah	Pah-han-nah.........	Dock-ah..........
Man	Hats-see........	Say-en	Tah-hah-ne-nah	Shu-o-tish...
Woman......	Nai-at-say	Ker.......	Clay-an-nah.........	Ste-osh........
Wife	Kar-nats-shu.....	Nah-ve-so ..	Could give no word...	Ne-ohoy...........
Boy	O-nue..........	An-noh	Dy-you-oo-nah........	
Boy (infant).	Sah-wish-sha..	....	....	Ah-cue...........
Girl	Koy-yah	An-ugh	Koo-ac-lon-nah.......	....
Girl (infant).	Sah-wish-sha....	....	....	Foud-o-hos-che ......
Head	Nash-can-ne	Pum-bah ...	Pi-ne-nah.............	Chit-cnous...........
Forehead	Cop-pay	Sic-co-vah ..	Pah-hem-nah	Wah-pay.
Face........	Ko-wah........	Cha-ay	Cha-gah-neem-may	Tcho-tah ....
Eye	Kan-nah.......	Chay......	Che-nay ,..........	Saech............
Nose	Kar-wish-she ..	Shay......	Poo-ae-nak ,.........	For-saech...........
Mouth......	Tseé-kah	Sho.......	Clah-mo-e-nah	E-ae-quah..........
Teeth.......	Har-at-chay-nay.	Moo-ah	Moo-en-nah-en-hay	Goo-whan ....
Tongue.....	Wah-at-chin.....	Hah	May-oon-on-en-ah	Ain-lah...........
Chin......	Tyars-kah.....	Sab-boh.....	Clah-bon-hay	Ah-tish...
Ear........	Kah-se-pah.....	O-ye-o	Tag-lay-o-nay.........	Wash-chish ......
Hair........	Har-tran	Poh	Pah-han-nay..........	Fore-lah...
Neck	Wit-trah-ne	Kah	Gah-ne-may	Toe .. ..
Arm	Kah-u-may	Ko.......	Hah-en-nay...........	Hah
Elbow.......		....	....	
Hand.......	Kah-mosh tay..	Mah	....	Mah-tish.
Finger......				
Breast	Quaist-pah ...	Pe-ah	Pah-ah-kay-nay-ne-may	Pay-lu ....
Leg........	Kay-ah-kah....		Pah-nay.............	Hong ....
Knee				
Foot.......	Kar-tay	Ah........	E-en-en-nah	Awn-dash .....
Deer.......	Ke-ah-ne......	Pah-ye	Tah-mean-mah	Pah-ah ....
Buffalo......	Moo-shats......	Kah	Kah-nah-neem-mah....	Toss-chach .....
Horse.......	Kah-yai-oh..... (Probably a corruption of the Span. caballo.)	As in Span..	Kah-wan-nah. (Probably a corruption of the Spanish.)	Gu-nah............
Serpent.....	Skers-ker.	Could give no word.	Hatch-oo-nah..........	Pay-chu-tah.........

246

dians of—		In the language of the wild tribes denominated—		
Zuñi. (5.)	Moqui. (6.)	Navajos. (7.)	Ticorillas, (a branch of the Apaches.) (8.)	Utahs. (9.)
Ho-ae-wo-nac-we-o-nah.	Toc-kill	Yuah-del-kill..	Dios. (Span.)	
	Toke-pay-lah ...			
Yat-tock-kah.............	Tah-wah.......	Cho-hae-nae-i..	....	Tap.
....	Moo-yah........	Old-chay.....	....	Mah-tots
Mo·yat-chu-way......	....	Del-gay-he....	Shah.........	Quah-lantz.
....	O-mow.........			
Ou-lock-nan-nay	Tou..h-quae......	Ne...........	Nay	
Oat-se.............	Se-ke-ah........	Ten-nay.......	Tin-lay	Toe-on-pay-ah.
O-care..	....	Es-ten-nay....	Tay-kay......	Nai-jah.
Could give no word....	....	Cha-at	Pe-aug-oo-le ..	
Art-se-ke.............	....		Is-ke-e	Ah-pats.
....	....	Che-yaz......		
Tya-nah	....		Mem-che-to....	Mah-mats.
			(Doubtless a corruption of *muchachitos*— Spanish.)	
We-at-zah-nah.........	....	Chay-way....		
O-shuck-quin-nay	Qua-tah........	Hut-se........	It-se	Tuts.
Huck-kin-nay	Col-ler........	Hut-tah......	Pin-nay	Mut-tock.
No-pon-ne-nay.........	....	Hun-ne	....	Koo-elp.
Too-nah-way	Po-se...........	Hun-nah	Pin-dah	Put-ty-shoe.
No-lin-nay	Ya-kuck........	Hut-chin	Witch-chess ..	Mah-vc-tah.
Ac-wah-tin-nay........	Mo-ah	Huz-zay	Huz-zay......	Timp.
O-nah-way	Tah-mah........	How-go......	E-gho........	Tong.
Ho-nin-nay	Ling-a	Hot-so........	E-zah-te......	Ah-oh.
Klay-which-chin-nay....	Ke-at	Hi-ot-ze......	E-zay-tah:....	Hah-nock-quell.
Sah-schuck-tin-nay	Nook-a-wuck...	Hut-chah......	Wick-yah	Nink.
Ti-ah-way	Hay-me........	Hot-se......	It-se	Su-ooh.
Kiss-sin-nay..........	Qua-pe........	Huck-quoss...	Wick-cost....	Kolph.
Ar-se-way............	Mah-at........	Hut-con.......	Wit-se	Poo-ir.
....	Cher-ber........			
Shon-che-way	Mock-tay.......	Hul-lah	Wis-lah.......	Mas-seer.
....	Mah-latz			
Po-at-tan-nay..........	Toe-witz-kah ...	Hay-yete.....	Ko-jay-ae.....	Pay.
Sack-que-way.........	Ho-kah :........	Hut-yah	Wit cha-te.....	
....	Tom-me.........			
Wake-que-a-way.......	Her-kuck.......	Hut-kay......	Wit-kay.....	Namp.
....	....	Pay-ye.......	Pay-ah.......	
Too-she-kay-one-na-way	....	A-yan-ne	Yah-nay	
Too-she.............	As in Spanish...	Kle	Shle..........	Kah-vah.
Che-to-lah.............	....	Kot-so	Ko-oh.........	Toe-weroe

Name of the object in English.	Santo Domingo, San Felipe, Santa Anna, Silla, Laguna, Pojuate, Acoma, Cochiti. (1.)	San Juan, Santa Clara, S. Aldefonso, Pojuaque, Nambe, Tesuque. (2.)	Taos, Picoris, Sandia, Isleta. (3.)	Jemez, (old Pecos.) (4.)
			In the language of the Pueblo In	
Rattlesnake..	Shrue-o-we.....	Pay-yoh....	Pi-ho-own............	Kae-ah-vae-lah.......
Dog........	Tish............	Cher.......	So-dor-nah..........	Caw-nu...........
Cat.........	Moos..........	Moo-sah....	Moo-se-e-nah.........	Moon-sah..........
Fire........	Hah-kan-ye.....	Tah........	Pah-an-nah..........	Twa-ah.............
Wood......	....	Sun........		....
Water......	Tseats..........	Ogh........	Poh-ah-oon...........	Pah...............
Stone.......	....	....		Ke-ah-ah...........
Cactus... ..	Ae-mocch-te....	Sow-wah....	....	Te-ah............
Corn.......				
Bean.......				
Bread.......	Pah. (Probably a corruption of the Span. pan.)	As in Span..	Ah-coon-nah.........	Zo-tane-bae-lah ....
Flesh.......	Ish-sha-ne......	Pe-we......	Zoe-an-nay...........	Gu-nay-nat-si........
Bow........	....	....	....	....
Arrow......				
Fusil.......	O-nistz..........	Pe-quar-re ..	Tah-we-nan...........	Tah-his-tah........
Sword......	....	....	....	....
Spurs.......				
Whip.......				
Pipe........				
Hat........				
Friend......	....	Ke-nah.....		

NOTES.

(1.) Obtained by Lieutenant Simpson from U-kat-te-wah, (all the world looks as the man that sings,) governor of the pueblo of Santo Dommgo.

(2.) Obtained by Lieutenant Simpson, through Mr. E. M. Kern, from an Indian belonging to the pueblo of San Juan.

(3.) Obtained by Lieutenant Simpson, through Dr. Horace R. Wirtz, U. S. A, from an Indian belonging to the pueblo of Taos.

(4.) Obtained by Lieutenant Simpson from an Indian belonging to the pueblo of Jemez, by name Da-he-du-lu, (eagle.)

(5.) Obtained by Lieutenant Simpson from an Indian belonging to the pueblo of Zuñi, by name, as he wrote it himself, Lilu. Mexican name, Juan Christoval.

(6.) Obtained by Lieutenant Simpson from a Moqui Indian who happened to be at Chelly when the troops were there.

(7.) Obtained by Lieutenant Simpson from a friendly Navajo chief, by name Tus-ca ho-gont-le. Mexican name, Sandoval.

(8.) Obtained by Lieutenant Simpson from an Apache Indian, a prisoner in the guard-house at Santa Fe.

(9.) Obtained by Lieutenant Simpson from an Utah Indian, a prisoner in the guard-house at Santa Fe.

diars of—		In the language of the wild tribes denominated—		
Zuñi. (5.)	Moqui. (6.)	Navajos. (7.)	Ticorillas, (a branch of the Apaches.) (8.)	Utahs. (9.)
....	....	Klish		
Wat-so-tah............	Po-ku..........	Klay-cho.	Klin-cha-ah...	Sah-reets.
Moo-sah		Moose.......	Moo-sah......	Moo-sah.
Mack-ke................	Day-bor.......	El-chin.......	Cone.........	Coon.
....	Ser-her-be	....	....	Oof.
Ke-a-o-way........... ..	....	Toe............	Ko...........	Pah.
Tze-nan-nay..........				
Melah	Kar-uk.........			
....	Se-ka-mo-se.....			
Moo-hen-nay	....	Pah. (Probably a corruption of the Span. *pan.*)	Klay-tun-che-chay.	
She-lay................	....	Et-se..........	It-se	
....	Au-ah..........			
....	....	Ho-huck		
Toe-o-an-nan-nay	A-muck-te......	Pay-dil-ston ..	Jeh-kay.......	
....	Le-po-wah......			
....	Le-pom-uck-ke..			
....	Wo-bock-pe			
....	Chong...........			
....	Pa-ta-nock-a-chee			

NOTES.

In all such syllables as ah, mah, nah, tah, &c., *a* has the same sound as in fat.

In all such syllables as ay, may, nay, kay, &c., *a* has the same sound as in fate.

The following Indian names were obtained by Lieutenant Simpson, through Mr. R. H. Kern, from Indians belonging to the pueblos named :

The Indian name of the pueblo of Santa Anna....is Tom-i-ya.

Do.............do..........Santo Domingo is Ge-e-way.

Do.............do..........Cochiti.........is Ko-cke.

Do.............do..........Silla.......... is Tse-ah.

Do............do..........San Felipe.....is Ka-lis-cha.

Do.............do..........Pecos..........is A-cu-lah.

Do.............do..........Jemez.........is Ha-waw-wah-lah-too-waw.

I am informed that the Indians of the Pueblo de Lentes have lost their original tongue, and now speak entirely the Spanish language.

The only tribes which, in the above vocabulary, discover any obvious affinity in their languages, are the Navajos and the Ticorillas. It is, however, somewhat remarkable that the word for cat, (moose,) with some slight variations, should be found common to them all.

Cañon de Chai, upper California
September 7, 1849

Sir: At your request, I send you a description of a room that I saw, in company with Mr. Collins, of Santa Fe, in the ruins of the Pueblo Bonito, in the Cañon of Chaco, on the 28th ult.

It was in the second of three ranges of rooms on the north side of the ruins. The door opened at the base of the wall, towards the interior of the building; it had never been more than two feet and a half high and was filled two-thirds with rubbish. The lintels were of natural sticks of wood, one and a half to two and a half inches in diameter, deprived of the bark, and placed at distances of two or three inches apart; yet their ends were attached to each other by withes of oak [willow] with its bark well preserved.

The room was in the form of a parallelogram, about twelve feet in length, eight feet wide, and the walls, as they stood at the time of observation, seven feet high. The floor was of earth, and the surface irregular. The walls were about two feet thick, and plastered within with a layer of red mud one-fourth of an inch thick. The latter having fallen off in places showed the material of the wall to be sandstone. The stone was ground into pieces the size of our ordinary bricks, the angles not as perfectly formed, though nearly so, and put up in break-joints, having intervals between them, on every side, of about two inches. The intervals were filled with laminae of a dense sandstone, about three lines in thickness, driven firmly in, and broken off even with the general planes of the wall—the whole resembling mosaic work.

Niches, varying in size from two inches to two feet and a half square, and two inches to one and a half feet in horizontal depth, were scattered irregularly over the walls, at various heights above the floor. Near the place of the ceiling, the walls were penetrated horizontally by eight cylindrical beams, about seven inches in diameter; their ends were on a line with the interior planes of the walls they penetrated, and the surfaces of them perpendicular to the length of the beam. They had the appearance of having been sawed off originally, except that there were no marks of the saw left on them; time had slightly disintegrated the surfaces, rounding the edges somewhat here and there.

Supporting the floor above were six cylindrical beams, about seven inches in diameter, passing transversely of the room, and at distances of less than two feet apart—the branches of the trees having been hewn off by means of a blunt-edged instrument. Above, and resting on these, running longitudinally with the room, were poles of various lengths, about two inches in diameter, irregularly straight, placed in contact with each other, covering all the top of the room, bound together at irregular and various distances, generally at their ends, by slips apparently of palm-leaf or marquez [yucca plant], and the same material converted into cords about one-fourth of an inch in diameter, formed of two strands, hung from the poles at several points.

Above, and resting upon the poles, closing all above, passing transversely of the room, were planks about seven inches wide and three-fourths of an inch in thickness. The width of the planks was uniform, and so was the thickness. They were in contact, or nearly so, admitting but little more than the passage of a knife blade between them, by the edges, through the whole of their lengths. They were not jointed; all their surfaces were level and as smooth as if planed, excepting the ends; the angles as regular and perfect as could be retained by such vegetable matter. They are probably of pine or cedar, exposed to the atmosphere for as long a time as it is probable these have been. The ends of the planks, several of which were in view, terminated in a line perpendicular to the length of the planks, and the planks appear to have been severed by a blunt instrument. The planks—I examined them minutely by the eye and the touch, for the marks of the saw and other instruments—were smooth, and colored brown by time or by smoke.

Beyond the planks nothing was distinguishable from within. The room was redolent with the perfume of cedar. Externally, upon the top, was a heap of stone and mud, ruins that have fallen from above, immovable by the instruments that we had along.

The beams were probably severed by contusions from a dull instrument [actually, stone axes] and their surfaces ground plain and smooth by a slab of rock; and the planks, split or hewn from the trees, were, no doubt, rendered smooth by the same means.

Very respectfully, your obedient servant,
J. F. HAMMOND
Assistant Surgeon, U.S. Army

First Lieutenant J. H. Simpson
Corps Topographical Engineers, U.S. Army.

Treaty of peace and amity made and entered into by the United States and the Navaho tribe of Indians.[1]

ARTICLE I

There shall henceforth exist between the people of the United States and the people of New Mexico during its occupation by the United States, on the one part, and the tribe of Navaho Indians, on the other part, a firm and lasting peace.

ARTICLE II

A mutual trade shall be carried on between the parties above mentioned; the people of the United States and those of New Mexico during its occupation by the United States, being permitted to visit parts of the Navaho country and the Navaho Indians to visit all parts of the United States and of New Mexico during its occupation as above, without molestation and with full protection; and the said trade shall be carried on in every respect, as between people of the same nation.

ARTICLE III

There shall be an entire restoration of all prisoners that are held at the date of this treaty by either of the parties, and the people of New Mexico; such restoration to be full and complete without regard to the number of prisoners held.

ARTICLE IV

The people of the United States guarantee during their occupation of New Mexico, the strict observance of this treaty by the people of the Territory.

ARTICLE V

The Navaho tribe of Indians will deliver immediately to the acting Assistant Quartermaster of the United States now here,

[1] This treaty was never ratified by Congress. The treaty text and Colonel Newby's accompanying letter are found in the War Records Division of the National Archives, NMRA, Army & Air Corps Branch.

three hundred sheep and one hundred head [of] mules and horses; such delivery to be made as indemnity in full for the expenses incurred by the people of the United States in this campaign.

The undersigned severally and fully empowered by their respective nations to pledge a full compliance with, and enforcement of, the above articles have hereunto signed their names and affixed their seals.

> *Done at Headquarters*
> *Camp at Monte del Cayatana*[2]
> *Navaho Country*
> *this 20th day of May, 1848.*
> E. W. B. NEWBY, *Col. Comg.*
> *1st Regt. Illinois Infantry vol.*

JOSÉ LARGO, *Principal Chief*
NARBONA, *second Chief*
CHAPITONE, *third Chief*
ZARCILLAS LARGO, *fourth Chief*
ARCHULETA, *fifth Chief*
JUAN LUCERO, *sixth Chief*
SEGUNDO, *seventh Chief*
PABLO PINO, *eighth Chief*

> *Headquarters, 9th Military Department*
> *Santa Fe, New Mexico*
> *June 17th, 1848*

SIR:

I have the honor to report that having received, for a long time previous almost daily intelligences of the the terrible outrages and devastation committed by the Navijo and other

---

[2] Monte del Cayantana is shown as Cayotano Mountain (named after a Navaho) on Captain Anderson's 1864 Map of the Military Department of New Mexico. A part of the Lukachukai Range, it is in modern times known as Beautiful Mountain, scene of the 1913 revolt of the medicine man Bi-joshii and his small band.

tribes of Indians within this Department upon the persons and property of the Mexican inhabitants, I departed against the former tribe on the first day of May last, with a command consisting of one hundred and fifty men, from the 3d Regt., Missouri Mounted Volunteers, and fifty [men of the] 1st Illinois Infantry, Mounted, for the occasion leaving on the fourth day the Pueblo town Jemez—which I had made my starting point on the frontier principally for the purpose of procuring able spies.

After an arduous march of six days, through a country of deep sand and almost entirely destitute of water and vegitation, I reached the outskirts of the Navijo Territory, and in the immediate vicinity of which, as informed by the spies, numbers of the Indians [were] herding their stock and preparing to sow their grain. Late in the evening of the sixth day I perceived some four or five men on horseback at a short distance in advance, and instantly ordered out the best mounted portion of my force to give chase. I soon perceived, however, from the extreme ease with which the Indians made their escape, that an attempt to march openly upon them would be folly and blast every prospect of the successful issue of the expedition. The difference between the speed of their animals and *ours* infinitely surpassed my expectations and convinced me that as much secrecy as possible would have to be used.

I therefor immediately encamped within some fifty feet of an extremely rugged and steep range of mountains, which forms the strongest possible barrier to the country of the Navijos. I knew that if the Indians should effect their retreat with their stock across the mountains that it would be next to impossible to even get up with them. Immediately after encamping, I saw in advance runners and immense clouds of dust, which I was informed by the spies indicated where the Indians were retreating, with immense herds of stock. Yet I still entertained light hopes of a successful issue, for the greater portion of the stock was sheep, which could be easily overtaken. I determined to give persuit as soon as possible, and consequently ordered Capt.

Stockton of the Missouri Volunteers to take fifty men and make the spediest preperations to march in persuit, and not to halt until he had overtaken them.

The next morning a man sent back by Capt. Stockton informed me that the Captain had proceeded but five miles, and having taken four prisoners, had encamped and was yet lying there. I immediately started with the rest of the command, and in a few minutes reached Capt. Stockton's encampment.

I was astonished to find that the Prisoners were mounted, well armed, and running at large through the encampment. I was still further surprised to find that there was a number of Indians in the hills around at a very short distance from the command, and that the men were scattered around, the greater number of them without their guns. I immediately ordered the prisoners to be disarmed, when they began to fly—firing at us as they ran, whilst at the same time we received a fire from the Indians around the encampment. I then ordered the command to fire upon them, when—after some forty or fifty rounds were fired, four of the Indians were killed. The remainder fled and all succeeded in affecting their escape, with the exception of one of the Prisoners who was seized before he could fire, and was in consequence surrounded.

Immediately [the command] followed with all possible speed, but had not proceeded far when an Indian was perceived flying rapidly, and leading a horse. I instantly sent Major Reynolds of the Missouri Volunteers with a few men in persuit. While persuing this one the Major suddenly came upon another who had been wounded severely and was supposed, when first seen, to be dead; he, however, suddenly raised himself, and after discharging one or two arrows, was shot by one of the men. After a short halt for the purpose of disencumbering myself of the greater part of the prisoners, I again started in persuit. I had not, however, been under way more than two hours when I was met by two of the Principal Chiefs who proposed making a treaty, and promising to visit our camp in a few days for that purpose.

I went back to the camp I had just left and made preperations to remain several days. According to promise, all the principal Chiefs came in and a treaty which is herewith enclosed was made and agreed to by all of them without exception. I deem it proper to state before closing my report in explination of the silence of the treaty on the subject of property taken by the Navijoes, that the Mexicans had succeeded previously to my departure from this place, in taking from the Indians by stealth, immense numbers of cattle and sheep, leaving the Indians with about as much as properly belongs to them.

I would also add that those stipulations of the treaty relating to the payment of the expenses of the expidition, and the exchange of prisoners have been fully complied with, and that twelve Mexican captives have been restored to their relatives.

I have the honor to be, Sir, your Obedient Servant,

E. W. B. Newby
Colonel commanding

Brig. Genl. R[oger] Jones
Adjutant General of the U.S.A.

The following acknowledgements, declarations, and stipulations have been duly considered, and are now solemnly adopted and proclaimed by the undersigned; that is to say, John M. Washington, governor of New Mexico, and lieutenant-colonel commanding the troops of the United States in New Mexico, and James S. Calhoun, Indian agent, residing at Santa Fe, in New Mexico, representing the United States of America, and Mariano Martinez, head chief, and Chapitone, second chief, on the part of the Navaho tribe of Indians:

I. The said Indians do hereby acknowledge that, by virtue of a treaty entered into by the United States of America and the United Mexican States, signed on the second day of February, in the year of our Lord eighteen hundred and forty-eight, at the city of Guadalupe Hidalgo, by N. P. Trist, of the first part, and Luis G. Cuevas, Bernardo Couto, and Mgl Atristain, of the second part, the said tribe was lawfully placed under the exclusive jurisdiction and protection of the Government of the said United States, and that they are now, and will forever remain, under the aforesaid jurisdiction and protection.

II. That from and after the signing of this treaty, hostilities between the contracting parties shall cease, and perpetual peace and friendship shall exist; the said tribe hereby solemnly covenanting that they will not associate with, or give countenance or aid to, any tribe or band of Indians, or other persons or powers, who may be at any time at enmity with the people of the said United States; that they will remain at peace, and treat honestly and humanely all persons and powers at peace with the said States; and all cases of aggression against said Navahos by citizens or others of the United States, or by other persons or powers in amity with the said States, shall be referred to the Government of said States for adjustment and settlement.

III. The Government of the said States having the sole and exclusive right of regulating the trade and intercourse with the said Navahos, it is agreed that the laws now in force regulating the trade and intercourse, and for the preservation of peace with the various tribes of Indians under the protection and guardianship of the aforesaid Government, shall have the same force and efficiency, and shall be as binding and as obligatory upon the said Navahos, and executed in the same manner, as if said laws had been passed for their sole benefit and protection; and to this end, and for all other useful purposes, the government of New Mexico, as now organized, or as it may be by the Government of the United States, is recognized and acknowledged by the said Navahos; and for the due enforcement of the aforesaid laws, until the Government of the United States shall otherwise order, the territory of the Navahos is hereby annexed to New Mexico.

IV. The Navaho Indians hereby bind themselves to deliver to the military authority of the United States in New Mexico, at Santa Fe, New Mexico, as soon as he or they can be apprehended, the murderer or murderers of Micente Garcia, that said fugitive or fugitives from justice may be dealt with as justice may decree.

V. All American and Mexican captives, and all stolen property taken from Americans or Mexicans, or other persons or powers in amity with the United States, shall be delivered by the Navaho Indians to the aforesaid military authority at Jemez, New Mexico, on or before the 9th day of October next ensuing, that justice may be meted out to all whom it may concern; and also all Indian captives and stolen property of such tribe or tribes of Indians as shall enter into a similar reciprocal treaty, shall, in like manner, and for the same purposes, be turned over to an authorized officer or agent of the said States by the aforesaid Navahos.

VI. Should any citizen of the United States, or other person or persons subject to the laws of the United States, murder, rob, or otherwise maltreat any Navaho Indian or Indians, he or they shall be arrested and tried, and, upon conviction, shall be subjected to all the penalties provided by law for the protection of the persons and property of the people of the said States.

VII. The people of the United States of America shall have free and safe passage through the territory of the aforesaid Indians, under such rules and regulations as may be adopted by authority of the said States.

VIII. In order to preserve tranquility, and to afford protection to all the people and interests of the contracting parties, the Government of the United States of America will establish such military posts and agencies, and authorize such trading-houses, at such time and in such places as the said Government may designate.

IX. Relying confidently upon the justice and the liberality of the aforesaid Government, and anxious to remove every possible cause that might disturb their peace and quiet, it is agreed by the aforesaid Navahos that the Government of the United States shall, at its earliest convenience, designate, settle, and adjust their territorial boundaries, and pass and execute in their territory such laws as may be deemed conducive to the prosperity and happiness of said Indians.

X. For and in consideration of the faithful performance of all the stipulations herein contained by the said Navaho Indians the Government of the United States will grant to said Indians such donations, presents, and implements, and adopt such other liberal and humane measures, as said Government may deem meet and proper.

XI. This treaty shall be binding upon the contracting parties from and after the signing of the same, subject only to such modifications and amendments as may be adopted by the Government of the United States; and, finally, this treaty is to receive a liberal construction, at all times and in all places, to the end that the said Navaho Indians shall not be held responsible for the conduct of others, and that the Government of the United States shall so legislate and act as to secure the permanent prosperity and happiness of said Indians.

In faith whereof, we, the undersigned, have signed this treaty, and affixed thereunto our seals, in the valley of Cheille, this ninth day of September, in the year of our Lord one thousand eight hundred and forty-nine.

J. M. WASHINGTON (L. S.)
Brevet Lieutenant-Colonel Commanding
JAMES S. CALHOUN (L. S.)
Indian Agent, residing at Santa Fe.
MARIANO MARTINEZ, *Head Chief,* his X mark, (L. S.)
CHAPITONE, *Second Chief,* his X mark. (L. S.)
J. L. COLLINS.
JAMES CONKLIN.
LORENZO TOREZ.
ANTONIO SANDOVAL, his X mark.
FRANCISCO HOSTA, *Governor of Jemez,* his X mark.

Witnesses—
H. L. KENDRICK, *Brevet Major, U.S. Army.*
J. N. WARD, *Brevet First Lieutenant, cd Infantry.*
JOHN PECK, *Brevet Major, U.S. Army.*
J. F. HAMMOND, *Assistant Surgeon, U. S. Army.*
H. L. DODGE, *Captain commanding New Mexico Volunteer Infantry.*
RICHARD H. KERN.
J. H. NONES, *Second Lieutenant, 2d Artillery.*
CYRUS CHOICE.
JOHN H. DICKERSON, *Second Lieutenant, 1st Artillery.*
W. E. LOVE
JOHN G. JONES.
J. H. SIMPSON, *First Lieutenant, Corps Topographical Engineers.*

Sources

ARCHIVAL COLLECTIONS

U.S. National Archives, War Records Division

Fort Wingate File 1251.

Muster Roll, Abiquiu, New Mexico, Record Group 94.

Muster Roll, Jemez, New Mexico, Record Group 94.

Muster Rolls, Volunteer Organizations, Record Group 94, Box 2550.

NMRA, Army and Air Corps Branch.

Post Returns, Abiquiu, New Mexico, Record Group 94, Box 94.

Post Returns, Albuquerque, New Mexico, Record Group 94, Box 6.

Post Returns, Cibolleta, New Mexico, Record Group 94.

Post Returns, Fort Marcy, New Mexico, Record Group 94, Box 387.

Quartermaster's Post Returns, Albuquerque, Record Group 92, Office of the Quartermaster General, Consolidated Correspondence, Box 9.

Quartermaster's Consolidated File, Colonel J. M. Washington, Record Group 92.

Record Group 15, 1817–SC–1773.

Record Group 15, 55–160–97627.

Record Group 77, Topographical Bureau S, Letters Received, 1845–50, Box 69.

Record Group 92, Office of the Quartermaster General, Consolidated Correspondence, 1794–1915, Boxes 9, 987.

Record Group 94, AGO, Letters Received, 514–W–1849, 515–W–1849, 520—W—1849.

Record Group 94, Academy Papers, 297–1824.

Record Group 94, Mexican War, K173, 1846.

Record Group 94, Mexican War, Muster Rolls.

Record Group 98, Records of U.S. Army Commands, Dept. of New Mexico, Letters Received, Box 1.

Sources

U.S. National Archives, Indian Records Division

New Mexico Superintendency, 1849–53, Letters Received, Micro. Roll 546; 1854–55, Micro Roll 547; 1856–57, Micro Roll 548.

OTHER MANUSCRIPT MATERIALS

Bradley, Zorro A. "Site Bc 236, Chaco Canyon." An unpublished report of Bradley's 1958 excavation of a small Chaco site indicating an early Mesa Verde occupation. Copy at superintendent's office, Chaco Canyon.

Fort Sutter Papers, 127–28–29, Huntington Library. Relating to the death of Dr. B. J. Kern.

Kern, Richard H. "Notes of a Military Reconaissance of the Pais de los Navajos in the Months of Aug & Sept 1849." Diary, Huntington Library, HM 4274.

———. "A Description of the Pueblo of Santo Domingo." Fragment of notes, Huntington Library, HM 4274.

Vivian, R. Gordon. "The Three-C Site, an Early Pueblo II Ruin in Chaco Canyon." Unpublished report of an excavation made in 1939, a copy in the author's possession.

REGISTERS, REPORTS, LETTERS, DIARIES, ETC.

Abert, Lt. James William. "Report of Lt. J. W. Abert on his Examination of New Mexico in the Years 1846–47." 30 Cong., 1 sess., *House Exec. Doc. 31.*

Appleton's Cyclopaedia of American Biography. Vol. II. New York, D. Appleton & Co., 1888.

Benevides, Alonso de. *Memorial of 1603.* Trans. and ed. by Federick Webb Hodge, George P. Hammond, and Agapito Rey. Albuquerque, University of New Mexico Press, 1945.

Bourke, John G. "Bourke on the Southwest" (ed. by Lansing B. Bloom), *New Mexico Historical Review,* Vol. XIII (1938).

Calhoun, James S. *The Official Correspondence of James S. Calhoun While Indian Agent at Santa Fe and Superintendent of Indian Affairs in New Mexico.* Ed. by Annie Heloise Abel. Washington, Government Printing Office, 1915.

Cullum, George W. *Biographical Register of the Officers and Graduates of the U.S. Military Academy at West Point, N. Y.* Boston and New York, Houghton, Mifflin & Co., 1891.

Dominguez, Fray Francisco Atanasio. *The Missions of New Mexico, 1776.* Trans. and annotated by Eleanor B. Adams and Fray Angelico Chávez. Albuquerque, University of New Mexico Press, 1956.

Dutton, Capt. Clarence E. "Mount Taylor and the Zuñi Plateau." U.S. Geological Survey, *Sixth Annual Report.* Washington, Government Printing Office, 1885.

Emory, Lt. William Hemsley. "Notes of a Military Reconnoissance from Fort Leavenworth, in Missouri, to San Diego, in California . . . 1846–47." Washington, Wendell and Van Benthuysen, 1848.

Hamersly, Thomas H. S. *Complete Regular Army Register of the United States.* Washington, T. H. S. Hamersly, 1880.

Heitman, Francis B. *Historical Register and Dictionary of the U.S. Army.* Washington, Government Printing Office, 1903.

Hewett, Edgar L. "Antiquities of the Jemez Plateau, New Mexico." Bureau of American Ethnology, *Bulletin 32,* Washington, 1906.

Jackson, William Henry. "Report on the Ancient Ruins Examined in 1875 and 1877; Ruins of the Chaco Cañon, Examined in 1877." U.S. Geological and Geographical Survey of the Territories, *Tenth Annual Report,* Washington, 1878.

Kappler, Charles Joseph. *Laws, Statutes, Etc.* Washington, Government Printing Office, 1904.

Loew, Oscar. "Report of the Ruins of New Mexico." Appendix J2 to Appendix LL of *Annual Report,* Chief of U.S. Engineers. Washington, Government Printing Office, 1875.

Magoffin, Susan Shelby. *Down the Santa Fe Trail and into Mexico: The Diary of Susan Shelby Magoffin, 1846–47.* Ed. by Stella M. Drumm. New Haven, Yale University Press, 1962.

Mallery, Garrick. "Sign Language Among North American Indians Compared with that Among Other Peoples and Deaf Mutes." Bureau of American Ethnology, *First Annual Report,* Washington, 1881.

"Report of the Secretary of War, U.S. War Dept., 1857–58," 35 Cong., 2 sess., *House Exec. Doc. 2.*

"Report of the Secretary of War, U.S. War Dept., 1859–60," 36 Cong., 1 sess., *Sen. Exec. Doc.*

Roberts, Frank H. H. "Shabik'eschee Village, a late Basket Maker Site in the Chaco Canyon, New Mexico." Bureau of American Ethnology, *Bulletin 92,* Washington, 1919.

Simpson, James Hervey. "Report of Exploration and Survey of a

Route from Fort Smith, Arkansas, to Santa Fe, New Mexico, Made in 1849, by First Lieutenant James H. Simpson, Corps of Topographical Engineers," 31 Cong., 1 sess., *House Exec. Doc. 45.*

———. "Report of Lieut. Col. James H. Simpson, Corps of Engineers, U.S.A., on the Change of Route West from Omaha, Nebraska Territory, Proposed by the Union Pacific Railroad Company," Washington, Government Printing Office, 1865.

———. "Report of Board Convened to Determine on a Standard for Construction of the Pacific Railroad, Made to Hon. James Harlan, Sec. of the Int., Feb. 24, 1866, with Accompanying Documents," Washington, Government Printing Office, 1866.

———. "Report of Explorations Across the Great Basin of the Territory of Utah for a Direct Wagon-Route from Camp Floyd to Genoa, in Carson Valley, in 1859," Washington, Government Printing Office, 1876.

Sitgreaves, Capt. Lorenzo. "Report of an Expedition Down the Zuñi and Colorado Rivers," 33 Cong., 1 sess., *Sen. Exec. Doc.*

Stevenson, Matilda Coxe. "The Zuñi Indians: Their Mythology, Esoteric Fraternities, and Ceremonies." Bureau of American Ethnology, *Twenty-third Annual Report,* Washington, 1904.

Washington, Col. John Macrae. *Letters.* 31 cong., 1 sess., *House Exec. Doc. 5,* Part I.

Wirtz, H. R. "How Bill Williams was Killed." The doctor's notebook account, published in the weekly *Arizona Miner,* August 20, 1870. The document is now in the collection of the Sharlot Hall Museum, Prescott, Arizona.

BOOKS, PAMPHLETS, AND MONOGRAPHS

Adair, John. *The Navajo and Pueblo Silversmiths.* Norman, University of Oklahoma Press, 1944.

Amsden, Charles Avery. *Navaho Weaving.* Albuquerque, University New Mexico Press, 1949.

Andrews, C. C., ed. "History of Saint Paul, Minnesota." Minnesota Historical Society *Publications,* 1890.

Bancroft, Hubert Howe. *History of Arizona and New Mexico, 1530–1888.* San Francisco, The History Co., 1889. New facsimile edition, Albuquerque, Horn & Wallace, 1962.

———. *History of Utah.* San Francisco, The History Co., 1891.

Brand, Donald D., F. M. Hawley, F. C. Hibben, *et al. Tseh So, A*

Small House Ruin, Chaco Canyon, New Mexico. Albuquerque, University of New Mexico Press, 1937.

Catlin, George. *North American Indians.* 2 vols. Edinburgh, John Grant, 1903.

Chávez, Fray Angelico. *Origins of New Mexico Families.* Santa Fe, Historical Society of New Mexico, 1954.

Cleland, Robert Glass. *This Reckless Breed of Men.* New York, Alfred A. Knopf, 1950.

Conard, Howard Louis. *Uncle Dick Wootton.* Chicago, W. E. Dibble and Company, 1890.

Davis, W. W. H. *El Gringo; or, New Mexico and Her People.* New York, Harper and Brothers, 1857.

Favour, Alpheus H. *Old Bill Williams, Mountain Man.* Norman, University of Oklahoma Press, 1962.

Frémont, John Charles. *Memoirs of My Life.* 2 vols. Chicago and New York, Belford, Clarke & Co., 1887.

Gallegos, Hernán. "The Gallegos Relation of the Rodríguez Expedition to New Mexico, 1581–1582." Trans. and ed. by George P. Hammond and Agapito Rey. *Historical Society of New Mexico Publication in History,* Vol. IV, Santa Fe, 1927.

Gladwin, Harold S. *A History of the Ancient Southwest.* Portland, Bond Wheelwright Co., 1957.

Goetzman, William H. *Army Exploration in the American West, 1803–1863.* New Haven, Yale University Press, 1959.

Gregg, Josiah. *Commerce of the Prairies.* Ed. by Max L. Moorhead. Norman, University of Oklahoma Press, 1954.

Hawley, Florence M. "The Significance of the Dated Prehistory of Chetro Ketl." *Monograph of the School of American Research, No. 2.* Albuquerque, University of New Mexico Press, 1934.

Hewett, Edgar L. *The Chaco Canyon and Its Monuments.* Albuquerque, University of New Mexico Press, 1934.

Hill, Willard W. "Navaho Warfare." Yale University *Publications in Anthropology, No. 5* (1936).

Hine, Robert V. *Edward Kern and American Expansion.* New Haven, Yale University Press, 1962.

Hodge, Frederick Webb. *History of Hawikuh, New Mexico: One of the So-Called Cities of Cíbola.* Publications of the F. W. Hodge Anniversary Publication Fund, Vol. 1. Los Angeles, The Southwest Museum, 1937.

Sources

——, ed. *Handbook of American Indians North of Mexico*. 2 vols. Bureau of American Ethnology, Bulletin No. 30. Washington, Government Printing Office, 1912.

Hughes, John T. *Doniphan's Expedition; Containing an Account of the Conquest of New Mexico*. Cincinnati, U. P. James, 1847.

Humboldt, Alexander von. *Vues des Cordillères et Monuments des Peuples Indigènes de l'Amerique*. Paris, 1810.

Judd, Neil M. "The Material Culture of Pueblo Bonito." Washington, *Smithsonian Miscellaneous Collections, Vol. 124*, 1954.

——."Pueblo del Arroyo, Chaco Canyon, New Mexico." Washington, *Smithsonian Miscellaneous Collections, Vol. 138, No. 1*, 1959.

Kidder, Alfred Vincent. *An Introduction to the Study of Southwestern Archaeology*. New Haven, Yale University Press, 1962.

Kluckhohn, Clyde, and Dorothea Leighton. *The Navaho*. Cambridge, Harvard University Press, 1948.

McNitt, Frank. *Richard Wetherill: Anasazi*. Albuquerque, University of New Mexico Press, 1957.

——. *The Indian Traders*. Norman, University of Oklahoma Press, 1962.

Moorhead, Max L. *New Mexico's Royal Road: Trade and Travel on the Chihuahua Trail*. Norman, University of Oklahoma Press, 1958.

Nevins, Allan. *Frémont, the West's Greatest Adventurer*. 2 vols. New York, Harper and Brothers, 1928.

New Mexico: A Guide to the Colorful State. Compiled by writers of the Works Projects Administration, American Guide Series. New York, Hastings House, 1940.

O'Kane, Walter Collins. *Sun in the Sky*. Norman, University of Oklahoma Press, 1950.

Pepper, George H. "Pueblo Bonito." *Anthropological Papers of the American Museum of Natural History, Vol. XXVII*. New York, 1920.

Prescott, William Hickling. *History of the Conquest of Mexico, with a Preliminary View of the Ancient Mexican Civilization*. New York, Harper and Brothers, 1848.

Prince, Bradford L. *Spanish Mission Churches of New Mexico*. Cedar Rapids, The Torch Press, 1915.

Reagan, Albert B. *Don Diego, or the Pueblo Uprising in 1680*. New York, 1914.

Sandburg, Carl. *Abraham Lincoln: The War Years*. Vol. I. New York, Charles Scribner's Sons, 1949.

Sawyer, Charles Winthrop. *Our Rifles.* The Cornhill Company, 1920.

Slater, John M. *El Morro: Inscription Rock, New Mexico.* Los Angeles, The Plantin Press, 1961.

Smith, Watson, *Kiva Mural Decorations at Awatovi and Kawaika-a.* Cambridge, Peabody Museum, 1952.

Stubbs, Stanley A. *Bird's-Eye View of the Pueblos.* Norman, University of Oklahoma Press, 1950.

Taft, Robert. *Artists and Illustrators of the Old West.* New York, Charles Scribner's Sons, 1953.

Thomas, Alfred Barnaby. *Forgotten Frontiers.* Norman, University of Oklahoma Press, 1932.

Underhill, Ruth. *Here Come the Navaho!* Washington, Bureau of Indian Affairs, 1953.

Van Valkenburgh, Richard. *Diné Bikéyah.* Paper, mimeographed in limited number of copies. Window Rock, Office of Indian Affairs, 1941.

———, and John C. McPhee. A *Short History of the Navajo People.* Paper, mimeographed in limited number of copies. Window Rock, U.S. Dept. of Interior, Navajo Service, 1938.

Vivian, R. Gordon. "The Hubbard Site and Other Tri-Wall Structures in New Mexico and Colorado." *Archaeological Research Series No. 5,* Washington, 1959.

———, and Paul Reiter. "The Great Kivas of Chaco Canyon and Their Relationships." *Monographs of the School of American Research and the Museum of New Mexico, No. 22.* Santa Fe, 1960.

Wall, Leon, and William Morgan. *Navajo-English Dictionary.* Window Rock, Navajo Agency, Branch of Education, 1958.

Wislizenus, Frederick Adolphus. *Memoir of a Tour to Northern Mexico, Connected with Col. Doniphan's Expedition in 1846 and 1847.* Washington, Tippin and Streeter, 1848.

ARTICLES

Bandelier, Adolph F. "Final Report of Investigations among the Indians of the Southwestern United States." Cambridge, Archaeological Institute of America, *Papers, American Series,* Vols. 2–3, Part I (1890–92).

———. "An Outline of the Documentary History of the Zuñi Tribe," *Journal of American Ethnology and Archaeology,* Vol. III (1892).

Bloom, Lansing B. "The Emergence of Chaco Canyon in History," in Edgar L. Hewett, *The Chaco Canyon and Its Monuments, q.v.* First published in *Art and Archaeology,* February, 1921.

Bryan, Kirk. "The Geology of Chaco Canyon, New Mexico" (ed. by Neil M. Judd). Washington, *Smithsonian Miscellaneous Collections,* Vol. 122, No. 7.

Fewkes, Jesse Walter. "Reconnaissance of Ruins in or near the Zuñi Reservation," *Journal of American Ethnology and Archaeology,* Vol. I, (1891).

Grinnell, George Bird. "Bent's Old Fort and its Builders," *Kansas Historical Society Collections,* Vol. XV (1919–22).

Hall, Edward T., Jr. "Recent Clues to Athapascan Prehistory in the Southwest," *American Anthropologist,* Vol. XLVI (1944).

Landgraf, John L. "Land-Use in the Ramah Area of New Mexico." *Papers of the Peabody Museum,* Vol. XLII, No. 1, (1954).

Parsons, Elsie Clews. "The Pueblo of Jemez." Department of Archaeology, Phillips Academy, *Papers of the Southwestern Expedition,* No. 3 (1925).

Reagan, Albert B. "Dances of the Jemez Pueblo Indians," Kansas Academy of Sciences *Transactions,* Vol. 20, No. 20 (1906).

———."Notes on Jemez Ethnography," *American Anthropologist,* n.s., Vol. 29, No. 4 (1927).

———. "The Jemez Indians," *El Palacio,* Vol. 4, No. 2 (1917).

———. "The Jemez Indians," *Southern Workman,* Vol. 44, No. 6 (1915).

———. "Symbolic Wall Painting in Jemez Kiva," *El Palacio,* Vol. 20, No. 8 (1926).

———."Symbolical Drawings by Jemez Pueblos," *El Palacio,* Vol. 12, No. 2 (1922).

Simpson, James Hervey. "Narrative of a Tour in the Navaho Country in 1849," Minnesota Historical Society *Annals,* St. Paul, 1852.

———. "Coronado's March in Search of the Seven Cities of Cibola and Discussion of Their Probable Location." *Annual Report of the Smithsonian Institution, 1869.* Washington, Government Printing Office, 1871.

Twitchell, Ralph Emerson. "The Story of the Conquest of Santa Fe, New Mexico, and the Building of Old Fort Marcy, A.D. 1846." *Publication of the Historical Society of New Mexico, No. 24* (n.d.)

———. "Colonel Juan Bautista de Anza . . . Diary of His Expedition to the Moquis in 1780," *Publication of the Historical Society of New Mexico, No. 21* (1918).

Van Valkenburgh, Richard. "Captain Red Shirt," *New Mexico* magazine, July, 1941.

White, Leslie A. "The Pueblo of San Felipe," American Anthropological Association *Memoirs*, No. 38 (1932).

———. "The Pueblo of Santo Domingo, New Mexico," American Anthropological Association *Memoirs*, No. 43 (1935).

Wilson, Lucy W. W. "Hand Sign of Avanyu," *American Anthropologist*, n.s., Vol. 20, No. 3 (1918).

MAPS

Maps are not often listed as a writer's tools. There are times when they should be. The E. M. Kern map of 1849 and the Lieutenant John Parke–R. H. Kern map of 1851—incomplete and not always accurate —still were the first and only maps of any dependability that the United States government had, until 1860, of the new southwest territory. For documenting place names, old stream courses and trails, and military routes, the maps are primary source materials. They are as invaluable now as they were to the military forces of occupation one hundred years ago. In his quarters at Fort Marcy, while planning the Navaho expedition, Colonel Washington at best could draw upon faulty maps of the region inherited from the Spanish colonial period, or rudely sketched by such old hands as Richard Campbell and Old Bill Williams. Such maps, if he had them, were grossly inaccurate. With nothing better he was forced to rely upon the knowledge of two guides—the amiable Hosta and the invaluable Carravahal. The maps listed chronologically below I have found in map collections at the National Archives, in the Library of Congress, the New York Public Library, and the Coe Memorial Library at the University of Michigan.

1845. Map [of] *New Mexico and the Southern Rocky Mountains,* made under the order of Captain J. C. Frémont, U.S. Topographical Engineers, and conducted by Lieutenant J. W. Abert, assisted by Lieutenant W. G. Peck, U.S.T.E. This is a partial map of Frémont's third expedition, showing the route of the Santa Fe Trail to Bent's Fort, and, through the High Plains country, the course of the Platte, Kansas, Arkansas, and Canadian rivers and their tributaries. Streams heading in the lower Rockies are figured, as are the familiar fur-trapping grounds of the Bayou Salade, Old Park, and New Park. Ceran St. Vrain's fort is shown on the south fork of the Platte. Farther north is shown Fort Laramie, and, in detail, the country south and west of the fort. The map also details the Cimarron and Bent's Fort routes to Santa Fe and Lieutenant Abert's route down the Canadian and Washita rivers to Fort Gibson. E. M. Kern in 1851 found serious inaccuracies: Bent's Fort, for example, was shown forty miles too far to the west.

1849. The Edward M. Kern *Map of the Route Pursued in 1849 by the U.S. Troops under the Command of Bvt. Lieut. Col. Jno. M. Washington, Governor of New Mexico, in an Expedition against the Navajo Indians.* The map is published with Simpson's journal of the campaign and figures the principal landmarks found on the route of march. The original of this map is in the collection of the Cartographic Division of the National Archives.

1851. Brevet Second Lieutenant John G. Parke and Richard H. Kern. *Map of the Territory of New Mexico.* Compiled by Parke and drawn by Kern, by order of Brevet Colonel John Munroe, commanding the Ninth Military Department, Santa Fe. The Bent's Fort routes to Taos and Santa Fe are from surveys by Brevet Major Emory and Lieutenants Abert and Peck. The Río Grande, from its head to Taos, and the San Juan country are from a map sketched by Old Bill Williams, with additional data supplied by Dr. H. R. Wirtz, E. M. Kern, Ceran St. Vrain, Antoine Leroux, John L. Hatcher, and others. The heads of the Arkansas and the south fork of the Platte, the Spanish Trail, and the Wasatch Mountains are figured from surveys by Frémont. The Doña Ana and Fort Smith–Santa Fe route is drawn from the survey by Lieutenant Simpson, assisted by E. M. Kern. The Río Pecos as far as the Bosque Grande and the *Jornada del Muerto* as far as El Paso are from the surveys by R. H. Kern. The Colorado of the West and adjacent country is according to Antoine Leroux and others. The Río Gila is from the survey of Major Emory. The original map is in the collection of the U.S. Topographical Engineers, War Department, Cartographic Division of the National Archives.

1853–58. Captain A. W. Whipple. *Preliminary Map of the Western Portion of the Reconnaissance and Survey for a Pacific Rail Road Route Near the 35th Par. . . . 1853–54 . . . with Additions Showing the Route of the Proposed Wagon Road from Fort Defiance to the Colorado, together with Several Lateral Explorations, by E. F. Beale, Supt., 1857–58.* From Albuquerque to Los Angeles, this map shows some of the major military routes to California, rivers and streams, springs and water holes, mountain ranges, and the location of Indian tribes. Whipple's map projects fairly closely the route followed in the 1880's by the Atlantic and Pacific Railroad.

1860. Captain J. N. Macomb, assisted by C. H. Dimmock. *Map of Explorations and Surveys in New Mexico and Utah, made under the direction of the Secretary of War.* This large map shows many important place names which have long since been changed or discarded and is particularly useful for determining major military routes through the country from 1845 to 1859.

1864 Captain Allen Anderson, Fifth U.S. Infantry. *Map of the Military Department of New Mexico,* drawn under the direction of Brigadier General James H. Carleton. For persons interested in frontier New Mexico and Arizona, this large map is probably richest in detail. It is a compilation of the works of all previous cartographers of the region and shows wagon roads, routes of exploration, military routes, military posts, and—most importantly—geographical place names no longer current but of historical interest.

1869. U.S. Army Engineers Department. *Military Map of the United States.* Western territories and states (longitude 125° west to longitude 99° east). This map is excellent in its detail of river courses, mountain ranges, towns, pueblos, trails, wagon roads, and military posts. It has been particularly useful in this work in tracing Lieutenant Simpson's Utah expedition to California. The map also shows Baja California and a sizeable part of northwestern Mexico.

1881–82. U.S. Geological Survey, J. W. Powell, director, Henry Gannett, Gilbert Thompson, A. H. Thompson, *et al. Northwestern New Mexico.* This is a contour map from Manuelito and Zuñi (west) to Cabezon Peak (east) and from Pueblo Pintado (north) to El Morro, Agua Fria, and El Rito (south). This excellent map shows the route of the Atlantic and Pacific Railroad, pueblos, towns, villages, springs, streams, rivers, mountains and mesas, Indian ruins, military posts, roads, and trails. Detail is remarkably clear and probably the most accurate of all the maps of the country to this time.

1886. U.S. Interior Department, General Land Office. *Map of the Territory of New Mexico.* This map shows towns and villages, railroads and railroad land-grant limits, military and Indian reservations, and private land grants.

1922. Robert P. Anderson. *Central Portion of the Chaco Canyon National Monument Showing the Location of Pueblo Bonito.* Drawn from surveys sponsored by the National Geographic Society, this contour map shows the canyon formation and major ruins, from Wijiji to Penasco Blanco. As far as it goes, the map is accurate and useful, but up to this time no one has attempted a truly adequate archaeological map of the Chaco.

1937–38. U.S. Interior Department, Geological Survey. *Canyon de Chelly National Monument, Apache County, Arizona.* This is a large highly detailed contour map of the canyon and its branches, showing roads, trails, and location of a few of the major ruins.

1937–56. U.S. Interior Department., Office of Indian Affairs. *Navajo Country.* (1937, revised 1956.) This map includes the Hopi and Zuñi reservations. Badly drawn, confused with crude overlays of the Navaho tribal council districts, this large map still is useful for its accurate topographical features and modern place names. Anyone seriously following the map's minor reservation roads is certain to get lost—a fairly accurate compass will serve far better.

1949. Records and Maps of the Old Santa Fe Trail, by Kenyon Riddle, published by the Raton *Daily Range,* Raton, New Mexico. Maps 4–a and 5, of eight. Drawn by Karl Riddle, these maps are the most painstakingly detailed of any I have found that show the principal cutoff routes of the trail. They were especially useful here in tracing Simpson's route in search of a site for Fort Union and in determining the geography of the region surrounding Fort Union and Barclay's fort.

1958. U.S. Interior Department, U.S. Geological Survey. *Western United States.* Four sectional maps were used in this work: *Albuquerque, Aztec, Shiprock, and Gallup.* These are contour maps, compiled from aerial photographs, with U.S. Geological Survey horizontal and vertical controls. Technically, these maps are unsurpassed. Combined, they show the country of the 1849 Navaho expedition, with the exception of the terrain between San Felipe Pueblo and Santa Fe. In retracing the Simpson route in 1961, I found the maps indispensable. When even the Land-Rover's compass failed, these maps pinpointed isolated hogans and wandering hogan roads.

Index

Abert, Colonel J. J.: 166n., 228–29, 231; orders for Sitgreaves Expedition, 215, 215n.

Abert, Lieutenant J. W.: xxiii–xxiv, 117, 117n.; on water supply at Acoma, 131, 131n.; at San Felipe Pueblo, 157n.

Abiquiu, New Mexico: xxxviii, xl, xli xlvii; Jicarilla raid on xlix, lxv; troops directed to, 5, 7, 192, 212

Acoma Pueblo, New Mexico: 139, 145; water problem of, 131, 131n; Henry L. Dodge agent for, 185, 210; comparative vocabulary, 246, 248

Agathla Peak (Arizona): 84n.

Agua Fria, New Mexico: xxii, 6–7, 158

Alameda, New Mexico: 154

Albuquerque, New Mexico: x–xi, xxvi, lxxix, 5, 26n., 108n., 158, 166n., 209; military post, xxvii, xxx, xxxiii; distance to Laguna Pueblo, 144n., 151; expedition reaches, 153–54; historical background, 153, 153n.; *Rio Abajo News*, 211n.; route from to Los Angeles, 215n., 217; routes from to Cebolletita, 245, 245n.

Albuquerque, Duke of: 153n.

Aldrich, Stephen E.: 182n.

Alexander, Brevet Lieutenant Colonel Edmund: 3, 6, 24; military record, lxx

Alexandro (Navaho): signs 1846 treaty, xxix

Algadones, New Mexico: 6, 154–55, 155n., 156

Alley, Lieutenant John W.: recovers body of Henry L. Dodge, 211n.

Alvarez, Manuel: lxivn.

Anáhuac (Mexico): 38n., 54–56

Anañe, Josea Ignacio: 90n., 98n.

Anaya, Juan: 192n., 197

Antelope Point (Canyon de Chelly): 92n.

Antelope Valley (Nevada): 237

Anton Chico, New Mexico: lvii–lxi

Apache Indians: xlvii, 100n., 193, 201; depredations, xxv, lxii, 88, 165, 165n., Calhoun recommends reservation for, 176; Calhoun refused escort for visit to, 178

Arapaho Indian: lv

Arbuckle, General Mathew: liii

Archuleta (chief of San Juan Navahos): signs 1846 treaty, xxix; at Chuska Valley council, 1849, 65–67; hostilities attributed to, 187, 188; sons in Peralta raid, 203ff.; signs 1848 treaty, 254

Archulette: *see* Archuleta

Arkansas River: xxi, xxxiii, lii, 192, 221, 238

Armijo (chief of Chuska Navahos): at Chuska Valley council, 1849, 67; surrenders murderer of soldier, 189–90, 191; at council of Laguna Negra, 196; for compromising Peralta raid, 204; with troops when Henry L. Dodge is captured by Coyotero Apaches, 208

Armijo, Governor Manuel: xxi; house at Albuquerque, 154

274

Index

Arvide, Father Martin de: 17n.
Ashley, General William H.: 160n.
Astialaqua ruin (New Mexico): 22n.
Atarque, New Mexico: 38n.
Atchison, Topeka and Santa Fe
Railroad: 219
Atlantic and Pacific Railroad: 219
Atrisco, New Mexico: 152, 152n.
Atsidi Sani (Navaho): 202, 202n.
Atsinna Ruin (New Mexico): 130n.
Aubrey, F. X.: murdered by Indians,
xlii, xliin.
Aztec Indians: 34, 35n., 38n., 53–55,
96, 115, 115n., 116–17, 117n.

Backus, Major Electus: 107n.
Badger Springs (New Mexico): 60n.,
61, 62n.
Baird, Spruce M.: 219; succeeded as
Navaho agent by Henry L. Dodge,
184–85
Bal, Father Juan de: 114n.
Banoso, Father, at Zuñi Pueblo: 116n.
Barclay's Fort (New Mexico): 213,
230
Barela, Elfego E.: owner of former
site of old Fort Wingate, 142n.
Barnabas, Father: 12n.
Barrionuevo, Francisco de: 12n.
BC 50 ruin (New Mexico): 52n.
BC 236 pueblo site (New Mexico):
41n.
Beall, Lieutenant Colonel Benjamin
Lloyd: xxxv, xxxvn., xxxvi, xxxviii,
xl–xli, xliii, xlvii–xlviii, lxxiv, 5, 7,
154n.
Bear River (Wyoming): 232
Bear Springs: see Ojo del Oso
Beaubien, Charles: lxivn.
Beautiful Little Canyon: see Cañon-
cito Bonito
Beautiful Mountain (New Mexico):
site of 1848 treaty, 254n.
Beckh, H. V. A. von: 235
Beckwith, Lieutenant E. G.: 220, 222
Bee, Colonel Fred A.: 236
Beheale, "Hosea" (Navaho): lxxvii
Bellows, John: 222–23, 223n.
Benevides, Father Alonzo de: 17n.
Bennett, Major Frank Tracy: 62n.
Bennett's Peak (New Mexico): 62,
62n., 63–64, 189

Bent, Charles: xxi, xxiv–xxv; murder of,
xxix–xxx; on Navaho population,
98n.
Bent, William: 183, 221
Bent's Fort (Colorado): xxi, xxxiii,
xxxv, lii, 213, 221, 229–30; Sumner's
meeting with Cheyennes near, 170;
Colonel Dodge camps at, 183
Bernalillo, New Mexico: 153n., 155
Berthoud Pass (Colorado): 238
Bi-joshii (Navaho): 254n.
Bill Williams Fork (of Verde River,
Arizona): 216
Bill Williams Mountain (Arizona): 216
Bill Williams River (Arizona): 216
Bird, W.: lxxv; with Simpson at El
Morro, 125–39
Black Beaver (Delaware Indians): lv
Black Creek (Arizona): 108n.
Black Falls (Arizona), of Little
Colorado: 216
Black Mesa (New Mexico): 157n.
Black Mountain (or Mesa, Arizona):
84n.
Bonneville, Colonel B. L. E.: 210–11,
211n.
Borrego Canyon (New Mexico): lxvii
Bosque Redondo (New Mexico):
lxxix, 142n.; see also Fort Sumner
Bourke, Lieutenant John G.: 21n.;
criticism of Fort Defiance, 171n.
Brady, Mathew: 239
Brent, Captain Thomas Lee: 13, 14n.,
24; military record, lxx; urges
military post west of Chuska Moun-
tains, 173
Brooke, Commander John M.: 224
Brower, Lieutenant Charles B.: 5–6,
90; military record, lxxi
Buford, Lieutenant John: 245
Bullock, Isaac: 232
Burgwin, Captain J. H. K.: xxvi–xxvii;
death of, xxx
Burnside, Lieutenant A. E.: 230

Caballada Mucho (Navaho): signs
1846 treaty, xxix
Caballo Mountains (New Mexico):
212n.
Cabezon Peak (New Mexico): 11,
25–26, 26n., 28, 31, 31n., 32n., 34,
108n., 147n.; caused by eruptions of

275

of which *Navaho Expedition* is Number 43, was started in 1939 by the University of Oklahoma Press. It follows rather logically the Press's program of regional exploration. Behind the story of the gradual and inevitable recession of the American frontier lie the accounts of explorers, traders, and travelers, which individually and in the aggregate present one of the most romantic and fascinating chapters in the development of the American domain. The following list is complete as of the date of publication of this volume.

1. Captain Randolph B. Marcy and Captain George B. McClellan. *Adventure on Red River:* Report on the Exploration of the Headwaters of the Red River. Edited by Grant Foreman. Out of print.
2. Grant Foreman. *Marcy and the Gold Seekers:* The Journal of Captain R. B. Marcy, with an Account of the Gold Rush over the Southern Route. Out of print.
3. Pierre-Antoine Tabeau. *Tabeau's Narrative of Loisel's Expedition to the Upper Missouri.* Edited by Annie Heloise Abel. Translated from the French by Rose Abel Wright. Out of print.
4. Victor Tixier. *Tixier's Travels on the Osage Prairies.* Edited by John Francis McDermott. Translated from the French by Albert J. Salvan. Out of print.
5. Teodoro de Croix. *Teodoro de Croix and the Northern Frontier of New Spain, 1776–1783.* Translated from the Spanish and edited by Alfred Barnaby Thomas. Out of print.
6. A. W. Whipple. *A Pathfinder in the Southwest:* The Itinerary of Lieutenant A. W. Whipple During His Explorations for a Railway Route from Fort Smith to Los Angeles in the Years 1853 & 1854. Edited and annotated by Grant Foreman. Out of print.
7. Josiah Gregg. *Diary & Letters.* Two volumes. Edited by Maurice Garland Fulton. Introductions by Paul Horgan.
8. Washington Irving. *The Western Journals of Washington*

Irving. Edited and annotated by John Francis McDermott. Out of print.

9. Edward Dumbauld. *Thomas Jefferson, American Tourist: Being an Account of His Journeys in the United States of America, England, France, Italy, the Low Countries, and Germany.*

10. Victor Wolfgang von Hagen. *Maya Explorer:* John Lloyd Stephens and the Lost Cities of Central America and Yucatán.

11. E. Merton Coulter. *Travels in the Confederate States:* A Bibliography.

12. W. Eugene Hollon. *The Lost Pathfinder:* Zebulon Montgomery Pike.

13. George Frederick Ruxton. *Ruxton of the Rockies.* Collected by Clyde and Mae Reed Porter. Edited by LeRoy R. Hafen.

14. George Frederick Ruxton. *Life in the Far West.* Edited by LeRoy R. Hafen. Foreword by Mae Reed Porter.

15. Edward Harris. *Up the Missouri with Audubon:* The Journal of Edward Harris. Edited by John Francis McDermott.

16. Robert Stuart. *On the Oregon Trail:* Robert Stuart's Journey of Discovery (1812–1813). Edited by Kenneth A. Spaulding.

17. Josiah Gregg. *Commerce of the Prairies.* Edited by Max L. Moorhead.

18. John Treat Irving, Jr. *Indian Sketches.* Taken During an Expedition to the Pawnee Tribes (1833). Edited and annotated by John Francis McDermott.

19. Thomas D. Clark (ed.). *Travels in the Old South, 1527–1860:* A Bibliography. Three volumes. Volumes One and Two issued as a set (1956); Volume Three (1959).

20. Alexander Ross. *The Fur Hunters of the Far West.* Edited by Kenneth A. Spaulding.

21. William Bollaert. *William Bollaert's Texas.* Edited by W. Eugene Hollon and Ruth Lapham Butler. Out of print.

22. Daniel Ellis Conner. *Joseph Reddeford Walker and the*

Arizona Adventure. Edited by Donald J. Berthrong and Odessa Davenport.

23. Matthew C. Field. *Prairie and Mountain Sketches.* Collected by Clyde and Mae Reed Porter. Edited by Kate L. Gregg and John Francis McDermott.

24. Ross Cox. *The Columbia River:* Scenes and Adventures During a Residence of Six Years on the Western Side of the Rocky Mountains Among Various Tribes of Indians Hitherto Unknown; Together with a Journey Across the American Continent. Edited by Edgar I. and Jane R. Stewart.

25. Noel M. Loomis. *The Texan–Santa Fé Pioneers.*

26. Charles Preuss. *Exploring with Frémont:* The Private Diaries of Charles Preuss, Cartographer for John C. Frémont on His First, Second, and Fourth Expeditions to the Far West. Translated and edited by Erwin G. and Elisabeth K. Gudde.

27. Jacob H. Schiel. *Journey Through the Rocky Mountains and the Humboldt Mountains to the Pacific Ocean.* Translated from the German and edited by Thomas N. Bonner.

28. Zenas Leonard. *Adventures of Zenas Leonard, Fur Trader.* Edited by John C. Ewers.

29. Matthew C. Field. *Matt Field on the Santa Fe Trail.* Collected by Clyde and Mae Reed Porter. Edited and with an introduction and notes by John E. Sunder.

30. James Knox Polk Miller. *The Road to Virginia City:* The Diary of James Knox Polk Miller. Edited by Andrew F. Rolle.

31. Benjamin Butler Harris. *The Gila Trail:* The Texas Argonauts and the California Gold Rush. Edited and annotated by Richard H. Dillon.

32. Lieutenant James H. Bradley. *The March of the Montana Column:* A prelude to the Custer Disaster. Edited by Edgar I. Stewart.

33. Heinrich Lienhard. *From St. Louis to Sutter's Fort, 1846.* Translated and edited by Erwin G. and Elisabeth K. Gudde.

34. Washington Irving. *The Adventures of Captain Bonneville.* Edited and with an introduction by Edgely W. Todd.

35. Jean-Bernard Bossu. *Jean-Bernard Bossu's Travels in the Interior of North America, 1751–1762*. Translated and edited by Seymour Feiler.
36. Thomas D. Clark (ed.). *Travels in the New South, 1865–1955:* A Bibliography. Two volumes.
37. John Lloyd Stephens. *Incidents of Travel in Yuctán.* Edited and with an introduction by Victor Wolfgang von Hagen. Two volumes.
38. Richard A. Bartlett. *Great Surveys of the American West.*
39. Gloria Griffen Cline. *Exploring the Great Basin.*
40. Francisco de Miranda. *The New Democracy in America:* Travels of Francisco de Miranda in the United States, 1783–84. Translated by Judson P. Wood. Edited by John S. Ezell.
41. Col. Joseph K. F. Mansfield. *Mansfield on the Condition of the Western Forts, 1853–54.* Edited by Robert W. Frazer.
42. Louis Antoine de Bougainville. *Adventure in the Wilderness:* The American Journals of Louis Antoine de Bougainville, 1756–1760. Translated and edited by Edward P. Hamilton.
43. James H. Simpson. *Navaho Expedition:* Journal of a Military Reconnaissance from Santa Fe, New Mexico, to the Navaho Country Made in 1849. Edited by Frank McNitt.